Hospitality Accounting

WILLIAM S. GRAY, C.A., B. Comm.

Southern Vermont College

Prentice Hall
Upper Saddle River, New Jersey 07458

Library of Congress Cataloging-in-Publication Data

Gray, William S.,
    Hospitality accounting / William S. Gray.
      p.   cm.
    Includes index.
    ISBN 0-13-142838-1
    1. Hospitality industry—Accounting.   I. Title.
HF5686.H75G7   1996
657′.837—dc20   95-36696
                             CIP

Acquisitions Editor: Robin Baliszewski
Editorial-Production Supervision: WordCrafters Editorial Services, Inc.
Interior Design: Adele Kupchik
Editorial Assistant: Rosemary Florio
Manufacturing Buyer: Ed O'Dougherty
Managing Editor: Mary Carnis
Director of Manufacturing & Production: Bruce Johnson
Marketing Manager: Frank Mortimer, Jr.
Cover Design: Carol Ceraldi

© 1996 by Prentice-Hall, Inc.
A Simon & Schuster Company
Upper Saddle River, New Jersey 07458

Printed in the United States of America

10 9 8 7 6 5 4 3 2 1

ISBN 0-13-142838-1

Prentice-Hall International (UK) Limited, *London*
Prentice-Hall of Australia Pty. Limited, *Sydney*
Prentice-Hall Canada Inc., *Toronto*
Prentice-Hall Hispanoamericana, S.A., *Mexico*
Prentice-Hall of India Private Limited, *New Delhi*
Prentice-Hall of Japan, Inc., *Tokyo*
Simon & Schuster Asia Pte. Ltd., *Singapore*
Editora Prentice-Hall do Brasil, Ltda., *Rio de Janeiro*

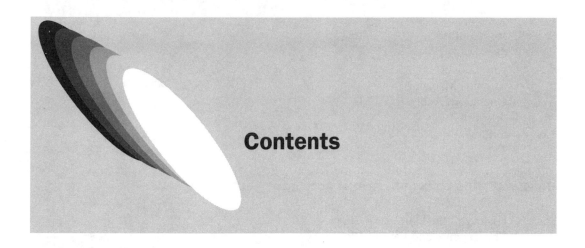

Contents

Chapter 3   The Uniform System of Accounts   16

SECTION II   ORIGINAL ENTRY   28

Chapter 4   Journal Entries and the General Ledger   28

Chapter 5   Night Audit   43

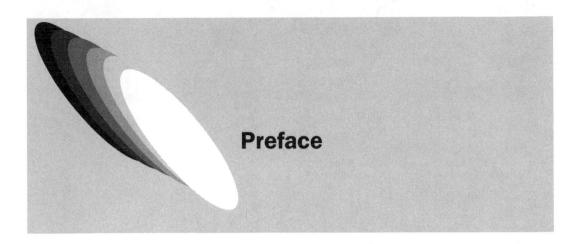

Preface

Since I commenced teaching on a full-time basis, I have become very cognizant of the need for an accounting textbook suitable for use by hospitality management students.

Other texts in the field are either outdated or are written in such technical terms that they are directed toward the needs of a student majoring in hospitality accounting rather than a student who is in one, or at the most, two accounting or finance classes as a part of overall program requirements.

Since I spent over twenty-five years in the hotel and restaurant industry, all of it accounting related, I feel that I have addressed the accounting requirements of the many areas of hospitality operations. Staying active as a consultant in the field has also permitted me to remain conversant with the latest developments in hotel systems. I have incorporated this knowledge into this text.

The easy-to-follow, step-by-step manner in which the procedures are explained should be well suited to students enrolled in both two- and four-year programs. I took the opportunity to test out various chapters on my students during a recent semester.

My earliest book, *Hotel and Motel Management and Operations* (Gray/Liguori, published by Regents/Prentice Hall, 3rd edition, 1994) contained a few chapters devoted to hotel accounting. While some of the content of those chapters is repeated in this text, some areas have been updated as a result of new thinking or increased technology and, of course, many areas not mentioned within the limited scope of those few chapters are now addressed in depth. I am particularly pleased to have been able to cover such areas as budget preparation, financial analysis, and long-range projections. "Hotel Grayscot," which is discussed throughout the book, is a hypothetical hotel used for illustrative purposes. These are areas that are of particular concern to students interested in any segment of hospitality management.

Lastly, I would like to dedicate this book to my colleague and long-time friend, Sal Liguori, who passed away last summer. Long-time members of the New York City Hotel industry will remember Sal not only for his hard work, but for his overwhelming belief in the integrity of the hotel controller. I like to feel that some of that fervor rubbed off on me.

1   The Role of Accounting

From the time of the ancient Chinese abacus to today's world of the computer, accounting has always been an integral part of business activity. Regardless of whether a business has a profit or a loss, someone has to calculate the results. However, the role of the accountant has changed dramatically over the last 50 years. Once relegated to the back room and a green eyeshade, today's accountant participates in the management process at all levels. This is perhaps more critical in service industries than in the manufacturing sector where the heaviest emphasis remains on research and product development. Among the many service industries, hospitality operations are some of the most complex.

People in the field of marketing refer frequently to the "intangibility of service." The success of a hospitality operation does not depend on the cost or quality of the service but on the customer's perception of the services. Decor and an overall feeling of comfort are more important than the thickness of the mattress. Similarly, presentation and service in a restaurant have more impact than the actual ingredients in the food. Thus, in a manufacturing operation, accounting focuses on the product costs in relation to sales. The hospitality accountant is faced with a wider range of costs related to the diverse elements of service.

In general, the scope of the accountant steadily increased as a result of government legislation which required businesses to maintain more accurate and more extensive records. Foremost among the legislation was the enactment in 1914 of personal income tax laws. Legislation related to Social Security, tax withholding, minimum wage, workmen's compensation, and the like required more extensive payroll records. The advent of the sales tax resulted in detailed bookkeeping related to revenue. The Internal Revenue Service set standards for documenting expenditures. Finally, for the protection of the public and the shareholders, the Securities and Exchange Commission enacted extensive legislation pertaining to publicly held corporations.

However, in the hotel field it was the invasion of conglomerates and multinational corporations via acquisitions that placed an even greater emphasis on financial

matters. Such corporations are run with the aid of financial analyses, budgets, forecasts, and business plans.

THE BASIC PHILOSOPHY OF THE ACCOUNTING DEPARTMENT

In the 1950s, hotel accountants were transformed into auditors, a title commonly applied to the chief accountant. Their principal responsibility was to control all hotel revenues and expenses and to set up safeguards to minimize losses, including those from theft. To this end, they worked very closely with all other department heads and personally supervised or test-checked all employees involved in the daily revenue-producing operations of the hotel. They and their staffs also performed the normal accounting functions of recording transactions; keeping records; preparing, analyzing, and interpreting statements; and providing management with all needed information.

In the 1980s, the auditor evolved into a hotel controller. Top management—in many cases, absentee management—changed its priorities for two principal reasons: the advent of electronic computers and the corporate need to show a profit in the face of the squeeze resulting from equal or lower revenues and higher operation costs.

Management soon discovered that many financial statements, reports, and statistics were readily available, and that computers could easily be programmed to produce them periodically. Finding this information very useful, management began asking for more reports, statistics, and comparisons. The controller was thus called upon to draw up new formats to present the desired information and to participate in frequent meetings with management to review and interpret the findings.

The profit squeeze led to a growing reliance on operating budgets. These reports will be discussed in detail in relation to the duties of the controller; they shall be commented on here only briefly. A budget is an estimate of revenue and expenses for a fiscal or calendar year which is normally submitted to top management for approval a few months before the starting date of the period covered. The key word here is *estimate*, an "educated guess" based on past performance, current price levels, and future bookings. Unfortunately, some general managers and home-office executives in chain-owned or -operated hotels tend to view the budget as the "Bible." They question any variation from it but may overlook a poor departmental operation if the actual results conform to the estimated figures.

This attitude, plus the sometimes unreasonable insistence that the figures reflect a desired result, necessitates many revisions to, and frequent updating of, the projections throughout the period covered. These changes require frequent consultations with other department heads and many meetings with management, both before and after final approval. All of this leads to the belief in some organizations that this function is a constant challenge, perhaps even the all-year-round, full-time job of the controller. Tragically, reliance on estimated projections of income and expenses may eliminate the incentive to closely monitor or control departmental operations, to consider them acceptable if they follow the pattern established in the budget. This may result in an accounting department that records transactions and transmits information to a computer without verifying the accuracy or checking the reasonableness of the figures submitted.

The preceding statements are not intended as an indictment of management policy or an implication that a well-planned budget is not a necessary tool in the overall supervision of a hotel's operations. Rather, caution should be taken against overreliance on estimated figures, a concern that is frequently voiced at local or national meetings of hospitality accountants. Present and future controllers should be alerted to the danger in disregarding the basic auditing and accounting standards and drifting into a routine of overemphasis on meetings and reports. Becoming a member of the top management team added new responsibilities to the position of the controller but did not take away the old ones. In order to understand the role of the controller and his or her department, it is essential to understand the overall structure of a hotel.

THE STRUCTURE OF A HOTEL

Figure 1–1 shows the organization of a hotel with more than 1,000 rooms. While smaller properties do not require the same number of department heads or subdepartment heads, the functions performed do not disappear. Instead, one person performs several functions. While certain departments are larger than others, they are all essential to the proper operation of the hotel. In the following paragraphs, the functions of each department are briefly described.

Rooms

The primary responsibility for the well-being of the guests is delegated to the head of the rooms department, known as the *resident manager*. He or she heads the numerically largest department in the hotel, many of whose members come into direct contact with the guests. In fact, from the moment the guests arrive until their departure, someone in this department is performing a direct service for them. Training, a must for all hotel employees, takes on an added significance for the members of this staff. Frequently, employees who come into personal contact with the guests not only must be trained in the functions and duties of their positions, but must be told how to interact with guests.

The resident manager carries out what may be the most important responsibility of the general manager: the day-to-day operation of the guest rooms. The various subdepartment heads, such as the executive housekeeper, executive assistant manager, front-office manager, chief telephone operator, and the garage manager, together with their respective staffs, register the guests, maintain and clean the rooms, and provide information on hotel facilities and local points of interest—cultural, recreational, or amusement. They also handle all guest complaints. The purchasing agent was not included in the list of subdepartment heads for two reasons. The first is that he or she performs no service directly affecting the guest. The other is that the position varies in importance with the size, type, and ownership of the hotel. In a small to medium-sized, individually owned hotel, the position may be little more than clerical, involving the typing of purchase orders for items previously requested, priced by the department heads, and approved by the general manager. In a large hotel that is not part of a chain, and excluding for the moment food and beverages, the position may require obtaining price quotations and possibly setting specifications for the merchandise needed. In any

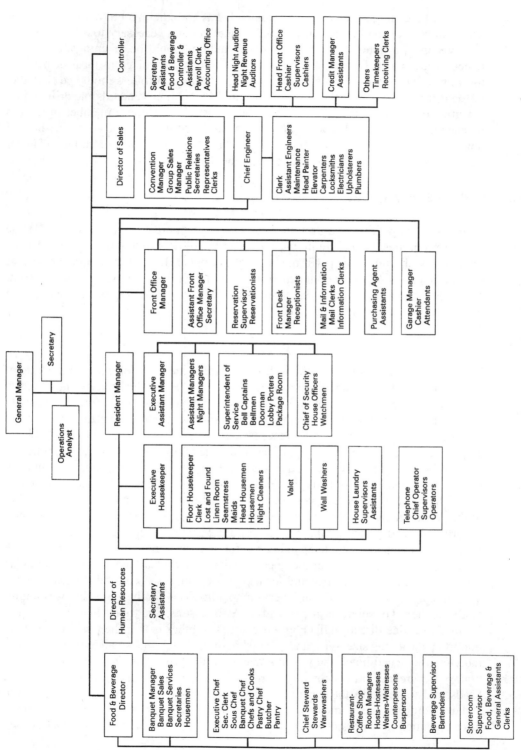

Figure 1-1 Hotel Organization Chart

4

size hotel that is part of a group, the position, again excluding food and beverages, often entails little more than the processing of requisitions to the central office for merchandise ordered by department heads. It is important to remember that this is another responsibility of top management. Thus, all requisitions and purchase orders should require the approval of the general manager or a designated representative.

The purchasing of food and beverages is a field in itself; the procedure is reviewed in a subsequent chapter. In many hotels, this purchasing is done by a person under the control and direction of the food and beverage manager. This is an undesirable arrangement because it seriously affects accounting controls. The food and beverage manager supervises the preparation of the food and the service, recommends or actually sets the specifications, and determines the quantities needed. He or she should not have the added authority to select the purveyor and the price to be paid for the food. Figure 1–1 shows the purchasing agent reporting to the resident manager, acting, of course, as the designated representative of the general manager.

Food and Beverages

The food and beverage director heads a department that also involves guest relations. The service staff in the restaurants, coffee shop, bars, and banquet rooms come into direct contact not only with resident guests but with members of the general public who use the hotel facilities.

This is the department that most clearly demonstrates the old hotelier's famous saying: "Service is our most important product." A good meal, well cooked and beautifully presented, can be easily spoiled by a careless or sloppy waiter or waitress. Proper attention to the table setup—silverware, china, glasses, and so on—and to guests' needs for such items as bread, water, and liquor are just as important as the food itself. How often we hear the complaint: "We wanted another round of drinks, but we could never get the waiter's attention." The attention given to the guests while they are eating can be as important as the prompt taking of the initial order. No one likes to be rushed, but most people need to feel that there is someone near to help them in case they want something. It has been said that more food and beverage repeat business has been lost by poor service than by poor or badly cooked food. Moreover, repeat business in the restaurants, banquet rooms, and sleeping rooms is the single most important factor in the success or failure of the hotel as a profit-making enterprise.

In the final analysis, all that advertising can accomplish is the attraction of new guests. Only the concerted efforts of the staff can create a satisfied guest—the repeater, the person who spreads the word among friends and business associates of the "wonderful hotel I stopped at." Word-of-mouth advertising is the most powerful medium in the service industry, for both good and bad. Many hotel owners have discovered that it is very difficult to build a good reputation and very easy to ruin one.

Engineering

The chief engineer is concerned with the appearance and physical condition of the building. Having limited personnel, the chief engineer depends on others, primarily the rooms department staff, to detect and report bad physical conditions and out-of-order

appliances in the guest rooms. This is one small example of the teamwork needed to operate a hotel successfully.

Human Resources

The main responsibility of the director of human resources is to staff the hotel. It is the employees who take care of the guests, and good service is the most important ingredient for the success of the operation. However, the human resources director also administers the various employee-related programs, maintains the records, and does the reporting required by the various government regulatory bodies, such as OSHA, the Department of Employment and Training, and the Department of Labor (relative to compliance with minimum wage, child labor, and so on).

Sales

The sales department is the lifeblood of the organization. Few outsiders realize that the director of sales is called upon to make more decisions about present and future earnings than any other department head.

Hotels—indeed, cities—compete fiercely to attract large groups, companies, and organizations. Conventions are sometimes booked years in advance, and hotels are called upon to guarantee room rates within a certain range, and to give such other inducements as free meeting rooms and discounts on banquets. These are decisions that should be made only with the knowledge and consent of the general manager. Huge national conventions, of such organizations as the American Legion, Shriners and the two major political parties every four years, are booked by the city officials with the aid of all hotels. They work through a citywide agency, such as the Convention and Visitors Bureau, or the local chamber of commerce. Rates and other inducements are set on a citywide basis. Practically the only decision an individual hotel has to make is the number of sleeping rooms to commit and guarantee to the central agency for the convention.

It is the smaller groups, those booked and handled by a single hotel, that require the most top management decisions and often create interdepartmental problems. Food and beverage and banquet managers rarely take very kindly to free meeting rooms. Public-room rentals are very important to them, particularly since the food and beverage department is usually charged for the labor in setting up and cleaning these rooms. Special food discounts increase food cost and adversely affect the department's profits. Another important consideration is the possible loss of food and beverage business; a banquet cannot be accepted if the room is reserved for a convention group. Many a banquet manager has tried to explain a poor operating result in a given month by citing that reason. There have also been heated discussions regarding accepting conventions during certain months of the year because of the possible loss of banquet functions, particularly repeat business. Sales personnel theorize that local organizations, companies, and groups that hold annual or more frequent functions will not return if they are driven to use another hotel and find it equally or more desirable. A healthy interdepartmental rivalry develops, the solution to which is the sole responsibility of the general manager.

Accounting

The structure of the accounting department is described in detail in Chapter 2. Along with engineering, sales, and human resources, the department provides various support services for the revenue-producing departments and for the other aforementioned support departments. The nature of these services is described in the following chapter and throughout the book.

General Manager

Certain activities are the direct responsibility of the general manager. These include labor relations, insurance, advertising (in conjunction with the hotel's advertising agency), and relations with tenants operating stores and concessions. Frequently, the booking of entertainment in the hotel's outlets is also handled through the general manager's office because its quality is highly reflective of the hotel's image. However, the area that absorbs the largest portion of the general manager's time is his or her role in sales and an active daily commitment to good public relations.

The Executive Committee

The executive committee, formed under the direction of the general manager, sets the hotel's operating policies. The structure of the committee can vary, but the overall intent is to have all departments represented so it is composed of all the senior department heads. It normally meets weekly and, in addition to setting policies, it addresses problems and reviews the coming week's activities within the hotel. The hotel controller is always on the executive committee as the financial advisor and representative of the accounting department.

RESTAURANTS AND CLUBS

In a smaller hospitality operation, the structure is less complex but many of the functions are the same. Larger restaurant operations usually have a general manager supported by a chef and one or more restaurant managers. A club operation usually requires a general manager to handle the membership-related responsibilities. This individual may also supervise the food and beverage operations with the support of a chef and restaurant manager.

1. Draw an organization chart for a hotel showing only the departments and not the job titles.

2. Prepare a list of the activities normally performed by a general manager.

3. Circle T or F to indicate whether the following statements are true or false:

   T   F   **a.** A budget is an estimate of revenue and expenditure for a calendar or fiscal year.

   T   F   **b.** The executive housekeeper is a member of the rooms department.

   T   F   **c.** It is desirable to have the purchasing done by the food and beverage director.

   T   F   **d.** National conventions are usually booked through a citywide agency.

   T   F   **e.** A minor responsibility of the director of human resources is to staff the hotel.

4. Circle the correct answer to the following statements:

   a. Personal income tax laws were enacted in:
   (1) 1892
   (2) 1914
   (3) 1934

   b. In the 1950s hotel accountants were known as:
   (1) Bookkeepers
   (2) Financial analysts
   (3) Auditors

   c. Entertainment in hotel outlets is frequently booked by:
   (1) The controller
   (2) The front-office manager
   (3) The general manager

2 The Organization of a Hotel Accounting Department

In Chapter 1 we examined the functions and responsibilities of the various departments in a hotel with the exception of accounting. The overall role of the controller and his or her department was also defined. In this chapter, we are concerned with the individual subsections of the accounting area, their respective goals, and the type of support they provide for the other departments. Within the department, certain functions can be carried out by one or possibly two individuals, while others are more diversified and complex. To understand these functions and their relationships, refer to the department's organization chart, Figure 2–1.

This chart reflects the generally accepted lines of authority in a large hotel, which is defined as 600 rooms and up. However, the number of rooms does not, by itself, determine the size and complexity of the accounting department. This is impacted also by the number of food and beverage outlets and by the existence of other large revenue-producing departments (e.g., casinos, golf courses, spas, etc.). In smaller operations, two or more functions may be combined but, as emphasized in the preceding chapter, the individual functions always exist and must be performed. However, their magnitude may not justify the need for a particular employee. Furthermore, the structure may be modified because of the desires of management or the preference of the individual controller. The order in which the individual subsections are reviewed here is based not on their respective sizes, but rather on the degree to which they are involved with the operating departments.

FRONT-OFFICE CASHIERS

The separation of duties between operations and accounting is one of the most fundamental principles of internal control in all businesses. However, in a hotel the operational position of receptionist is often combined with an accounting function, that of the front-office cashier. Except in very large hotels, there are times of the day or periods of the year when two people at the front desk cannot be economically justified. The

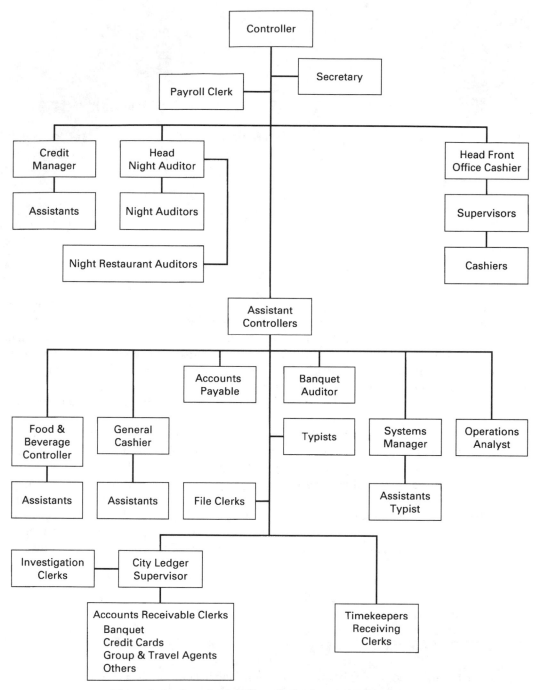

Figure 2–1 Organization Chart for the Accounting Department

receptionist greets and registers the incoming guest; the cashier checks out and obtains settlement from the departing guest. Both functions must be performed in the same area—the front desk. Therefore, combining the two roles can be easily accomplished.

NIGHT AUDIT

A similar situation occurs when the cost of a night receptionist cannot be justified and the night reception function is covered by the night auditor. During the day, the cashiering function is performed by a receptionist, an employee whose line of reporting is to the front-desk manager, a part of operations (see Figure 1–1). At night, the night auditor carries out an operational function, but always reports to accounting. The responsibilities of the night auditor and the front-office cashiers are explained in detail in Chapter 5.

CREDIT

While a medium-sized or larger hotel generally has a credit department, or at least a credit manager, in a smaller hotel, the function is frequently divided between the front-office manager or an assistant manager and the city ledger department. The granting of credit and the monitoring of in-house credit often requires direct contact with the guest and can be delegated to rooms department management, while the follow-up and collection of overdue accounts is delegated to the city ledger employees. Again, the function exists but the volume cannot support or justify an employee to carry it out. The credit function is covered in detail in Chapter 11.

ASSISTANT CONTROLLERS

While small properties frequently have no assistant controller, a very large property may have two or more assistants; it is strictly a function of size and volume. The functions and areas within the accounting department are divided up between the assistants on an arbitrary basis. However, when there are two assistants, the most common practice is to delegate the day-to-day bookkeeping and accounting, including the month-end closing (described in Chapter 8), to one assistant while the other is responsible for reports, systems, budgeting, and special projects.

BANQUET AUDITOR

The banquet auditor can be considered an extension of the night audit inasmuch as the function involves the verification of revenue. However, as will be explained in Chapter 5, it necessitates working closely with both accounts payable and the banquet sales and service staff. Consequently, it is much easier to perform the banquet audit during normal working hours rather than at night.

ACCOUNTS PAYABLE

Chapter 6 is devoted exclusively to the accounts payable function. Accounts payable is a key area in the accounting process because it is the mechanism that audits and controls most of the operating costs and expenditures and determines to which department expenses should be charged. The responsible individual or individuals must deal with both management and vendors on a friendly but firm basis and always be alert to the possibility of error or impropriety.

Accounts payable works extremely closely with puchasing and receiving as incorrect vendor billings usually result from incorrect pricing or the failure to deliver the proper quantity or quality. Delivery of an incorrect item resulting in it being returned for credit also involves these two areas. However, the frequent need for management approvals requires interfacing with all departments of the hotel.

FOOD AND BEVERAGE CONTROLLER

The food and beverage controller's normal activities fall into the scope of both food and beverage operations and accounting. Operationally, the food and beverage controller is the analytical arm of the food and beverage director. As such, his or her diversified duties may include:

1. Testing menu items for quality and taste.
2. Obtaining samples from purveyors of both ingredients and supplies in order to complete a survey on quality and price.
3. Working with the chef on menu yields.
4. Eating and drinking in competitive restaurants or lounges—known as *competitive shopping.*
5. Preparing comparisons of the productivity of individual servers or kitchen personnel.
6. Analyzing sales to determine the popularity and profitability of various items—called *abstracting the menu.*

The responsibilities related to accounting involve the preparation of various reports on inventory consumption and costs, explained in detail in Section IV.

GENERAL CASHIER

General cashier is a purely accounting function which is principally related to revenue control and accounts receivable. A detailed description of the duties related to revenue control can be found in Chapter 5, while the other elements of the function are described in Chapter 10. Communication with other departments occurs with both the front desk and the food and beverage outlets on a daily basis. Within the accounting department, communication with the accounts receivable personnel is also very important.

CITY LEDGER

In a large hotel, you may find more employees in city ledger than there are in the entire accounting department in a small property. Volume in terms of numbers of accounts and transactions is the determining factor in establishing the requisite staffing for this area.

The supervisor must be very well organized and possess excellent communicative skills as there is daily contact, both by mail and on the telephone, with former and potential guests. It is quite possible for the responsibilities to reach a level where the supervisor of the department acquires the title of assistant controller.

Internally inaccurate billings result from mistakes at the front desk or in the food and beverage department. Good communication with these departments is, therefore, essential. Differences on group billings between numbers or amounts charged and the contractual agreements also requires a close working relationship with both the sales and banquet staffs. Chapter 10 describes the function and responsibilities of the city ledger in detail.

SYSTEMS MANAGER

As mentioned previously, systems management is frequently the responsibility of an assistant controller. While the major function of computer systems in hotels involves servicing the accounting area, various operating departments also have computer requirements. The need to place all computer system decisions in the hands of one individual cannot be overemphasized. Without it, the proper integration of the various systems in use cannot be attained. Property management systems are described in Chapter 5. In addition to accounting, these systems serve reservations, the front desk, the bell staff and, provided they contain a guest history segment, sales and marketing.

Other systems serving operations are telephone and communications, purchasing, utility consumption and environmental control, sales and marketing information, banquet booking, recipe and menu specifications, and, as described in Chapter 14, various segments of the point-of-sales systems.

While Chapter 26, Systems Management, primarily relates to the accounting area, additional coverage on other systems is provided.

OPERATIONS ANALYST

This position should, perhaps, be shown on the organization chart with a dotted line, because the role of the operations analyst is to provide operations with any form of analysis requested in the interest of improving operations or making changes to specific areas. However, as many hotels cannot justify the cost of a full-time operations analyst, the function is frequently delegated to the controller and his or her assistants. Additionally, when a full-time analyst is employed, the necessary research for the assigned project usually requires information or numbers, the source of which is the accounting department.

PAYROLL

Chapter 7 emphasizes that payroll preparation for most hotels is done by a payroll service company. The hotel accounting function is one of verification and input of hours and periodic audit of master file information normally provided to the computer service by the human resources department. Support is sometimes provided by timekeepers whose primary duty is surveillance of the time clocks. These duties are frequently delegated to security or receiving.

However, good relationships with the other departments are essential. An employee who feels that the hours for which he or she was paid are incorrect usually heads for the accounting department first. However, the final resolution usually involves the employee's direct supervisor.

SUMMARY

In Figure 2–1, typists and clerks are indicated in various areas. The degree to which they are required or necessary depends on the volume of work and proper consideration as to whether time-consuming tasks should be performed at a lower labor cost.

Ultimately, a major function of the accounting department is to provide support for all areas of operations. When called upon for that support, the staff must always be ready and willing to provide it.

In restaurants and clubs, the accounting function usually requires very limited personnel, normally a controller and one or two bookkeeping assistants. Additionally, in those operations many of the administrative functions are also handled by the accounting department.

1. Draw an organization chart of a hotel accounting department.
2. Write a paragraph explaining the growth of the role of the hotel accountant from 1914 to present.
3. Circle T or F to indicate whether the following statements are true or false:

   T F **a.** The required staffing of the accounting department is not affected by the number of outlets.

   T F **b.** Front-desk cashiering is an accounting function.

   T F **c.** The night auditor reports to operations.

   T F **d.** The size of a hotel can affect the number of employees required in city ledger.

   T F **e.** Timekeeping duties are frequently performed by security or operations.

4. Circle the correct answer to the following statements:

   a. The following is not a duty of the food and beverage controller:
      (1) Testing menu items for quality and taste
      (2) Approving credit for banquets
      (3) Eating and drinking in competitive restaurants

   b. The easiest time to perform a banquet audit is:
      (1) Between 10 P.M. and 2 P.M.
      (2) Between 5 A.M. and 7 A.M.
      (3) During normal working hours

   c. Computer systems are often used to provide:
      (1) Utility consumption and environmental control
      (2) Telephone and communications service
      (3) Sales and Marketing information
      (4) All of the above

3 The Uniform System of Accounts

HISTORY OF THE UNIFORM SYSTEM

The first edition of the Uniform System of Accounts for Hotels was prepared in 1925/1926 by a group of accountants at the request of the Hotel Association of New York City. In March 1926, it was formally accepted and copyrighted by that organization. In September of that year, the American Hotel and Motel Association, then operating as the American Hotel Association of the United States and Canada, at the recommendation of the local association, passed a resolution adopting the Uniform System of Accounts for Hotels.

Another important accomplishment of the accounting committee was the organization of the Hotel Accountants Association of New York City. Through the years, the accounting committee of the organization has periodically updated and revised the manual. The eighth edition has been in use since 1986, and as of this writing, no committee has been formed to undertake the ninth edition. However, it continues to be the Bible for the hotel industry.

In a similar manner, the Uniform System format was used to create systems for restaurants and clubs. Specifically, the Uniform System of Accounts for Restaurants was developed by the National Restaurant Association and the Uniform System of Accounts for Clubs by the Club Managers of America. The uses and advantages subsequently described in this chapter apply equally to the other two systems. Their format is similar but with fewer departments and complexities.

THE EXPENSE AND PAYROLL DICTIONARY

A companion booklet published by the American Hotel and Motel Association is the *Expense and Payroll Dictionary.* The dictionary was originally created by a firm of hotel accountants for their staff to use in classifying expense and payroll items in conformity with the Uniform System of Accounts and has been updated and revised by the

American Hotel and Motel Association to conform with each revision of the Uniform System.

The dictionary is divided into two parts. Part One lists just about every conceivable item or product that can be purchased, or service contracted for, in the operation of a hotel. (Excluded are items purchased for resale, such as food and beverages, since their costs are charged against sales in the affected department.) Opposite each item is listed the expense department and subclassification to which it should be charged. Here are some examples:

Baggage tags	Rooms	Printing and stationery
Boiler repairs	Repairs and maintenance	Plumbing and heating
Burglary insurance	Administrative and general	Insurance—general
Napkins—linen	Food and beverage	Linen
Napkins—paper	Food and beverage	Paper supplies

Similarly, Part Two lists the various job classifications and opposite each, the department and subclassification. All wages for each department are normally shown in one amount; the subclassifications are used only for comparison purposes when analyzing or preparing special payroll reports. Examples are:

Bellmen	Rooms	Service front
Cashiers—restaurant	Food and beverage	General cashiers
Cashiers—front office	Administrative and general	Front-office accounting
Painters	Repairs and maintenance	Painters and paperhangers

Despite its name, the dictionary does not define any of these items or job classifications; it merely lists them alphabetically. Nevertheless, there is no question that it has contributed to the universal acceptance and success of the Uniform System of Accounts.

CONCEPT OF THE SYSTEM

The Uniform System is not merely a recommended accounting system for hotels. It formalizes the entire structure and departmentalization now commonly in use in the industry. The Uniform System provides for a series of departments into which the organization of the hotels is structured. These departments can be divided into two broad categories: revenue-producing departments or, as they are called, operated departments, and overhead departments. Operated departments exist for each type of revenue derived by the hotel operation. Obviously, this can vary from hotel to hotel, but the most common are rooms, food and beverage, telephone, laundry and valet, and garage. Where there are individual shops within the hotel that the hotel actually operates, these require individual departments. Such other sources such as golf courses and swimming pools would, if they were revenue-producing, similarly become operated departments. Hotels have the option of operating the food and beverage department as a combined entity or as two separate departments. In truth, preparation in the two elements can conceivably be separated, but the service is too interrelated to justify separation.

The overhead departments, as contained in the eighth edition of the Uniform System, are: administrative and general; marketing (sales and advertising); energy costs; and property operation and maintenance.

The Uniform System defines the organization of each department in terms of classification of the employees and the expenses that must be charged against the department. The defining of individual positions or their assignment to a specific department serves not only to provide a payroll breakdown by department for cost purposes, but also to determine the reporting responsibility for each job classification. For example, all employees whose job classification falls within the rooms department in the Uniform System should be reporting either directly or indirectly to the person who is responsible for managing that department. Table 3–1 is an example of a chart of accounts for a hotel operation using the Uniform System format. As with all hotels, it has been customized.

The first pages of the table set out the balance-sheet accounts by category and the individual asset and liability accounts that fall within each subheading. The detailed description of each account is provided by the Uniform System. On the following pages, the accounts that make up the operating statement, both revenue and expenditure, are shown in detail. In this example, there are only four operated departments: rooms, food and beverage, telephone, and laundry and valet. An additional income category, store rentals and other income, is also listed in the chart of accounts. The overhead departments are the standard four: administrative and general, marketing, energy costs, and property operation and maintenance. Allocated departments and fixed charges are also included.

Each department is set out in a vertical column, with the applicable revenue and expense classifications listed by department. Note that in both the revenue and expenditure areas, a certain type of revenue or expense may appear in more than one department. For example, "payroll" is shown in all departments, and "printing and stationery" is applicable to six of the seven departments. Many accounts, however, fall only into one specific department; for example, "bad debts" is applicable only in administrative and general. Again, the Uniform System provides a detailed description of every expense applicable to every department. Within the scope of the Uniform System, there is the opportunity for a hotel to expand the chart of accounts to show material items separately. This has been done in Table 3–1 with those items most common to hotels.

The advantages of the Uniform System to the hotel industry are substantial. It provides a uniformity of departmentalization and of classification of assets and liabilities, revenue, and expenditures. What this means to the industry is that job classifications do not vary from hotel to hotel, nor are they included in one department in one hotel and elsewhere in another. Thus, formalized guidelines are available consistently for use by management and personnel as well as accounting throughout the industry.

This consistent classification, particularly of revenue and expenditures, permits comparison of one operation to another. Several firms prepare annual studies on hotel operations, not only in the United States but worldwide. These studies provide averages and medians for hotel operations within various forms of classification, for instance, old and new, city and resort, owned and managed; and by geographical location. These statistics are prepared and categorized in the format determined by the

Uniform System. Thus, any owner or manager is in a position to readily compare his or her operation to the average. This is particularly useful where a large number of hotels are owned by a company whose headquarters is based some distance away. Similarly, the Uniform System provides the chains with the ability to compare their operations with those of individual hotels. Individual hotel managers can make comparisons among themselves, with the knowledge that within any particular area, they are talking about the same thing.

The Uniform System also facilitates staff training and reduces the amount of time required to familiarize a new employee with the system in use. An employee leaving one hotel that uses it requires only a limited amount of training or indoctrination because he or she is already familiar with the overall concepts of the system in use.

Finally, the Uniform System provides the ability to exercise strong budgetary control. By reference to the system, each department head can be conversant with those expenses, both payroll and other, for which the department has a responsibility. He or she can budget with a full understanding of what must be included, and also police those items of expense charged against the department's budget. Thus, management is enabled not only to demand a high level of budgetary control but to effectively provide the department head with the tools to control the department's results.

Table 3–1 *Chart of Accounts, Uniform System Format*

ACCOUNT TITLE	ACCOUNT NUMBER
Cash	
House Banks	11-1000
Payroll Acct.	11-1005
Operating Acct.	11-1006
Escrow Acct.	11-1007
Accounts Receivable	
Guest Ledger	13-1024
City Ledger	13-1025
Miscellaneous	13 1026
Allowance for Doubtful Accts.	13-1012
Inventories	
Food	15-1062
Beverage	15-1063
Miscellaneous	15-1068
Prepaid Expenses	
General Insurance	23-1101
Maintenance Contracts	23-1102
Workers' Compensation	23-1105
Licenses	23-1106
Miscellaneous	23-1108
Fixed Assets and Depreciation	
Building	18-1210
Furniture, Fixtures, and Equipment	19-1282
Automotive Equipment	19-1272
Land	17-1220
Accumulated Depreciation	22-1300

(Continued)

Table 3–1   *(Cont'd.)*

Other Assets
Preopening Expenses	23-1401
Security Deposits	23-1405
Investments	23-1410

Accounts Payable—Trade and Concessions
Trade Creditors	37-1500
Tenant Lease Security Deposits	37-1501
Unclaimed Wages	37-1518
Banquet Tips	37-1516
Valet	37-1503
Store #1	37-1504
Store #2	37-1505
Store #3	37-1506
Concessions #1	37-1507
Concessions #2	37-1508
Concessions #3	37-1509
Banquet Miscellaneous	37-1510
Safe Deposit Box Deposits	37-1515
Others	37-1520

Accounts Payable—Banquet
Banquet Payable—Florist	37-1581
Banquet Payable—Newsstand	37-1582
Banquet Payable—Musicians	37-1583
Banquet Payable—Checkroom	37-1584
Banquet Payable—Other	37-1585

Taxes Payable and Accrued
Federal Income Tax	38-1601
State Unemployment Insurance	39-1602
Federal Unemployment Insurance	39-1603
F.I.C.A. Tax	39-1604
State Sales Tax	37-1605
Occupancy Tax	37-1606
State Use Tax	39-1607
Deferred Federal Income Tax	45-1608
Beverage Tax	37-1609
Entertainment Tax	37-1610

Accrued Expenses
Salaries and Wages	37-1625
Vacations	37-1626
Electricity	37-1627
Water and Sewer	37-1628
Gas	37-1629
Telephone	37-1630
Audit Fees	37-1631
Group Insurance	37-1632
Savings Plan	37-1633
Workers' Compensation	37-1634
Retirement Plan	37-1635
Sundry	37-1636

Reserves, Deferred Credit, Debt, Capital Stock, and Surplus
Reserve for Replacement—Rooms Linen	44-1650
Reserve for Replacement—Food Linen	44-1651

Table 3–1

Reserve for Replacement—China & Glassware	44-1652
Reserve for Replacement—Food Silverware	44-1653
Paid-in Surplus	54-1675
Retained Earnings	55-1676

Rooms

Sales—Transient (Individual)	310-1801
—Golf (Individual)	310-1802
—Corporate (Individual)	310-1803
—Group (Corporation)	310-1804
—Group (Tour & Travel)	310-1805
—Group (Association)	310-1806
—Group (Sports)	310-1807
Sales Allowances	310-1808

Salaries and Wages

Salaries and Wages—Front Office	310-2021
Salaries and Wages—Housekeeping	310-2022
Salaries and Wages—Bell Staff	310-2033
Holiday and Vacation Pay	310-2060
Employee Payroll Taxes and Benefits	310-2065
Employee Meals	310-2070

Expenses

Cable TV	310-5008
China and Glassware	310-5009
Cleaning Supplies	310-5010
Commissions	310-5011
Contract Cleaning	310-5012
Contract Services	310-5013
Decorations	310-5016
Dry Cleaning	310-5017
Equipment Rental	310-5023
Guest Entertainment	310-7010
Guest Supplies	310-5027
Guest Parking and Transportation	310-5028
Laundry	310-5040
Linen	310-5042
Office Supplies and Postage	310-5050
Printing and Stationery	310-5056
Reservation Expense	310-5060
Telephone	310-5067
Travel Expenses	310-5068
Uniforms	310-5072
Miscellaneous	310-5099

Food and Beverage

Food Sales

Sales—Outlet 1	320-1825
—Outlet 2	320-1826
—Room Service	320-1827
—Banquets	320-1828
Sales Allowances	320-1829

(Continued)

Table 3–1   *(Cont'd.)*

Beverage Sales	
Sales—Outlet 1	330-1851
—Outlet 2	330-1852
—Bar	330-1853
—Room Service	330-1854
—Banquets	330-1855
Sales Allowances	330-1856
Other Income	
Cover Charges	320-1875
Public Room Rentals	320-1876
Banquet Miscellaneous	320-1877
Ice Sales	320-1878
Cost of Sales	
Food	320-3001
Beverage	320-3002
Cost of Employee Meals	320-3003
Salaries and Wages—Kitchen	320-2121
—Service	320-2122
—Administration	320-2123
—Beverages	330-2221
Holiday and Vacation Pay	320-2060
Employee Payroll Taxes and Benefits	320-2065
Employee Meals	320-2070
Expenses	320-5002
Advertising	320-5003
Bar Expense	320-5004
China and Glassware	320-5009
Cleaning Supplies	320-5010
Commissions	320-5011
Contract Cleaning	320-5012
Contract Labor	320-5013
Decorations	320-5016
Dry Cleaning	320-5017
Dues and Subscriptions	320-6015
Entertainment	320-7010
Equipment Rental	320-5023
Guest Supplies	320-5027
Ice	320-5032
Kitchen Fuel	320-5036
Laundry	320-5040
Licenses and Permits	320-5041
Linen	320-5042
Menus and Wine Lists	320-5045
Music and Entertainment	320-5046
Office Supplies	320-5050
Paper Supplies	320-5054
Postage and Telegrams	320-5055
Printing and Stationery	320-5056
Silver	320-5064
Telephone	320-5067
Travel	320-5068
Uniforms	320-5072

Table 3–1

Utensils	320-5073
Miscellaneous	320-5099
Telephone	
Revenue—Local	350-1901
—Long Distance	350-1902
—Pay Phone Commissions	350-1903
Allowances	350-1905
Cost of Calls—Local	350-3006
—Long Distance	350-3007
Rental of Equipment	350-3008
Salaries and Wages	350-2321
Holiday and Vacation Pay	350-2060
Employee Payroll Taxes and Benefits	350-2065
Employee Meals	350-2070
Equipment Changes	350-5024
Printing and Stationery	350-5056
Uniforms	350-5072
Miscellaneous	350-5099
Laundry and Valet	
Sales—Valet	600-1925
—Laundry	600-1926
Cost of Sales	600-3009
Salaries and Wages	600-2421
Holiday and Vacation Pay	600-2060
Employee Payroll Taxes and Benefits	600-2065
Employee Meals	600-2070
Contract Cleaning	600-5012
Printing and Stationery	600-5056
Supplies	600-5099
Miscellaneous	600-5099
Transfer to Rooms	600-8001
Transfer to Food	600-8002
Transfer to Beverage	600-8003
Store Rentals and Other Income	
Store Rentals—#1	450-1951
—#2	450-1952
—#3	450-1953
Concessions —#1	450-1954
—#2	450-1955
—#3	450-1956
Commissions—#1	450-1957
—#2	450-1958
—#3	450-1959
Other Income—Forfeit Deposits	450-1960
—Cash Discounts	450-1961
—Salvage Sales	450-1962
—Miscellaneous	450-1963
Administrative and General	
Salaries and Wages—Accounting	500-2521
—Administrative	500-2522

(Continued)

Table 3–1 *(Cont'd.)*

Holiday and Vacation Pay	500-2060
Employee Payroll Taxes and Benefits	500-2065
Employee Meals	500-2070
Audit Fees	500-6002
Bank Charges	500-6004
Cashier's Short (and Over)	500-6006
Contract Services	500-5013
Corporate Office Expense	500-6008
Credit Card Commissions	500-6009
Credit and Collection Expenses	500-6010
Data Processing Expenses	500-6013
Donations and Contributions	500-6014
Dues and Subscriptions	500-6015
Entertainment	500-7010
Equipment Rental	500-5023
Guest Loss and Damage	500-6018
Insurance—General	500-6022
Legal Fees	500-6025
Licenses and Permits	500-6026
Manager's Expenses	500-6030
Office Supplies	500-5050
Postage and Telegrams	500-6034
Printing and Stationery	500-5056
Provision for Bad Debts	500-6035
Telephone	500-5067
Travel Expenses	500-5068
Uniforms	500-5072
Miscellaneous	500-5099

Marketing
Sales

Salaries and Wages	520-2621
Holiday and Vacation Pay	520-2060
Employee Payroll Taxes and Benefits	520-2065
Employee Meals	520-2070
Contract Services	520-5013
Dues and Subscriptions	520-6015
Entertainment	520-7010
Equipment Rental	520-5023
Guest History	520-7015
Operating Supplies	520-7020
Photography	520-7025
Postage and Telegrams	520-6034
Telephone	520-5067
Travel	520-5068
Trade Shows	520-7035
Miscellaneous	520-5099

Advertising and Merchandising

Agency Fees	530-7501
Brochures	530-7504
Direct Mail	530-7507
Franchise Fees	530-7510
Hotel Representatives	530-7512
In-House Graphics	530-7515

Table 3–1

Local Media	530-7520
Marketing Fees	530-7525
Point of Sales Materials	530-7530
Print—Directories	530-7541
—Magazines	530-7542
—Newspapers	530-7543
Production	530-7548
Radio and TV	530-7550
Trade Agreements	530-7560
Miscellaneous	530-5099
Energy Costs	
Electric Bulbs	570-8001
Electricity	570-8002
Fuel	570-8005
Sewage	570-8008
Steam	570-8009
Water	570-8012
Property Operation and Maintenance	
Salaries and Wages	580-2721
Holiday and Vacation Pay	580-2060
Employee Payroll Taxes and Benefits	580-2065
Employee Meals	580-2070
Air Conditioning	580-8501
Building	580-8502
Contract Labor	580-5013
Curtains and Drapes	580-8505
Electrical and Mechanical Equipment	580-8508
Elevators	580-8510
Engineering Supplies	580-8512
Equipment Rental	580-5023
Floor Coverings	580-8515
Furniture	580-8516
Grounds and Landscaping	580-8520
Kitchen Equipment	580-8524
Laundry Equipment	580-8528
Office Supplies	580-5050
Painting and Decorating	580-8532
Plumbing and Heating	580-8535
Printing and Stationery	580-5056
Refrigeration	580-8538
Removal of Waste	580-8539
Service Contracts	580-8543
Snow Removal	580-8544
Swimming Pool	580-8545
Television	580-8548
Uniforms	580-5072
Vehicles	580-8553
Miscellaneous	580-5099
Allocated Departments	
Personnel Department, Payroll Taxes, and Employee Relations	

(Continued)

Table 3–1 *(Cont'd.)*

Salaries and Wages	620-2821
Holiday and Vacation Pay	620-2060
Payroll Taxes	
FICA/Medicare	620-2062
Federal Unemployment	620-2063
State Unemployment	620-2064
Social Insurances	
Health Insurance	620-2067
Workers' Compensation	620-2068
Savings Plan	620-2069
Employee Relations and Other Personnel	
Employee Relations	620-9001
Medical Expenses	620-9004
Personnel Recruitment	620-9006
Postage and Telegrams	620-6034
Printing and Stationery	620-5056
Telephone	620-5067
Miscellaneous	620-5099
Employees' Cafeteria	
Salaries and Wages	630-2921
Holiday and Vacation Pay	630-2060
China and Glass	620-5009
Cleaning Supplies	620-5010
Paper Supplies	620-5054
Printing and Stationery	620-5056
Silver	620-5064
Uniforms	620-5072
Miscellaneous	620-5099
Allocation to Other Departments	
(Separate Entry for Each Cost Center)	
Rooms	620-8010
Food and Beverage	620-8011
Telephone	620-8012
Laundry and Valet	620-8013
Admin. and General	620-8014
Marketing	620-8015
Property Operations and Maintenance	620-8016
Fixed Charges	
Capital Leases	650-9001
Insurance on Buildings and Contents	650-9005
Taxes—Real Estate	650-9010
—Personal Property	650-9011
Interest—Mortgages	650-9020
—Notes	650-9021
—Other	650-9023
Depreciation—Buildings	650-9030
—Furniture and Equipment	650-9031
—Operating Equipment	650-9032
Management Fees	650-9050
Preopening Expense Amortization	650-9060

1. After reviewing the chart of accounts, suggest a probable account number for the following items:
   a. Kleenex for guest rooms
   b. Cooks' aprons
   c. Specialty drink tentcards
   d. Cocktail cherries
   e. Repair of a lobby table
   f. Propane gas for kitchen ranges
   g. Copy paper for accounting department
   h. Rental of fax machine for sales office
   i. Paper placemats for coffee shop
   j. Detergent for dishwashing machine

2. List three accounts that could be found under these balance-sheet classifications:
   a. Prepaid expenses
   b. Accounts payable
   c. Taxes payable

3. Circle T or F to indicate whether the following statements are true or false:
   T F a. The Uniform System assists in training.
   T F b. Golf is an overhead department.
   T F c. Telephone is an operated department.
   T F d. Food and beverage are always operated as two separate departments.
   T F e. Hotel employees can be classified by department.

4. Circle the correct answer to the following statements:
   a. The following expense can be found in more than one department
      (1) Legal fees
      (2) Electricity
      (3) Guest supplies
   b. The following department is an overhead department
      (1) Guest laundry
      (2) Casino
      (3) Property operation and maintenance
   c. The following expense can be found in the food and beverage department
      (1) China and glassware
      (2) Music and entertainment
      (3) Guest history
      (4) All of the above

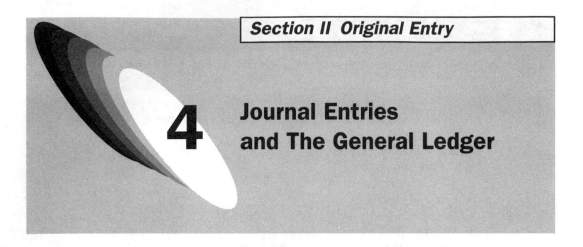

4 Journal Entries and The General Ledger

Hospitality accounting can be described as fundamental accounting principles and procedures customized for the hotel and restaurant industry. Accordingly, this chapter reviews these fundamentals. The foundation of accounting is double-entry bookkeeping, which means that for every entry in the books there must be an equal and opposite entry ensuring that at every step the books will be "balanced" and the final result will be in balance.

There are four basic types of accounts: assets, liabilities, revenue, and expenses. The first two are balance-sheet accounts which means that the balances represent the amount of the asset or liability at a specific point in time. Assets are items owned by the business while liabilities are debts owed. Examples of assets are:

> Cash
> Accounts receivable
> Inventories

Examples of liabilities are:

> Accounts payable
> Taxes payable
> Mortgage payable

Since the assets normally exceed the liabilities, the difference is known as *capital* (or *net worth*).

A listing of the balances in these accounts at a point of time is called a *trial balance*. In such a listing, the asset balances are normally in the left-hand column and termed *debit balances,* while the liability and capital balances are in the right-hand column and termed *credit balances*.

Thus, a trial balance of a small bed and breakfast operation could, at the beginning of the year, look like this:

Grayscot Bed and Breakfast
Trial balance as at January 1, 199X

	Debits	Credits
Cash	$3,210	
Accounts receivable	715	
Inventory—food	1,622	
Inventory—beverage	205	
Land	52,000	
Building	210,000	
Furniture & equipment	38,212	
Accumulated depreciation		$31,620
Accounts payable		1,117
Mortgage payable		160,000
Capital (Net worth)		113,227
	$305,964	$305,964

The other two types of accounts, revenue and expenses, known as *operating accounts*, represent the amount of revenue earned or expenses incurred for a specific period of time. Examples of these accounts are:

Revenue:
   Room and board sales
   Beverage sales

Expenses:
   Payroll
   Cost of food
   Cleaning supplies
   Heating expense

At the end of a business year, these accounts are zeroed out and the net result is added or deducted from capital. Therefore, a trial balance of Grayscot Bed and Breakfast at a point during the operating year could look like the following:

Grayscot Bed and Breakfast
Trial balance as at April 30, 199X

	Debits	Credits
Cash	$2,709	
Accounts receivable	922	
Inventory—food	1,708	
Inventory—beverage	176	
Land	52,000	
Building	210,000	
Furniture & equipment	39,712	
Accumulated depreciation		$32,740
Accounts payable		1,382
Mortgage payable		158,000
Capital		113,227

Room and board sales		28,210
Other food sales		2,710
Beverage sales		1,260
Miscellaneous revenue		412
Cost of food	11,206	
Cost of beverage	363	
Payroll expense	2,760	
Cleaning supplies	820	
Other supplies	762	
Linen service	1,820	
Heating expense	4,705	
Electricity	3,208	
Depreciation expense	1,120	
Interest expense	3,950	
	$337,941	$337,941

JOURNAL ENTRIES

The most basic method by which transactions are recorded is known as a *journal entry*. A journal entry simply records the net change to each account by showing the amount and the account affected in the form of balancing debits and credits. Journal entries can show changes in both balance-sheet and operating accounts or only in one of them. Also, the entries can be made to two or several accounts. Examples of some entries for Grayscot Bed and Breakfast for May 1 are:

		Debits	Credits
1.	Cash	$ 652	
	Room and Board Sales		$ 652
	To record checkouts for May 1		
2.	Interest Expense	1,266	
	Cash		1,266
	To record payment of mortgage interest for May		
3.	Accounts Payable	1,382	
	Cash		1,382
	To record payment of April's accounts payable		
4.	Cost of Food	217	
	Accounts Payable		217
	To record liability for groceries delivered by Smith Wholesale.		

GENERAL LEDGER

The collective grouping of the individual accounts is known as the *general ledger* and the accounts are termed *general ledger accounts*. A simplified method of viewing general ledger is to view each account in the form of a "T" with debits to the left of the "T" and credits to the right. Thus, the general ledger for Grayscot Bed and Breakfast at May 1, before recording any May entries, would appear as follows:

	Cash			Accounts Receivable	
Bal/Fwd 5/1	$2,709		Bal 5/1	$922	

	Inventory—Food			Inventory—Beverage	
Bal/Fwd 5/1	$1,708		Bal 5/1	$176	

	Land			Building	
Bal/Fwd 5/1	$52,000		Bal 5/1	$210,000	

	Furniture & Equipment			Accumulated Depreciation	
Bal/Fwd 5/1	$39,712		Bal 5/1		$32,740

	Accounts Payable			Mortgage Payable	
Bal/Fwd 5/1		$1,382	Bal 5/1		$158,000

	Capital			Room & Board Sales	
Bal/Fwd 5/1		$113,227	Bal 5/1		$28,210

	Other Food Sales			Beverage Sales	
Bal/Fwd 5/1		$2,710	Bal 5/1		$1,260

	Miscellaneous Revenue			Cost of Food	
Bal/Fwd 5/1		$412	Bal 5/1	$11,206	

	Cost of Beverage			Payroll Expense	
Bal/Fwd 5/1	$363		Bal 5/1	$2,760	

	Cleaning Supplies			Other Supplies	
Bal/Fwd 5/1	$820		Bal 5/1	$762	

	Linen Service			Heating Expense	
Bal/Fwd 5/1	$1,820		Bal 5/1	$4,705	

	Electricity			Depreciation Expense	
Bal/Fwd 5/1	$3,208		Bal 5/1	$1,120	

	Interest Expense	
Bal/Fwd 5/1	$3,950	

After recording the May 1 entries (known as *posting*), the following reflects the changes to the accounts affected:

	Cash			Accounts Payable	
Bal/Fwd 5/1	$2,709	5/1 $1,266	Bal Fwd 5/1		$1,382
	$ 652	5/1 $1,382		$1,382	5/1 $ 217

	Room & Board Sales			Cost of Food	
Bal/Fwd 5/1		$28,210	Bal Fwd 5/1	$11,206	
		$ 652		$ 217	

	Interest Expense	
Bal/Fwd 5/1	$3,950	
	$1,266	

At the end of the month, each account is totaled and balanced so that the balance can be carried forward to the following month. For example,

		Cash		
Bal/Fwd 5/1	$2,709		5/1	$1,266
5/1	652		5/1	1,382
5/31	122		5/31	381
5/31	538		5/31	1,101
Total	10,029			6,922
	6,922			
Bal 5/31	$3,107			

After the accounts are balanced at month end, a trial balance for the month end, similar to the April 30 trial balance shown on page 29, can be prepared. It is essential that the general ledger be in balance. If it is not, the individual entries must be rechecked and each account readded to find the error.

Certain entries are normally made only at month end. The most common of these are entries to adjust the inventory and to record expenses for which invoices have not been received or expenses paid in advance. The entry to adjust the inventory is simply a debit or credit to "Cost of food (or beverage)." For example,

	Debit	Credit
Inventory—Food	$222	
Cost of Food		$222
To record the increase in the inventory at month end.		

For the other entries mentioned, two balance-sheet accounts must be added: an asset account "Prepaid expense" and a liability account "Accrued expense."

Examples of possible entries to these accounts are:

	Debit	Credit
Electricity Expense	$432	
Accrued Expense		$432
To record an estimate for electricity for May—bill not received.		
Prepaid Expense	$210	
Heating Expense		$210
To adjust for fuel paid for in May but which will be used in June.		

The recording of prepayments and accruals commonly found in the hotel industry will be discussed in more detail in later chapters.

Recording Guest Charges

The night audit (the daily recording of revenue) is not practiced by many of the small bed and breakfast operations which continue to use manual bookkeeping. Instead, the revenue is recorded at the time of guest checkout. The actual charges for each guest are

Room No. _____		No. of Guests _____		
Name of Guest _____				
Rate _____		Checked in _____		

Date	Description	Charge	Payment	Balance

Figure 4–1 Guest Account Card for Bed and Breakfast

tracked manually on an account card (one for each room), such as the one shown in Figure 4–1. The charges and settlements for all checkouts are analyzed, totaled, and recorded on a daily basis.

Monthly Journal

Since making a journal entry for each day's transactions is a tedious task, it is much simpler to record the daily transactions in a monthly journal format in which the daily

amounts are accumulated and a single journal entry is made for the month's transactions. Figure 4–2 is a sample of a combination cash receipts and revenue journal. While separate journals could be maintained for cash receipts and revenue, they are frequently combined. This is particularly true in the hotel industry as a high percentage of revenue is collected in cash at checkout. The end-of-month journal entry for Figure 4–2 would be:

	Debit	Credit	Explanation
Cash	$10,022.65		Daily deposits
Accounts receivable	452.70		Customer charges
Accounts receivable		$ 481.30	Customer payments
Bed and breakfast		7,208.35	Daily sales
Other food revenue		1,810.10	Daily sales
Beverage revenue		902.10	Daily sales
Telephone expense		12.00	Guest reimbursement
Miscellaneous revenue		61.50	Ski rental

Similarly, Figure 4–3 is an example of a purchase journal recording the purchases for the month. The monthly entry would be:

	Debit	Credit	Explanation
Accounts payable		$17,279.39	May purchases
Cost of food	$ 3,702.10		May purchases
Cost of beverage	53.00		May purchases
Cleaning supplies	282.12		May purchases
Other supplies	138.40		May purchases
Travel agent commiss.	26.00		May purchases
Advertising expense	40.00		May purchases
Linen service	600.00		May purchases
Electricity	982.00		May purchases
Heating expense	385.00		May purchases
Telephone expense	81.40		May purchases

Figure 4–4 is a sample of a check register (or cash disbursements journal). Since most of the checks written are to settle accounts payable, the number of columns needed is limited. The monthly entry would be:

	Debit	Credit	Explanation
Cash		$11,428.26	May payments
Accounts payable	$ 8,445.26		May payments
Payroll bank a/c	1,002.00		Transfers to payroll a/c
Federal tax withheld	344.00		May withholding
State tax withheld	94.00		May withholding
Social Security withheld	142.00		May withholding
Interest expense	1,280.00		Interest payment —May
Travel advance	121.00		Advance to Grayscot

Grayscot Bed and Breakfast

Date	Bank Deposit	Accounts Receivable		Room and Board Revenue	Other Food Revenue	Beverage Revenue	Other	
		Dr	Cr				Account	Amount
May 1	304.45	40.00		262.45	14.00	28.00		
2	404.90	62.50	23.00	388.40	12.50	31.50	Telephone	12.00
3	293.05		39.20	202.85	19.00	32.50		
May 31	309.65	29.40	33.85	148.70	61.20	33.80	Ski Rental	61.50
TOTAL	10022.65	452.70	481.30	7208.35	1810.10	902.10		73.50

Figure 4–2   Example of Simple Cash Receipts and Revenue Journal

$\mathcal{G}$rayscot Bed and Breakfast

Date	Supplier	Amount	Cost of Food	Cost of Beverage	Cleaning Supplies	Other Supplies	Travel Agent Commissions	Advertising	Other Account	Other Amount
May 1	Smith Foods	402.20	402.20							
2	Grace Produce	117.65	117.65							
3	James Liquor	18.00		18.00						
4	Brown Meats	116.08	116.08							
5	General Supplies	286.79			170.50	116.29				
6	New York Travel	6.00					6.00			
7	Local News	40.00						40.00		
7	Linen Co.	120.00							Linen Sv.	120.00
29	Brown Meat	212.40	212.40							
30	Louis Wines	35.00		35.00						
31	Upstate Power	982.00							Electr.	482.00
	TOTALS	6290.02	3702.10	53.00	282.12	138.40	26.00	40.00		2048.40

Figure 4–3 Example of Purchase Journal

Grayscot Bed and Breakfast

Date	Supplier	Check Nos.	Amount	Accounts Payable	Payroll Transfers	Other Account	Other Amount
May 1	Smith Foods	62	812.40	812.40			
1	Brown Meats	63	621.65	621.65			
3	General Supplies	64	685.11	685.11			
4	Local News	65	164.00	164.00			
28	Our Bank	118	496.00		496.00		
28	I.R.S.	119	172.00			Fed. Tax W/H	172.00
28	State of Mind	120	47.00			St. Tax W/H	47.00
31	Grace Produce	121	162.10	162.10			
31	Our Mortgage Co.	122	1280.00			Interest Exp.	1280.00
TOTAL			11428.26	8445.26	1002.00		1981.00

Figure 4–4 Example of a Check Register

37

Grayscot Bed and Breakfast

Payroll for Period Ending May 14

Name	Gross Earnings	Fed. Tax W/H	State Tax W/H	Social Security	Health Ins.	Total Deductions	Net Pay	Check No.
Tom Grayscot	400.00	96.00	32.00	32.00	5.00	165.00	235.00	1101
Sally Sales	300.00	62.00	15.00	24.00	5.00	106.00	194.00	1102
Iam Parttime	88.00	12.00	2.00	8.00	---	22.00	66.00	1103
Sue Covers	64.00	8.00	1.00	6.00	---	15.00	49.00	1104
TOTAL	852.00	178.00	50.00	70.00	10.00	308.00	544.00	

Figure 4–5 Example of a Payroll Journal

Figure 4–5 is an example of a payroll journal for one pay period. Normally, a separate journal is necessary for each pay period and a journal entry must be made for each. The following would be the entry for Figure 4–5:

	Debit	Credit	Explanation
Payroll expense	$852.00		Payroll—5/14
Federal tax withheld		$178.00	Payroll—5/14
State tax withheld		50.00	Payroll—5/14
Social Security withheld		70.00	Payroll—5/14
Health insurance payable		10.00	Payroll—5/14
Payroll bank account		544.00	Payroll—5/14

A separate journal entry will be made for employer contributions such as Social Security. This will be covered in more detail in Chapter 7.

Financial Statements

At the end of each accounting period, the cycle is completed by the preparation of financial statements, principally a statement of income and a balance sheet. A statement of income is prepared for the period and the year to date. This can be two separate statements or can easily be combined into one statement using two columns.

To provide an example of these statements, I have used the trial balance as at April 30, 199X shown on page 29. Figure 4–6 is the income statement for the four

Grayscot Bed and Breakfast
Income Statement as at April 30, 199X

Month of April	Revenue	4 Months to April 30
	Room and board sales	$28,210
	Other food sales	2,710
	Beverage sales	1,260
	Miscellaneous revenue	412
	Total revenue	$32,592
	Expenditure	
	Cost of food	11,206
	Cost of beverage	363
	Payroll expense	2,760
	Cleaning supplies	820
	Other supplies	762
	Linen service	1,820
	Heating expense	4,705
	Electricity	3,208
	Depreciation expense	1,120
	Interest expense	3,950
	Total Expenditure	30,714
	Net Income	$1,878

Figure 4–6 Example of Income Statement

months, while in the left-hand column there is a space for the April amounts. This statement incorporates all the revenue and expense amounts for the four months. The net result is then incorporated into the end-of-period balance sheet, as reflected in Figure 4–7.

The statements have been prepared in a very basic format to illustrate the necessary steps. For most hotels, the number of accounts is much larger and the format of the financial statements is more complex. In Chapter 8, the end-of-period process and the preparation of financial statements for a full hotel operation are discussed in detail.

Subsequent chapters explain how customized versions of these journals are used in hotel accounting. Also described is how, by use of computer technology, the basic recording steps have been simplified.

Grayscot Bed and Breakfast
Balance Sheet
as at April, 30, 199X

Assets		
Cash		$2,709
Accounts receivable		922
Inventory—food		1,708
Inventory—beverage		176
Land	52,000	
Building	210,000	
Furniture and equipment	39,712	
	301,712	
Accumulated depreciation	<32,740>	268,972
		$274,487

Liabilities		
Accounts payable		$ 1,382
Mortgage payable		158,000
Capital—Balance January 1	$113,227	
Net Income—per		
Income Statement	1,878	115,105
		$274,487

Figure 4–7   A Sample Balance Sheet

1. Using the following trial balance, prepare a balance sheet of the Catamount Inn as at June 30 and an income statement showing the year-to-date results:

Catamount Inn
Trial Balance as at June 30

	Debits	Credits
Cash	$11,122	
Accounts receivable	6,048	
Inventories	5,836	
Accounts payable		$9,547
Taxes payable		1,208
Capital		2,574
Room sales		38,715
Food sales		14,032
Beverage sales		7,112
Cost of sales—food	4,128	
—beverage	1,763	
Rent expense	18,000	
Payroll expense	17,012	
Operating supplies expense	3,137	
Utilities expense	6,142	
	$73,188	$73,188

2. Using the chart of accounts in Chapter 3, prepare a separate journal entry for each of the following transactions (show account numbers):
   a. A guest charge to a room for lunch in Outlet 1; the check has the following breakdown: food $35, beverage $12.80, tax $4.70.
   b. A purchase from Smith Hotel Supplies Company of the following:

Dinner napkins	$322.00
Dishwashing soap	172.00
Toilet tissue	318.00
Laundry soap	731.00
Name tags for maintenance employees	68.00

   c. A bill received from the electric utility company for $3,105.
   d. Transfer from one department to another of 11 hours @ $6 per hour for an engineering employee who worked in banquet.
   e. A telephone bill received comprising $2,122 in charges for guest calls and $1,171 in calls received by reservations on their 800 number.

3. Circle T or F to indicate whether the following statements are true or false:
   T F **a.** In all journal entries, the total debits must equal the total credits.
   T F **b.** Revenue and expense accounts in the general ledger are zeroed out at year end.

T F **c.** Inventory adjustments are usually recorded on a daily basis.

T F **d.** An accrual account is used to record an estimated expense for which a bill has not been received.

T F **e.** Weekly payrolls usually require separate journal entries.

4. Circle the correct answer to the following statements:

   a. The financial position of a business at a specific point in time is reflected in:
   (1) An income statement
   (2) A balance sheet
   (3) A trial balance

   b. The daily sales are recorded in:
   (1) A purchase journal
   (2) A receipts and revenue journal
   (3) A check register

   c. The following account is not an asset account:
   (1) Inventories
   (2) Taxes payable
   (3) Accounts receivable

5 Night Audit

In the preceding chapter, the use of a revenue journal was described as the method by which daily revenue could be recorded and recapped for posting to the general ledger.

In most hotels, the recording and control of revenue occurs through a process known as the *night audit*. A hotel "day" is considered to end after the restaurants and lounges close, usually between midnight and 3 A.M. Therefore, the night-audit function derives its name from being performed during the night and the person or persons performing the work are known as *night auditors* and usually work from 11 P.M. to 7 A.M.

Few people realize that hotels charge for their rooms by the night, rather than by the day. Regardless of what time he or she arrives, from early morning to late at night, the guest will be charged for one day's (night's) lodging if he or she leaves before checkout time on the following day. Thus, the posting of the room rentals—plus taxes where required—is one of the fundamental duties of all night auditors. Other charges are usually posted as soon as they are received by the daytime cashiers, but late charges—those incurred in facilities still open after the cashiers leave or any left by the cashiers—are also the responsibility of the night auditors. The charges come in various forms, the most common being restaurant checks signed by guests or other customers but also include telephone charges, metered in some manner, laundry and valet charges recorded on slips by the laundry, and miscellaneous other charges recorded on some form of document.

Thus, the primary functions of the night auditor are the posting of guest charges and the balancing and recording of all revenue. They are also required to handle any cashiering necessary, but this is rather limited as very few guests check out after 11 P.M. or before 7 A.M. and the making of change for a guest is the most common cashiering requirement. In smaller hotels, night auditors may also be required to handle check-ins, but this is neither a night-audit nor an accounting function.

In describing the night-audit process, we first look at it from the historical manual method using a hand transcript (see Figure 5–1) which is still used in some very small properties.

Hotel Grayscot

Night Audit Transcript For Jan. 18, 1966

Room No.	Name of Guest	Room	Food	Bev.	Tax	Tips	Tel.	Laun.	Misc.	Total	Bal. Fwd.	Paid	City Ledger	Closing Bal.
101	Smith J										188.50	188.50		-0-
102	Walters B	50.00	36.20	8.00	5.00	6.00	1.00			106.20	59.45			165.65
103	Jones C		7.10			2.00				9.10	104.60		113.70	-0-
105	Roberts G.	50.00	18.80	7.00	5.00	4.00		7.00	①1.00	92.80	—			92.80
106	Williams S	50.00	21.20		5.00	3.00	1.50			80.70	202.20			282.90
107	Jackson M	75.00	46.70	11.00	7.50	10.50			②3.80	154.50	162.85			317.35
108	Brown B	75.00	70.20	9.00	7.50					161.70	—			161.70
101	Casey S	50.00	21.65	4.00	5.00	5.00				85.65	—			85.65
	①Postage ②Telegrams													
Total		350.00	221.85	39.00	35.00	30.50	2.50	7.00	4.80	690.65	717.60	188.50	113.70	1106.05

Figure 5–1 Night Audit Hand Transcript

Our purpose in examining the hand transcript is to relate it to the revenue journal in the preceding chapter and to understand how it evolved into the electromechanical systems and, ultimately, the computerized property management systems now in use in most hotels.

THE HAND TRANSCRIPT

The use of a hand transcript required that an individual account be maintained on a daily basis for each occupied room. The individual charges and credits could be posted to each account either manually or using some form of posting mechanism that might or might not have the ability to pick up a prior balance and add in the individual transaction to arrive at a new total. If not, the new balance was calculated manually. The night auditor's responsibility was to arrive at a daily total for each type of transaction for each individual room and enter those totals on the hand transcript on a room-by-room basis as shown in Figure 5–1. The opening balances (bal. fwd.) were transferred from the prior night's transcript. The daily charges were totaled, added to the prior night's balance and settlements, either by payment or transfer to accounts receivable (city ledger), and were deducted to arrive at a new balance. It should be noted that when a room was vacated and reoccupied, it appeared twice on the hand transcript (see Room 101 in Figure 5–1). The final step in the night-audit process was simply to total each column and crossfoot to ensure that it was in balance.

Usually, the daily numbers were transferred to the general ledger by recording them on a daily basis in a revenue journal similar to Figure 4–2 and entering the monthly totals in the general ledger. However, an alternative involving slightly more work would have been to post the daily totals directly into the general ledger. In journal entry format, the entry for Figure 5–1 would be:

	Debit	Credit
Cash	$ 188.50	
Accounts Receivable—Guest Ledger	388.45*	
Accounts Receivable—City Ledger	113.70	
Room revenue		$350.00
Food revenue		221.85
Beverage revenue		39.00
Sales tax payable		35.00
Tips payable		30.50
Telephone revenue		2.50
Laundry revenue		7.00
Postage		1.00
Telegrams		3.80

*Charges of $690.65 less credits of $188.50 and $113.70.

THE NCR CLASS 42

The NCR Class 42 (Figure 5–2) played an important role in the transition from the manual transcript to the computerized systems in use today. The NCR 42 was discontinued in 1975 and, except for a few isolated properties, is no longer in use. However, the initial

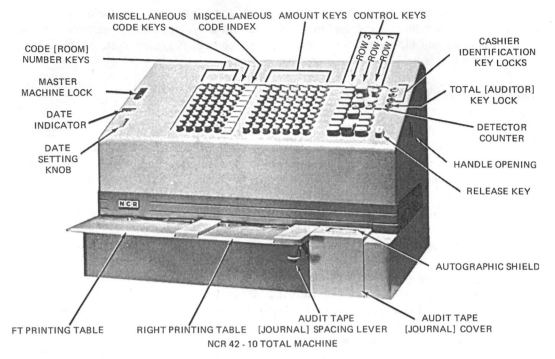

MISCELLANEOUS CODE KEYS MISCELLANEOUS CODE INDEX AMOUNT KEYS CONTROL KEYS

ROW 3 ROW 2 ROW 1

CODE [ROOM] NUMBER KEYS

MASTER MACHINE LOCK

DATE INDICATOR

DATE SETTING KNOB

CASHIER IDENTIFICATION KEY LOCKS

TOTAL [AUDITOR] KEY LOCK

DETECTOR COUNTER

HANDLE OPENING

RELEASE KEY

AUTOGRAPHIC SHIELD

FT PRINTING TABLE RIGHT PRINTING TABLE AUDIT TAPE [JOURNAL] SPACING LEVER AUDIT TAPE [JOURNAL] COVER

NCR 42 - 10 TOTAL MACHINE

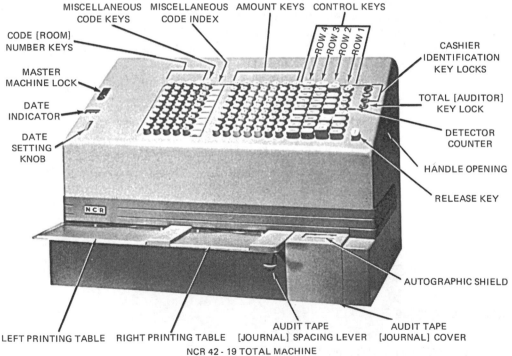

MISCELLANEOUS CODE KEYS MISCELLANEOUS CODE INDEX AMOUNT KEYS CONTROL KEYS

ROW 4 ROW 3 ROW 2 ROW 1

CODE [ROOM] NUMBER KEYS

MASTER MACHINE LOCK

DATE INDICATOR

DATE SETTING KNOB

CASHIER IDENTIFICATION KEY LOCKS

TOTAL [AUDITOR] KEY LOCK

DETECTOR COUNTER

HANDLE OPENING

RELEASE KEY

AUTOGRAPHIC SHIELD

LEFT PRINTING TABLE RIGHT PRINTING TABLE AUDIT TAPE [JOURNAL] SPACING LEVER AUDIT TAPE [JOURNAL] COVER

NCR 42 - 19 TOTAL MACHINE

Figure 5–2   NCR 42 Machines (Courtesy of AT&T Global Information Solutions)

computer systems were computerized replicas of the functions and the reports produced by the NCR 42. Some of the first computer systems even referred to their daily reconciliation of charges and credits as "D" cards, a term used for that function on the NCR 42.

The NCR 42 is introduced here not to suggest that it is a system currently in use, but to better facilitate the understanding of the modern computerized system.

The NCR 42, like the other posting machines, was, in essence, nothing more than a multitotal printing adding machine which performed the same function as the hand transcript. A greater number of keys made it possible to obtain a more detailed breakdown of income and other charges. Additionally, it had some special features, such as a "Paid in full" key which, after picking up the opening balance, automatically zeroed the balance due and updated the paid total in the machine.

Most charges were posted to the individual guest accounts during the day while the night auditor posted any late charges in addition to posting the room charges on a room-by-room basis. The final report, known as a "D Card" (Figure 5–3), was printed by the night auditor at the end of the audit and displayed totals for all posting keys. The night auditor corrected any errors manually on the "D" card. The "D" card format and method of compilation of data formed the basis for the systems in use today. Figure 5–4 shows the various phases in the development of night audit systems.

The final totals could then be transferred to a monthly income journal or used to prepare a daily journal entry in the same manner as previously described for a hand transcript.

WEAKNESSES OF THE MANUAL SYSTEM

The illustrations and the comments in the preceding paragraphs should make many of the weaknesses of manual systems apparent:

1. The posting of the room and tax was done room by room and was therefore time consuming.
2. As with other charges, the posting was a manual process and subject to human error.
3. An extensive amount of manual balancing was required, particularly if errors were made.
4. The number of totals available was limited. Even though the keys could be changed from the basic format (Figure 5–3 is an example), the grouping of classifications was necessary. A separate breakdown of "Miscellaneous" had to be made for entry into the income journal. Furthermore, the restaurant charges were sometimes grouped in one number and a further entry was required to break down food and beverages.

COMPUTERIZED NIGHT AUDIT

Automation, in the form of computers using sophisticated software packages specifically designed for hotels, has changed the night-audit process dramatically.

The industry term to describe these software packages is *property management systems (PMS)*. The advent of these systems moved the emphasis of front-desk systems

D—NIGHT AUDITOR'S MACHINE BALANCE NO.＿＿＿＿

DATE ＿＿＿＿＿＿

DEPARTMENT	DATE	DESCRIPTION	NET TOTALS	CORRECTIONS	MACHINE TOTALS	
ROOM		ROOM	4500.–	10.–	4510.00	
TAX		RMTAX	225.–	–.50	225.50	
TELEPHONE		REST	3900.–	20.–	3920.00	
LONG DISTANCE		PHONE	300.–		300.00	
LAUNDRY		LDIST	250.–		250.00	
VALET		LDRY	175.–		175.00	
GARAGE		VALET	150.–		150.00	
TELEGRAM		GARGE	250.–		250.00	
BEVERAGE		CL–DR	2100.–		2100.00	
MISCELLANEOUS		TR.DR	500.–		500.00	
RESTAURANT		MISC	125.–		125.00	
TRANSFER CHARGE		PDOUT	100.–		100.00	
PAID OUT	TOTAL DEBITS		12575.–			
TOTAL DEBITS						
TRANSFER CREDIT		PAID	9200.–	90.–	9290.00	
ADJUSTMENT		ALLOW	50.–		50.00	
PAID		TR.CR	500.–		500.00	
TOTAL CREDITS		CL–CR	1000.–		1000.00	
NET DIFFERENCE	TOTAL CREDITS		10750.–			
OPENING DR. BALANCE						
NET OUTSTANDING	NET DIFFERENCE		1825.–			
TOTAL MCH. DR. BALANCE		DR.BAL			8375.00	
TOTAL MCH. CR. BALANCE		CR.BAL			250.00	
NET OUTSTANDING	OPENING BAL		6300.–			
CORRECTIONS	NET OUTSTANDING		8125.–		8125.00	

DETECTOR COUNTER READINGS:

AUDITOR'S CONTROL ＿＿＿＿＿＿＿＿

MACH. NUMBER ＿＿＿＿＿＿＿＿＿

☐ DATE CHANGED

☐ CONTROL TOTALS AT ZERO

☐ MASTER TAPE LOCKED

☐ AUDIT CONTROL LOCKED

AUDITOR

NCR B-6777

＿＿＿＿＿＿＿＿＿＿＿＿＿＿＿

NOTE: Description and machine totals are printed by the machine. All other figures, with descriptions where required, are calculated and inserted by the night auditor.

Figure 5–3 The "D" Card (Courtesy of AT&T Global Information Solutions)

from specialized hardware designed for hotels to specialized software using standard computer hardware (see Figure 5-5). The newer systems have the flexibility to utilize hardware made by a number of manufacturers, rather than being limited to one specific brand.

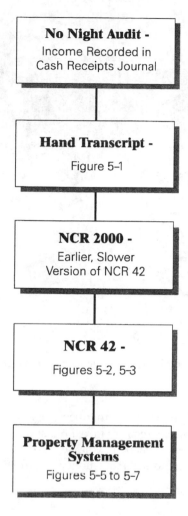

Figure 5–4 Phases in the Development of Night Audit Systems

The property management systems were designed to perform four primary functions: reservations, check-in and checkout, guest ledger, and night audit. However, most systems also provide a guest history: information on checked-out guests that is not only invaluable in researching information for billing problems or inquiries but can be used for marketing purposes. Additionally, the use of standard computer equipment provides the ability to interface directly with back-office accounting systems, energy management systems, in-room movies, and other functions not directly related to the recording or control of revenue or guest ledger.

Hotel revenue-recording procedures have always followed a format whereby room revenue (and directly related items such as tax or service charges) is posted at the end of the day by the night auditors, while all other charges (food, beverage, telephone, etc.) are posted during the day as close as practical to the time at which the charge was incurred. Automation has not changed this policy. However, the use of computer interfaces has dramatically reduced the amount of manual posting by cashiers. The inter-

Figure 5–5 Guest Checking Out at Computerized Front Desk (Photograph by Chris Alexopoulos)

face programs automatically transmit the room charges from the restaurant registers to the guest accounts. Telephone charges are measured and recorded by an automatic call accounting system (discussed in detail in Chapter 16). Manual postings are reduced, therefore, to miscellaneous items such as laundry or gift shop charges (unless the interface malfunctions).

POSTING OF CHARGES

We have previously discussed how the "D" card was used to analyze charges and credits to the guest's account and to provide the information for creation of an income journal entry. More standard accounting principles are followed in posting on the new property management system. The act of posting not only accomplishes the debit to the guest folio but also the credit to the revenue, or in certain instances, the liability account. The transaction is directed to the accounts through the use of "charge codes" which are entered into the computer along with the amount. A listing of common charge codes is shown in Figure 5–6. The codes are identified with general ledger account numbers and account types (1 = balance-sheet account, 2 = revenue account). However, hotels with several food and beverage outlets will have more extensive lists.

The postings are entered by keying in the charge code number and the amount. The charge codes are programmed to reflect a usual entry as a credit or a debit de-

CHARGE CODE	DESCRIPTION			GL ACCOUNT	TYPE
10	Front Desk—	Cash		11-1527	1
11		Amexco		11-1527	1
12		Visa/MC		11-1527	1
13		Diners		13-1025	1
14	Restaurant—	Cash		11-1527	1
15		Amexco		11-1527	1
16		Visa/MC		11-1527	1
17		Diners		13-1025	1
18	Bar—	Cash		11-1527	1
19		Amexco		11-1527	1
20		Visa/MC		11-1527	1
21		Diners		13-1025	1
30	Front Desk Paid Outs			11-1527	1
35	Rooms—	Transient		310-1005	2
36		Group—	Corporate	310-1105	2
37			Association	310-1107	2
38			Tour & Travel	310-1106	2
40		Adj—	Transient	310-1005	2
41			Group—Corporate	310-1105	2
42			Association	310-1107	2
43			Tour & Travel	310-1106	2
45	Restaurant—	Food		320-1301	2
46		Liquor		330-1401	2
47		Wine		330-1402	2
48		Adjustment		320-1301	2
50	Bar—	Food		320-1302	2
51		Liquor		330-1401	2
52		Wine		330-1402	2
53		Adjustment		320-1301	2
55	Rooms Tax			37-7004	1
56	Food & Beverage Tax			37-7003	1
57	Local Telephone			350-1601	2
58	LD Telephone			350-1602	2
59	Laundry			600-1702	2
60	Valet			600-1701	2
61	Telegrams			450-1834	2
62	Fax			450-1834	2
63	Flowers			37-1021	1
64	Shops			37-1024	1
65	Banquet Gratuities			37-2016	1

Figure 5–6 Standard Charge Codes

pending on the item; for example, hitting "Front Desk Cash" and $10 will post a $10 credit to a guest's account, while hitting "Restaurant Food" and $10 will post a debit. Negative entries or corrections can be entered with a minus (–) sign. In certain categories, it is common to provide "Adjustment" keys for the front-desk cashier to use to adjust items disputed at checkout.

In order to fully record the revenue for the day, it is necessary to record the revenue that is not charged to a guest account. This is accomplished through the use of a

house folio. A *house folio* is an account set up in the guest ledger in the same manner as a room folio, but it is used for nonguest transactions. The posting to the house folio for cash sales is made by posting the revenue to the house folio on the revenue charge key and recording the settlement by using a settlement charge code, usually "cash" or "credit card." Thus, the house folio is zeroed out at the end of the day. Figure 5–7 is an example of house folio entries for one day. House folios are also used to record city-ledger charges, that is, charges to other than hotel guests. The charges are cleared out of the guest ledger and into city ledger at the end of the day or the end of the period. House folios are also used for adjustments and corrections in addition to recording cash sales and other sales to nonguests. It is important to note that postings to house accounts are normally done by the night auditors rather than the cashiers.

NIGHT AUDITOR

The property management system has materially reduced the workload of the night auditor, with the emphasis shifting from the recording of charges and revenue to the running and review of reports.

The recording function is limited to the balancing of food and beverage revenue (described later in the chapter) and the recording of all revenue not automatically posted directly to the guest accounts. House account entries, as described earlier in the chapter, must be made for cash sales, allowances, adjustments, and corrections. Long-distance telephone revenue, usually posted automatically, should also be balanced.

Perhaps the night auditor's most important function is to review the "preliminary" night audit—a review of various reports on activity for the day. The preliminary night audit usually involves a review of the following:

1. The end-of-shift report run by each cashier. This report shows all entries made by that cashier.
2. The room charges report. This report shows, on a room-by-room basis, all charges, such as room revenue, tax, gratuities, food, or special items included in a package. Care should be taken to identify and correct rate errors and to review rate variances (rates that are other than the normal rate for that room).
3. Transfers to the city ledger for the day.
4. The printout by charge code of all transactions for the day.

If the preliminary night audit is done with proper care, the final audit is simply a matter of running a final report, which usually takes 40 to 60 minutes for a medium-sized hotel. The final report is a complete history of hotel activity for the day, including not only a record of guest charges and revenue but also all reservation and advance deposit activity.

ADVANCE DEPOSITS

When a reservation is entered, it receives a reservation number which also functions as a folio number in the advance deposit section of the guest ledger. (In some systems, it is a separate ledger but functions in the same manner as the guest ledger.)

N/A Journal Entries		Arrival Jan 1/93 Exp Dep Dec 31/93 Rate 00.0 Payment DB Page 1 Resv #000	

DATE		DESCRIPTION OF CHARGES	CHARGES	CREDITS
Mon	Feb 01	Restaurant Food	$2,412.05	
"	"	Restaurant Liquor	732.86	
"	"	Restaurant Wine	306.00	
"	"	Beverage Tax	103.89	
"	"	Food Tax	205.37	
"	"	Cost of Wine	4.80	
"	"	Cost of Liquor	7.30	
"	"	In-House Entertainment		$18.32
"	"	Rest. Room Charge	1,360.97–	
"	"	Rest. Cash		698.33
"	"	Rest. Amexco		972.60
"	"	Rest. Visa/MC		722.05
"	"	Bar Liquor	322.11	
"	"	Bar Wine	108.54	
"	"	Beverage Tax	42.99	
"	"	Bar Room Charge	180.12–	
"	"	Bar Cash		112.72
"	"	Bar Amexco		82.60
"	"	Bar Visa/MC		98.20
"	"	Bar Wine Correction	22.00–	
"	"	Bar Liquor Correction	22.00	
			$2,704.82	$2,704.82
		Total Account 0.00		

Figure 5–7   Example of a House Folio

When an advance deposit is received, it is posted to the folio in the same manner as a cashier posts a payment to an in-house folio. Thus, a reservationist posting advance deposits must print a shift report, make a cash drop, and so on, in the same fashion as a cashier. This permits a cashier to function as a reservationist and post advance deposits during his or her regular shift. This flexibility in the system aids reduced staffing in slow periods.

ACCOUNTING OFFICE REVIEW

Under the old mechanical systems, an extensive review of the night-audit work was carried out by the income controller. This function has been reduced to a review of the night-audit printout and report with an emphasis on functions performed manually by night audit: principally, adjustments made and the manual postings of revenue not automatically recorded. This, however, pertains mostly to food and beverage revenue.

FOOD AND BEVERAGES

In this area, also, mechanical cash registers have been replaced by electronic registers which capture the sales analysis and provide ready information for the recording of income. The principle for balancing food and beverage remains unchanged: Food + Beverage + Tax + Tips = Cash Sales + Charges (room, city ledger, and credit card).

The registers can produce balanced readings in report form which can be readily entered by the night auditor into the property management system. This provides sales information for the daily revenue report which subsequently flows into the general ledger. Many of the new food and beverage systems are fully interfaced with the property management system, providing an automatic flow of information and eliminating the need for re-entry. However, in addition to providing the cash and charge breakdown and the revenue analysis, these systems incorporate control features which provide detailed analyses of revenue, inventory consumption, and costs. These functions are described in greater detail in Chapter 14.

While a certain level of management supervision is still necessary, much of this control has now been transferred to the computers. By having various levels of computer access, certain functions can be restricted to management. The more common of these functions are the ability to void charges, to post charges to entertainment expense, and to transfer the responsibility for a check from one server to another. The final clearing of the day's information (commonly called the "z" report) still remains a night-audit function. While under the old mechanical systems the information was fully deleted, the new systems retain all information in computer memory subject to printing and purging either weekly or monthly. The purging is, however, controlled by accounting management and should not be done at the individual outlet level.

DEPOSIT PROCEDURES

The procedure for the physical dropping of deposits remains basically unchanged. All cashiers (front-office, restaurant bar, garage, and so on) must compute their new receipts, place them in a deposit envelope (Figure 5–8), and drop the envelope in a slotted safe-deposit box provided for this purpose. The envelope should show a breakdown of cash, checks, and other items included in the deposit. On the following day, the general cashier removes them, checks the contents of each against the figures entered on the outside of the envelope, and makes up the daily deposit.

Although the contents are rarely verified until the general cashier opens them, the number of envelopes dropped into and removed from the safe should be controlled by having another front-office or accounting department employee witness both acts. For this purpose, an individual sheet for each day (or a bound book) should be provided, with columns for the date, number of envelopes, and signatures of the cashiers and witnesses. When the drop is made, the witness's signature attests that he or she actually saw and counted the number of envelopes deposited into the safe. The following morning, the general cashier totals the number listed, opens the

```
            CASHIER'S REPORT

Date.......................... Watch ..........A.M.
                                          P.M.
Cashier...........................................

RECEIPTS                              |        |
LESS—DISBURSEMENTS                    |        |
NET RECEIPTS                          |        |
      CONTENTS OF ENVELOPE            |        |
CHECKS AND LIST ENCLOSED              |        |
CURRENCY                              |        |
COIN                                  |        |
HOUSE VOUCHERS (List separately)      |        |
                                      |        |
                                      |        |
                                      |        |
                                      |        |
                                      |        |
TOTAL AMOUNT ENCLOSED                 |        |
LESS—NET RECEIPTS                     |        |
EXCHANGE DUE CASHIER                  |        |

      EXCHANGE WANTED                 |        |
CURRENCY—                             |        |
      $20—and over                    |        |
         10—                          |        |
          5—                          |        |
          1—                          |        |
COIN—                                 |        |
         .50                          |        |
         .25                          |        |
         .10                          |        |
         .05                          |        |
         .01                          |        |
                                      |        |
             TOTAL                    |        |
                                      |        |
                                      |        |

William Allen & Co. (A Division of A. J. Bart & Sons, Inc.) • 718-821-5550 • Stock Form #9248
```

Figure 5–8 Cashier's Deposit Envelope (Courtesy of William Allen & Company)

safe in the presence of a witness, and counts the number of envelopes in it. If the total agrees, both the cashier and the witness initial the total on the sheet. The general cashier prepares a deposit analysis and summary (Figure 5–9) which compares the deposits of the individual cashiers and their respective computer readings and computes the overage/shortage amount by individual and in total. Where the individual

GENERAL CASHIER'S DEPOSIT SUMMARY

Day _____   Date _____

Station	Cashier	Witnessed By	Net Deposit	Breakdown From Envelopes						Received By	Do Not Include as Part of Deposit
				Cash	Checks	Travelers' Checks	Petty Cash Vouchers	Total Deposit	Due Back		Foreign Currency At Cost
Front Office											
AM			1200.00		1200.00	200.00		1400.00	200.00		
AM			1600.00	600.00	1000.00			1600.00	-0-		
PM			850.00		450.00	500.00		950.00	100.00		
PM			850.00		1100.00	200.00		1300.00	450.00		
Night			100.00	100.00				100.00	-0-		
Sub Total			4600.00								
City Ledger			2000.00		2000.00			2000.00			
Total F.O.			6600.00								
Restaurant*											
Banquets											
Total Restaurant			1800.00	1800.00				1800.00			
Bar*											
Total Bar			1200.00	1200.00				1200.00			
Total Food & Beverage											
Grand Totals			9600.00	3700.00	5750.00	900.00		10350.00	750.00		

"D" Card Recap

Cash   9700.00

Paid Out   100.00

Net Deposit as Above   9600.00

Deposit Recap

Total Deposit   10350.00

Less: Due Back   750.00

Net Deposit   9600.00

Number of Envelopes _____

Witness _____

List each outlet separately with one line for each shift, plus relief cashier where used.

Figure 5-9 General Cashier's Deposit Summary and Analysis

server also functions as a cashier (server banking is described in Chapter 14), a large number of deposit drops will be made. Where tips paid out exceeds the cash taken in, the difference must be repaid to the cashier out of other receipts. This is known as a *due back*.

BANQUET CONTROLS

Banquet revenue must be checked and verified by an experienced night auditor. The bills often include so many items and must be so detailed that the possibility of errors is great, making it almost mandatory to assign this function to a well-trained, banquet-oriented person. Banquet bills are prepared by the banquet manager, head waiter, or a designated assistant as soon as a function is over. It is the responsibility of the banquet auditor to check that the items listed were correctly priced and extended and to determine that no items were omitted.

All banquet functions should be covered by a contract or written confirmation, at the discretion of management. Either should include the full menu and complete details of the agreement. Attendance figures can only be estimated, since most functions are booked months, and even years, in advance. However, the customer should be informed of the hotel's policy on guarantees and be required to submit definite figures, in writing, before the day of the function. This information is needed not only for billing and control purposes, but by the banquet manager and chef to prepare for the function. The guarantee determines the number of waiters needed, the number of tables to set, and the amount of food to order and prepare.

Banquets benefit almost every revenue-producing department in the hotel. Guests attending a function very often use some of the other facilities. To alert the other department heads and to keep management informed of all bookings, the banquet managers prepare various reports of actual bookings. The period covered and the information included vary according to each hotel's management policy. At a minimum, these reports should be issued once a month, listing all functions booked for the next month, and updated at the end of each week for the following week. The contents should include the date, the name of the person or organization holding the function, type of function (dinner, dance, dinner dance, or whatever), number of people expected, and any special requirements that might affect other departments. In addition, the banquet manager should prepare a separate sheet for each function, including the full menu and all other pertinent information.

Copies of contracts or confirmations that were sent when the functions were booked, all function sheets, and final guarantees must be sent to the banquet auditor. In addition, the banquet manager should be instructed to send a memo of any last-minute changes on guarantees or other terms of the agreement. The banquet auditor needs and uses all this information to properly control the banquet revenue.

In some hotels, to verify the number of covers, the chefs are required to enter on the menu the number served and send that sheet to the banquet auditor. Each auditor must set up his or her own routine to verify revenue, but it should include the following procedures:

The auditor must determine that a bill was prepared and processed for each function held. This is easily done by checking each bill received against those listed on the weekly function sheet for that day. If possible, the number of covers charged should be verified with the number served, and the charge per cover, as well as the unit charge of all items included on the bill, verified with the function sheet. The bill should then be compared with the function sheet to determine that all items listed separately that call for an additional charge are on the bill. Included in this category are such items as public-room rentals, flowers, music, microphones, photographers, and any extra charge for bartenders. For weddings, extra charges could include wedding cakes, specially printed napkins, matches, and favors.

Verifying beverage sales requires an additional step. The function sheet lists only the brands requested by the guest and, if they are to be purchased by the bottle, a minimum quantity and the unit cost. The bar manager, or a designated assistant, reports the actual number used. This is usually done on a sheet showing the number of bottles issued, the number returned to the storeroom, and the number used. Some will have two additional columns for the unit costs and the total charges. The auditor, after verifying the unit price, can compare the quantities used as shown on this report against the guest's invoice. The final step is to check the extensions, the computations for tax and gratuities, and the total shown on the bill.

What action, if any, the banquet auditor takes for differences between the number of covers charged and the number in the final guarantee depends entirely on the policy established by management. Policies vary between hotels, with guarantees strictly enforced in some while serving only as a guide in others. They may even vary within a hotel, depending on the type of function, sponsor, and so on. All the banquet auditor can do is try to enforce the policy and report any deviation to the hotel controller. Only the controller should make the decision on whether to pursue the matter further.

Finally, the banquet auditor prepares a report (Figure 5–10) which becomes a source document for entering the information into the property management system. Copies of this report are then distributed to designated executives.

ENTRY INTO THE GENERAL LEDGER

The final night-audit report includes a total summary of activity for the day shown in a journal entry format. Figure 5–11 is an example of this report using the account numbers shown in Figure 5-6.

When the property management system encompasses both front-office and back-office accounting in the same system, the entry is automatically transferred into the general ledger. Even when the two systems differ, an automatic transfer can sometimes be made provided the two systems are compatible and a software interface can be written. If an automatic transfer is not feasible, the entry must be manually keyed into the general ledger.

DAILY REVENUE REPORT

The last step accomplished by the final night-audit run is the printing of a daily revenue report (Figure 5–12). The format of the report can be customized to meet the in-

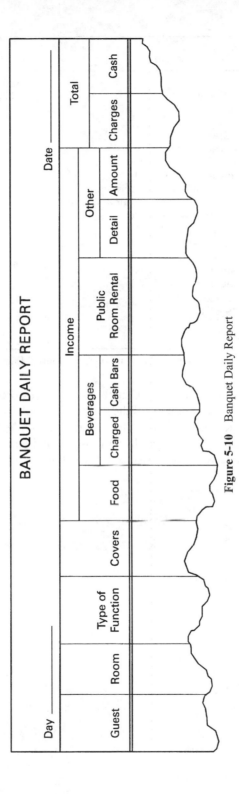

Figure 5-10 Banquet Daily Report

A/C No.	ACCOUNT	DEBIT	CREDIT
11-1527	Cash	$31,105.20	
13-1025	Accounts Receivable	17,640.05	
37-1021	Flowers		$ 62.00
37-1024	Shops		268.30
37-2016	Banquet Gratuities		1,172.60
37-7003	Food & Beverage Tax		1,705.00
37-7004	Room Tax		1,231.00
310-1005	Rooms Revenue—Transient		16,508.00
310-1105	Rooms Revenue—Group—Corporate		4,702.50
310-1106	Rooms Revenue—Group—Tour & Travel		1,520.75
310-1107	Rooms Revenue—Group—Association		2,128.60
320-1301	Food Revenue—Restaurant		9,622.70
320-1302	Food Revenue—Bar		628.45
330-1401	Liquor Revenue		2,128.40
330-1402	Wine Revenue		4,803.65
350-1601	Local Telephone		240.25
350-1602	Long Distance Telephone		1,633.20
450-1834	Telegrams & Fax		120.00
600-1701	Valet		109.50
600-1702	Laundry		160.35

Figure 5–11   End-of-Audit Journal Entry

formational needs of management. Usually this involves presenting the daily revenue on a grouping basis with subtotals for the various types of revenue and a grand total for the day. Key statistics, available from the information collected by the property management system, are also provided. Month-to-date and year-to-date numbers are normally included, along with comparisons to budget and prior year.

DAILY REVENUE REPORT

Tuesday, October 21, 19___

	Today	MONTH TO DATE Actual	MONTH TO DATE Budget	MONTH TO DATE Last Year
ROOM REVENUE				
Transient Room Revenue				
Transient Individual	5,178	241,564	92,525	216,542
Golf/Ski Individual	0	7,730	44,489	0
Corporate Individual	665	7,435	3,677	16,133
Total Transient Revenue	5,843	255,729	140,641	232,675
Group Room Revenue				
Group Corporate	0	53,858	107,768	90,921
Group Tour and Travel	0	61,946	22,677	20,898
Group Association	0	21,965	11,974	0
Total Group Room Revenue	0	137,769	142,419	111,819
Total Room Revenue	5,843	394,496	283,261	344,494
FOOD & BEVERAGE REVENUE				
Food Revenue				
Main Dining Room Food	480	83,571	40,343	59,546
Tavern Food	1,807	79,319	34,059	35,360
Room Service Food	0	92	0	0
Banquet Food	918	52,079	71,470	55,173
Total Food Sales	3,204	215,161	145,872	150,079
Beverage Revenue				
Main Dining Room Liquor	0	2,367	3,675	2,920
Main Dining Room Wine	0	7,262	4,519	2,952
Tavern Liquor	236	23,735	15,037	14,902
Tavern Wine	299	13,213	1,739	6,743
Pool Terrace Liquor	0	0	0	0
Pool Terrace Wine	0	0	0	0
Banquet Liquor	54	7,134	9,116	7,211
Banquet Wine	21	4,606	7,265	4,697
Total Beverage Revenue	610	58,317	41,350	39,425
Misc Food & Beverage Income				
Public Room Rentals	0	1,000	1,368	100
Banquet Miscellaneous Comm.	0	0	0	246
Audio Visual Rentals	0	130	0	1,165
Total Food & Bev Misc Income	0	1,130	1,368	1,511
Total Food & Beverage Income	3,815	274,608	188,590	191,016
TELEPHONE REVENUE				
Local & Long Distance Revenue				
Local Telephone	6	266	175	95
Long Distance Telephone	105	4,189	6,196	4,265
Total Local & Long Distance	111	4,457	6,371	4,360
Telephone Commissions	0	0	516	1,861
Total Telephone Revenue	111	4,457	6,887	6,221
GIFT SHOP REVENUE				
Sales Clothing & Gifts				
Sheppard's Store Clothing	21	2,068	5,037	1,542
Sheppard's Store Gifts	142	10,015	5,037	4,797
Total Sales-Gifts and Clothing	163	12,083	10,075	6,339

	Today	MONTH TO DATE Actual	MONTH TO DATE Budget	MONTH TO DATE Last Year
Sales Other				
Magazines and Paperbacks	28	534	206	437
Newspapers	26	1,260	413	808
Vermont Food Products	16	2,150	413	145
Sundries	3	634	0	537
Gift Shop Commissions	0	2,616	0	463
Total Sales - Other	73	7,194	1,032	2,389
Total Gift Shop Revenue	236	19,277	11,107	8,728
GUEST LAUNDRY & VALET REVENUE				
Sales - Laundry	23	385	0	2
Total Guest Laundry & Valet	23	385	0	2
STORE RENTALS & OTHER INCOME				
Store Rentals #1	0	10,799	5,161	13,065
Concessions - Game Room	0	0	0	0
Concessions Vending Room	0	0	0	116
Concessions #1	5	0	40	0
Concessions #2	5	35	323	0
Concessions #3	0	0	0	0
Forfeit Deposits	0	1,648	281	700
Miscellaneous	0	5,872	400	292
Total Store Rents & Other Income	5	18,355	6,205	14,172
COUNTRY CLUB REVENUE				
Sales - Food & Sodas				
Country Club Food	8	5,683	8,281	0
Total Sales - Food & Sodas	8	5,683	8,281	0
Sales - Liquor & Wine				
Country Club Liquor	172	2,363	5,092	0
Country Club Wine	4	229	454	0
Total Sales - Liquor & Wine	176	2,592	5,545	0
Total Country Club Revenue	184	8,274	13,826	0
SPA REVENUE				
A La Carte Services	107	8,894	5,781	4,951
Facility Charge	400	1,164	0	3,444
Local Programs & Misc Spa	58	3,070	4,645	1,635
Spa Pro Shop	25	1,434	1,032	0
Total Spa Revenue	590	14,562	11,458	10,030
GOLF REVENUE				
Greens Fees	5	55,290	68,952	0
Carts	175	13,462	16,012	0
Pro Shop Sales	58	8,230	10,069	0
Other Golf Income	0	0	0	0
Total Golf Income	238	76,982	95,033	0
Total Hotel Income	11,043	811,398	616,167	574,663

Figure 5–12 Daily Revenue Report

1. Sketch a hand transcript for a small, 10-room hotel for one night, create names for guests, and record the following transactions:
   a. Room charges of $60 for rooms 101, 104, 107, and 108.
   b. Room charges of $50 for rooms 103, 105, and 106.
   c. The only checkout is room 103 which had a balance from the prior night of $182.40. The guest checked out after breakfast and paid cash.
   d. Other rooms were occupied from the prior night and the balances were carried over:

104	$162.20
107	88.65

   e. Breakfast charges:

103	$7.80 + $2.00 Tip
104	6.40 + 1.00 Tip
107	9.10 + 1.00 Tip

   f. Dinner charges:

101	Food, $21.90; Tip $3.50
103	Food, 26.00; Beverage, 7.10; Tip, 5.00
108	Food, 33.00; Beverage 11.00; Tip, 6.00

   g. Telephone:

104	$6.00
105	4.50

   Total and balance the transcript and prepare a journal entry to record the revenue.

2. Record the following items on a night auditors' house folio:
   a. Restaurant revenue as follows:

   Revenue:

Food	$762.10
Beverage	432.15
Tip	108.25
Tax	62.80

   Method of settlement:

Cash	$1,072.10
Visa	108.30
Amexco	184.90

   b. Write-off of complimentary food charges of $162.20 with tax of $8.00 and tip of $24.00 at a food cost of 35 percent.

3. Circle T or F to indicate whether the following statements are true or false:
   T   F   a. Rooms revenue is recorded at the end of the day.
   T   F   b. House account posting is usually done by front-office cashiers.
   T   F   c. Night audit is one of the functions of property management systems.

T F **d.** The general ledger treatment of guest ledger postings is indicated through the use of charge codes.

T F **e.** Posting of telephone charges is usually handled by a call accounting system.

T F **f.** The night auditor usually posts advance deposits.

T F **g.** The "x" report is the final clearing of the day's information from point-of-sale systems.

T F **h.** The dropping of cash deposits in the safe should be witnessed by another employee.

T F **i.** Night auditors usually work from 7:00 P.M. to 3:00 A.M.

T F **j.** Property management systems utilize routine software but require specialized hardware.

4. Circle the correct answer to the following statements:

   a. The following is a function of a property management system:
   (1) Reservations
   (2) Night audit
   (3) Guest history
   (4) All of the above

   b. Charge codes are used in the night-audit process to:
   (1) Designate the outlet where the charge originated
   (2) Direct the charge to the proper general ledger account
   (3) Distinguish between guest charges and house charges

   c. House folios are zeroed out on:
   (1) A daily basis
   (2) A weekly basis
   (3) A monthly basis

6 Accounts Payable

If all billings received by a hotel were accurate in all areas, the processing of accounts payable would be relatively simple. Although somewhat more complex due to the need to allocate expenses to departments as well as individual accounts, the recording process follows the basic principles explained earlier in Chapter 4 and illustrated in Figure 4–3. Unfortunately, however, the control over accounts payable, and hence, expenses, must start at a much earlier point. Paying for merchandise never received, or for more merchandise than received, or even twice for the same merchandise, can be regular occurrences when control is lacking. While many of these overpayments result from honest mistakes and are readily rectified by the creditors, others are due to misrepresentation on the part of the vendors, collusion between the vendors and the buyers' employees, or dishonest accounts payable clerks. Whatever the immediate reason, the underlying cause is usually the difficulty of handling the enormous volume of paper associated with this accounting function. This is particularly true in the hotel field, where the very nature of the operation generates a tremendous number of bills every day.

The heavy volume of bills has caused accounts payable, like payroll, to automate. However, this trend has not materially reduced the incidence of overpayment. Computers are used to accumulate the amount due each vendor, compute cash discounts where allowed, print and sign the checks owed to the creditors, distribute the expenses to the designated subclassifications in each department, accumulate the monthly and month-to-date totals for profit-and-loss statements, and even check the extensions on each invoice. But they cannot verify the receipt of the merchandise or the accuracy of the number of units and unit prices shown on the invoices. They cannot check the quality of the merchandise, its delivery in accordance with desired specifications, or the return of all or part of an order to the vendor. In short, a computer can only substantially reduce the workload in the accounting department, often permitting a reduction of staff and, equally important, freeing the remaining employees to better check and control expenses.

Controlling expenses most successfully requires a complete payables system involving the department heads, management, and accounting staff. The department heads must initiate requests for merchandise, management must approve purchases, and accounting must check, verify, record, and pay the invoices; distribute the expenses; and prepare financial statements.

This chapter divides the accounts payable process into four phases: purchasing, receiving, recording, and payment. Computerization has materially reduced the workload of the latter two phases. In a hotel, those two steps do not differ widely from the recording and payment procedures in use in most businesses. Therefore, adapting computer programs to meet the needs of hotel accounting was relatively simple. Due to the complex departmental structure of hotels, the same statement cannot be made for purchasing and receiving. In the following sections, each of the four phases is discussed in detail. Purchasing and receiving of food and beverages is covered in Chapter 11. Discussion of food and beverages in these two areas only will, therefore, be omitted from this chapter.

PURCHASING

Department heads are expected to requisition needed supplies on a timely basis. This may or may not trigger a purchase order. When space is available, a hotel should keep all operating supplies in a central general storeroom. In a large hotel, the general storeroom should be under the control of a storekeeper or possibly a receiving clerk who reports to accounting. However, in many hotels, payroll economies have dictated that the purchasing agent perform that function. Some hotels are structured in such a manner that the storekeeper or receiving clerk reports to the purchasing agent. In those circumstances, the principles of internal control are ignored since receiving and inventory control are control/accounting functions while purchasing is an operational function.

Regardless, the individual who controls the general storeroom must assume the responsibility for maintaining adequate inventory levels. This can be done on a *bin card* (see Figure 6–1) on which the quantity of an inventory item received or issued is recorded and the balance on hand is reflected. A minimum quantity on hand should be indicated clearly on the card so that when the balance drops below that level a purchase requisition is initiated. It is particularly important that supplies used by more than one department be controlled in a central storeroom as this avoids excess quantities of the item being spread around the hotel and at the same time ensures that when the item has to be purchased, maximum use will be made of volume discounts. The existence of a central storeroom permits the individual department head to operate with a very limited quantity of supplies under his or her physical control which in turn reduces the chance of employee pilferage. However, requisitioning on a daily basis places too large a burden on the storeroom and leaves very little margin for error or misjudgment by the department head. A policy should be set that each department should requisition on a weekly basis based on its normal seven-day consumption. A posted schedule for requisitioning should ensure that too many departments do not requisition on the same day, thus balancing the workload on the storekeeper. A sample of a storeroom requisition is shown in Figure 6–2.

BIN CARD

No._____   Product _____   Size_____

Minimum Quantity _____

Date	Supplier	Quantity Received	Quantity Issued	Balance On Hand

Figure 6–1   Bin Card, General Stores

Unfortunately, many hotels have a very limited central storeroom, frequently a few shelves in the purchasing agent's office for the most widely used items (e.g., office supplies). The burden of controlling inventory levels and initiating purchases then falls on the department head. This should be accomplished by preparing, in duplicate, a purchase requisition (Figure 6–3). Purchase requisitions should differ from storeroom requisitions in order to avoid confusing the purchasing agent. The purchase requisition must briefly describe the items, quantity requested, date of the last order, quantity received, and vendor's name. The originals are sent to the general manager or other designated executive for written approval. Once approved, they are forwarded to the purchasing agent, who is responsible for ordering the merchandise.

Specifications as to size, type, or quality of any item should be originally approved by top management in consultation with the purchasing agent and affected de-

STOREROOM REQUISITION

Date _____

Department Ordering _____

Initiated By _____

Vendor*

Approved By
Dept. Head _____
Manager _____
Other _____

Quanity	Unit	Item Description**	

Figure 6–2 Storeroom Requisition

partment heads. Any deviation from these specifications when reordering should be approved.

Most requisitions are for items previously purchased, and many purchasing agents routinely reorder from the same vendor. However, they should periodically check the unit prices with those of other suppliers. Unit costs, particularly of printed forms, are materially reduced with increased quantities. Bulk buying, however, results in a net savings only if such purchases are carefully monitored and controlled. Adequate, safe storage and the rate of consumption should be prime considerations. Many hotels have ordered large quantities of stationery, office supplies, and cleaning supplies only to have them stolen or misused by their employees, or to see them become obsolete long before the supply was exhausted. To help reduce this waste, the controller should review and approve all requisitions for printed forms.

When the price, quantity, and specifications have been checked, the purchasing agent should prepare a purchase order (see Figure 6–4). Purchase orders should be sequentially numbered and printed in at least five parts. The distribution, starting with the original, should be as follows:

1. Vendor
2. Accounts payable (accounting)
3. Department head initiating the purchase
4. Receiving, or the department head in hotels with no receiving clerk
5. Purchasing

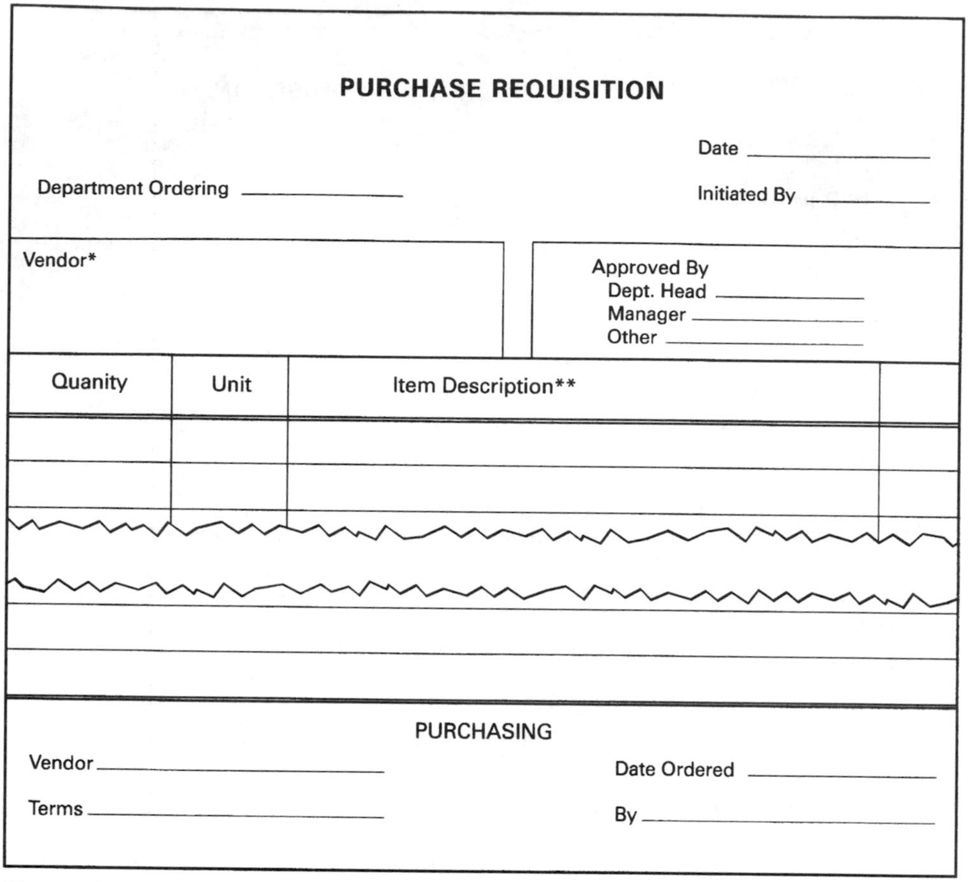

PURCHASE REQUISITION

Date _____

Department Ordering _____

Initiated By _____

Vendor*

Approved By
Dept. Head _____
Manager _____
Other _____

Quanity	Unit	Item Description**	

PURCHASING

Vendor _____

Date Ordered _____

Terms _____

By _____

*From previous order
**As complete as possible

Figure 6–3 Purchase Requisition

Department heads, by issuing a requisition, attest to the need for the merchandise and management approves the expense. Obtaining quotations and selecting vendors is the responsibility of the purchasing agent. But the controllers have the overall responsibility for controlling expenses. They must exercise this responsibility by determining the reasonableness of the price charged and the quantity ordered. Prices can be periodically test-checked by calling rival suppliers for their prices, and care should be taken that the quality of the merchandise offered meets the requirements of management. Quantity can be checked only by estimating the usage based on the volume of business and comparing this figure to the actual consumption. To determine the consumption, the accounts payable clerk need only maintain a worksheet listing all purchases of selected items, showing the date, quantity received, and unit cost for each order. Items usually listed are guest stationery, guest bills, registration cards, restaurant checks, and guest and cleaning supplies.

Although it was stated earlier that the impact of computerization in the purchasing area has not had a substantial impact on the workload, some progress has been

Hotel Grayscot

1 MAIN STREET
ANYTOWN, U.S.A.

PURCHASE ORDER
5900

The above number must appear on all invoices, shipping bills, packing slips and all correspondence pertaining to this order.

VENDOR

SHIP TO:

DATE		TERMS	DELIVERY	F.A.B.	
DEPT		REQUISITION	EXPENSE CODE	☐ Prepay freight charges and add to your invoice ☐ No freight charges to be billed	

QUANITY	UNIT	DESCRIPTION	UNIT PRICE	AMOUNT

OTHER CONDITIONS REVERSE SIDE

TOTAL

Director Purchasing

Purchasing Agent

SUPPLIER

Figure 6–4   Purchase Order

made. Most suppliers now provide the purchasing agent with a computerized list, preferable in quadruplicate, of available products and prices. The purchasing agent marks the quantities ordered and any agreed price changes on both copies of the list. A summary purchase order can then be prepared reflecting "as per order form." One copy of the list is attached to the vendor's copy of the order while the three copies are attached to the purchasing, receiving, and accounting copies.

In Chapter 2, purchasing was mentioned as an area where computer systems are being developed. Such systems focus primarily on the food and beverage area where the number of individual items ordered on a daily basis greatly exceeds the volume of other types of purchases. The intent of such systems is to automate the payment to vendors, which eliminates the need to manually process and input their invoices. This concept has not yet received widespread use in the hotel industry, but if it is accomplished successfully in the area of food and beverages, it will be expanded to other types of purchases. The process is explored in greater detail in Chapter 26.

RECEIVING

While purchasing is an operational function subject to monitoring and audit by the controller's staff, receiving is an accounting and control function for which the controller is directly responsible. Whether or not the hotel actually has a receiving clerk is determined largely by the size of the operation. Larger hotels need, and usually have, a separate receiving department. Others will either assign this function to their timekeepers or route deliveries directly to the department heads. The receipt of merchandise may be recorded on a special receiving form, usually favored in hotels with separate receiving departments, or on the receiving copy of the purchase order. In effect, these are the only two receiving procedures. In both, the department heads should be solely responsible for the contents of all packages. Receiving clerks and timekeepers should only indicate the number of packages received and immediately forward them to the right department heads. Furthermore, for proper control, the complete cycle of the receiving-form routing should take no longer than 48 hours. With this in mind, here is an examination of the two methods.

Where a special form is used, it should be printed in four parts (see Figure 6–5). When the merchandise is received, the receiving clerk should complete the form and indicate the number of packages received. The packages and three parts of the form are sent to the department head who ordered the merchandise. The department head then signs one copy of the receiving form (keeping the other two) and returns it to the receiving clerk, indicating that the number of packages shown was received. The clerk should attach it to the copy of the purchase order and file it in a processed folder. The fourth copy is sent, that night, to accounts payable, where it is checked for numerical sequence and filed. The fourth copy can also serve as a check on the department heads in the event the cycle is not completed within the specified time.

If a receiving form is not used, the receiving clerk should indicate the number of packages received on the copy of the purchase order. The delivery should then be listed on a sheet showing the purchase order number, the name of the department or depart-

```
                                                      No. _____
                         RECEIVING SLIP              Date _____


Supplier _____
         Name


         _____
         Address                              Department
                                              Routed To _____
         _____


Purchase Order No. _____


Merchandise Received
Description; No. of
Packages _____


                        Statement of Condition

              ☐ All in good condition      ☐ Damaged

Remarks and Disposition


                                          _____
                                          Receiving Clerk's Signature
```

Figure 6–5   Receiving Slip

ment head, and the number of packages received. The purchase order is then forwarded with the packages to the department head. Each night, the list should be sent to the accounts payable clerk. In hotels with no receiving department, the timekeeper or other authorized personnel would perform the same functions.

In the last stage of the receiving cycle, the department head should have in his or her possession the unopened packages and two copies of the receiving form, or the receiving copy of the purchase order. As the final step, the department head opens the packages and checks the quantity and quality of the merchandise against the specifications on the purchase order. If the number of items is correct and the quality satisfactory, the department head should attest to both facts with a signature. The purchase order, since it shows the number of items ordered as well as the number of packages received, requires only a signature as a sign of approval. However, the receiving form shows only the number of packages received and, where this form is used, the department head must enter the quantity received on both copies before signing. Then, one copy is sent to accounts payable, and the other is attached to the departmental copy of the purchase order and filed. If there is anything wrong with the quantity or quality, this fact must be noted on the receiving slip so that accounting may adjust the vendor's invoice and take whatever other action is deemed necessary.

Proper handling of the receiving slips by all concerned is the key to minimizing losses due to overpayment. These forms are essential in checking the vendors' invoices and serve, along with the purchase orders, as authority for the accounts payable staff to process and pay the invoices.

RECORDING ACCOUNTS PAYABLE

As stated in Chapter 4, a purchase journal is used to record the accounts payable on a monthly basis and to make a summary entry for posting into the general ledger. Historically, hotel accounts payable were recorded in the same manner. The effect of departmentalization resulted, of course, in a much wider distribution of expenses with the requisite posting to a wide range of accounts.

For most businesses, the purchase journal is now obsolete. In the 1930s, the manual entry method of accounting was replaced by electromechanical accounting machines with enough memory capacity to accumulate totals for each account and print a journal which provided a complete distribution for entry into the general ledger. Those machines were, in turn, replaced by computers. Both the electromechanical machines and, subsequently, the computer systems were fully capable of meeting the needs of the hotel industry. In particular, computers had no problems in handling the large number of accounts found in the Uniform System. The computer software provides several options relative to the accumulation of totals and entry into the general ledger. Due to the ease in the recording process, many hotels have opted to revert to having each invoice individually posted in the general ledger. However, given a proliferation of invoices for a specific account, each of which has the same characteristics (e.g., same account number, same vendor, same date), hotels will usually group those particular invoices into a single entry. The actual recording of an invoice can only follow the completion of various audit procedures conducted by the accounts payable personnel.

When the approved receiving slip reaches the accounts payable department, it should be matched immediately against the purchase order copy sent to the department by the purchasing agent. Where the receiving copy of the purchase order is used, the clerk need only attach the two forms together and file them in a pending file until the vendor's bill is received. Where a special receiving form is used, the quantities shown must be carefully matched with the purchase order and a notation of the receiving slip's number made on the purchase order before it is placed in the pending file. Any bills received before the receiving slip should be attached to the purchase order and filed in the pending file until the approved slip is received. A few vendors may enclose their bills with the delivery slips, but the vast majority mail them shortly after the merchandise is delivered. The employee opening the hotel mail should be instructed to forward all bills directly to the accounts payable department.

At least once a month, every purchase order in the pending file should be carefully examined. The purpose of this review is to clear the files of all purchase orders except those calling for deliveries at a future date. Purchase orders in the files that call for delivery on a prior date, and those with either a bill or a receiving slip attached, should be immediately investigated. To ensure future compliance, the controller should personally review any infractions of the receiving regulations with the offending department heads.

The audit procedures for checking, recording, and processing invoices for payment start when all three forms—purchase order, approved receiving slip, and invoice—are on hand. The accounts payable clerk only records and processes food and beverage invoices for payment. Verifying the receipt of food and beverage purchases, and the quantity, price, and total due as shown on each invoice, is the responsibility of the food and beverage controller.

All invoices for food and beverages received (accompanied by a receiving sheet which shows each vendor's name, invoice number, itemization, and cost of merchandise received) should be forwarded to accounts payable on a daily basis. Verifying the accuracy of those invoices is described in detail in Chapter 12. To ensure that no invoices were lost in transit, the accounts payable clerk should check each bill against the receiving sheet immediately upon receipt.

Checking all other invoices starts with matching the quantity received, as shown in the approved receiving slip, to the purchase order. When the invoice is received, the quantity and unit cost billed are checked against the purchase order. If they are in order, the extensions are checked and the invoice total verified. The accounts payable clerk performing this function should initial the totals shown on the invoices to signify that the quantities, unit costs, extensions, and totals were checked.

Normally, it is not necessary for the department heads to review or approve the invoices. They initiated the orders, they have a copy of the purchase order on file, and they have signified their approval for payment by signing the receiving slip. Any action taken regarding the invoices depends entirely on the desires of the individual managers.

There are many options available to management. Some authorize payment of all invoices without their approval. Others insist on personally approving each invoice before it is processed for payment. For the controller's protection and, in a sense, better control, the latter is much more desirable. However, it would certainly not be feasible to ask the managers of large hotels to personally approve the thousands of invoices processed each month. Alternatively, requiring no approvals by management is even less desirable. A procedure followed in many hotels is a compromise between the two extremes: invoices for nonrecurring expenditures exceeding a specified amount must be approved by the manager; all others can be processed for payment without his or her approval.

CODING AND INPUTTING THE INVOICES

When all the necessary approvals are affixed, the invoices are ready for coding and input. Many hotels require the department head to record the department and number of the account to be charged on the purchase requisition. This procedure not only helps the department heads to understand what each item on the operating statement represents, but should also permit them to track expenses against their budget on a monthly basis. This does not, however, relieve the accounts payable personnel of ensuring that the coding is correct. Each invoice must have a designated department and expense classification in accordance with the guidelines established by the Uniform System of Accounts.

Computerization permits the processing of each bill individually. However, it is common practice to attach a simple purchase voucher (Figure 6–6) to the invoice. The

INVOICE NUMBER _____	DUE DATE _____	INVOICE DISTRIBUTION	AMOUNT
		_____	___
		_____	___
DATE _____	AMOUNT _____	_____	___
		_____	___
		_____	___
CHECK STUB MESSAGE _____		_____	___
		_____	___
		_____	___

Figure 6–6 Purchase Voucher

completed purchase voucher permits easy entry of the invoice into the computer or, if not computerized, a mechanical or manual accounting system.

The key information to be recorded on the purchase voucher is:

1. Vendor number: This should be a combination of the vendor's name and a number, e.g., Wilcox Dairy could be WILC 01. This permits the accounts payable clerk to recall the vendor numbers without looking each one up.
2. The vendor's invoice number: This specifically identifies each invoice.
3. The date of the invoice: This permits aging.
4. The total of invoice and discount (if any).
5. The breakdown by account number to be charged.

The account numbers are based on the chart of accounts in use, which, in conformity with the Uniform System, consists of both the department number and the individual expense account within the department.

Consideration always should be given to any discounts reflected on the invoice or generally received from the vendor; such discounts are known as *trade discounts* and should be reflected on the purchase order. These should be automatically taken and accounted for as reductions in the invoice price. Cash discounts, however, are inducements to settle the invoices promptly. Whether they are taken or not depends on management policy as related to the overall financial resources of the hotel. Cash discounts should be taken when possible as they usually exceed the rate of interest which could be earned by investing the funds. However, when taken, the discount should be recorded separately as a credit to "Other Income— Cash Discounts."

Care should be taken when entering invoices that are more than five or six weeks old. While the computer should be programmed to redflag any invoices previously entered, an additional review should be made to ensure that payment was not made under another invoice number. This is extremely important in a noncomputerized system.

Certain invoices—such as insurance, dues, subscriptions, service contracts, and so forth—cover an expense for a period of several months. Such items should be

charged to a prepaid expense balance-sheet account and recorded on a worksheet. They become the basis for standard monthly journal entries as described in Chapter 17.

Similarly, invoices may be recorded for items that have been accrued, by standard journal entry, for several months—such as taxes or utilities. To the extent that they relate to prior periods and are covered by an accrued expense liability account, they should be charged to those accounts.

A category of invoices that merits special attention is for items exclusively ordered for and charged to a particular guest. These purchases, usually made for banquet guests, are of such items as flowers, wedding cakes, printed matchbooks, or other wedding favors; they might also be rentals of special audio or other electronic equipment by sponsors for their meetings. The invoices should not be vouchered and processed for payment unless approved by the income controller or other employee responsible for checking them with the guest charges. A detailed worksheet should be set up to properly control these disbursements. Checking the invoices against the guest bills without adequate notations may increase, rather than reduce, the possibility of error. When receipts and disbursements for such items cannot be matched, there is no alternative but to write off the difference, the *open balance*. With inadequate records, it is difficult to analyze the account and so discover and try to correct the error causing the open balance. Hence the importance of up-to-date worksheets checked monthly against the balance in the general ledger accounts.

Regardless of who is designated to approve the invoice, the worksheet, or the list of all such guest charges that is then transcribed into the worksheet, should be prepared by the income controller as part of the daily routine. The total charges listed each day should equal the total entered, either in one amount or by category, in the earnings journal. At the end of each month, they are posted as credits to the contra accounts in the general ledger. Worksheets need only be spreadsheets with sufficient columns to record the following data:

> Date of function
> Name of guest
> Banquet check number
> Description of item
> Total guest charge
> Vendor name
> Invoice number
> Total amount due
> Markup, if any
> Date invoice is approved

All headings, with the possible exception of "Markup, if any," are self-explanatory. Markup is a service charge, added at management's instructions to the cost of many of these items. Thus, the total amount due on the invoice plus the required markup should equal the total guest charge. On all invoices, the employee approving them should indicate the account number to be charged. In addition, where there is a markup, the employee should enter, with appropriate account numbers, the total guest charge as a debit to the contra account, the markup as a credit to income, and the net as the amount due to the vendor. In any month, when invoices are not processed in time

to offset the revenue, the net balance in all contra accounts in shown on the balance sheet as a current liability. The net balance should also equal the total on the worksheets of all open items.

While Figure 6–6 is a suggested format for a purchase voucher, the most important factor in designing the voucher is to have the information available for quick and easy entry into the computer. Therefore, the computer software design for accounts payable input is the most determining factor in the voucher layout.

The vouchers should be batched, that is, assembled in a stack, alphabetically by vendor, and totaled to arrive at a control total. A schedule should be established for entering batches once or twice a week, depending on volume. Since certain vendors may have a seven-day due date, at least one batch per week should be entered. The computer will automatically provide a total amount entered, which should match the batch total.

PAYMENT OF INVOICES

Most accounts payable programs provide the ability to print an "authorization for payment" list by due date. This list should be reviewed relative to the intended due date through which it is the intention to make payment. Where necessary, due dates should be changed to add or delete invoices from the intended payments. After these corrections are made, checks can be printed through the designated date.

In certain instances, it may be necessary to create a "pro forma" invoice for payments (such as sales tax) which must be made periodically but for which invoices are not received.

Accounts payable checks should be signed by at least two people, usually the general manager and the controller. All supporting documents, invoices, purchase orders, and so on should be attached to the checks when presented for signature. When paid, the invoices should be voided with a "paid" stamp to avoid reuse and filed with a copy of the check. As a further element of internal control, the checks, when signed, should be given to, and mailed by, someone other than the accounts payable clerk, purchasing agent, or anyone else involved in the purchasing process. In most computer systems, issuing checks and printing a check register (a listing of checks issued for a specific date) initiates an automatic entry in the general ledger that debits the accounts payable account and credits the bank account with the total amount of checks issued. If this does not happen, the same can be accomplished by a manual journal entry.

SUPPLIERS' STATEMENTS

Most vendors send out monthly statements showing balances owed and outstanding invoices. These statements should never be used as a basis for recording or paying invoices. However, they should be reconciled to the accounts payable balance in the books, and copies of missing invoices should be requested from the vendor.

1. Prepare a flowchart showing the flow of a purchase of supplies in a hotel from the initiation of the order to the payment to the vendor.
2. List the information that should be obtainable from the following forms:
    a. Bin card
    b. Storeroom requisition
    c. Purchase requisition
    d. Purchase order
3. Circle T or F to indicate whether the following statements are true or false:
    T   F   **a.** Requests for merchandise should be initiated by the purchasing agent.
    T   F   **b.** The receiving clerk or storekeeper should report to accounting.
    T   F   **c.** Receiving clerks should be responsible for opening and verifying the contents of packages.
    T   F   **d.** The status of all pending purchase orders should be reviewed every month.
    T   F   **e.** In a computerized system, each bill can be processed individually.
4. Circle the correct answer to the following statements:
    a. A bin card is used to:
    (1) Identify new inventory items received for the first time
    (2) Track quantities of inventory items on hand
    (3) Show the most recent price paid for an item
    b. Purchases of supplies are initiated by:
    (1) Calling the purchasing agent
    (2) Filling out a purchase order
    (3) Filling out a purchasing requisition
    c. The reasonability of quantities ordered can be checked by:
    (1) Calling rival suppliers
    (2) Estimating usage based on volume of business
    (3) Comparing to the quantity purchased previously
    d Incorrect quantities received should be noted on the:
    (1) Receiving slip
    (2) Purchase order
    (3) Invoice
    e. Cash discounts should be credited to:
    (1) The same account as the purchase
    (2) Other income—Cash Discounts
    (3) Interest expense

7 Payroll

Payroll is the largest single item of expense in hospitality operations. Inclusive of taxes and benefits, it can range from under 30 percent of total revenue in hotels with no restaurants to almost 50 percent in large transient and resort hotels. Consequently, it is an area continuously under scrutiny by management and is the first point of attack when cost trimming is necessary. However, as in all industries, there is a point beyond which the loss of revenue due to reductions in staff can exceed the savings realized by the reduction in total payroll.

The requirement, enacted in 1943, that federal income taxes be withheld from worker's pay was one of several enactments that complicated the payroll preparation process. The only prior requirement resulted from the Social Security tax laws enacted in 1937. Additional deductions resulted from the enactment of state and city income taxes and the impact of unionization.

Unionization brought requirements for new deductions. Not only do union contracts contain a clause requiring deductions for union dues and fees, but also for many of the fringe benefits that unions obtained. These benefits indirectly created a whole new area of possible deductions from salaries of nonunion employees. Since most of the fringe benefits enjoyed by union members are entirely financed by the hotels, management felt obliged to give similar benefits to their department heads and other salaried, nonunion employees. And because of the scarcity of qualified, experienced people to fill these key positions even in periods of high unemployment, their benefits soon outdistanced those negotiated for the union employees.

Many of these benefits offer options requiring voluntary contributions from the employees: hospitalization, dental and major medical policies, pension and savings plans, and additional life insurance coverage over a specified amount that is issued without cost to every nonunion employee. The list of possible voluntary deductions from both union and nonunion employees' salaries is almost endless. The mandatory deductions are limited mainly to taxes and court-ordered garnishments of wages.

PAYROLL SYSTEMS

As shown in the preceding chapters, the degree to which hospitality accounting has become very specialized or customized varies from area to area, from highly customized in the recording of revenues to a much lower level of customization in the recording of purchases and the payments related thereto.

However, specialization virtually disappears in the realm of payroll. In fact, the only element in payroll preparation unique to the hotel and restaurant industry is the handling of tips, an area that in recent years has become more complex due to changes in their income tax treatment. Consequently, a review of the history of hotel payroll systems is simply a review of systems commonly used in industry.

Early Systems

Prior to 1914, when the federal personal income tax laws were enacted, detailed payroll records were not necessary in most hotels. The payroll process was simply the multiplication of hours worked by the hourly rate. These calculations could be made on a single sheet of paper listing the names of the employees and the hours worked. Since most employees were paid in cash, they could be paid simply by putting the money in an envelope, usually with the calculation shown on the outside.

Even with the introduction of Social Security taxes, the initial payroll journals were very simple, similar to the one shown in Figure 4–5, with the addition, perhaps, of two columns on the left-hand side to show the hours worked and the hourly rate. Personal income tax withholding brought the need for detailed earnings records by individual fully into focus. Early attempts at earnings records involved simply transcribing the weekly amounts from the payroll journal to individual earnings cards. However, this process was error-prone and time-consuming. The obvious next step was to eliminate the duplication of work and the potential for errors by accomplishing both tasks at the same time. The solution was the introduction of a variety of systems all founded on the concept termed *"one-write" systems.*

The one-write systems were designed to prepare a payroll journal, an individual employee's earnings record, and a check or employee's receipt if payment was made by cash. Carbon paper was placed between the earnings record and the payroll journal while the top line of the check or receipt was carbonized on the back. Thus, by placing the check or receipt on top of the other two records, the information recorded on the check would be entered in the other two records simultaneously. The earlier versions were referred to as *pegboard systems* because the three records were placed on a wooden board and held in place by wooden pegs on each side.

A more sophisticated one-write system is the "One-Write Bookkeeping System" manufactured by McBee Systems. The board is replaced by a compact (when folded) poster-binder with a firm writing surface and textured vinyl exterior. It employs the same "one-write" principle: recording the check, the employee's earning record, and the payroll journal in one step. A pressure bar on the left-hand side holds the forms securely in place. An example is shown in Figure 7–1. These systems are still used extensively in small restaurants and private clubs and to some degree in small lodging

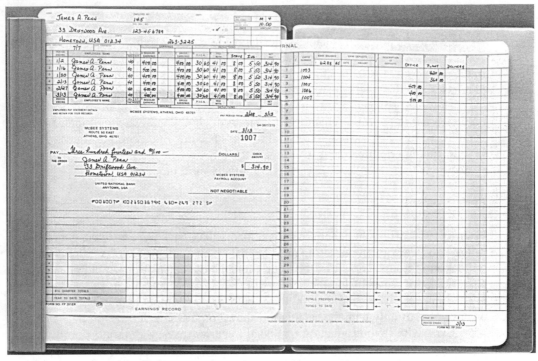

Figure 7–1 One-Write Payroll System (Courtesy of McBee Systems)

establishments which do not have enough employees to use a computer or do not use a payroll service.

Current Systems

The introduction, in the 1920s, of electromechanical payroll machines, usually with typewriter attachments, virtually eliminated the use of manual systems in the large hotels. Checks and payroll journals were printed mechanically and the machines were programmed to pick up and accumulate deduction totals for the individual employee's records. It should be noted that the only change in the appearance of the final payroll journal from those illustrated in Figures 4–5 and 7–1 is the ever-increasing number of deductions. Not only have the deductions increased in number, but the manner in which they are determined has become more and more complex. It was, therefore, natural for companies providing computer services to businesses to concentrate first on payroll. Since, as previously mentioned, the preparation of a hotel payroll is similar to that of other businesses, it was natural that hotels would follow the direction of other businesses in contracting out their payroll preparation to service bureaus.

While many of the large hotels have extensive computer installations, most choose to use service bureaus rather than prepare their payrolls in house. Keeping up with the continually changing formulas for deductions, not only state and federal taxes but also insurance, union dues, and so on, requires continuous program changes—too time-consuming for in-house computer staffs. As a result, the large majority of hotels,

both large and small, and larger restaurants and clubs find it appropriate to place their payroll preparation function in the hands of the service bureaus. In fact, most service bureaus prepare all necessary tax reporting forms as well as filings required by insurance companies, banks, unions, and other regulatory bodies. They frequently mail the checks to the employees, handle the various tax remittances, and sometimes even reconcile the payroll bank account. Thus, the role of the accounting department is one of control over input and entry of the final results into the hotel accounting system.

Payroll Control

Since the majority of hotel and restaurant employees are paid on an hourly basis, the most important area of input to control is the hours worked. However, it is also important to control the rate of pay and the calculation of deductions and even to verify the actual existence of the employee. It is not unknown in the industry for an unscrupulous department head to place fictitious or nonworking persons on the payroll.

Hiring and Processing of New Employees

Payroll control fails if an unnecessary employee is hired. This can be avoided by establishing proper guidelines for staffing of the various positions. The initial effort at staff planning should take place during the preopening period of a hotel. The feasibility study in which the viability of a hotel project is analyzed should contain the rationale for the estimates of payroll costs. This rationale should provide estimated staffing required for varying levels of business as well as anticipated rates of pay. This is, in effect, the initial staff planning guide. After the start-up period is over, those guidelines should be revised in line with actual experience. While in the larger hotels, this will be the responsibility of a full-time staff planner, the function in smaller properties is frequently entrusted to the controller working with the human resources department.

Staffing guidelines should be determined for all departments. The staffing in the overhead departments will essentially be fixed, while the staffing in the revenue-producing departments will be fixed in some positions but for the most part variable relative to volume. Following are some of the more common measurements used in setting guidelines for variable positions:

> Receptionists—in relation to expected number of arrivals
> Reservationists—in relation to reservation activity expected
> Maids and floor housekeepers—in relation to anticipated number of rooms occupied
> Servers, buspersons, and cooks—in relation to anticipated number of covers
> Bartenders—in relation to anticipated volume

Based on the forecast, staffing requirements for the following week should be determined in advance and a schedule prepared. A daily "flash forecast" should also be issued by the front-office manager to alert managers to a significant change from the original forecast. The schedule will not only provide for the proper staffing in the following week but, if additional staff must be hired, will provide the human resources department with the information and justification. Otherwise, hiring should only occur when an employee has left or been terminated or in the event of a fully approved and

documented organizational change. In the case of the former, the employment authorization form should clearly state the name and position of the person being replaced.

While some operations have individual forms for each process, the use of a multipurpose form, as shown in Figure 7–2, can better serve the purpose. Since these forms are completed by the department heads, it is much simpler for them to use a single form. The use of several forms frequently creates confusion, resulting in the wrong form being used. After the required approvals have been affixed, the forms are sent to human resources. There they are reviewed and checked, and copies inserted or proper notations made in the employees' permanent files. The originals, after being initialed by the human resources managers or their designated representatives, are then forwarded to the payroll department.

For proper control, this input into payroll must be checked and verified. Since most payrolls are computerized, this is relatively simple. All it requires is a program designed to automatically produce a weekly list of all new hires, terminations, and changes. These three listings will be described separately, although they are usually incorporated into one list.

For new hires, the list should show all the pertinent information: department, employee number, name, address, Social Security number, salary (both regular and overtime hourly rates), number of dependents, and so forth. If the employee is entitled to meals, that should also be shown, as well as the proper code for those classified as tip employees. If these reports are properly checked with the authorization forms by the designated employees in both the personnel and accounting departments, the possibility of error is almost eliminated. The termination report should show the department, employee number, name, and salary. The last figure should then be checked against the amount shown on the authorization for that employee's replacement. For the list of changes, the only information needed, in addition to the department, employee number, and name, is the new status, salary, address, number of dependents, and such data.

Tip Employees

Earlier in this chapter, reference was made to tipping as the area where hotel and restaurant payroll preparation requires additional customization. The taxation of tips has always been a major problem for the Internal Revenue Service. The IRS maintains a firm policy that all tips received must be reported by the employee and requires that any employee earning over $20 a month in tips must maintain a daily record of tips received. However, the requirement that hotels and restaurants pay FICA on all declared tips has discouraged employers from enforcing the rules. The 1994 regulation permitting employers to take a credit against federal income taxes equal to FICA paid on excess tips has reduced the impact.

However, the main instrument used by the IRS to encourage tip declaration is the Tax Equity and Fiscal Responsibility Act of 1982 (TEFRA). This act requires that to the extent that actual declared tips do not equal at least 8 percent of sales, the employer is required to allocate the shortfall among the offending employees. This requires filing Form 8027 and creates a bookkeeping headache for employers. To avoid the bookkeeping, many employers encourage employees to declare 8 percent of sales. However,

Hotel Grayscot
PAYROLL AND STATUS AUTHORIZATION

CHECK PERSONNEL ACTION TO BE INITIATED BY THIS FORM		
☐ New Hire	☐ Personal Data Change	☐ Leave of Absence - Depart
☐ Job Change	☐ Contract Change	☐ Leave of Absence - Return
☐ Rate Charge	☐ Termination	☐ Other (Explain in Comments)

EMPL. #	SOCIAL SECURITY #	LAST NAME	FIRST	MIDDLE

*ACTION EFFECTIVE ON >

*SALARY CHANGES EFFECTIVE ONLY ON FIRST DAY OF PAY PERIOD.

FROM — COMPLETE BELOW ON ALL ACTIONS			TO — ENTER ONLY INFORMATION TO BE CHANGED		
DIVISION	LOCATION - CITY	Bldg. & Floor	DIVISION	LOCATION - CITY	Bldg. & Floor
DEPARTMENT		Dept./CC#	DEPARTMENT		Dept./CC#
POSITION TITLE		Sal Gr/Ex. Lev.	POSITION TITLE		Sal Gr/Ex. Lev.
IMMEDIATE SUPERVISOR			IMMEDIATE SUPERVISOR		

SALARY STATUS

	WEEKLY	ANNUAL	LAST INCREASE	REASON FOR CHANGE	IF MERIT, INDICATE PERFORMANCE LEVEL	POSITION IN RANGE
PRESENT SALARY	$	$	Date:	☐ Merit:		
				☐ Promotion:	☐ Meets Expectations	$ Increase
CHANGE	$	$	Amount:	☐ Reclassification:	☐ Above Expectations	
				☐ Contract:	☐ Exceptional	New Position in Range
NEW SALARY	$	$	Reason:	☐ Other:	☐ Other	

EMPLOYMENT, TRANSFER OR PROMOTION

Date of Birth	Date of Hire	Telephone (Area Code and Number)	Sex	EEO DESIGNATION	
				☐ White	☐ American Indian
Name of Person Replaced		Last Salary	Date Left Position	☐ African Indian	☐ Oriental
				☐ Spanish Surname	☐ Other

TERMINATION OR LEAVE OF ABSENCE

	WORKING DAYS	REASON FOR TERMINATION		ELIGIBLE FOR REHIRE?	LEAVE OF ABSENCE	
Severance Pay Due		☐ Resignation ☐ Layoff ☐ Death		☐ Yes ☐ No	☐ Disability ☐ Pregnancy	HOW LONG? _____
Vacation Pay Due		☐ Dismissal ☐ Retirement ☐ Other			☐ Military ☐ Other	

COMMENTS

APPROVAL / DATE

	DEPARTMENTAL		EXECUTIVE		PERSONNEL	
	IMMED. SUPVR.	DEPT. HEAD	DIVISION	CORPORATE	OPERATIONS	COMPENSATION
APPROVAL						
DATE						

PERSONNEL USE ONLY

Unit Rate	EEO	Sal. Chg.	MS	Term	Special Payment Amount & Reason
					$

NOTE: Minimum required is original and two copies: Original to Payroll Department, copies to Personnel and Originating Department head.

Figure 7–2 Multipurpose Form

this remains the prerogative of the individual employee and cannot be mandated by the employer.

In order to facilitate the handling of tips for payroll tax purposes, gratuities are divided into two categories: optional (tips) and prearranged (fixed gratuities). For this reason, the special coding referred to in the preceding section is necessary. Gratuities to bellmen when rooming or checking out individual guests and to waiters and waitresses in the restaurants and coffee shops are optional, although 10–15 percent is considered good etiquette. The guests may give as little or as much as they please. However, for group or tour guests registering simultaneously, the bellmen's gratuities are often prearranged on a per-bag basis and charged to the sponsors. Banquet tips are always prearranged at a fixed percentage of the total food and beverage charges and are included as a separate item on the banquet bills.

Both types are subject to all payroll and withholding provisions of the tax laws. In other words, for tax purposes they are treated the same as cash wages. At the end of each year, both totals are added to the employees' wages to arrive at the reported annual earnings. However, there is a difference in the payroll treatment. Prearranged gratuities are processed through the payroll, included in the employees' cash wages, and offset in the general ledger against the amount collected from the guests. Declared tips are also processed through the payroll, taxed, but then deducted, since obviously they cannot be included in the employees' net pay.

Time Cards

Most hotel restaurant employees punch a time clock. (In most hotels, exceptions are made only for department heads, their assistants, and possibly clerical employees if they are nonunion.) However, time cards reflect only the time the employees entered and left the hotel, not the number of hours they worked. For proper control, department heads should record on a time sheet, without reference to the time cards, the number of hours each of their employees worked each day. At the end of each pay period, the time cards should be sent by the timekeepers directly to the payroll clerks in accounting. There, as a test-check that should include at least 10 percent of the cards for each department, the hours punched are extended and compared with the hours worked as entered on the time sheets. In many hotels, however, there is not enough time for such extensive test-checks. In such cases, they can be made after employees have received their pay, and any differences, after a thorough investigation and review with each responsible department head, can be adjusted in the following pay period.

Overtime

Overtime pay is another area that requires careful analysis and strict controls. Most hotel and restaurant employees are entitled to overtime pay for all hours worked in excess of their normal work week. The federal minimum-wage laws mandate this for all employees except executives, their assistants, and other members of the administrative staff. For union members, the terms of their contracts would be in effect, if more favorable to the employees.

The most important factor in the handling of overtime is not *if* it is authorized, but *when* it is authorized. Authorization after the fact is pointless. If the employee has worked, he or she is certainly going to be paid. Except for emergencies or unusual circumstances, overtime should not be allowed unless it is authorized in advance. Properly planned occasional use of overtime saves money. However, analyses of overtime payments have often been unfavorable. They have shown that the establishments could have reduced their payroll costs by hiring one or more additional employees, thus minimizing the need for overtime. Later in this chapter we will address overtime reports.

Vacations

Vacations are necessary but costly, and only through careful planning and with proper scheduling can this expense be controlled. Vacation lengths are fixed, determined by the period of employment. Management's only prerogative is to establish the time during which they can be taken. Obviously, the best time to schedule vacations is during slow periods, which depend on the location, type, and clientele of the hotel. Efficient department heads also try to spread their employees' vacations to minimize the cost of replacements. They should determine whether to cover for vacationing employees by paying other employees overtime or by hiring temporary, part-time help. Then, too, many employees request additional time off without pay. In such a case, if a replacement is not necessary, or if the cost of one is less than the employee's salary, the request should be not only granted, but encouraged.

Vacation scheduling is the responsibility of department heads. To perform this function properly, they must have a record of the employment date for each of their employees so they can determine the amount of vacation to which each is entitled. Then, wherever possible, they can give a choice of dates, based on seniority. Meanwhile, accounting checks the payroll to ensure that employees receive only the amount of vacation pay to which they are entitled. This would be simple if all employees took their full vacations at one time. But many, with the consent of their department heads, break up their vacations. Some may elect to take an extra day or days off; others may divide the multiple weeks to which they are entitled into two or more single-week vacations.

The department heads should keep records and exercise reasonable control over their employees' vacation pay. Accounting must do so.

A computer can be programmed to print out a monthly report and keep a record of each employee's vacation days due and taken. At the beginning of each year, the total number of vacation days due each employee is entered in the computer as part of the payroll data. A separate program is then designed to deduct from that total any vacation days taken and paid for. It should also provide for an immediate printout, listing by department the names of any employees exceeding their allowed vacations and showing the total vacation days due and paid to each employee so listed.

Test-Checks

At least two test-checks should be made by the controllers or their assistants. The first, a periodic review of wage rates, should be made at least once a month for two or more departments at a time. It requires the cooperation and assistance of the staff in the hu-

man resources department, since it is best accomplished by comparing the rates on the payroll with the wages in the personnel files. If a complete check of all employees' rates is preferred, then the comparisons should be made every three or four months. As with every other control, differences must be thoroughly investigated; if any fraud is uncovered, the offending employee should be fired and, if the amount warrants, arrested.

The second test-check of the distribution of payroll checks should be made weekly. Its purpose is to verify that there is an actual employee for each check issued. The usual procedure on payday is for department heads to sign for, receive, and distribute the checks to all the employees in their departments. For the test-check, each week the checks for one department, chosen at random, are instead distributed by an accounting clerk. Either the affected employees are asked to come to the auditing office for their pay, or the clerk goes to their department to distribute the checks. Because personal recognition is almost impossible, the employees should be made to sign for their checks. One method of obtaining the signatures is to list all employees, usually in numerical order by employee number, and have each sign next to his or her name. Some hotels go one step further. They have some signatures verified each week by comparison with the ones in the personnel files.

Cash Payments

Cash wages have become almost extinct in the hospitality industry. In the event of immediate termination of an employee, a call to the payroll service will immediately provide the information on deductions required to prepare a manual check. This check can then be recorded in the preparation of the next payroll with specific coding so that a second payroll check is not issued. In circumstances where an employee is underpaid but will be receiving a payroll check the following period, a nonpayroll check can be issued for a payroll advance based on the estimated net underpayment. This advance can then be deducted in the following week.

Advances against future earnings are extremely poor policy. This only places the employee in the position of playing a continual game of "catch up." Furthermore, such requests usually come from an employee who has a prior history. In situations of dire emergency, with the approval of management, a loan may be necessary. However, when such a loan is granted, the repayment should be spread over a period of time within which the financial situation of the employee can be reasonably expected to allow repayment. Furthermore, a loan document, in writing, should be executed so that in the event employment is ended, legal action can, if appropriate, be instituted to recover the balance.

Cash wages are still made in some major cities, in particular, New York City. In these locations, it is common practice for banquet employees, in response to the need, to work in several hotels over the period of a week. This group of temporary employees includes dishwashers and housemen who are at the lower end of the pay scale. Need, combined with long-established practice, has resulted in these employees being paid in cash at the end of each shift. To facilitate these payments, a payroll clerk must prepare a cash payroll voucher (Figure 7–3) from which the payment is subsequently entered into the payroll records. This area is wide open to abuse and requires continu-

CASH PAYROLL VOUCHER

79-80-2-0

DATE _____   W/E _____

WAGES WILL NOT BE PAID EXCEPT ON PRESENTATION
OF THIS CARD

AUTH. DEPT'S HEADS SIGNATURE

1-2 HOTEL	EXPLANATION / REASON	3-6 DEPT. #

7-15
SOCIAL SECURITY #

PRINT NAME OF EMPLOYEE AND ADDRESS

22-36 LAST	37-47 FIRST	48 INT.

	49 M/S	50-51 Fed Ex	55 Sex	67 Res.	77 R	78 Un.

79-80-2-1

22-48
STREET ADDRESS

49-68 CITY	69-73 STATE (ABBN)	74.79 ZIP

79-80-6-0 — EARNINGS — AMOUNT

		EARNINGS	AMOUNT
28-31 REGULAR	HRS. @	36-41	
32-35 OVERTIME	HRS.	42-46	
47-48 OTHER CODE		49-53	
57-60 VACATION	HRS.	61-66	
SERVICE CHARGES		67-72	

79-80-6-1
GROSS EARNINGS — 73-78 — $

FICA	16-20
FED. W/TAX	21-25
STATE TAX	26-29
CITY TAX	30-33
UNION DUES	34-37
UNION FEES	38-41
OTHER (58)	59-62

TOTAL DEDUCTIONS $

NET PAY 63-68 $

RECEIVED PAYMENT IN FULL FOR SERVICES TO DATE AND CERTIFY THAT
THE NUMBER OF WITHHOLDING EXEMPTIONS CLAIMED ABOVE DOES NOT
EXCEED THE NUMBER TO WHICH I AM ENTITLED.

SIGNATURE _____

ADDRESS _____

PUNCHED		VERIFIED	

Note: Requires multiple copies, one for the employee and others according to distribution specified by controller.

Figure 7–3 Cash Payroll Voucher

ous audit and scrutiny. A periodic "check-off" should be held where the names of the employees are noted as they leave the hotel and the list is immediately checked against the payroll vouchers prepared. Additionally, a specific schedule of hours to be worked should be prepared in advance and matched against the recorded hours.

Control of Deductions

As previously indicated, control over deductions is also a very necessary procedure. Employers act as temporary custodians of the money deducted from their employees' wages. Every deduction must be separately reconciled for each employee and in total. Separate forms are used to balance and file the deductions. Hotels, as a service industry, need many more employees in relation to size and volume of sales than any other type of business. They also employ a higher percentage of unskilled workers, which results in a larger turnover. Including part-time, temporary help such as banquet waiters and dishwashers, it is not unusual for a hotel to process through the payroll each year three or four times the number of employees on its permanent staff. Needless to say, the more employees involved, the more difficult it is to reconcile each deduction.

State and local laws regarding taxes and employees' benefits differ in their provisions, so it would not be feasible to try and describe all the varied reports needed to satisfy these requirements. However, employees in most hotels enjoy many similar benefits. Unionization of employees is quite common, and all hotels are subject to federal laws and IRS regulations. A brief review of the reporting forms and deposit requirements follows.

Reports and payments to the proper agency, at all levels of government, should be made on time. The interest and penalties if they are delayed can be very costly. Two separate reports must be submitted to the IRS; one combines the Social Security, Medicare, and Federal Income Tax withheld and the other is for unemployment taxes.

The Social Security, Medicare, and Income Tax Report (Form 941) is due on the last day of the month following each calendar quarter. When the laws were originally enacted, payment in full was made quarterly and included with the returns. Regulations have since been changed to require deposits during each quarter. At the present time, they range from no advance deposit, if the combined taxes are less than $500 in any quarter, to weekly deposits for the larger hotels whose combined taxes exceed $50,000 per year. For the latter, deposits are due three banking days after the date wages were actually paid.

Withholding Tax Statements (W-2s) are prepared for the calendar year and are due by January 31 of the following year. The IRS allows employers an additional month, until the end of February, to file copy A with them. They are individual multi-copy, multipurpose forms, headed with the hotel's operating name, address, and employer number. Each employee is identified by name, address, and Social Security number. The figures reported must show the total amount of each tax deduction made during the year and the gross wages used to calculate each one: Federal Income Tax, Social Security and, where required, state and local income taxes.

Two sets of W-2s are prepared simultaneously for each employee. One set is used to send reports to each taxing authority (the original to the IRS) and one is retained as a file copy. The other set, with the same number of copies, is given to the employee. The total deductions must be reconciled to the amounts shown on the quarterly reports, which in turn are reconciled to the deposits or payments as required. For every deduction, a tape, run on a computer or adding machine, must be sent to the taxing authority with whatever summary sheet they provide. The IRS requires the annual summary to be made on Form W-3, shown with the W-2 in Figure 7–4. In the 1980s,

a Control number	22222	Void ☐	For Official Use Only ►		
b Employer's identification number			**1** Wages, tips, other compensation		**2** Federal income tax withheld
c Employer's name, address, and ZIP code			**3** Social security wages		**4** Social security tax withheld
			5 Medicare wages and tips		**6** Medicare tax withheld
			7 Social security tips		**8** Allocated tips
d Employee's social security number			**9** Advance EIC payment		**10** Dependent care benefits
e Employee's name (first, middle initial, last)			**11** Nonqualified plans		**12** Benefits included in Box 1
			13 See Instrs. for Box 13		**14** Other

15 Statutory employee ☐	Deceased ☐	Pension plan ☐	Legal rep. ☐	942 emp. ☐	Subtotal ☐	Deferred compensation ☐

f Employee's address and ZIP code					
16 State Employer's state I.D. No.	**17** State wages, tips, etc.	**18** State income tax	**19** Locality name	**20** Local wages, tips, etc.	**21** Local income tax

Cat. No. 10134D   Department of the Treasury—Internal Revenue Service

Form **W-2** Wage and Tax Statement **1993**

Copy A For Social Security Administration

For Paperwork Reduction Act Notice,
see separate instructions.

OMB No. 1545-0008

a Control number	33333	For Official Use Only ► OMB No. 1545-0008		
b Kind of Payer	941/941E ☐ Military ☐ 943 ☐ CT-1 ☐ 942 ☐ Medicare govt. emp. ☐	**1** Wages, tips, other compensation		**2** Federal income tax withheld
		3 Social security wages		**4** Social security tax withheld
c Total number of statements	**d** Establishment number	**5** Medicare wages and tips		**6** Medicare tax withheld
	e Employer's identification number	**7** Social security tips		**8** Allocated tips
f Employer's name		**9** Advance EIC payments		**10** Dependent care benefits
		11 Nonqualified plans		**12** Deferred compensation
		13 Adjusted total social security wages and tips		
		14 Adjusted total Medicare wages and tips		
g Employer's address and ZIP code				
h Other EIN used this year		**15** Income tax withheld by third-party payer		
i Employer's state I.D. No.				

Under penalties of perjury, I declare that I have examined this return and accompanying documents, and, to the best of my knowledge and belief, they are true, correct, and complete.

Signature ►   Title ►   Date ►

Telephone number (   )

Form **W-3 Transmittal of Wage and Tax Statements 1993**   Department of the Treasury Internal Revenue Service

Figure 7–4   Federal Forms W-2 and W-3

the IRS issued a new ruling requiring employers filing more than 250 W-2s to use magnetic media instead of individual W-2s. Most states are now either requiring or accepting similar filings.

Federal unemployment taxes are entirely paid by the employer and require no detailed reporting forms. Like all payroll taxes, they are based on a calendar year, with the maximum taxable wages for each employee set by Congress. The tax return (Form 940) is due by January 31 for the preceding year. Substantial credit is given for payment made to states for unemployment insurance. When this tax was originally enacted, and for many years thereafter, the gross tax rate was 6 percent. The employer was then permitted to deduct up to 90 percent, assuming that the payments to the state equaled or exceeded that amount. In the 1980s, Congress increased the gross rate to 6.2 percent but left the maximum credit at 5.4 percent, in effect increasing the net rate from .06 percent to .08 percent. The higher rate was due to expire at the end of 1987. However, Congress extended the 6.2 percent rate through 1995. The advance deposit requirements are relatively simple. If the accumulated tax liability exceeds $100 in any quarter, which is the case with most hotels, deposit of the total tax due is required before the end of the month following the quarter.

State laws have different deposit requirements and different regulations as to when or how their residents qualify for unemployment benefits. The amount of the payment, up to each state's maximum, depends on the individual applicant's earnings. Some states, commonly called *reporting states,* require detailed quarterly returns listing each employee's Social Security number, name, and taxable or total wages. Others, known as *request states,* require only quarterly summaries showing the computation of the total tax due. If a former employee files for unemployment benefits, a special form requesting detailed payroll information is sent to the hotel. This form must be completed and returned, usually within 7 to 10 days; otherwise a penalty for noncompliance may be assessed against the hotel.

Other Deductions

Employee benefits and union contracts account for most of the other payroll deductions. All require special programming so that the necessary figures, statistics, and reports are automatically produced or available on demand.

Union Contributions.   Even though almost all benefits to union members require no employee contributions, the hotel's liability to the trustees administering each fund must be separately calculated, recorded, and paid. The benefits vary, but they usually include hospitalization, medical and life insurance, and pensions. Some contracts include dental benefits. Contributions are not necessarily based on cash wages; gratuities and meal allowances may be included, and the amount due a fund may be based on the total number of union employees in the hotel or on the total number of hours they worked. The percentages used to determine the cost of the benefits, regardless of base, are usually different. These factors must be analyzed and taken into account when setting up a computer program for processing the payroll.

Detailed reports listing the names of covered employees are usually not required. The unions control their membership through the dues and fees deduction reports. Dues are normally payable monthly and are deducted, by agreement with the union, in

the same week of each month. Most unions either maintain their own employment bureaus or work very closely with their state's employment offices. A hotel is usually obligated under the contract to try to hire all replacements of union employees through these offices. If they cannot provide a qualified union member to fill a position, the hotel is free to hire any applicant that meets the requirements. However, since most union contracts call for a closed shop, new employees must join the union within a specified time and pay a fee for the privilege. These fees are rarely deducted in full in any one week; the usual procedure is to spread the total over a period of weeks.

Dues and fees thus require two separate functions to process and control them. The first is to deduct them and produce a detailed report listing the name, position, and amount deducted for each employee. The other controls the number of deductions for fees and stops them when the total amount due has been paid.

Shared Benefits.   Many hotels and restaurants offer their employees the option to upgrade some of their benefits by sharing the additional cost, that is, by making voluntary contributions through payroll deductions. The internal administration of these programs may be a personnel or an accounting function, depending on company policy. Control of the income and expense is, as always, the controller's responsibility. However, this is an area where administration and control are so intermingled that it is often difficult to know where one ends and the other begins. Only through the complete cooperation of all concerned can the interest of the employees and the hotel be fully protected.

These plans usually involve a third party: a trustee, an insurance company, or a bank. The operation pays the total cost and is partially reimbursed by the employees' contributions. But this system can cause unnecessary expenses for the hotel and even loss of benefits for a few employees.

The insurers or administrators of the plan must have at all times a current list of all covered employees. Benefits such as hospitalization, major medical, dental, and life insurance cease when employment terminates (although the employee may have the option to convert to direct payments). Yet, unless they are so notified, the outside administrators will continue billing the hotel for its former employees. Conversely, in order to arrange for proper coverage, they must also be notified as new employees become eligible for the benefits, or when employees are given increases in wages that entitle them to an increase in benefits.

The other side of the coin involves the payroll. Obviously, when employees are terminated, their deductions are no longer made, but deductions for new employees should start on the day they become eligible for benefits. Also, many employees are allowed to take time off without pay during slow periods. Since the benefits cannot be canceled, the deductions should not be stopped. If the time off is sufficient to create payless periods, then the deductions should be doubled up when the employee returns until the lost amounts are recouped. Any additional benefits due to a promotion or a raise in pay may require an increase in the employee's contributions. All this points out the absolute necessity of communication and cooperation between the internal administrator and the paymaster.

But the dissemination of information, essential as it is, does not ensure proper coverage for the employees or control over expenses. Both can be achieved only by

thoroughly analyzing the bills received from the administrators and in some way checking them with the payroll summary sheets. The totals shown in each pay period for each deduction should also be verified. This requires a worksheet listing, by name and department, the employees for whom changes in the amount of any deduction were processed during each pay period. The correct totals for any period are then the previous period's totals adjusted by the net differences of the listed additions and deletions. Prudence also dictates that each change be checked with the payroll to verify that it was not only correct in amount, but was processed for the named employee.

Some companies, such as Blue Cross and Blue Shield, submit itemized lists showing the name and charge for each covered employee as part of their bills. The charge denotes the type and amount of coverage. This is helpful if the plan includes an option for employees to upgrade their benefits. When checking the listings against the latest payroll summary sheet to verify that each person listed there is currently employed, the clerks can also verify the deductions for those employees with excess coverage.

On bills for life insurance premiums, most companies will usually show, in addition to the rate per thousand, only the number and total dollar amount of all the policies then in effect. They should also attach a statement giving the figures at the close of the last billing period, itemization of all changes and adjustments in the interim, and the net totals for the current billing period. Most plans give the eligible employees a basic coverage with an option to purchase additional amounts of insurance. This way, any worksheet set up to control these bills must start off with the number of eligible employees, which will always be the number of policies in effect, and the total basic coverage. As options are exercised, only the dollar amount need be adjusted. Once the original totals are set up, all that is required to keep the worksheets current is to enter all additions, deletions, and adjustments as they are processed. If they are properly updated and the insurance company is promptly advised of all changes, the totals on the worksheet as of any billing date should agree with the figures shown on the bills.

However, verifying the amount billed does not prove that each employee's share and the total deductions are correct. The amount of each deduction must be checked with the payroll when the employees first exercise their options and rechecked as soon as any changes are processed. The total deductions should be checked every month, since a fixed monthly amount is usually charged for each thousand dollars of optional insurance. The total optional insurance is the difference between the total amount of insurance in effect at the end of any month and the total amount given to all eligible employees without charge. This difference, multiplied by the rate per thousand charged for the optional insurance, should equal the total deductions made each month for insurance.

RECORDING OF PAYROLL

As discussed in Chapter 4, the customary procedure is to prepare a journal entry to record each individual payroll, either weekly or biweekly. The journal entry must break down the payroll by department and subdepartment so that each expense category is properly charged. Similarly, a separate account must be credited for each deduction.

Since the individual employees are classified by department and subdepartment when they are originally set up on the computer, the payroll will automatically classify them in their respective departments and the completed payroll will provide a breakdown by department and subdepartment. However, occasions do occur when an employee may work a certain number of hours in a department other than his or her own. If this is a rare occurrence, a separate journal entry may be made for each payroll crediting the employee's department for the applicable cost and charging the department in which he or she worked. However, if this is a regular occurrence, a method of recording such hours should be a part of the payroll input process. The payroll service will then prepare a second payroll summary for the distribution side of the payroll in which the costs of the hours are included in the department in which they were actually incurred. Following is an example of a payroll journal entry assuming that the hotel's departmentalization follows the chart of accounts displayed in Table 3–1:

	Debit	Credit
Salaries and Wages—Front office	$3,524.71	
Housekeeping	6,408.22	
Bell staff	1,724.11	
Kitchen	4,850.48	
Service (F&B)	5,111.75	
Administration (F&B)	2,727.08	
Beverages	2,024.17	
Telephone	780.52	
Laundry	1,511.28	
Accounting	2,628.57	
Administrative (A&G)	2,175.36	
Marketing	3,021.80	
Maintenance	4,029.63	
Human resources	1,782.59	
Federal Income Tax		$8,911.72
State Income Tax		2,308.61
FICA/Medicare		3,256.07
Group Insurance		1,108.21
Payroll Bank A/C		26,716.66

The Social Security liability (6.2 percent of gross wages at present) and the Medicare liability (1.45 percent) can be credited to the same account, as the remittance to the federal tax authorities is a combined payment.

A separate entry is necessary to record the liability for the employer's matching contribution to FICA. This is a simple entry charging the Employee Payroll Taxes and Benefits account in each department for its respective share and crediting the liability account. Thus, the relative entry for the preceding example would be a debit to the Payroll Taxes and Benefits accounts in each department and a credit to FICA in the amount of $3,256.07. The distribution to the departments of the cost of group insurance is usually made in the accounts payable processing of the invoice from the insurance company. The Payroll Taxes and Benefits account in each department is charged

with the employer's contribution while the Group Insurance liability account is debited with the amount of the employee contributions.

A journal entry is also required at the end of the period to accrue for the days worked from the end of the last payroll to the end of the period. The calculation thereof and the required entry are discussed later in Chapter 8.

MANAGEMENT REPORTS

As noted in the opening paragraph of this chapter, payroll is the largest single item of expense in a hotel, and top management requires detailed reports, statistics and analysis in order to properly control this area.

The most basic of these reports relates to overtime. For proper control, on both manual and computerized payrolls, an overtime report should be prepared each week. It should be reviewed by the controller with the affected department heads, and proper explanations of any unauthorized payments should be forwarded to management. In addition, a schedule showing the dollar cost of overtime by department in each pay period should be maintained. This schedule will enable management to concentrate its efforts on those departments showing a consistent or excessive amount of overtime.

The most important report, however, is a daily labor report (Figure 7–5). This report is prepared only for hourly employees and compares scheduled hours and dollar cost against actual hours and dollar cost. The dollar cost figure is, for the sake of simplicity, determined by multiplying the hours by an average rate for the people included in that category. A further comparison of actual dollars against budgeted dollars is also provided. In addition to being prepared for each day, a second page in exactly the same format should be prepared for the period to date.

This report permits management to review the effectiveness of scheduling and highlights problem areas where excessive hours were incurred. The results must, of course, be reviewed with due consideration to the actual level of business activity compared to the amount of business expected as shown at the foot of the report. Accurate forecasting contributes materially to the value of this report. Furthermore, this report becomes extremely valuable in the budget preparation for the following year and for the evaluation of the productivity standards used in the preparation thereof.

A productivity report (Figure 7–6) should also be prepared on a daily basis either as a third page to the daily labor report or as a separate report. This report measures the actual productivity achieved compared to the productivity levels used in preparation of the schedule. Number of rooms occupied and number of covers served are the key standards used in the measurement of productivity, but other factors such as number of arrivals may be used where appropriate. Also, in measuring the productivity for the housekeeping area, a fairer measurement is to compare hours against rooms occupied for the preceding night as in fact those are the rooms that were cleaned during any given day rather than the rooms that will be occupied on the day in question. For that reason also, the period to date numbers are more significant than the daily numbers when looking at housekeeping numbers in the daily labor reports.

—— HOTEL GRAYSCOT ——

Daily Labor Report For September 19, 199__

Department	Actual Hours	Scheduled Hours	Variance	Actual Dollars	Scheduled Dollars	Variance	Budgeted Dollars	Variance
Rooms								
Maids	182	180	2	1084	1080	4	960	124
Floor Supervisors	48	48	0	336	336	0	342	(6)
Reception	48	48	0	288	288	0	294	(6)
Reservations	30	32	(2)	180	192	(12)	215	(35)
Bell	34	30	4	136	120	16	140	(4)
Other Hourly	20	16	4	120	96	24	130	(10)
Total	362	354	8	2144	2112	32	2081	63
Food & Beverage								
Cooks	86	80	6	860	800	60	880	(20)
Dishwashing	43	40	3	258	240	18	240	18
Servers/Bus	194	196	(2)	711	720	(9)	700	11
Hostess/Cashier	24	24	0	168	168	0	180	(12)
Captains	31	32	1	253	262	(9)	240	13
Bartenders	38	40	(2)	228	240	(12)	230	(2)
Other Hourly	16	16	0	112	112	0	120	(8)
Total	432	428	4	2590	2542	48	2590	0
Telephone	32	32	---	194	194	---	200	(6)
Laundry/Valet	60	64	(4)	370	394	(24)	360	10
Admin & Gen'l								
Accounting	40	40	0	320	320	0	340	(20)
Administrative	8	16	(8)	64	128	(64)	64	0
Night Audit	18	16	2	144	128	16	128	16
Other Hourly	8	8	0	48	48	0	48	0
Total	74	80	(6)	576	624	(48)	580	4
Marketing	8	8	0	64	64	0	60	4
Engineering	60	56	4	540	504	36	590	(50)
Grand Total	1028	1022	6	6478	6444	34	6461	17

Number of Rooms Occupied   ---   Actual 264   Scheduled 258

Number of Covers Served   ---   Actual 708   Scheduled 722

Figure 7–5 Daily Labor Report

Hotel Grayscot

Daily Productivity Report for September 19, 199x

Rooms Dept.	Today		Period to Date	
	Actual	Schedule	Actual	Schedule
Hours worked				
Maids	182	180	3,320	3,370
Floor supervisors	48	48	902	912
Reception	48	48	930	912
Reservations	30	32	602	608
Bell	20	16	312	300
Rooms occupied				
(prior night)	308	310	6,140	6,128
Rooms occupied				
(today)	264	258	6,404	6,386
Arrivals	42	46	2,101	2,211
Reservations				
taken	72	N/A	2,310	N/A
Hours per occup. room				
Maids	0.59	0.58	0.54	0.55
Supervisors				
	0.16	0.15	0.15	0.15
Hours per arrival				
Reception	0.88	0.96	0.44	0.41
Bell	0.48	0.33	0.15	0.14
Hours per reservation	0.42	—	0.26	—
Food & beverage				
Hours worked				
Cooks	86	80	1,582	1,560
Dishwashing	43	40	840	810
Servers	194	196	2,092	2,111
Captains	31	32	608	640
Number of Covers	708	722	14,511	15,800
Covers per hour				
Cooks	8.23	9.03	9.17	10.13
Dishwashing	16.47	18.06	17.27	19.50
Servers	3.65	3.68	6.93	7.48
Captains	22.84	22.56	23.87	24.69
Dollars per hour				
Bartenders	80	76	92	77

Figure 7–6   Productivity Report

1. Prepare a list of payroll deductions you might expect to find on a hotel payroll.
2. Suggest a measurement of productivity that might be used for the following positions:

Bell person	Laundry worker
Cook	Bus person
Floor supervisor	Reservationist
Gift shop sales clerk	Dishwasher
Receptionist	Bar server

3. Circle T or F to indicate whether the following statements are true or false:

   T F **a.** Payroll is one of the most specialized areas in hotel accounting.

   T F **b.** The majority of hotel workers are paid on an hourly basis.

   T F **c.** Staff planning should take place immediately after the hotel opens.

   T F **d.** Staffing in overhead departments varies heavily with volume.

   T F **e.** Cash wages are common in the hotel industry.

   T F **f.** Payroll costs must be broken down by department.

   T F **g.** The most important payroll report is the daily labor report.

   T F **h.** Employee advances are normal in hotels.

   T F **i.** Tips are subject to tax withholding.

   T F **j.** Payroll costs in a hotel rarely exceed 30 percent.

4. Circle the correct answer to the following statements:

   a. Overtime should be authorized:

   (1) After the work is completed

   (2) When the weekly schedule is prepared

   (3) Before the work is done

   b. Productivity of maids can be measured:

   (1) In relation to hours worked

   (2) In relation to number of floors in the hotel

   (3) In relation to number of rooms cleaned

   c. Banquet gratuities are:

   (1) Very rarely paid

   (2) Usually charged as a fixed percentage of the total charges

   (3) Usually left to the customer's discretion

8

Closing the Financial Period: Prepaids, Accruals, and Other Entries

The results of all hospitality operations are computed at the end of a financial period. While the financial period for most hotels is the calendar month, certain other options are available and sometimes used. One option is to divide the year into 13 periods each consisting of four weeks. The odd day (or two days) in each year results in variances in the length of the first and/or last period. Another approach, which retains the 12 periods in a year concept, is to use four-week periods with every third period having five weeks. The thinking behind the four-week period approach is that each period has the same number of weekends, which eliminates variances from period to period or year to year that are the result of large differences between weekend business and weekday business. This concept is heavily used in retail operations, particularly by department stores and supermarkets. There is less rationale for this approach in the hotel industry because more variances occur due to seasons of the year than to days of the week. Also, there is little similarity in volume patterns between commercial hotels and resort hotels.

However, it is extremely important to record the revenues and expenditures accurately on a period-by-period basis. Failure to do so not only distorts the results for the period, but violates one of the most important tenets of accounting: the proper matching of revenue and expenditures. Therefore, the closing of a financial period requires a series of accounting entries in order to properly state the results.

The closing of the period is greatly facilitated by the preparation and maintenance of a complete set of workpapers. *Workpapers* are schedules prepared and maintained to verify and support the accuracy of the month-end asset and liability accounts in the general ledger. At the end of the year, proper workpapers also facilitate the work of the independent auditors in verifying the balance sheet and certifying the financial results for the year.

The format of period-end workpapers depends on the nature of the asset or liability account they support. Some change completely each period, resulting in new schedules or listings, while others are updates of schedules that are revised each period

but maintained on a continuing basis throughout the year. The following sections cover the broad categories and describe the nature of each.

TRIAL BALANCES

These are detailed listings prepared at the end of each period for various assets and liabilities. They include various forms of accounts receivable, amounts owed to the hotel in such subcategories as guest and city ledger, and sundry accounts receivable and travel advances due from employees. Also included in this category are listings of trade accounts payable to suppliers (including commissions due to travel agents), advance deposits received from guests for future reservations, and gift certificates that have been sold and not yet redeemed for services. These trial balances represent support or substantiation for general ledger numbers and do not normally result in period-end entries, although failure to balance to the appropriate asset and liability accounts may necessitate an adjustment.

CASH RECONCILIATIONS

These are comprised of a listing of all house banks or floats held by the staff and reconciliations of all bank accounts. Figure 8–1 shows a sample of a bank reconciliation; the steps required in its completion are addressed later in the chapter, along with the period-end entries that may result.

INVENTORIES

These are listings of the food, beverages, consumables, and other inventories on hand at the end of the period. They include inventories of goods for resale in gift shops and

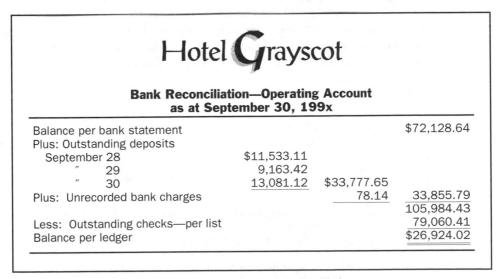

Hotel Grayscot

Bank Reconciliation—Operating Account
as at September 30, 199x

Balance per bank statement		$72,128.64
Plus: Outstanding deposits		
September 28	$11,533.11	
" 29	9,163.42	
" 30	13,081.12	$33,777.65
Plus: Unrecorded bank charges		78.14 33,855.79
		105,984.43
Less: Outstanding checks—per list		79,060.41
Balance per ledger		$26,924.02

Figure 8–1   Sample Bank Reconciliation

tennis or golf pro shops. The accounting entries related to these listings are reviewed later in the chapter.

PREPAIDS AND ACCRUALS

Schedules are prepared to reflect calculations of expenditures already made which relate to future periods and estimates of liabilities for expenses incurred for which the billings have not yet been received. The schedules are carried forward from period to period and are adjusted to reflect changes in the amounts. They cover a broad area and are the major generators of month-end adjustments. The preparation of these schedules and the adjusting entries are described extensively later in this chapter.

In addition to these general categories, other schedules should be prepared or, if unchanged, carried forward for any other assets and liabilities. The more frequently required are analyses of reserves for bad debts, fixed assets and accumulated depreciation, tax liabilities of all types, and long-term debt. The remainder of this chapter is devoted to detailed explanations of the various workpapers and the end-of-period entries resulting from them.

BANK RECONCILIATIONS

The purpose of a bank reconciliation (Figure 8–1) is to reconcile the balance shown on the end-of-period bank statement with the bank balance shown in the general ledger. The normal reasons that the amounts differ are because deposits and checks recorded during the period have not, due to the time lag, cleared the bank as of the month end. Deposits recorded but not yet reflected on the bank statement are known as *outstanding deposits* and must be added to the balance. Checks that have not yet cleared are termed *outstanding checks* and must be deducted from the bank balance. Most accounts payable/check disbursement computer programs now have an added feature where the check numbers for checks cashed by the bank can be input into the cash disbursements records. The computer then produces a listing of the un-cashed (i.e., outstanding) checks. This eliminates the tedious task of making a manual listing.

No accounting entries are required because of outstanding deposits or checks since they will automatically clear in a subsequent period. However, other reconciling items probably will necessitate an entry. The most common of these is bank charges debited to the bank account but for which no entry has yet been made. In Figure 8–1, the resultant entry would be:

Dr.	Administrative and General—Bank Charges	$78.14	
Cr.	Operating Account		$78.14
	To record bank charges for September.		

Similarly, an entry would be required for any checks deposited but charged back against the account due to insufficient funds.

PREPAID INSURANCE

The most commonly found prepaid expense of a significant amount is prepaid insurance (Figure 8–2). For this reason, it usually warrants a separate account in the general ledger and, therefore, a separate analysis in the workpapers. As seen in Figure 8–2, calculations must be made to determine what portion of each premium is prepaid, that is, applies to future periods. An entry must then be made to adjust the ledger balance to the calculated total:

Dr.	Fixed Charges—Insurance	$11,071	
Cr.	Prepaid Insurance		$11,071

To adjust prepaid insurance to the correct amount as at September 30 (assumes a prior ledger balance of $94,284)

PREPAID ADVERTISING

Another prepaid expense that is frequently a considerable amount in a hotel operation is prepaid advertising (Figure 8–3). Because payments are usually made to an advertising agency that in turn pays the individual media, the hotel is often required to make substantial payments in advance. When this occurs, an entry must be made at the end of the month to record the expense for that month. The entry for Figure 8–3 would be as follows:

Dr.	Advertising—Print—Newspaper	$1,985	
	" " —Magazine	2,000	
Cr.	Prepaid Advertising		$3,985

To expense advertising for September.

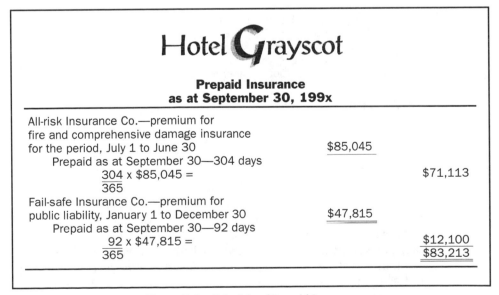

Figure 8–2   Schedule of Prepaid Insurance

Hotel Grayscot

**Prepaid Advertising
as at September 30, 199x**

Paid to Johnson, Smith & Brown—			
Advertising in *New York Daily*			
September 1 to October 31	$3,970		
Monthly expense	1,985	Prepaid	$1,985
Advertising in *New Jersey Monthly*			
September 1 to December 31	8,000		
Monthly expense	2,000	Prepaid	6,000
			$7,985

Figure 8–3   Schedule of Prepaid Advertising

PREPAID—OTHER

The most common type of prepayment is the various maintenance contracts a hotel is required to have. These are usually grouped in the general ledger under "Prepaid—Other" (Figure 8–4). The monthly entry to charge the individual accounts with the monthly expense would be:

Dr.	Rooms—Contract Services	$4,000.00
	Telephone—Equipment Maintenance	1,133.33
	Admin. & General—Data Processing	1,393.33
	Food & Bev.—Contract Services	2,633.33
Cr.	Prepaid—Other	$9,159.99

To expense monthly portion of other prepayments.

ACCRUED SALARIES AND WAGES

Unless the end of the pay period coincides exactly with the end of the accounting period, it will be necessary to make an entry to accrue payroll costs and related expenses for those additional days not included in the payroll. Various methods can be used to arrive at the amounts to be accrued, the simplest being to prorate the last payroll of the month based on the number of days. This does not, however, take into account variances caused by different days of the week or increases/decreases in volume. The more accurate method is to make an accrual (Figure 8–5) based on the daily labor reports, the preparation of which was explained in Chapter 7. Since payroll taxes and benefits remain fairly constant, on a department-by-department basis, as a percentage of cash payroll, the year-to-date percentage can be used to calculate the estimated taxes and benefits. The accounting entry is relatively simple:

Dr.   Salaries and wages—in each category based on schedule
      Payroll taxes and benefits—in each category based on schedule
Cr.   Accrued Salaries and Wages $37,839
To accrue payroll September 28–30

However, it is very important that an entry also be made to reverse any accrual made for the prior month (e.g., August in this case).

ACCRUED UTILITIES

Very few utilities bill on a calendar-month basis, and even when they do, the billings are received too late to be incorporated into the accounting period. It, therefore, becomes necessary to make accruals for such items as electricity (or gas), water, and telephone. While it may also be necessary to accrue for fuel, this can be avoided by having the tanks refilled on the last day of each period. In that way, the billings will also reflect the consumption for the month. The value of full tanks can then be carried as a fixed inventory of supplies.

The calculation of the various utility accruals (Figure 8–6) depends on the ability of the engineering department to read meters reflecting consumption. Electricity

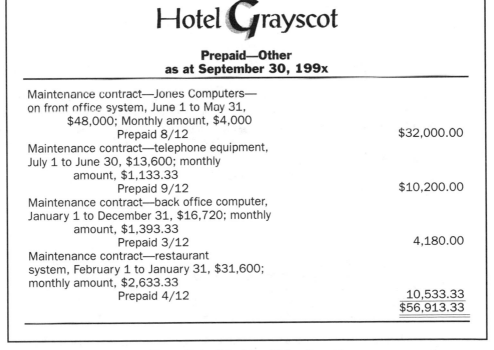

Figure 8–4   Schedule of Other Prepaids

Hotel Grayscot

**Accrued Salaries and Wages
as at September 30, 199x**

Accrual for payroll from September 28–30 based on daily labor reports:

	SEPT 28–30 PER DAILY REPORTS	EST. P/R TAXES	TOTAL
Rooms—Front Office	$2,183	$ 520	$2,703
Housekeeping	4,027	1,007	5,034
Bell Staff	1,154	288	1,442
Feb—Kitchen	5,600	1,400	7,000
Service	5,102	1,275	6,377
Admin.	2,031	508	2,539
Beverages	1,142	285	1,427
Telephone	641	160	801
Laundry	868	217	1,085
A&G—Accounting	2,472	618	3,090
Admin.	2,146	536	2,682
Marketing	1,043	261	1,304
Engineering	1,862	493	2,355
	$30,271	$7,568	$37,839

Figure 8–5   Schedule of Accrued Salaries and Wages

and water are usually metered in a manner that the consumption for a period can be determined by deducting the reading at the end of the prior period from the current reading. The total telephone cost is usually available from the printouts from the call accounting system for the days not billed. The printouts show the actual cost of administrative calls and frequently also show in total the cost of the guest calls. If the guest calls are only displayed at selling price, the costs can be calculated by applying the markup percentage in reverse.

As reflected in Figure 8–6, the entry required at the end of the period to reflect the accruals is:

Dr.	Energy Costs—Electricity	$13,550.00	
	Energy Costs—Water	6,242.20	
	Telephone—Cost of Calls, Long Distance	10,790.20	
	All depts. as per distribution, Telephone Expense	2,716.10	
Cr.	Accrued Utilities		$33,298.50

To record utility accruals for September.

Again, it is important to remember to reverse the accrual from the prior month.

Accrued Utilities
as at September 30, 199x

Electricity—per readings—$271,000	
Kilowatt hours @ 0.05 per thousand	$13,550.00
Water—per readings 312,110 gals.	
@ 0.02	6,242.20
Telephone—per call accounting	
reports, September 11 (billed through September 10)	
to September 30—Admin. $2,716.10	
Guest 10,790.20	13,506.30
	$33,298.50

Figure 8–6 Schedule of Accrued Utilities

ACCRUED INTEREST

If interest on long-term debt is paid other than on a monthly basis, it is necessary to make an accrual.

In Figure 8–7, the accrual is for two months. Assuming that an entry was made for an accrual in the prior month, the easier way (rather than to reverse the prior accrual) is to increase the existing accrual by one month's interest.

Dr.	Fixed charges—Interest expense	$15,833	
Cr.	Accrued interest		$15,833
To accrue interest for September.			

Accrued Interest
as at September 30, 199x

Accrual for months of August and September—10% of	
$1,900,000 for two months	$31,666

Figure 8–7 Schedule of Accrued Interest

Hotel Grayscot

**Accrued Credit Card Commissions
as at September 30, 199x**

American Express 2.5% of	$716,522	$17,913
Visa/MC 2.0% of	633,011	12,660
		$30,573

Figure 8–8   Schedule of Accrued Credit Card Commissions

ACCRUED CREDIT CARD COMMISSIONS

The credit card companies usually bill the hotel for commissions in the following month. Therefore, it is necessary to make an accrual (Figure 8–8) based on charges for the period. As shown, the required entry would be:

Dr.	Admin. & General—Credit card commissions	$30,573
Cr.	Accrued credit card commissions	$30,573

To accrue credit card commissions—September.

Once more, the accrual from the prior month must be reversed.

RESERVE FOR BAD DEBTS

Proper accounting procedures require that a reserve be set up to cover possible losses due to accounts receivable being uncollectible. At the year end, a very exact formula based on the age of the accounts is used to calculate the reserve. However, during the course of the year, the entry for the provision is usually a rounded amount—frequently based on the budget. A detailed schedule (Figure 8–9) should be maintained and updated at the end of each period to support the general ledger balance. The monthly entry for the provision is:

Dr.	Admin. & General—Bad debt expense	$1,000
Cr.	Reserve for bad debts	$1,000

To record monthly provision—September.

FIXED ASSETS AND ACCUMULATED DEPRECIATION

Depreciation is usually described as writing off the cost of an asset over its useful life. An asset usually requires a life of five years or more to be considered a fixed asset. Land and certain untangible assets such as good-will are considered to have indefinite life spans and are, therefore, not depreciable.

Hotel Grayscot

**Reserve for Bad Debts
as at September 30, 199x**

Balance—January 1		$24,500.00
Monthly provision: 9 x 1,000		9,000.00
		$33,500.00
Write-offs		
Smith Travel Agency	$3,032.50	
Green Corporation	2,761.50	
Credit card chargeback		
losses	476.00	$ 6,261.00
Balance—September 30		$27,239.00

Figure 8–9   Reserve for Bad Debts

Most companies in the United States follow the rules and regulations as set down by the Internal Revenue Service. This avoids the need to be continually reconciling book profits (losses) with tax profits (losses).

The method of depreciation, or *cost-recovery* as they refer to it, the IRS uses is the modified Accelerated Cost Recovery System (MACRS). MACRS provides for various classes of assets from 3 years (race horses) to 50 years (railroad gradings). However, in hotel accounting the two classes most commonly used are the 7-year, into which most furniture and equipment falls, and 31.5-year for nonresidential commercial buildings.

The seven-year class permits the use of a 200 percent write-off on a declining-balance basis. Simply stated, seven years means a depreciation rate of 14.68 percent (100 divided by 7). This means that the first year's write-off will be 200 percent or 2 x 14.68 = 29.36 percent of the cost of the asset. *Declining balance* means that in the second year the write-off will be 29.36 percent of the cost of the asset minus the first year's depreciation.

Let us assume a table cost $100. The depreciation taken in the first year would be 29.36 percent of $100 or $29.36. However, in the second year depreciation would be 29.36 percent of $70.64 ($100 minus $29.36).

Depreciation in the 31.5-year class is straight-line. The total cost is simply divided by 31.5 and an equal amount is written off each year.

There are numerous other regulations related to part-years, disposals, and so on with which a hotel controller must be acquainted. However, for purposes of this chapter, the preceding information is adequate.

A schedule (Figure 8–10) must be maintained so that a monthly entry can be made. This means that any additions must also be analyzed and entered on the schedule so that the amount can be updated.

Hotel Grayscot

Fixed Assets and Accumulated Depreciation as at September 30, 199x

FIXED ASSETS

	Balance Jan. 1	Additions	Disposals	Balance Sep. 30
Land	$4,000,000			$4,000,000
Building	8,232,000			8,232,000
F&E	3,011,719	$159,905		3,171,624
Operating Equipment	368,722			368,722
	$15,612,441	$159,905		$15,772,346

ACCUMULATION DEPRECIATION

	Balance Jan. 1	Additions	Balance Sep. 30
Building	$1,567,998	$195,999	$1,763,997
F&E	1,227,620	516,150	1,743,770
	$2,795,618	$712,149	$3,507,767

Figure 8–10   Fixed Assets and Accumulated Depreciation

When an asset is depreciated, the asset account is not credited with the write-off. Instead, the depreciation is credited to a reserve account known as "Accumulated depreciation." The asset account remains at original cost while the reserve increases each year by the amount of depreciation.

Another asset common to hotels is "Operating equipment," the term applied to linen, china, glass, and silver. The proper accounting procedure is to write off 50 percent of the cost of the original equipment over a period of five years (10 percent per year). The asset account is reduced rather than creating a reserve. The remaining 50 percent is left on the books as a permanent asset and all replacements are immediately written off. The theory behind the 50 percent asset is that for every cup or knife put into service, one is about to be broken or lost. Therefore, 50 percent is a fair value of the total equipment in use.

In Figure 8–10, the total additions to accumulated depreciation of $712,149 represent nine months, January through September. The entry required at the end of a period for one month would be:

Dr.	Fixed Charges—Depreciation—building	$21,777	
	" F&E	57,683	
Cr.	Accumulated depreciation		$79,460

To record depreciation expense for September.

Hotel Grayscot

**Sales Taxes Payable
as at September 30, 199x**

Food tax—September	$52,111
Beverage tax—September	18,108
Use tax—September	8,873
	$79,092

Figure 8–11 Schedule of Sales Taxes Payable

TAXES PAYABLE

Taxes payable do not normally require a period-end entry because the liabilities are created by revenue or payroll entries during the course of the period. An adjusting entry might be required if, for some reason, the calculated amounts did not agree with the general ledger. However, schedules should be prepared. An example of sales taxes payable (Figure 8–11) and payroll taxes payable (Figure 8–12) are prepared for the benefit of the reader.

LONG-TERM DEBT

It is very unlikely that any end-of-period entry will be required relative to long-term debt. However, a schedule (Figure 8–13) should be prepared.

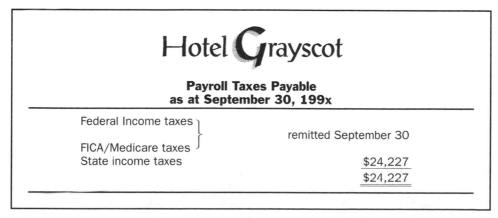

Hotel Grayscot

**Payroll Taxes Payable
as at September 30, 199x**

Federal Income taxes ⎤		
⎬	remitted September 30	
FICA/Medicare taxes ⎦		
State income taxes		$24,227
		$24,227

Figure 8–12 Schedule of Payroll Taxes Payable

Hotel Grayscot

**Long-Term Debt
as at September 30, 199x**

Smith Mortgage—due July 1, 201x	
Balance as at September 30	$1,900,000

Figure 8–13 Schedule of Long-Term Debt

INVENTORIES

At the end of each period, an entry is required to adjust the opening inventories to the closing inventories by debiting or crediting the difference to cost of sales. Let us assume, for example, that the inventories in Hotel Grayscot were as follows:

	September 30	August 31
Food	$22,481.10	$19,308.72
Beverages	14,122.18	15,302.21
Gift Shop	20,313.08	19,722.02
Golf Pro Shop	26,151.00	24,803.00

The required entries are as follows:

Dr.	Inventory—Food	$3,172.38	
Cr.	F&B—Cost of Food Sold		$3,172.38
Dr.	F&B—Cost of Beverage Sold	1,180.03	
Cr.	Inventory—Beverages		1,180.03
Dr.	Inventory—Gift Shop	591.06	
Cr.	Gift Shop—Cost of Sales		591.06
Dr.	Inventory—Golf Pro Shop	1,348.00	
Cr.	Golf—Cost of Sales		1,348.00

To adjust closing inventories to physical.

While hotels also carry inventories of operating supplies, such as office supplies, a physical count of these inventories is not normally made monthly. However, the requisitions signed by each department can be totaled at the end of the month and an entry made to charge the department. If inventories are carried, they should be counted twice a year and adjusted to physical. Many hotels, however, do not carry an inventory of supplies but charge each department as purchased.

OTHER ENTRIES

Each hotel has its own set of required additional entries, most of which relate only to income and expense accounts. These include the monthly food and beverage entries

(described in Chapter 13) and any allocations between departments of payroll or other expenses. Similarly, a review of final numbers may reveal errors that must be corrected. Such departments as golf frequently create additional entries.

USE OF A STANDARD JOURNAL

In order to avoid entering a recurring journal entry each month, use should be made of standard journal entries. Under a manual system, this simply consisted of a sheet (see Figure 8–14) on which the entries were recorded with columns for each month or period of the year.

Computerized programs provide for the creation of monthly standard journal entries which, once entered, will post automatically each month unless changed. While nothing prevents changing the amounts of the entries each month, the use of standard journal entries is much more valuable and time-saving if the amounts do not change or only change periodically as seen in Figure 8–14.

FINANCIAL STATEMENTS

Almost all computerized accounting systems provide for the automatic printing of financial statements. While this process is, for many businesses, the printing of only a balance sheet and income statement, the full complement of hotel financial statements also includes individual departmental schedules, both operating and overhead, and one or more pages of statistics.

Various formats are in use in hotel financial statements. These are described in detail in Section VI. The formats used in financial presentations for clubs and restaurant operations are described in Chapter 18.

Hotel Grayscot

STANDARD JOURNAL - Page 1

	JANUARY		FEBRUARY		MARCH	
	Dr.	Cr.	Dr.	Cr.	Dr.	Cr.
Depreciation Expense	21,777.00		21,777.00		21,777.00	
Accumulated Depreciation		21,777.00		21,777.00		21,777.00
To Record Depreciation						
Insurance Expense	9,071.00		11,071.00		11,071.00	
Prepaid Insurance		9,071.00		11,071.00		11,071.00
To W/O Insurance						
Advertising - Print	1,685.00		1,685.00		1,985.00	
Advertising - Magazine	2,000.00		2,000.00		2,000.00	
Prepaid Advertising		3,685.00		3,685.00		3,985.00
To W/O Advertising						
Rooms - Contract Service	4,000.00		4,000.00		4,000.00	
Telephone - Equip. Maint.	1,133.33		1,133.33		1,133.33	
A&G - Data Processing	1,393.33		1,393.33		1,393.33	
F&B - Contract Services	2,633.33		2,633.33		2,633.33	
Prepaid Other		9,159.99		9,159.99		9,159.99
To W/O Other PP's						

Figure 8–14   Extract from Standard Journal

1. Draw up journal entries to reflect prepayments or accruals for the following as at July 31:
   a. Payment on July 15 of a fire insurance policy covering the year May 1 to April 30 which was charged fully to Prepaid Insurance—$36,600.
   b. Payment of a telephone maintenance contract for one year starting July 15 which was charged to Prepaid—Other—$13,800.
   c. Payment on July 20 of newspaper advertising for August and September charged fully to Prepaid Advertising—$3,122.
   d. Interest on a loan of $6,400,000 at 5 percent; interest has already been accrued through June 30.

2. Draw up the journal entries for inventory adjustments as at July 31 based on the following:

INVENTORY	JUNE 30	JULY 31
Food	$29,072.11	$31,062.58
Beverage	17,522.80	19,537.10
Gift Shop	21,018.72	20,571.12
Golf Pro Shop	37,668.69	38,592.83

3. Circle T or F to indicate whether the following statements are true or false:
   T F a. The 13-period year is used most frequently for retail operations.
   T F b. Workpapers should be prepared only at year-end.
   T F c. Accruals are required for expenses incurred but not invoiced.
   T F d. Prepayments are required for bills received but not recorded.
   T F e. On a bank reconciliation, outstanding deposits must be added to the bank balance.

4. Circle the correct answer to the following statements:
   a. A bill was received on August 12 for September advertising but was not recorded. The required entry at August 31 is:
      (1) A prepayment
      (2) An accrual
      (3) None
   b. If the end of the month coincides with a payday, the month-end accrual:
      (1) Should be calculated based on the last week
      (2) Should be calculated based on the daily labor report
      (3) Should be ignored
   c. The best way to accrue for electricity is to:
      (1) Use the prior month's invoice
      (2) Use meter readings
      (3) Use the same amount every month

d. Straight-line depreciation means:
  (1) The amounts should always be rounded to the nearest $100
  (2) The depreciation is spread evenly over the life of the asset
  (3) The first year's depreciation is 200 percent of the cost divided by the useful life
e. Original operating equipment costs should:
  (1) Be written off at 10 percent per year until written down to 50 percent
  (2) Be written off completely at 10 percent per year
  (3) Not be depreciated

9 Credit Card Processing

Prior to the advent of credit cards, the granting of credit to the individual guest or restaurant patron was a major, time-consuming process for the hospitality industry. First, a determination had to be made prior to, or quite frequently, at the point of, check-in as to whether the guest could be granted credit. This process involved asking for various types of identification and other information relative to the financial status of the customer. A negative response to a request for credit was, at best, embarrassing for both guest and hotel or restaurant employee and, at worst, resulted in confrontation, arguments, and possibly loss of business. Second, the actual billing process consumed substantial hours of effort and paperwork by the accounting department. On short stays, the cost of billing the guest eroded much of the profit margin. Finally, there was always the possibility of a bad debt loss, not necessarily always because the customer turned out to be a bad credit risk. Improper addresses resulting in returned mail often left the hotel with no alternative but to write the account off.

Certainly the most irritating and sometimes the most costly of all the problems was the after-departure charges, late restaurant or telephone charges which were posted after the guest had settled his or her bill and checked out. These were either written off immediately or perhaps billed once or twice before being written off. The rate of recovery of after-departure charges was rarely better than 30 percent. Thus, one would assume that the arrival of credit cards as a method of collection was heartfully welcomed by hotels, but this was not the case. Since they involved a substantial expense— the discount on charges submitted that is retained by the credit card companies—hotels were initially reluctant to accept them. Even through the middle 1960s, many hotels strictly limited the number of cards honored and actually discouraged their guests from using them. They preferred to bill the guest directly, using the credit card for identification purposes only. The restaurant industry has been even more resistant to credit cards as the commission rates are higher for self-standing restaurants.

Slowly this attitude began to change, from reluctance to gradual acceptance, and finally to active solicitation. There were several reasons for this change. The most ob-

vious was the tremendous increase in the number of credit cards (owing in large part to the emergence of bank credit cards) and their growing popularity and increased use by the public. Undoubtedly, this in itself would have forced the acceptance of most cards, but the complete reversal of attitude was a purely financial decision. In line with all other operating expenses, the cost of direct billing began to climb, while at the same time the competition among the companies for outlets where their cards would be honored not only stabilized the cost of accepting them, but often reduced it. In addition, cash flow became a very important consideration in hospitality operations, since the tightening money supply slowed down collections and made borrowing difficult and expensive when additional funds were needed. Acceptance of credit cards was a natural outcome.

Today there are very few hotels either in the United States or overseas that do not honor one or more of the major credit cards and some, particularly the motels, will honor credit cards issued by the oil companies. Most restaurants, while still resisting the cards with higher commission rates, now accept the low-rate bank cards.

THE MAJOR CREDIT CARDS

Let us review the credit cards most commonly accepted in hotels and restaurants.

American Express

American Express can rightly be regarded as the father of the credit card industry. As the leading purveyor of travelers' checks, American Express found that the issuance of credit cards was a natural avenue for business expansion. While the later credit cards were issued as a means by which the general public could obtain ready credit for a wide variety of purchases and services, the American Express card was and continues to be primarily a convenience vehicle by which a traveler can avoid carrying cash or writing checks. It continues to be the most commonly used card by the business traveler because it provides easy support for expenditures, facilitates reimbursement by employers, and provides a monthly record that reduces the chance that a reimbursable expense will be overlooked. The requirements for obtaining an American Express card, even the lowest level "Green" card, are still much stricter than for other credit cards. In addition to the "Green" card, American Express issues "Gold" and "Platinum" cards with higher credit limits. American Express card holders are, except for the Optima card, required to settle their accounts fully each month, as opposed to having a revolving balance.

From the viewpoint of the hotelier, the American Express card probably receives a slightly higher level of acceptance than the other credit cards. This is not the case with the restaurants which in many areas have organized campaigns against the use of the card. However, there are fundamental reasons why the card is more attractive to hoteliers than to restaurateurs. The commission charged by American Express to the acceptor is principally determined by the average dollar amount of the individual charge. This is rational if you consider that the overhead cost of processing a $125 charge is the same as the cost of a $25 charge. A second factor in determining the rate is the total annual volume of charges. Thus, while a restaurant may pay a 4.5 percent

commission, more than twice the rate of the bank cards, some hotels pay as little as 2.25 percent, only slightly higher than the bank cards. Additionally, hotel chains can negotiate a lower chainwide rate.

Another factor that attracts hoteliers is a "guaranteed no-show" policy agreement executed by American Express. Under the terms of this agreement, American Express enforces the payment of "no-show" charges when the reservation deposit has been guaranteed by an American Express card number. The manner in which American Express guarantees settlement of returned checks cashed by their card holders is also a determining factor in their level of acceptance.

Visa/MasterCard

Although Visa and MasterCard are two different cards in appearance, they are both issued in the same manner by banks and financial institutions and their processing is similar. In fact, individual card holders frequently receive one billing for both cards. While separate submissions must be computed by the hotel, they can usually be transmitted or delivered to the issuing bank at the same time. Furthermore, the commission rate charged by the issuing bank is usually the same for both cards. While the average charge is a factor in determining the rate, the total volume is the principal consideration. Rates for hotels run in the 1.6 to 2.0 percent range. Rates for restaurants and retail merchants are slightly higher, but there is not as much disparity as with American Express rates. Since the cards are issued by individual banks and institutions, the field is highly competitive. The competition for business has become more fierce with the entry into the field of major corporations, such as General Electric and Sears and organizations such as the American Association for the Advancement of Retired People (AARP) and some of the major unions, such as the Postal Workers Union.

Diners Club

Diners Club and Carte Blanche, which was absorbed by Diners Club, were originally the principal competition to American Express. However, the arrival of the bank cards cut heavily into their market, and while American Express was able to fight back, Diners Club has lost a large portion of its market share. Today it must be considered a minor operator in the credit card field.

While the hotels continue to accept the card, the charges represent, for most hotels, a small portion of the total credit card business. Commission rates currently run in the 3.2 percent range.

Discover

The Discover card is relatively new but has received a high level of acceptance by the consumer and, as a result, is now widely accepted not only by hotels but by restaurants and retail merchants. The initial success of the card can be attributed to its policy of offering a cash rebate annually based on the actual volume of charges. However, this feature has now been copied by some of the bank cards, and it is difficult at this time to

determine whether Discover will ultimately become a significant force in the battle for credit card business. Its commission rate is modest—in the same range as the bank cards.

PREAUTHORIZATION

The greatest advantage of credit cards to the hotel industry is the ability to obtain credit card information at the point of the reservation and to store it in the computer for future use. Credit cards, like travelers' checks, eliminate all risk of credit losses to the hotel provided they are authenticated.

Originally, each credit card company furnished hotels with a list of its canceled credit cards, so all a credit department clerk had to do was check each card presented by the guests against the appropriate list to determine if it was still valid. In addition, each company had its own telephone number, which had to be called to validate all guest charges when the total exceeded a specified amount.

In the 1980s, modern technology eliminated the need for both of these time-consuming steps. Today, one terminal will validate all major credit cards. Several types of equipment are needed for this purpose. One is completely automatic and can only be used when the cashier has the actual credit card on hand. There is a slot through which the card is processed and keys to punch in the total amount due. The authorization number appears on a small screen if the charge is accepted. If the charges are not accepted, the screen will so indicate without giving any reason for the rejection. For all valid charges, the cashier need only record the authorization number on the credit company's charge slip and then accept the credit card in full settlement of the guest's account.

However, the actual credit card is not normally available to the reservationist. Therefore, the reservationist must manually input the credit card number and expiration date at a terminal. The terminal issues an authorization number verifying that the card is valid and provides a guarantee of the first night's stay. Should the card prove to be invalid, the reservationist must call the guest to obtain a different form of guarantee. In some of the newer property management systems, the keying of the card number directly into the appropriate space will generate an authorization. Where an authorization terminal is not available, authorization can be obtained over the telephone. The authorization terminal service is usually provided by the bank handling the bank card processing or possibly by American Express. Additional authorization charges result when an additional card (or cards) is added to the system. Therefore, hotels sometimes refrain from using the authorization terminal for the lesser used cards, opting instead to obtain authorization by telephone or to determine validity by referring to printed cancellation lists.

At the point of check-in, an actual imprint of the credit card should be taken. Authorization should then be obtained, usually by the credit department, for the estimated bill based on the length of stay. If, at checkout, the guests' charges are less than the authorized amount, the account can be processed with no further approvals. Otherwise, the card can be processed for the full billing as previously described.

SUBMISSION OF THE CHARGES

There are presently three methods of submitting credit card slips for reimbursement: by mail, by direct deposit in the bank, or by transmission over telephone lines.

The mail was originally the only method by which submissions could be made. Similarly, the credit card companies sent settlement checks by mail. The submission process involves running an adding machine tape of all charges and a separate tape of credits. The tapes are then wrapped around the hard copies of the credit card vouchers and a total is entered on the summary slip. The individual slips, the summary slip, and mailing envelopes are all provided by the credit card companies. There are certain time limits within which submissions must be mailed. Samples of the individual credit card slips are shown in Figure 9–1.

Direct deposit was initiated by the bank card issuers as the preferred method of submission. The charge slips are submitted to individual banks, frequently the bank with which the hotel has the rest of its banking arrangements. If not, a hotel may sign a contract with a bank that has a branch in the immediate area. The choice of a bank primarily depends on commission rates, but lines of credit offered, privileges for employees banking, and so on are other considerations. Generally, two banks are involved: the bank to which the submission is made and the bank that issued the card and must ultimately bill the cardholder. The packaging of the submission is similar to that of a mail submission except that a deposit slip must be prepared. American Express will make a deposit directly into the hotel's bank account but charges one half of one percent for the privilege. The advantage to making direct deposits into a bank account is that the funds are immediately credited and available for use. With mail submissions, both American Express and Discover will make settlements directly into a designated bank account instead of sending checks. When this procedure is followed, the credit card companies charge the applicable commission to the account on a monthly basis in the same manner as Visa/MasterCard.

Transmission of credit card charges over telephone lines is a relatively new phenomena. The advantages of this is the elimination of paperwork and an immediate credit to the hotel's account. The terminals required for on-line processing may be purchased or rented. This is usually handled by the bank that processes the bank card submissions. Any number of terminals can be installed, not only at the cashiers' stations to handle checkouts but also in the restaurants, bars, and other outlets to handle charges made directly to a credit card. The only limiting factor is cost because each terminal requires a dedicated phone line to handle the transmissions. Some of the more sophisticated point-of-sale terminals now have a feature where transmission can be effected at the same time that the settlement of the check is entered.

While the on-line transmission process was instituted primarily to handle bank card settlements, American Express and other cards can also be transmitted for an additional surcharge. A warning: American Express presently considers each terminal as a separate outlet and, as a result, the lower commission rate provided for high volume may be lost or impacted. This can, of course, be avoided by processing all the American Express transmissions through a specific terminal. If several terminals are used, a separate bank account should be opened to handle the transmissions.

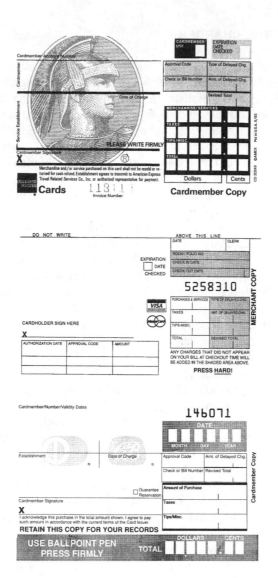

Figure 9–1 Samples of Credit Card Slips

While the individual charges are not transmitted, proper control procedures mandate that a transmission be made at the end of each shift. Thus, if a hotel has five outlets, each with two shifts, and possibly two terminals at the front desk and one in reservations, also with two shifts each, then a total of 16 transmissions, that is, 16 bank deposits, will be made daily. To commingle these with the regular hotel deposits can make the reconciliation of the bank account a horrendous task. Transfers from the special credit card bank account to the operating account can be made in total daily or periodically as required. Some of the banks have now designed a feature where individual transmissions are accumulated in the system, then grouped and reflected on the bank statement in one total. Additional problems may arise when one or more outlets or shifts fail to make their transmission on the proper day and the transmission then gets mixed up with the following day's charges. This can be prevented by making it a responsibility of the night auditors to make the final transmissions for all areas or at least to verify that all required transmissions have been made.

The importance of reconciling bank accounts used for transmitting credit cards cannot be overstated. The age of computer technology has also brought with it the problem of electronic fraud—the ability of computer experts to intercept transmissions to a specific bank account and redirect them to a bank account they control.

CREDIT CARD PROBLEMS

In addition to the reconciliation problem discussed in the preceding paragraph, certain other problems resulting from credit card acceptance should be mentioned. One of the most common mistakes is imprinting the charge on the wrong voucher or, if on-line transmission is in use, to transmit the charge to the wrong credit card company. Unless the error is caught or corrected in the accounting department, this causes confusion, possible loss, or at least delay in obtaining reimbursement. Often, such errors also make it difficult to reconcile the balances due from each credit card company. Similarly, duplicating a transaction will result in similar problems and will alienate the customer who ends up with two charges on his or her monthly billing for the same transaction.

Chargebacks are, however, the primary cause of problems. Chargebacks may occur for several reasons: unauthorized charges over the limits specified by the credit card companies, unauthorized charges on stolen or invalid cards, duplicate charges, and charges disputed by the customer. In the case of disputed charges, the credit card companies will request explanations which must be returned within specific time limits. The credit card companies must then become judges or arbitrators between the hotel and the complaining customer. This situation becomes, in the case of bank card disputes, further complicated as the disputed item must be resolved both with the hotel's bank and with the issuing bank responsible for billing the customer. As a result, bank card disputes are usually more time consuming and difficult to resolve then those of the other credit cards. This is particularly true in the case of charges for no-shows as the banks vary in their attitude and policy in regard to such charges.

Hotels and restaurants should never lose focus on the costs of credit card acceptance. The bank card field is very competitive, and every establishment must shop around to obtain the best rate possible. While the same situation does not exist with

American Express, consideration should be given to joining an organization, such as a hotel affiliation group or a similar organization, which obtains a lower rate for its members based on the total volume of all members. Frequently, the savings in reduced credit card commissions exceeds the cost of belonging to the organization.

ACCOUNTING ENTRIES RELATED TO CREDIT CARDS

The credit card charges become either a part of the total bank deposit or a part of the daily city ledger charges depending on whether they are a direct deposit in the bank or are mailed to the credit card company. In either instance, the general ledger entry, a debit to cash or accounts receivable, is made as a part of the daily income entry transferred to the general ledger by the night auditor as described in Chapter 5.

Additional journal entries are necessary to record the commissions and chargebacks if they cannot be resolved and must be written off. If the charge comes via the bank as a debit on the bank statement, the entries are made after reconciliation of the bank statement, usually a month-end function. The entry requirement is a debit to the applicable expense and a credit to the bank account as shown below:

	DEBIT	CREDIT
Commissions Expense	$682.50	
Bad Debt Reserve	122.00	
Operating Account		$804.50

If the chargebacks are deducted from remittances received, the entry required is similar but the credit is made to accounts receivable.

BENEFITS RESULTING FROM CREDIT CARD ACCEPTANCE

No chapter on credit cards would be complete without a discussion of the benefits to be derived from their acceptance. At the beginning of the chapter, the savings in labor and paperwork in the billing area as a result of accepting credit cards was mentioned. We also addressed the elimination of after-departure charges, reduced check-in time due to predetermined credit, and the value of the immediate use of funds rather than waiting out the billing cycle. These factors must be weighed against the costs resulting from commission charges and the degree to which chargebacks result in bad-debt losses.

Other benefits may be realized from acceptance of certain credit cards. Both American Express and Visa/MasterCard frequently feature client hotels in their advertising, both print and television, at no cost to the hotels. Valuable marketing information can also be provided by the credit card companies, some of which is free and some of which requires a nominal payment. Their periodic reports provide a detailed analysis of the origin of the hotel's clientele, average amounts expended, frequency of visits, and so on. Such information can also be obtained, usually for a fee, with comparisons to the hotel's competitors and on a regional and geographic basis. Every hotel that accepts credit cards should investigate what types of analyses are available as many of them are invaluable in making marketing decisions.

1. Write a brief description of the different features of American Express, Visa/MasterCard, and Discover.

2. What are the three methods of submitting credit cards for reimbursement?

3. Circle T or F to indicate whether the following statements are true or false:

    T   F   **a.** The commission charged by American Express is principally determined by the amount of the average charge.

    T   F   **b.** Hotel chains can negotiate a lower commission rate on credit cards.

    T   F   **c.** Credit card numbers are usually obtained by a hotel at check-in.

    T   F   **d.** Restaurants normally pay a higher commission rate on American Express than hotels.

    T   F   **e.** Visa and MasterCard always send separate bills.

4. Circle the correct answer to the following statements:

    a. The following card is the most difficult of the three cards to obtain:

    (1) American Express
    (2) Diners Club
    (3) Visa/MasterCard
    (4) Discover

    b. The "Gold" card concept was first used by:

    (1) American Express
    (2) Diners Club
    (3) Visa/MasterCard

    c. The concept of a cash rebate was first initiated by:

    (1) American Express
    (2) Visa/MasterCard
    (3) Discover

    d. One half of one percent additional charge for the privilege of direct deposit into a bank account is charged by:

    (1) American Express
    (2) Visa/MasterCard
    (3) Discover

    e. Chargebacks can result from:

    (1) Disputed charges
    (2) Duplicate charges
    (3) Charges on invalid cards
    (4) All of the above

10 City Ledger

Figure 2–1 showed an organization chart for the accounting department of a major hotel. One of the major branches of that chart was the city ledger area and the various positions reporting to the city ledger supervisor. In Chapter 5, *city ledger* is referred to briefly as accounts receivable other than amounts owed by guests still in the hotel. At this point, it is appropriate to more clearly define and explain the term.

In a hotel there are only two basic types of accounts: guest ledger and city ledger. The distinction between the two is simple. The guest ledger includes only the amounts due from guests currently occupying a sleeping room; the city ledger includes all other amounts due. Normally, the two amounts are shown separately on the balance sheet. The origin of the term *city ledger* probably relates back to when the only nonguest accounts receivable were amounts owed by local, that is, "in the city" patrons, of the restaurants and lounges. In spite of this very clear distinction, some hotels carry regular local patrons in their guest ledger during the month and then transfer their balances to city ledger at month end. This only occurs if the customer is being billed monthly and is done as a matter of expedience to avoid having to make daily transfers to the city ledger. The balancing and control of the guest ledger is a function of the front-desk cashiers and night audit. These procedures were previously described in Chapter 5. As with all other accounting areas, the final responsibility for the guest ledger rests with the hotel controller.

Accounts receivable are not a significant factor in restaurant operations. Billing privileges are frequently available for banquets, particularly if the customer is a business or an organization such as the Rotary Club or the local chamber of commerce. Otherwise, credit may be extended to a few regular customers, but credit card acceptance avoids the need for any extensive billing activity.

Clubs normally maintain individual accounts for members. While annual dues or monthly fees are the common factor in billings to members, charge privileges are usually extended for food and beverage and, where applicable, recreational activities. Where monthly billings do not produce settlement on a current basis, the usual prac-

tice is to post the names of members whose accounts are in arrears on a notice board. The ultimate action is, of course, the cancelation of membership.

However, neither restaurants nor clubs require the extensive billing and credit procedures found in a hotel.

RESPONSIBILITIES OF THE CITY LEDGER DEPARTMENT

In a large hotel, the level of staffing in the city ledger area can be such that it becomes a department within the accounting department. The primary responsibility of the city ledger department is to mail bills and statements to guests who, having been granted credit privileges, did not pay their bills, either partly or fully, at time of departure and to others who did not occupy a room but used other hotel facilities and were granted credit. Included in the responsibility is the mailing of charge vouchers and summaries to those credit companies not being handled as direct deposits in the bank account. This procedure is described in the preceding chapter. While the assembling of charge slips and the completion of summaries for credit card bank deposits is normally done by the general cashier, many hotels delegate the function to the city ledger department. However, in this circumstance, the completed package is then turned over to the general cashier for completion of the deposit slip and delivery to the bank. An alternative procedure is for the general cashier to accomplish the complete process. Because of the problems that result from charges processed on the incorrect charge voucher, all credit card processing should be done by the same person or persons. The billing process, other than credit cards, can, however, be divided into specific classifications or segments which are described in the following paragraphs.

INDIVIDUAL BILLINGS

Individual billings were, at one time, the largest single segment, in terms of number of accounts, in the city ledger. However, the introduction of credit cards has had the most impact on this segment. It is strongly recommended that billings to individuals be discouraged through strong enforcement of a credit card only policy. Vigorous enforcement of such a policy should keep the opening of new accounts to an absolute minimum while, over a period of time, accounts that predate the advent of credit cards will slowly die out. It is realistic to expect that any business traveler and most vacation travelers will possess at least one of the commonly accepted cards. In fact, it is becoming increasingly difficult for any individual to make a hotel reservation without one. Additionally, it would be inadvisable to grant credit to a person without a credit card. In today's world, the main reason for not owning a credit card is the inability to obtain one due to a poor credit history.

There is, however, one circumstance under which such accounts will continue to be opened. Many local patrons of the restaurants and other facilities do not like to have a bunch of small charges placed on their credit cards. They prefer to receive a monthly statement from the hotel listing their charges. This type of business is highly desirable and hotels do considerable marketing to acquire it. However, even this type of account can be regulated by issuing some form of numbered card or I.D. which the patron should present when signing his or her restaurant check. It is important that all outlets

have on hand an up-to-date listing of these patrons so no embarrassment is caused because of a lost or mislaid card. Fortunately, these customers are usually well known to the staff.

In the case of individual guest folios, the initial billing should be sent out within 24 hours of checkout, along with a copy of the guest folio. Care should be taken to ensure that the guest signs the folio at checkout.

CORPORATE ACCOUNTS

These accounts are similar in nature to individual billings in that they involve folios, individual stays, or individual charges in the outlets. The difference is, of course, that one company or organization is paying the bills for a varying number of individuals who incur charges at various times during the month. Certain precautions should be taken and a defined policy established relative to such accounts.

The company or organization should, upon opening a corporate account, provide the hotel with a list of persons authorized to sign room accounts or other charges on its behalf. An updated listing should be obtained at least annually. On all other individuals, a letter, signed by an officer of the company, should either be forwarded to the hotel at the time of the reservation or hand carried by the guest and presented at check-in. Both the hotel's registration card and the signature section on the folio should clearly state that the guest has the primary liability for payment of the charges and that in the event the company or organization does not pay, the individual guest will be held responsible.

It is recommended that the hotel obtain a credit card number and imprint from the individual, not only for identification purposes, but in the event that certain charges are disputed or unpaid, they can be charged back to the individual. Where overnight stays for that company or organization are significant in number, it is normal policy in the hotel industry to grant such customers a special rate, usually referred to as a *corporate rate*. However, the hotel should send a letter of agreement stating any discounts to the customer. It should clearly specify that any failure to reach the required levels of volume will result in discontinuance of the special rate. However, monitoring of the volume levels is usually done by the sales or reservations department utilizing the guest history records and is not normally a function of the accounting department.

The hotel must determine whether corporate charges will be billed monthly or immediately after the charges are incurred. To prevent confusing the customer, restaurant charges should be billed only monthly. A decision on handling room folios should be the subject of an agreement between the hotel and the customer with due consideration to the volume and dollars involved. A high level of volume would certainly justify billing on a weekly basis or even within 24 hours after checkout. In the latter instance, a complete statement of charges for the month should be sent at month end. However, if complete supporting documents and backup have been sent at checkout, it should not be necessary to repeat the process. While it is common practice in other industries to send billings on a cycle basis other than a monthly basis, the hotel industry has usually adhered to a calendar-month cycle. Attempts to do otherwise have not been successful, although the lack of acceptance of this concept by hotel patrons

may mostly result from the failure of the industry as a whole to make a serious attempt at adopting it.

GROUPS AND TRAVEL AGENTS

These accounts can also involve substantial amounts, but the principal reason for segregating them is that they require special and rather prompt handling. Groups, and especially conventions, usually entail the accumulation of many individual guest bills into one master account. Some groups or companies pay for all their members' charges; others assume responsibility for room and tax only, with the individual paying his or her own sundry charges. In some, the individual is liable for all charges—room, tax, and sundries. A special invoice format (see Figure 10–1 for an example) should be designed for group billings. While it is recognized that the accumulation of the billing elements is time-consuming and frequently requires research, a general policy should be established in writing that such billings should be sent out within 48 hours. However, the most important factor of all is accuracy. A small error of $5 in a $25,000 billing may result in settlement being delayed for a month. In preparing the billing, all elements (e.g., room rates, number of nights, meal prices, and so on) should be checked back against the original contract. While errors in these areas should have been caught by the front desk or night audit, city ledger still has the final responsibility for the accuracy of the billing.

Travel agents' referrals also require a variety of billing procedures. An agent may book a package tour for any number of guests which can include room, meals, cocktails, and a show if the hotel has a nightclub, plus tax and possibly even gratuities. The plan might also embrace outside activities such as theater tickets, local sightseeing trips, nightclubs, and so on. The guests pay the travel agent for the complete package and receive a prepaid tour coupon plus, either from the agent or from the hotel at registration, a coupon or ticket for each item included in the itinerary. When using the hotel restaurant, bar, or nightclub, the guest is asked to give the appropriate coupons to the person taking the order so that he or she may properly set up the charge to the travel agent. At that time, the guests should be advised of their personal liability for any item ordered that is not included in the package. The same procedure applies to outside restaurants or nightclubs. Sightseeing companies will usually accept a hotel coupon if this has been prearranged, and theater tickets are normally obtained from a theater agency, often a concessionaire in the hotel. All of these outside firms bill the hotel at an agreed price per person, with the total charge supported by individual coupons, which should be submitted with the invoice. The hotel, in turn, bills the travel agent for the fixed price of the whole plan, enclosing the prepaid tour coupons collected from the guests at registration time to justify the total charges. Obviously, each tour group requires a rather detailed worksheet.

Travel agents also refer individual guests and small groups on a commission basis, which varies. These accounts are normally handled in one of three ways:

1. The travel agent only makes the reservation; the guest is responsible to the hotel for the full amount of his or her charges. The hotel must pay the agent a commission

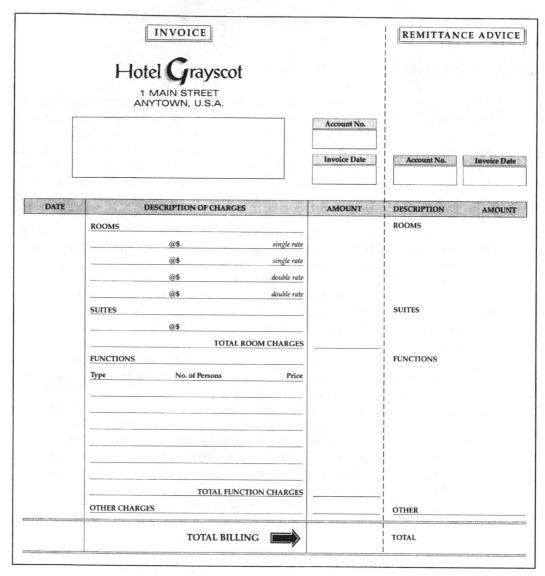

Figure 10–1   Invoice for Group Billing

and, to maintain good relations, should do so as soon as the guest checks out, whether the account is paid or not.

2. The travel agent collects the room charges from the guest, either partially or in full, and remits the net amount (total received less commission) to the hotel as a deposit on the reservation. The guest gets a prepaid coupon, which is presented at registration, and receives full credit for the amount paid when checking out.

3. The travel agent collects a deposit from the guest but does not remit any part of it to the hotel. The prepaid voucher, in this instance, serves a dual purpose. It ensures

that the guest receives the correct credit at departure, and it substantiates the invoice that the hotel must send to the agent, again for a net amount. Hotels allow this type of settlement only when prior arrangements have been made and the travel agent's credit has been approved.

BANQUET ACCOUNTS

In some hotels, banquet accounts may represent a sizable percentage of the total city ledger, whereas in other properties, the number of accounts may be insignificant enough not to justify a separate section in the city ledger. The governing factors are the capacity of the function area and the hotel policy relative to local functions. The determining factor in hotel policy is the degree to which function space must be protected to service groups and conventions.

Weddings are the largest type of local banquet business and they are usually booked well in advance. This requires a major decision on the part of the hotel unless the guest rooms have already been reserved to near capacity for that date. A hotel cannot afford to lose a group or convention because it cannot provide enough meeting or function space. Therefore, hotels that do a high level of group and convention business must make a policy decision as to how long in advance of a date they will protect function space in order not to lose business because the space is fully booked with local functions. An exception to this situation would be a hotel that, at certain times of the year, hosts weddings in outside areas. Normally, the hotel can protect against bad weather by using tents. However, in locations where the temperature in May and June, the heaviest wedding months, is not suited to outdoor functions, a major policy decision must be made. The proper approach is to protect the public areas within reason because function business is not good business if it results in empty guest rooms. The ideal situation is, of course, to have a large block of rooms committed to by wedding attendees.

Weddings and other social functions present a higher than average credit risk so it is advisable to require a large deposit based on the estimated bill with full settlement on the day of the function. To do otherwise may result in the responsibility for the balance being tossed back and forth from the bride's family to the groom's family.

In Chapter 5, the procedures required to ensure proper billing are described in detail. If those procedures are adhered to vigorously and combined with a stringent credit policy, the volume of banquet city ledger and, hence, the risk of bad debt loss can be kept to a low level. For hotels that cater principally to individual transient room business but that have sizable function space, local banquets can be a significant portion of their total volume.

OTHER ACCOUNTS

The final billing responsibility encompasses all other city ledger balances. Included in this group are *after-departure charges*. As the term indicates, these represent items that were not included on the bill when the guest checked out. If the guest paid the account in full, these charges create an unpaid balance. If the guest charged the account, the amount due increases. Merely billing the guest is not sufficient. An explanation, some-

times an apology, and always a photocopy of the charge should accompany the statement. This approach not only promotes good guest relations, but aids tremendously in the collection of the item. Fortunately, as discussed in the preceding chapter, the common practice of requiring a credit card number at the time of the reservation has significantly reduced the volume of after-departure charges.

INVESTIGATION CLERKS

Maintaining good guest relations is the principal—really, the only—responsibility of the investigation clerks. Indeed, they are sometimes referred to as members of the customer service department. All their tasks must be directed toward that goal. They are often the final contact the guests have with the hotel, and sometimes the only one after they check out—a very important contact, since it occurs only when a guest asks for assistance. There is nothing more infuriating or frustrating than a feeling of being ignored. A prompt reply, whether to comply with the guest's wishes or to ask for additional information, is the only way to ensure the guest's good-will. The investigation clerks handle all requests, questions, or disputes relating to the guest's account, ranging from a simple request for a duplicate bill to a claim that partial or full payment was made and no credit was shown on the statement. They also handle requests from travel agents for unremitted commissions.

Because of the voluminous correspondence, most large hotels have set up form letters (see Figure 10–2) to facilitate the handling of these requests. Some go as far as to immediately acknowledge receipt of the request, assign a reference number to it in case additional correspondence is necessary, and advise the guest that the inquiry will be processed as soon as possible. Caution: In the attempt to expedite these requests, a hotel may incur unnecessary expense that in the aggregate can amount to a substantial loss. Two mistakes in judgment are most common, and both can occur on a single transaction: a guest's justifiable complaint of an erroneous charge. To illustrate:

A guest complains that although he or she had no restaurant charges while in the hotel, one appeared on the bill. The investigation clerk pulls out the restaurant check and verifies the fact that it was an erroneous charge. The fastest and easiest way to adjust the error is to write off the charge and send the guest a refund for the amount. The guest is satisfied, but the hotel has incurred a loss, possibly double the amount of the charge. Obviously, the fact that a restaurant check exists indicates that some guest incurred the charge. Thus, the correct procedure is to identify the other guest, obtain a billing address through a folio or registration card, set up a city ledger account if none exists, and transfer the charge to this account. In this way, the account of the guest who was incorrectly charged is automatically credited and the hotel suffers no loss of revenue.

The second mistake is to authorize a refund without first verifying that the account was paid in full. If it was not, then the transfer reduced the balance due and all that need be done is to send a corrected bill, with a letter thanking the guest for calling attention to the overcharge. The invoice to the guest who incurred the charge, with a photocopy of the restaurant check, should be enclosed in a letter explaining and apologizing for the delay in billing the item.

Hotel Grayscot

1 MAIN STREET · ANYTOWN, USA

(Insert name and address
of travel agent)

Dear ———————

      We acknowledge receipt of your request for commission on the stay of _(name of guest)_ for the period from _(date of arrival)_ to _(date of departure)_.

      We will follow up on your request and research our records immediately. Since this process involves searching historical records there may be a short delay before we respond.

      If however you do not receive payment or an explanation within 14 days please contact us immediately.

Yours Sincerely

Janet Smith
Accounts Receivable Supervisor

Figure 10–2   Form Letter to Respond to Commission Requests

The refund of an overcharge to a guest whose account is still open does not necessarily result in a loss to the hotel. Most guests will subsequently pay the full amount, including the overcharge, but some will not. There have been many cases where the guest accepted the refund but still deducted the erroneous charge from the remittance. Collecting this balance is at best time-consuming and expensive, and it is frequently ir-

ritating to the guest, who cannot understand why he or she should pay for a charge that was not incurred. The greatest loss results from a refund to someone who never pays the account, which eventually has to be written off as a bad debt. Fortunately, this does not happen very often, but it does happen.

Some years ago, I encountered a very substantial bad debt write-off that included the account of a bus tour operator in bankruptcy. The itemization of this account showed that the company had erroneously been given a refund by check of over $2,000 for room rental overcharges on a tour it had booked just two months before declaring bankruptcy.

Such an incident not only demonstrates the need for internal controls, it also shows that the responsibilities of the accounting department extend beyond the universally accepted functions of controlling the income and operating expenses of a hotel.

GENERAL CASHIER

In Chapter 5, the duties of the general cashier, as they relate to the auditing and recording of daily front-office and food and beverage deposits, was described. Earlier in this chapter, a further reference was made to the general cashier's responsibility to assemble and deposit the credit card submissions. In addition to the aforementioned, the daily deposit contains two other elements: accounts receivable remittances and miscellaneous other receipts.

Most payments of accounts are received through the mail and necessary safeguards to protect those receipts must be established. The primary point of control is at the opening of the incoming mail. All mail should be opened by an employee who is neither an accounting department employee nor has any participation in the recording of revenue or receipts. Most commonly, the task is delegated to the general manager's secretary. A list of incoming checks should be prepared in triplicate—one copy being retained in the mail openers' file, the second accompanying the checks when they are forwarded to the general cashier for deposit, and the third going to the city ledger department to provide detailed information for posting to the individual accounts. After posting, the city ledger department must verify its total against the total city ledger credit recorded by the general cashier. The copy retained by the mail opener serves two purposes: (1) to be available in the event that a problem occurs and the receipt of a check must be verified, and (2) to be used by the controller as an internal control mechanism to audit and verify the actual deposit detail against the checks received.

Miscellaneous payments, such as telephone commissions, receipts from the sale of waste, and so on, will be received through the mail and should be subjected to the same listing procedure. The nature of these receipts and their accounting treatment becomes a responsibility of the general cashier who must consult with his or her superior when necessary.

The daily front-office and food and beverage receipts, as entered on the general cashier's deposit summary (Figure 5–9) are automatically recorded in the general ledger through the property management system in the manner described in Chapter 5. A second cash receipts journal entry must be made on a daily basis to record the city ledger payments and the miscellaneous receipts. This can be in the form of a standard

journal entry posted daily or the amounts can be recorded in a monthly cash receipts journal and posted at month end.

The general cashier is also responsible for the control and audit of the *house banks*. These are funds in varying amounts issued to front-desk and food and beverage cashiers primarily to make change but also to cash travelers' checks and, when approved, guests' personal checks. Other outlets dealing with the public require house banks and even such areas as receiving may need a small bank to handle CODs, freight charges, and so on. The general cashier also has the responsibility for maintaining the hotel petty cash fund from which authorized cash expenditures are made when required. However, payments in cash should, except for emergencies or extenuating circumstances, be limited to under $25. The general cashier should periodically, at least weekly, prepare a summary of all expenditures and submit it with the supporting vouchers, to accounts payable in order to receive a check which, when cashed, will replenish the petty cash fund. The general cashier is also required to keep a large central cash bank from which to make change for the individual house banks. In total, the house banks in a large hotel can exceed $10,000 and, on holiday weekends, it may be necessary to temporarily increase the regular amount.

The general cashier should retain the receipts for all house banks issued and, with another accounting employee, audit/count all banks monthly. The controller is responsible for counting the funds under the direct control of the general cashier. Since the general cashier has access to large amounts of cash, including, of course, the daily deposit, proper procedures are essential to good control. Deposits must be made daily, in consecutive order, and all weekend and holiday deposits must be made on the next banking day. Manipulating the sequence of deposits and misusing the cash included is a method frequently used by dishonest cashiers to cover up their thefts. Checking the consecutive order of the deposits and immediately investigating a missing receipt eliminates this possibility.

ACCOUNTING ENTRIES

The principal reasons for journal entries initiated by the city ledger area are billing errors and disputes. These entries will result in debits to the affected revenue or liability (in the case of incorrect taxes or gratuities) and a credit to accounts receivable. Only in the event that an account is written off purely because it is uncollectible should the debit be made to the bad-debt reserve account. Disputes or errors should also be charged back against the revenue accounts. Not only is this proper accounting procedure, but it usually results in saving the sales taxes related to the adjustment. Payments of travel agents' commissions or refunds should be processed through the accounts payable system as described in Chapter 6.

1. List and describe the various types of accounts that are usually segmented in the city ledger.

2. Describe the three ways in which accounts of individual guests and small groups are handled between a travel agent and the hotel.

3. Circle T or F to indicate whether the following statements are true or false:

    T   F   **a.** City ledger includes accounts due from guest currently occupying a sleeping room.

    T   F   **b.** Local patrons of the facilities prefer to be billed separately for each visit.

    T   F   **c.** A hotel's registration card should state that the guest has the primary liability for payment of charges.

    T   F   **d.** The city ledger department normally monitors volume levels of corporate accounts.

    T   F   **e.** The hotel industry was the first to use cycle billings on other than a calendar-month basis.

4. Circle the correct answer to the following statements:

    a. A hotel should only permit new individual billing accounts for:

    (1) Politicians

    (2) Local patrons of the restaurants

    (3) Traveling salesmen

    b. Group billings should be sent out:

    (1) Within 12 hours

    (2) Within 7 days

    (3) Within 48 hours

    c. Weddings present a credit risk that is:

    (1) Average

    (2) Higher than average

    (3) Lower than average

    d. A refund should not be authorized until it is verified that:

    (1) Payment was made by credit card

    (2) The account was paid in full

    (3) The guest intends to return

    e. All incoming mail should be opened by:

    (1) The controller's secretary

    (2) Any employee of the accounting department

    (3) An employee who is not in the accounting department and doesn't record revenue or receipts.

11 Credit

Control of credit is the most serious problem confronting business today. More than half of all Americans carry at least one credit card, a fact that makes the credit industry the biggest in the nation. But such widespread use of credit can foster, and even encourage, impulse buying and overspending, all too often beyond the individual's means.

Credit management is not a new business. The Bible and other ancient writings frequently make reference to debtors and creditors. However, the greatest growth in this field came in the twentieth century. There are many reasons for the increase in the use of credit—and the resulting need for more and better credit management—but most of them are related directly or indirectly to two factors: inflation and business and industrial expansion.

Inflation directly affects the use of credit. As the purchasing power of the dollar shrinks and the cost of an article increases, the desire and the ability of the consumer to make immediate payment decreases.

Business growth in this century quickly outdistanced the ability of owners to provide the necessary capital from their personal funds. They were faced with two alternatives: to share their businesses by selling stock or to borrow the funds needed to expand; most used both. As the demand for borrowing increased, so did the cost. Businesses and individuals not only increased the use of credit for their purchases, but delayed payments as much as possible. *Slow pay,* letting bills sit a little longer, an easy and cheap way of stretching cash reserves, caused serious problems for creditors, whose need for cash in many cases exceeded that of their customers.

The hotel industry has, throughout its history, been particularly plagued with credit problems. The innkeeper, as the genial host, was never particularly inclined to enforce credit procedures. Guests were accepted at face value, with little if any attempt made to get proper identification. Losses due to skippers—guests who registered under fictitious names and addresses and left without paying their bills—were considered a normal operating expense, a necessary risk of doing business.

As the concept of hotel operations changed and innkeepers became profit-oriented businesspeople, excessive credit losses could no longer be tolerated. The increased use of credit, the longer time taken by guests to pay their bills, and the cash requirements of the operation also contributed to the greater stringency of the credit procedures now in effect in most hotels.

A credit policy based solely on sound financial principles is difficult, and a uniform policy, even for a group of hotels under one management, is impossible to establish. A hotel room is the most perishable article sold in any type of business. The income from today's vacant room is lost forever, as is the income from a banquet or other function lost to a competitor. Often, a hotel must accept business, whether for a guest room or a banquet, even though it may involve a credit risk. Determining what is an acceptable degree of risk must be a management decision; it cannot be incorporated into written credit policies or procedures. Credit limits obviously depend on the operation, the level of charges, and the type of guest.

ELEMENTS OF A CREDIT POLICY

A hotel chain's general credit policy rules may be interpreted, changed, or modified by the management to fit their particular hotel. This authority is necessary if the managers are to be held responsible for the success or failure of their operation.

Since it can affect every facet of the operation, a credit policy must take into account the marketing objectives of the organization. A liberal policy tends to expand the market, but it entails a certain amount of risk; conversely, the tighter the policy, the most restricted the market. A new hotel has a greater need to solicit and attract business than does a well-established hotel, which can depend on its reputation to attract new guests and repeat business from former guests. Within the hotel itself, a more liberal credit policy may be adopted in a dining room with empty tables than in a busy coffee shop.

Distinction must also be made between in-house guests and nonhotel guests. In-house guests are those who occupy sleeping rooms; nonhotel guests are those who do not, but who use one or more of the hotel's other facilities. Credit privileges extended to in-house guests are for room charges, food, beverages, laundry, valet, items purchased in the stores and concessions, telephone services, entertainment, and cash. Every item except cash represents profit. Hotels are not banks, but they usually permit their guests to cash personal checks. Like every other service performed for the convenience of their guests, this is intended to build good-will, ensure repeat business, and evoke a recommendation from the guest to his or her friends and business associates. Obviously, the only result of an increase in the number of checks cashed is the possibility of greater losses. For this reason, the "sale" of cash must be tightly controlled.

FUNCTIONS OF THE CREDIT DEPARTMENT

The credit department in a hotel is small. In the largest hotels, it consists of only a credit manager, a secretary, and a few assistants. They are members of the accounting department staff, and the credit manager reports directly to the controller.

In most industries, the credit department has two primary functions: to investigate the financial standing of and approve limits of credit for each prospective client, and to try to collect the amount due if the customer fails to live up to the terms established for payment of the account. In the hotel industry, there is never enough time to check the financial status of each guest, so individual credit limits are impossible to establish. Rather, an attempt must be made to control credit while charges are accumulating, with no idea as to what the final total will be. Bad debts can be prevented, or at least kept within reasonable limits, only while the guest is still in the hotel; after check-out, it is too late.

Automation has reduced the workload of the credit department personnel. A computer program provides a daily list of guest balances that exceed authorized amounts and other analyses of the individual guest bills that the credit manager requires. A specific limit can be established for each guest based on the limit on the credit card or type of credit card used to guarantee the account. Obviously, that eliminates the tedious and time-consuming daily review of each guest bill. But full automation of the front office does not change the basic principles of a good credit policy or the credit manager's responsibility to carry them out. Ideally, each guest's bill should be under constant surveillance by one of the credit personnel. However, there may be a thousand or more bills and only a few people to monitor them. Furthermore, the staff has many other duties to perform and, thus, cannot devote full time to this function. Other than hiring more credit people than are economically feasible, the only solution to this imbalance is to make credit everyone's business. In a hotel, it must be. In fact, this cooperation is so necessary that it requires the expertise of the controller to organize and supervise the training needed to obtain it and the authority of top management to enforce it. Some of the ways in which others can help the credit department succeed in its job follow.

INTERDEPARTMENTAL COOPERATION

The bellman who rooms the guests should note on every rooming slip the number and condition of the bags. Some record only negative comments, such as poor or light baggage. If no such comment appears, a member of the credit staff who is reviewing the slips cannot be certain that the guest had good or excellent baggage; the bellman could have overlooked or forgotten to record its true condition.

The room service cashiers should immediately alert the credit department of any unusually large orders of food and, more particularly, beverages. The room service waiter or waitress should report unusual activity in a room—a large number of people, a party, many bottles of liquor not ordered from the hotel, and the like, as well as unusually large tips, over 25 percent of the check. Skippers usually prefer room service to restaurants, order the finest food and beverages available, and are generally very liberal tippers.

The maid indicates the status of the room in her morning report, but she should be trained to recognize and report any conditions that might indicate that the guest has departed without notice. A favorite trick of skippers is to remove all personal toilet articles except, perhaps, a half-empty can of shaving cream or hair spray and to leave an old dress or pair of trousers hanging in the closet and an old, broken-down bag in the

room. The maid's report will not help to stop the skipper, but it will prevent the accumulation of additional room charges and, possibly, a loss of revenue if the room could be rerented that day. Restaurant, bar, and nightclub cashiers should also alert credit personnel of any unusually large gratuities authorized by guests on their checks.

The most important aid to the credit manager is, however, the actual activity on a guest account. The front-desk staff and the night auditors are, for a variety of reasons, continually looking at guest folios. They are in the best positions to spot unusual activity, both in the numbers of charges and in the amounts involved. If guests, immediately after arrival, start ordering from room service, incur charges in the restaurants or bars, send out clothes to the valet or laundry, or charge purchases from the stores and concessions, they are suspect, and someone in credit should be advised to review their bill. This is particularly important if the guest has made no long-distance telephone calls. Of all possible guest charges, long-distance calls are the only ones that can be used to trace a former guest when the hotel does not have a valid address.

The night auditors should be instructed to monitor the high balance report (a listing of guest balances exceeding predetermined limits) and ensure that copies go to the credit manager, front-office manager, and controller.

THE CREDIT POLICY IN DETAIL

The assistance given the credit department does not in any way alter or reduce the credit manager's responsibility to carry out the hotel's credit policy, or to maintain adequate controls over all guest charges. Others can only alert the credit departments; they cannot make any determination as to a guest's honesty or ability to pay. Once alerted, the credit staff must review the charges and determine what action, if any, to take.

Excluding city ledger billing and collection procedures, the credit policy should cover three periods:

1. Prior—before a function or registration.
2. During—while the function is in progress or while the guest is in residence.
3. After—at the end of a function or at the checkout of the registered guest.

Prior to the Event

The credit manager's efforts during this period are primarily confined to checking the financial standing of small or relatively unknown companies, associations, groups, or individuals who have booked banquets or conventions.

To assist the credit manager in checking ratings, most hotels with banquet and convention facilities sign up with one or more credit bureaus or national or local credit associations. The larger hotels sign with Dun & Bradstreet (D&B).

Subscribers to D&B receive a reference book listing the estimated financial strength and credit rating of thousands of companies and individuals. Financial ratings are shown by a series of symbols, each indicating a dollar amount, ranging from under $5,000 to over $50 million. A separate symbol, a number from 1 to 4, is used to designate the credit rating. The four classifications are high, good, fair, and limited. Cards

issued to subscribers explain the dollar range for each symbol and the credit classifications. In the case of listings that are not rated, the absence of the rating is also explained. When a name is not listed in the reference book, D&B will provide on request a special report on that company or individual. Many hotels extend or refuse credit solely on the basis of a D&B rating.

Credit managers who have no access to the D&B reports can obtain similar information from credit bureaus or associations. Other valuable sources of credit information are the bank used by the sponsor of the affair and, if a company is responsible for the bill, its suppliers or creditors. References can also be requested from other hotels who have previously hosted the group or convention.

Most credit policies do not establish definite procedures or define the class of guests whose financial standing should be checked. They leave the decision to the credit and sales department heads in consultation with the controller and, if necessary, with the general manager. Since the credit manager cannot know of any future business until notified by sales, the credit policy must require sales to notify credit immediately when a banquet or convention is booked. It should also mandate frequent meetings between these department heads to review the coming events and the steps needed to ensure prompt and full payment.

Verifying credit in advance on individual guests has become a very minor element of the credit process as almost all hotels require a credit card guarantee on individual reservations. The credit card information is entered into a computer at the time the reservation is made and its validity is verified. For those guests who make cash deposits or have no reservations, little can be done prior to arrival.

During the Event

For this period, specific rules and procedures for individual guests can be incorporated into a credit policy, applicable either to one hotel or to a group of hotels under one management. The following paragraphs discuss the areas generally covered, the procedures, and, wherever possible, the rationale behind the rules.

Guest registration.   As management has become more aware of credit problems, new credit policies have been formulated and, more to the point, enforced. All arrivals, except well-known former guests, are asked for some form of identification. Hotels go one step further and ask for a national credit card that the guest will use to settle his or her account at departure. The average traveler carries more than one credit card, and the controller can reduce the credit card commission expense by taking advantage of this fact. The room clerk should mention first the card with the lowest discount rate, pause for a few seconds, and then mention the other cards accepted by the hotel. Many guests will automatically use the first card mentioned.

When a guest presents a credit card, the room clerk should immediately imprint it on the back of the registration card. If it will be used to settle the bill, the clerk should also imprint it on the proper charge slip and staple the slip to the registration card. Some credit policies require the room clerk to indicate in code, on the hotel's copy of the guest bill, walk-ins, same-day telephone reservations, and claimed reservations.

Finally, the policy should clearly indicate the responsibility of the bellmen to note on the back of the rooming slip the condition of the guest's baggage. All rooming slips for guests with light or no baggage should be immediately returned to the room clerk, who should then note that fact on the back of the registration card and have it initialed by a member of the credit department staff.

Credit-department billing procedures. Most credit policies require the credit manager or a member of the credit staff to review each day every guest bill that exceeds its authorized limit and to contact the guest to either make a payment or to provide some additional form of guarantee. A brief review should be made of all other bills, listing for special attention those accounts that exceed a specified amount, those that seem to have an unusual number of charges—especially when coded or marked for light or no baggage—and, finally, any bill that, for a few days, has no charges other than room and tax. The reason for checking the last-mentioned accounts is that the guest may have checked out but for some reason the bill was not pulled, and the room continues to be carried as occupied when in fact it is vacant.

The policy should also specify the number of days a guest can remain as a resident before receiving a bill for all charges to date. Formerly, most credit managers were instructed to bill every guest except those with established credit at the end of three days, and to follow up the three-day bills on the next day with a request to establish credit or a demand for immediate payment. Today, because of the better credit procedures at registration, the three-day bills have been phased out. However, all guests, regardless of affiliations, should be billed at the end of each seven days. The night auditor should bring the total balance forward to a new bill and forward all copies except the guest's to accounting. The guest's copy is left for the credit manager, who should review the account and, if it is a personal charge, see that it is placed in the guest's box; he or she is also responsible for following through for payment. If the account is to be charged to a firm, the credit manager should determine the requirements for billing and, if they are in order, give the bill to the city ledger clerk with proper mailing instructions. Every account, regardless of the credit rating of the firm involved, should be followed through for payment, and any deviation in the payment from the amount billed should be questioned immediately—principally because, after a long stay, it is difficult to analyze and break down the unpaid balance of any account with partial or on-account payments.

Group and convention billing. A uniform policy cannot be established for billing an organization, company, or corporation hosting these functions. Not only do the charges for which they will accept responsibility vary, but most will specify exactly how their bill is to be prepared and to whose attention it is to be mailed. This is very important, particularly when dealing with a large company. Many hotel bills have been lost or payments seriously delayed because the mailing address did not include the department and name of the person authorized to process them. These varied requirements emphasize once more the need for cooperation between the sales and accounting departments.

Salespeople make the contacts, sell and supervise the functions, and are usually the only people privy to the billing instructions. Therefore, management should require

that all billing instructions, whether written or verbal, be immediately turned over to the controller, who then issues the proper instructions to his or her staff. In fact, because the salesperson may misunderstand or misinterpret the billing instructions, the controller should meet with the group's representative to review the billing procedures personally, particularly in the case of large companies or groups.

Since group billing—the master bill as well as the individual members' charges—must be closely monitored and frequently reviewed, the billing instructions should be updated daily if necessary, while the guests are in residence in the hotel rather than after the function is over or the group has checked out.

Check cashing. Every state has a "bad-check law" that makes it a crime to issue a check with intent to defraud, that is, in the knowledge that insufficient funds are on deposit to cover the amount of the check. In most states, the act of issuing a bad check is in itself proof of intent to defraud and, depending on the amount, is a misdemeanor or a felony, punishable by a fine, a jail sentence, or both. Therefore, it is essential that the credit manager be thoroughly familiar with the bad-check law of the state in which the hotel is located and at least have access to the general provisions of these laws in other states.

Management in each property must set its own limits on the total dollar amount of checks it will cash for guests during any one stay or period of time. Here are some guidelines and restrictions that should be incorporated into an overall credit policy:

1. *Credit cards.* Cards are used primarily to settle the guest's accounts, but some cards carry certain check-cashing privileges. National companies—American Express, Diners Club, and Discover, among others—will guarantee their cardholders' checks up to a specified amount, provided that the cardholder is a registered guest of the hotel, that the credit card is valid, that the card is imprinted on the back of the check, and that at departure the full amount of the bill is charged to the credit card. If all conditions are met, the company will reimburse the hotel, deducting only the normal discount, for any bad checks cashed by its cardholders. Every member hotel is given a form specifically designed for filing these claims. The credit policy, therefore, should list the companies extending this privilege, the dollar limits, and the restrictions involved.

2. *Approvals.* A credit policy should clearly define, with a definite dollar limit, the responsibility and authority of all employees or executives empowered to cash a guest's check. These are the front-office cashiers, the credit manager and staff, assistant managers, night auditors, night managers, and all other department heads, as well as the general manager and controller. The last two are usually given unlimited authority in this matter, and if so, this should be stated in the policy.

3. *Restrictions.* Certain types of checks should not be approved for cashing, but may be accepted in payment of a guest's account. These are:

    a. *Postdated checks.* A postdated check is in effect a note receivable, a promise to pay at some future time. The hotel cannot deposit it and should not record the payment until the date shown on the check. Also, the hotel loses its rights to prosecute and recover under the bad-check law if the check is returned for nonpayment. However, it is at least a written acknowledgment of the debt, and

if that is all a guest can or will give, the controller may have no choice but to accept it in payment of an account.

b. *Second-party checks.* A check may be drawn to the order of the guest by a second party—an individual, association, company, or corporation. A second-party check should be cashed or accepted in payment of an account only if the payee is personally known to the hotel executive who is specifically authorized to approve such a transaction. Otherwise, no credentials should be accepted for purposes of identification because they, as well as the check itself, could be found, stolen, or forged.

c. *Checks payable to a corporation, company, or organization.* Such checks should never be cashed or accepted in payment of a guest's account even if the guest is known to be the president of the company or organization involved. By accepting such a check, the hotel would be subject to a lawsuit by any stockholder or member of the organization should the guest be convicted of misappropriating funds, and might even be in trouble with the tax authorities if the guest was siphoning company funds to hide income and reduce taxes.

d. *Money orders.* Few people carry money orders or purchase them for any reason except to mail in payment of a debt or for a purchase. Therefore, they should never be approved for cashing unless the payee is personally known to the hotel executive. As with second-party checks, credentials are worthless. It is no exaggeration to say that more than 50 percent of all money orders cashed at hotels without personal identification are found to be stolen; the hotels never recover their money.

4. *Recording.* There is only one way to control the number and the dollar amount of all checks cashed by each guest during any one stay, and that is by keeping an accurate and complete record of every check cashed. For a registered guest, the entry can be made on the back of the registration card. The only information needed is the date, the bank on which the check is drawn, the amount, and the initials of the person who approved it for cashing. This means that the entry should be made by that person, not by the front-office cashier who actually pays out the money, unless he or she is authorized to cash the check without other approval. The reason is obvious. No one can intelligently approve a check without knowing the number and amount of any checks previously cashed for that guest. Where this rule is not strictly enforced, bad-debt write-offs could include three or more checks cashed in one day by a guest, each one approved by a different executive so authorized. Recording the payor bank is helpful only in that rare instance when a guest presents a check drawn on a different bank from the one on which a prior check was cashed, and then only to indicate the possibility of fraud. People rarely carry blank checks drawn on more than one bank, so such a deviation from normal custom should be thoroughly investigated, even to the point of calling both banks to verify the validity of the checks.

For nonregistered guests, if they are permitted this privilege, a similar entry should be made, again by the person approving the check, on a card with the guest's name and address. The cards, filed in alphabetical order, should be kept in a secure place, but must be readily available during the hours that such transactions are permitted.

5. *Travelers' checks.* It is common knowledge that travelers' checks can be freely accepted without risk of loss if a few simple rules are followed. Each check must be countersigned on its face in the presence of the cashier, who can accept it without further identification. Yet this simple safeguard has all too often been disregarded by both the guest and the hotel cashier, and travelers' checks are sometimes improperly accepted. Some have only one signature on the face, with the second, usually affixed in the presence of the cashier, on the back as an endorsement. Others are correctly signed in both places, but before the guest comes to the cashier's desk. And in neither case does the cashier verify the signatures.

Accepting these improperly signed checks may not result in any loss to the hotel, provided that the guest was the purchaser. But the most important reason for carrying travelers' checks is that if they are lost or stolen, the purchaser can notify the issuing company of the loss and receive prompt replacements. The company then stops payment, and anyone improperly accepting them suffers a financial loss. It is for this reason that the procedures for accepting or cashing travelers' checks must be included in the overall credit policy, and that the credit manager be specifically given the full responsibility for enforcing them.

6. *Restaurant and other cashiers.* The credit policy should limit or prohibit the handling of any type of check, except travelers' checks, by any cashier in the hotel other than the front-office cashiers. Restaurant, bar, garage, and other cashiers may be authorized to accept travelers' checks up to a specified amount in payment of an account and to give cash for the excess over the amount of the charge. If a restaurant or bar guest is not required to pay at the cashier's station, then the second signature should be witnessed at the guest's table by the person in charge of the room, who should then initial the check as proof.

7. *Stamp.* Whenever a cashier gives cash on any check (with the possible exception of travelers' checks), whether for the full amount of the check or for the excess over an amount applied to the guest's bill, the guest should be required to sign for it. The cashier needs only a stamp to imprint on the back of the check, with spaces for the amount of cash paid out, the amount applied to the bill, the guest's room number, and a blank line for the guest's signature, all to be entered in ink. This procedure not only helps the hotel control its cashiers and avoid serious disputes with the guests, but it should be implemented primarily for the benefit of the guests, to help them verify the amount paid on their bill and to have any error easily corrected.

8. *Group and convention guests.* The procedures outlined regarding checks cashed for individual guests apply equally to personal checks presented by in-house guests who are members of a group or convention. However, second-party checks issued to their members by the company or organization holding the function are normally accepted or cashed without further approval by the front-office cashiers. Advance arrangements should always be made to handle these checks, not only so that the controller can set up proper controls, but also to make sure the cashiers have enough money on hand to cash them. The payor should provide a list of those authorized to sign the checks, the dollar range with a maximum amount that can be accepted, an estimate of the total dollar amount to be issued, and, if possible, the amount the ho-

tel cashiers may be expected to handle in any one day. The payor should also assume full responsibility for lost or stolen checks, unless either the controller, the credit manager, or, in their absence, the hotel salesperson servicing the account is immediately notified of such a loss. The person so notified must then alert the front-office cashiers and post in a conspicuous place the check number, name of the payee, and the amount. He or she should also alert the staff of all nearby hotels, in case some members of the group or convention are registered there.

Guest charges.   Guests may purchase almost anything and charge it on their room bills. Normally, these charges are incurred within the hotel itself, but sometimes they involve COD purchases from outside stores and even outright cash advances.

Obviously, not every guest charge that originates within the hotel can be checked; rather, the credit staff must try to monitor and control them through the daily review of each guest's bill. The credit policy can only require that procedures ensure that all charges, whether posted automatically from a point-of-sale terminal or physically given to the front desk, are posted promptly to the guest account.

CODs and cash advances, where they are permitted, are not sales for profit but an outlay of the hotel's cash, so they must be strictly and individually controlled. The front-office cashiers should not have the authority to pay out any cash without the written approval of the credit manager or other authorized executive. Packages sent COD should not be accepted unless the guest has left written instructions stating that an article was being delivered, by whom, and the amount of the total charges—in effect approving in advance the charge to his or her account. This authorization should be stapled to the COD voucher, which should be signed by the person delivering the package.

Charges from nonregistered guests.   Few hotels, except those owned by companies issuing their own credit cards, will accept charges from their stores and concessionaires for persons who are not registered guests of the hotel. However, they all permit charges in the hotel-operated restaurants, bars, or other facilities. Most of these charges are made through national credit cards and, if properly accepted, pose no credit problems. Many hotels also establish individual or company accounts for executives of firms whose offices are located nearby.

All these charges, whether on credit cards or on company or individual accounts, should be processed through the front-office system. However, instead of being posted to individual room folios, they are posted to house account folios. For customers with frequent charges, separate house accounts should be opened. Such accounts can be closed out through a transfer to city ledger and billed monthly. Other charges can be posted to a city ledger control account and cleared to the individual city ledger accounts daily.

After the Event

At checkout.   The general tightening of credit procedures prior to guest arrival and at the time of registration has greatly eased the burden of the credit staff and front-office cashiers at checkout time. And by reducing the time needed for this process, it has also contributed to better guest relations. Long lines and delays at the checkout counter

frequently lead to complaints, which former guests remember and may mention when discussing the service they received and the efficiency of the hotel staff.

The procedures themselves have not changed, and the front-office cashiers still have the principal responsibility for checking out guests. The manner in which they carry out these duties directly affects the present and future earnings of a hotel. The correct procedure follows.

The guest usually asks for the bill by room number. After printing the bill and pulling the registration card from the pit, the cashier should check for unposted charges and then ask the guest, by name, if he or she made any telephone calls or incurred any restaurant or other charges within the last few hours. Since many guests make a telephone call or order a meal, particularly breakfast, immediately before checking out, these two items should be specifically mentioned, and most cashiers are required to do so. The guest should be addressed by name if for no other reason than that it is good guest relations; most people relate better to the hotel staff when so addressed. However, there is a more pressing reason: to prevent the guest from settling the wrong account. The cashier may pull another bill or the guest may give a wrong room number and, in the rush to check out, the guest may not immediately catch the error. When this happens, the result is not easy to straighten out, and it is certain to irritate two guests, the one who settled the wrong account and the one whose account was wrongly settled.

Since the method of settlement was established for most guests at the time they registered, and since the credit staff has had sufficient time to check it where necessary, the cashier can then proceed to close out the account. If a guest's payment method was not established, or if it has been changed, the cashier must determine if he or she has the authority to complete the transaction, and if not, must refer the guest to the credit manager. A disputed charge, if incurred on the day the guest is checking out, should be checked and adjusted by the cashier. Previous days' charges must, if time permits, be referred to the credit manager, if the vouchers are not available. If the guest is unable to wait, the cashier should circle the item, mark it "disputed charge," deduct it from the total, and settle the balance with the guest, leaving the amount of the disputed charge open. The night auditor should transfer this open balance to the city ledger, and the city-ledger clerk then has the responsibility to check it the next day and take whatever action is necessary to properly charge and collect the item. Charges for local calls, in hotels with telephone registers, are not subject to these restrictions, and most cashiers have the authority to allow them if disputed by a guest.

Although cashiers rarely are given authority to cash personal checks for guests without approval, many are permitted to accept them in payment of an account up to a specified amount, provided the check is made payable to the hotel and is in the exact amount of the bill. A guest whose account exceeds that limit, or who writes a check for an amount greater than the total bill and requests cash for the excess, should be referred to the credit manager for approval.

Charge accounts fall into two categories, those charged to a personal or business account in the city ledger and those charged on a credit card. The information regarding the method of settlement, requested from most guests at registration, can greatly facilitate and speed the handling of either transaction. During daily review of the guests' bills, the credit staff should use this information to check the guests' credit or,

if the account is to be charged to a credit card, take some of the steps necessary for the proper acceptance of these cards. Credit approval should be indicated by initialing the bill; then the cashier need only make sure all charges are posted and obtain the guest's signature to show acceptance of the total amount due.

All checkout procedures outlined here apply both to individual guests and to those who are with a group or attending a convention, insofar as their personal charges are concerned. The master bill, as previously mentioned, should be under constant review by the credit manager or a member of the accounting staff. In addition, it is often advisable for the controller and credit manager to periodically review the account with the group's representative or the person in charge of the function. Review and approval of the charges while the group is still in the hotel usually result in more prompt payment of the bill.

Collection.   When guests check out, their bills are printed and any open balance is transferred by the night auditor to the city ledger. This includes all charge accounts and paid bills that, because of a disputed or after-departure charge, were not settled in full. Restaurant, bar, banquet, and other charges for nonregistered guests are charged directly to the city ledger. It then becomes the responsibility of the city-ledger clerk or clerks to bill these accounts.

There is one primary credit principle: the only way to collect an account is to bill it. Any delay in billing automatically delays payment. This means that the first bill should be sent out by the city-ledger clerk as soon as possible after the guest has checked out or the function has been held. This is followed by monthly statements, on whatever billing dates are established by the hotel. Nonregistered guests with either personal or business accounts in the city ledger are rarely billed after each restaurant or bar charge. Rather, they are billed once a month for the total charges incurred through the billing date.

Since credit policies are exclusively a management decision, they can vary from hotel to hotel, or among groups of hotels. Most policies do not mandate any special collection effort, assuming the address is correct, until at least the second monthly statement has been mailed out. A possible exception might be a message printed on this second statement asking the guest if payment has been held up because of an error or question regarding the charges. With the third statement, most hotels will include a formal demand for payment, which, depending on the amount due, may be followed by a telegram, a personal call, or even an attorney's letter, especially if the hotel is owned by a company with an in-house legal department. Hotels with outstanding banquet or convention accounts will often include the banquet or sales managers and their staffs in this collection effort, on the theory that, since they booked and supervised the functions, they are known to the people involved and should be more successful than the credit clerk in collecting. However, many salespersons are reluctant to press for payment because they feel that any such pressure will alienate their clients and cause them to lose business. Therefore, a wise policy will limit the time given the banquet or sales staff to effect a collection and will require that, at the expiration of that time, the account be returned to the controller for whatever action is deemed necessary.

Almost all small balances (under $10) can be traced to disputed charges at check-out that are subsequently found to be correct in whole or in part or to after-departure charges. Each require different handling.

Every guest who disputes or questions a charge at departure should be given the courtesy of a letter of explanation, with an apology if the charge was totally or partially incorrect. A photocopy of the actual charge and a duplicate or corrected bill should always be included to substantiate any remaining balance.

After-departure charges on a paid account should be billed as soon as possible after the guest's departure. Many hotels use a preprinted form, which merely states that a copy of the charge that had not reached the cashier in time to be included on the guest's bill at departure is enclosed, expresses regret for any inconvenience caused, and requests payment. Accounts under two or three dollars are rarely rebilled and are often transferred directly to a house account in the city ledger. Any money received from the one-time billing is credited to this account, with no attempt made to identify the original charge. The net balance of the account is usually written off each month. Late charges from stores or concessions, which some hotels even refuse to accept, and for long-distance calls in states where the telephone company will accept responsibility for uncollected calls must be segregated and controlled so that they can be charged back in the event payment is not received within a specified time.

After-departure charges on charge accounts require a slightly different billing procedure. For a personal or business account, a form letter of explanation, with a copy of the late charge and a corrected bill, will usually suffice. Guests who charged their accounts on credit cards must also be informed but, in addition, the charge slip must be corrected or a supplementary one (in the amount of the late charge) prepared. The amount signed for by the guest should never be altered. Some charge slips have a blank space where the city ledger clerk can enter the corrected total, which will be accepted by the credit card company subject to the cardholder's approval.

Collection efforts, like controls, must be carefully evaluated and studied before being put into operation. Costs, salaries, and other expenses involved sometimes exceed the amount collected. Collection staffs are relatively small, and the time and effort needed to collect a $1,000 account is approximately the same as that to collect a $100 account. For these reasons, many collectors are instructed to concentrate their efforts on accounts with a minimum past-due balance of at least $200.

However, at some point, all unsuccessful efforts by the hotel personnel must cease and other collection methods be employed. At what point the outside assistance is to be implemented, and the form it should take, should be clearly spelled out in the overall credit policy, particularly since most controllers and credit managers are understandably reluctant to write off uncollected accounts or to turn them over to an attorney or collection agency. Unfortunately, waiting too long will sometimes cause an uncollected account to become uncollectible.

The following procedures are recommended for consideration and inclusion in a credit policy:

1. Imprint an "Address Correction Requested" stamp on the first billing to any guest who did not have a confirmed reservation. If the debtor has moved, the post of-

fice will send the new address, providing your correspondence was sent by first class mail.

2. Immediately investigate all return mail. Sending further statements without first verifying the address on the bill, registration card, or reservation correspondence, if any, is a waste of time and money. If no other address is available, then that guest must be considered a "skipper" and a decision must be made as to the disposition of the account. Unless there are long-distance calls or a record of checks cashed by the guest, which might enable the hotel staff or an outside collection agency to trace the guest, the only available alternative is to write off the balance due.

3. Small balances—say, from under $10 to $25—if not paid in 90 days, should be deemed uncollectible and written off.

4. Accounts from under $50 up to $200, depending on the type of hotel and the rates, should not be assigned to the hotel collection staff for personal attention. Collection efforts should be limited to the normal billing routine: monthly statements, demands for payment, and attorney's letters. After 90 to a maximum of 120 days, all unpaid balances should be turned over to an outside agency for collection. Many agencies offer a so-called letter series, whereby for a nominal amount they send three to eight letters to the guest. The hotel retains full control over the accounts, and the letters normally specify that all payments be made directly to the hotel. By introducing a third party, hotels have been fairly successful in collecting a substantial percentage of their accounts, and many hotels use this service before turning accounts over, on a percentage basis, to a collection agency of their choice.

5. With the small balances written off and other accounts assigned for routine billing, the hotel's collection staff can concentrate its efforts on accounts with substantial open balances. Letters on hotel stationery, like repeated monthly statements, are often completely disregarded by the former guests. They are fully aware of the outstanding balance, and until they are ready to settle the account, mail from the hotel is discarded without being read. The best way to contact such people and be sure of getting their personal attention is to call them. If the telephone number is not available, because of a private listing or for any other reason, a telegram or registered letter should be sent requesting immediate payment. If that is not possible, the guest should be asked to call the person assigned to collect the account. Complete and accurate records must be kept of all telephone conversations, and any promises to pay that are not kept should immediately be followed up by another call. Some collection managers instruct their staffs to make these follow-up calls collect if they are outside the local call area.

Even though the overall credit policy cannot prescribe detailed credit procedures, it can and should be very specific as to the point at which accounts should be assigned to the collection staff and when these efforts, if unsuccessful, should cease. The suggested timetable is to assign these accounts to specific collectors at 90 days and terminate their efforts on all balances still unpaid when they are 180 days past due. At that time, all accounts, except those specifically withheld by the general manager or controller, should be turned over to an outside agency for collection.

At 90 days, no special collection efforts need be made. The collector should be given statements demanding payment, the attorney's letter, and any form letters normally sent. These should be mailed and a file opened for the account. Ten to 15 days later, if no payment is received, the first contact is made. During this waiting period, the collector should obtain the original bills, individual charge vouchers, and any other pertinent information in order to discuss the open balance with the guest intelligently and answer any questions that arise.

Of course, this process can be carried out only if the aged trial balance is received and analyzed each month by the controller, along with the credit manager, an investigation clerk who keeps the data on skippers and disputed charges, and a collection clerk to report on the status of the over-90-day accounts. The general manager may participate in some of these meetings; if not, he or she should be briefed on any actions taken and should review the monthly trial balances with the controller.

Checks returned unpaid by the bank require special and immediate attention. Many hotels redeposit them on the next business day without notifying the guests on the theory that their own bank will let them know when the checks are returned for "insufficient funds" or "drawn against uncollected funds." The results are excellent; most checks clear on the second try. Those that don't, as well as checks returned for other reasons—"account closed," "payment stopped," and the like—should be turned over to the credit manager for immediate action and, if not paid within 30 days, given to an attorney for collection.

Bad debts. Few city ledger accounts, except those of skippers, are deemed to be uncollectible in the same accounting period, fiscal or calendar year, in which the charges were incurred. Therefore, a reserve for bad debts is set up each year, the expense being charged to current operations, to offset any such losses that might occur in the future. When the account is actually written off, it is charged against the reserve and does not affect the operating results for a future year. The amount set up as a reserve is usually a percentage of room sales, from .25 percent to 1 percent. The reserve should be reviewed at least twice a year to determine if the balance is sufficient to cover any possible losses from doubtful accounts. A percentage of the totals shown on the city ledger aged trial balance as being 60 days or older should be considered uncollectible. In addition, 2 percent of 60 days; 5 percent of 90 days; 10 percent of 120 days or more; and 50 percent of all accounts not yet written off but turned over to outside agencies or attorneys for collection should be considered uncollectible. If the reserve is more or less than the total of these percentages, the monthly provision can be decreased or increased.

Comparisons between hotels is difficult, even between hotels under one management. Too many factors must be considered: deterioration of the neighborhood, a change in the class of guests, and, of course, the charge-sales percentage (excluding credit cards) of total sales—before the annual amount written off as bad debts can be properly evaluated. A hotel with 75 percent of its total sales paid for in cash or charged on credit cards should certainly have a smaller annual bad-debt loss than one with the same volume but 75 percent of sales charged and only 25 percent paid in cash or through credit cards. In any event, barring very unusual circumstances, the annual

write-off should not exceed 1 percent of net room sales. If it does, the credit policy should be reviewed and its enforcement strengthened.

Legal aspects of collection.   Until well into the twentieth century, collection practices were rarely challenged; debtors could be harassed and coerced into paying their accounts. Slowly at first, but accelerating very rapidly in the 1960s and 1970s, consumer-protection laws were enacted at all levels of government—local, state, and federal. In addition, the courts have been very liberal in interpreting these laws in favor of the debtor. Today, credit managers must be aware of what actions are illegal. However, they should also be made aware of what steps they can take to properly protect the hotel and must make a strong and determined effort to collect the amounts due. Management can help by incorporating in the credit policy some general information as to which actions are proper and which are illegal.

If possible, this section of the credit policy, as well as the formats of all collection letters and telegrams, should be reviewed and approved by an attorney. Too many creditors have found themselves not only accused but convicted of extortion or of committing a libelous action while trying to collect a just debt. The courts tend to judge any action calculated to harass or coerce a debtor a form of extortion. Some of the more common credit procedures found to be offensive are repeated telephone calls at all hours of the day or night, collection letters that appear to be legal documents, summonses or complaints intended to frighten the debtor into paying, threats of criminal prosecution, and dissemination of an unfavorable credit report to force the debtor into bankruptcy. Naturally, the creditor can legally threaten to turn the account over to a collection agency or to an attorney for legal action if the debt is not paid within a specified time.

Libel laws prohibit the publication of any material that might injure a person's reputation or invade his or her right to privacy. Defamatory telegrams and postcards, or envelopes on which are written words or symbols indicating that the debtor is delinquent, have been judged to be libelous actions, on the ground that they could be seen by others. Mailing such cards or envelopes is also in violation of postal laws and subject to a fine, imprisonment, or both.

Collection agencies should be thoroughly investigated before they are used. Any illegal acts they commit as agents will reflect on the hotel's reputation and possibly subject the hotel to legal action. Most reputable agencies have, or will purchase, an insurance policy to protect the hotel against such a possibility.

Credit policy should also include some reference to the provisions of the Equal Credit Opportunity Act and the Truth-in-Lending Act. The first is not of much concern to most hotels. It prohibits discrimination in the extension of credit on the grounds of sex, marital status, race, color, religion, national origin, or age. It does not prohibit any credit practices that are uniformly administered. Thus, a policy is legal that requires everyone without a confirmed reservation to produce proper and sufficient identification before being accepted as a guest and allowed to register.

The other, the Truth-in-Lending Act, does mandate certain procedures. It requires that a notice outlining specific procedures for handling disputes be enclosed with any statement of a current charge that is mailed to a guest. The notice is not re-

quired if the statement shows only a previous balance due. However, since it is too costly to sort the statements, most hotels enclose it with all of them.

The act not only outlines the procedures but sets a time limit for each step. It specifies the time within which a guest must file a written complaint and the time within which the hotel personnel must acknowledge receipt of the complaint and handle it. The guest is then given the option to accept or reject the settlement within a specified time. Finally, the act outlines the rights of each party during and after each interval.

Any local and state laws or statutes that deal with the extension of credit, particularly in the sale of alcoholic beverages, should be reviewed by management and included in the overall credit policy.

1. List the responsibilities of the bell staff, room-service cashiers, and maids relative to credit.

2. List the guidelines and restrictions, relative to check cashing, that should be incorporated into an overall credit policy.

3. Circle T or F to indicate whether the following statements are true or false:

   T   F   **a.** A credit policy must take into account the marketing objectives of the hotel.

   T   F   **b.** A D&B rating is used to evaluate a customer's credit status.

   T   F   **c.** All long-stay guests should be billed each seven days.

   T   F   **d.** Most hotel cashiers have the authority to make an adjustment to the guest's account for disputed local calls.

   T   F   **e.** Small balances under $10 should be written off it not paid within 90 days.

4. Circle the correct answer to the following statements:

   a. A high balance report is:
   1. A list of overdue city ledger accounts
   2. A list of guest accounts exceeding predetermined limits
   3. A list of authorized maximum balances for regular guests

   b. Credit policy should cover:
   1. Prior—before a function or registration
   2. During—while the function is in progress or while the guest is in residence.
   3. After—at the end of a function or at checkout
   4. All of the above

   c. The hotel should *never* accept in payment of an account:
   1. A postdated check
   2. A check payable to a corporation
   3. A second-party check

   d. The hotel should not redeposit returned checks marked:
   1. Insufficient funds
   2. Drawn against uncollected funds
   3. Payment stopped

   e. The hotel that has the highest percentage of cash and credit card sales should have:
   1. A lower bad-debt expense than other hotels
   2. A higher bad-debt expense than other hotels
   3. The same bad-debt expense as other hotels

12 Purchasing and Receiving

In Chapter 7 the importance of payroll control in food and beverage operations was stressed. Expenses and costs related to payroll constitute the largest single expenditure in those areas, frequently reaching 50 percent of revenues. Efforts to control payroll are, however, wasted if profitability has already been rendered impossible due to a very high cost of sales. The price paid for food and beverages is not the only determinant in excessive costs. The selling price plays a major role in the relationship of cost to revenue and, in certain instances, deliberately low prices may be justified if more than offset by increases in volume. However, the relationship of demand to price should be carefully analyzed as underpricing with no resultant increase in volume is simply bad management. Poor receiving procedures (discussed later in this chapter) and inadequate storeroom controls (reviewed in the following chapter) can both result in high costs. Too much waste at the preparation level and losses incurred in the service process either from employee theft or carelessness can also contribute. However, control must start at the initial point in the process—purchasing.

FOOD PURCHASING

Many hotel and restaurant chains have a policy of centralized purchasing—a procedure that can result in substantial savings in operating equipment (e.g., linen, china, glass, or silver) and in the area of operating supplies (e.g., paper goods or cleaning supplies). When these items can be purchased in large quantities, there is substantial savings. Such a policy can be very successful because such items can be centrally stored and drop-shipped to a hotel on a scheduled basis. Such a policy can also be practiced with reasonable success with canned goods and even packaged goods provided the useful life of the packaged item lends itself to such treatment. However, the major cost elements in a food operation are meat, fish, produce, and like commodities whose limited life expectancy makes centralized purchasing impractical. The responsibility for purchasing those items normally rests with an individual within the operation. For most

medium-sized and large hotels, this responsibility is vested in the purchasing agent through whose office all purchasing should flow. However, since a large part of the process involves issuing purchase orders and receiving quotations, a secretary is needed.

Certain characteristics of food purchasing are determinants of the procedures used. Food is, in varying degrees, a perishable commodity. In particular, fresh fruit and vegetables, milk and bread, and fresh meat and fish have a limited life; even frozen meat and vegetables cannot be stored indefinitely. On the other hand, canned and packaged products, known as dry goods, have an extended life, anywhere from three months to a year depending on the product. As a result, purchase orders can be used for dry goods but by necessity all other food purchasing is a telephone process.

Except for emergencies, food purchasing for the restaurants should be done on a regular, scheduled basis. Meat and fish are normally ordered twice per week while at certain times of the year produce may be ordered four to six times per week. Bread and dairy products are usually delivered daily with the exception, perhaps, of Sundays.

For operations with a large banquet volume, it is not feasible to buy and store all food items required to service these functions. Consequently, buying for banquets may be done on a daily basis according to requirements.

A very important factor to consider is price fluctuation. The prices of fresh produce change daily. Meat and fish prices are also volatile, often changing more than once a week.

Quotations are obtained by the purchasing department, by telephone or fax, from the approved vendors. There may be five or six vendors quoting on certain items, whereas only two or three vendors may be considered suitable for others. The selection of a vendor depends on its established record as a supplier to the industry in general and on the past experience the hotel has had with the vendor in regard to reliability, price, and product quality.

The product quality can be measured by matching the food received against pre-established specifications and standards set out by the purchasing agent. Specifications should cover size, weight, portion size, market form, and origin, as well as quality. The U.S. Department of Agriculture standards or specifications issued for all produce and dairy products are commonly used for those items. Meat standards are established by the *Meat Buyer's Guide to Standardized Meat Cuts,* published by the National Association of Meat Purveyors. Fish does not, however, lend itself to regulated standards and the quality must be checked on each purchase. Shellfish are ordered based on size, the number of units per pound (termed the *count*), specified by the buyer.

For the protection of the hotel, vendors should be instructed to advise the hotel promptly of any price change in items it regularly purchases. Prices for frozen and canned goods are less subject to fluctuation, and quotations can be obtained less frequently.

The quotations obtained are entered on a daily quotation sheet (sometimes referred to as a *market list*), an example of which is shown in Figure 12–1. This provides a ready comparison of prices. The sheets should be maintained on file for at least a year to permit verification, by auditors and others, that the lowest prices were obtained. The order is marked on the quotation sheet and then placed with the vendor by telephone.

Market Quotation Sheet columns (ON HAND | ARTICLE | WANTED | QUOTATIONS):

BEEF
- Corned Beef
- Corned Beef Brisket
- Corned Beef Rump
- Corned Beef Hash
- Beef Chipped
- Beef Bread
- Butts
- Chuck
- Fillets
- Hip Short
- Hip Full
- Kidneys
- Livers
- Loin, Short
- Strip
- Shell Strip
- Ribs Beef
- Shins
- Suet, Beef
- Tails, Ox

VEAL
- Breast
- Brains
- Feet
- Fore Quarters
- Hind Quarters
- Head
- Kidneys
- Legs
- Liver
- Loins
- Racks
- Saddles
- Shoulder
- Sweet Breads

MUTTON
- Fore Quarters
- Kidneys
- Legs
- Racks
- Saddles
- Saddles, Hind
- Shoulder
- Suet

LAMB
- Breast
- Fore Quarters
- Feet
- Fries
- Kidneys
- Lambs
- Legs
- Lamb, Spring
- Racks, Double
- Racks, Spring
- Saddles
- Shoulder

PROVISIONS
- Bacon
- Bologna
- Bologna
- Crepinette
- Salami
- Hams, Corned
- Hams, Fresh
- Hams, Polish
- Hams, Smoked
- Hams, Virginia
- Hams, Westphalia
- Head Cheese
- Lard
- Lyon Sausage
- Phil. Scrapple
- Smoked Butts
- Pig's Feet

Provisions (Cont'd)
- Pig's Head, Corned
- Pig's Knuckles Fresh
- Pig's Knuckles Corned
- Pig, Suckling
- Pork, Fresh Loin
- Pork, Larding
- Pork, Spare Ribs
- Pork, Salt Strip
- Pork, Tenderloin
- Sausages, Country
- Sausages, Frankfurter
- Sausage, Meat
- Shoulders, Fresh
- Shoulders, Smoked
- Shoulders, Corned
- Tongues
- Tongues, Beef Smoked
- Tongues, Fresh
- Tongues, Lambs
- Tripe

POULTRY
- Chickens
- Chickens, Roast
- Chickens, Broilers
- Chickens, Broilers
- Chickens, Supreme
- Cocks
- Capons
- Ducks
- Ducklings
- Fowl
- Geese
- Goslings
- Guinea Hens
- Guinea Squabs
- Pigeons
- Poussins
- Squabs
- Turkeys, Roasting
- Turkeys, Broiling
- Turkeys, Spring

GAME
- Birds
- Partridge
- Pheasant, English
- Rabbits
- Quail
- Venison, Saddles

SHELL FISH
- Clams, Chowder
- Clams, Cherrystone
- Clams, Little Neck
- Clams, Soft
- Crabs, Hard
- Crabs, Meat
- Crab, Oyster
- Crabs, Soft Shell
- Crabs, Self Shell Prime
- Lobster, Meat
- Lobster, Tails
- Lobsters, Chicken
- Lobsters, Medium
- Lobster, Large
- Oysters, Box
- Oysters, Blue Points
- Oysters
- Scallops
- Shrimps
- Turtle

FISH
- Bass, Black
- Bass, Sea
- Bass, Striped
- Blackfish
- Bluefish
- Bloaters

FISH (Cont'd)
- Butterfish
- Carp
- Codfish, Live
- Codfish, Salt Boneless
- Codfish, Salt Flake
- Eels
- Finnan Haddie
- Flounders
- Flounders
- Flounders, Fillet
- Fluke
- Haddock
- Haddock, Fillet
- Haddock, Smoked
- Halibut
- Halibut, Chicken
- Herring
- Herring, Smoked
- Herring, Kippered
- Kingfish
- Mackerel, Fresh
- Mackerel, Spanish
- Mackerel, Salt
- Markerel, Smoked
- Perch
- Pickerel
- Pike
- Porgies
- Pompano
- Redsnapper
- Salmon, Fresh
- Salmon, Smoked
- Salmon, Nova Scotia
- Scrod
- Shad
- Shad Roes
- Smelts
- Sole, English
- Sole, Boston
- Sole, Lemon
- Sturgeon
- Trout, Brook
- Trout, Lake
- Trout, Salmon
- Weakfish
- Whitebait
- Whitefish
- Whitefish, Smoked

VEGETABLES
- Artichokes
- Asparagus
- Asparagus
- Asparagus, Tips
- Asparagus, Fancy
- Beans
- Beans, Lima
- Beans, String
- Beans, Wax
- Beets
- Beets, Tops
- Broccoli
- Brussels Sprouts
- Cabbage
- Cabbage, Red
- Cabbage, New
- Carrots
- Carrots
- Cauliflower
- Celery
- Celery Knobs
- Chicory
- Chives
- Corn
- Corn
- Chervil
- Cranberries
- Cucumbers
- Dandelion
- Escarole

Vegetables (Cont'd)
- Endive
- Estragon
- Egg Plant
- Garlic
- Horseradish Roots
- Kale
- Kohlrabi
- Lettuce
- Lettuce, Ice Berg
- Lettuce, Place
- Leeks
- Mint
- Mushrooms
- Mushrooms, Fresh
- Okra
- Onions
- Onions, Yellow
- Onions, Bermuda
- Onions, Spanish
- Onions, White
- Onions, Scallions
- Oyster Plant
- Parsley
- Parsnips
- Peppermint
- Peas, Green
- Peas
- Peas
- Peppers, Green
- Peppers, Red
- Potatoes
- Potatoes, Bermuda
- Potatoes, Idaho
- Potatoes, Idaho
- Potatoes, Sweet
- Potatoes, New
- Potatoes, Yams
- Pumpkins
- Romaine
- Radishes
- Rhubarb, Fresh
- Rhubarb, Hot House
- Sage
- Shallots
- Sorrel
- Sauerkraut
- Spinach
- Squash Cooked Neck
- Squash Hubbard
- Tarragon
- Thyme
- Tomatoes, New
- Tomatoes, Hot House
- Turnips, White
- Turnips, Yellow
- Turnips, New
- Watercress

FRUIT
- Apples, Cooking
- Apples, Baking
- Apples, Crab
- Apples, Table
- Apricots
- Bananas
- Blackberries
- Blueberries
- Blueberries
- Cantaloupes
- Cantaloupes
- Honey Balls
- Melons, Casaba
- Melons, Honeydew
- Melons, Persian
- Melons, Spanish
- Cherries
- Cherries
- Cherries
- Currants

FRUIT (Cont'd)
- Chestnuts
- Dates Figs
- Gooseberries
- Grapes
- Grapes
- Grapes, Concord
- Grapes, Malaga
- Grapes, Tokay
- Grapefruit
- Grapefruit
- Guavas
- Lemons
- Lemons
- Limes
- Limes, Florida
- Limes, Persian
- Mushmelons
- Oranges
- Oranges
- Oranges
- Peaches
- Peaches
- Pears
- Pears
- Pears, Alligator
- Pineapples
- Plums
- Plums
- Pomegranates
- Quinces
- Raspberries
- Strawberries
- Strawberries
- Tangerines
- Watermelons
- Watermelons

BUTTER
- Prune
- Quicking
- Sweet

EGGS
- White
- Brown
- Mixed Colors
- Pullets

CHEESE
- American, Kraft
- American, Young
- Bel Paese
- Camembert
- Camembert
- Cheddar
- Cottage
- Cream
- Cream, Phila.
- Cream, Phila.
- Edam
- Gorgonzola
- Liederkranz
- Parmesan, Grated
- Rusquefort
- Roquefort
- Roquefort, Broken
- Salton
- Store
- Swiss
- Swiss, Gruyere
- Swiss, Gruyere

Miscellaneous

WILLIAM ALLEN & CO., A DIVISION OF ALVIN J. BART & SONS, INC.   STOCK FORM #222

Figure 12–1   Market Quotation Sheet (Courtesy of William Allen & Company)

If the order did not go to the lowest quotation, the purchasing agent must be prepared to justify this deviation from policy, which usually results from variance in quality. A copy of the quotation sheet must be supplied to the receiving clerk to permit verification of quantity and price.

In order to ascertain quantities needed, food inventories should be scheduled daily. Even if the next day is not a normally scheduled ordering day, heavy usage can require emergency purchasing. While a regular slate of vendors is normally used for most purchasing, certain specialty items can only be obtained from vendors specializing in gourmet or select foods.

Since fresh meat and fish and all produce go directly into the kitchen, requisitioning of these items is the responsibility of the chef. Based on the daily inventories, items and quantities needed are marked on a quotation sheet, usually approved by the chef, and forwarded to the purchasing agent who is then responsible for placing the orders. Frozen items and dry goods, normally placed in storerooms, are requisitioned by the food and beverage director and ordered by the purchasing agent. The requisitioning of bakery supplies is usually handled by the pastry chef.

The accounting department should periodically review the quotation sheets, and where the lowest prices are not obtained, request a satisfactory explanation from the purchasing agent.

BEVERAGE PURCHASING

Although storage space is a consideration in beverage purchasing, perishability is not a factor (although certain wines can go bad), and prices do not fluctuate erratically. Consequently, there is adequate time to obtain written quotations and to issue purchase orders for beverages.

However, whether or not quotations can actually be obtained, or provide any benefits, depends on the state's liquor laws. In approximately half the states, the purchase of liquor, and in some even beer and wine, can only by done through state outlets. Under those circumstances, prices are controlled on a statewide basis and everyone purchases at the same price. In other states, only one liquor dealer handles each brand. While this permits a certain amount of flexibility, available by considering alternative brands or possibly negotiating volume discounts, true competitive pricing does not exist. Volume discounts usually apply to the *bar brands,* the brand the hotel will pour when no brand is specified by the customer. Usually, for this reason, there is a higher margin of profit on bar brands. In other states, there is complete competition and each dealer may handle any brand it pleases.

The existence of monopolies in some states and full competition in others results in highly varying costs from one state to another. This situation is further magnified by taxing policies; some states tax the sale of alcohol very heavily while others impose little or no tax.

Every hotel should have a list of brands approved by management for sale in the bars and at banquet functions. This list includes the designated bar brand and the selected group of other labels for each type of liquor. *Par stocks,* that is, predetermined quantities, not only of hard liquor but of beer, wine, and soft drinks should be set for each outlet and for the storeroom. The pars in the outlets are levels to be maintained through daily requisitioning from the storeroom. When quantities in the storeroom drop below the par level, the purchasing process is initiated.

When possible, competitive quotes should be obtained from vendors and, since quality is not a factor in purchasing a selected brand, the lowest price should always be obtained. In determining a bar brand, quotations should be obtained on the various labels available. However, selecting bar brands is done by management with consideration to image and customer perception and quality as well as price. Sometimes a decision may be made to use a cheaper brand in mixed drinks while using a better brand for straight drinks. Management decides the types of beer to be carried and again

considers customer perception and preference, as well as practicality. Savings can be achieved by using larger bottles (e.g., one gallon) but these are usually only used with automatic pourers or beverage-control systems. While most operators consider such systems appropriate for use in service bars, their use in front bars must again be evaluated in terms of image and customer perception.

When storeroom levels drop below the par level, the individual responsible for storeroom management must send a requisition to the purchasing agent who in turn selects a vendor and issues a purchase order. Purchase orders should be used for all beverage purchasing. However, a standing order may be acceptable where a daily delivery of such items as draft beer is necessary. Where purchasing must be done from a state-owned outlet, most states require that orders be placed on their preprinted order forms.

RECEIVING

Receiving is the natural next step in the control process after purchasing, but the two should be completely separate and under different control. Whereas purchasing is a management function and the purchasing agent reports to the resident manager, receiving is a control function and the receiving clerk should report to the controller. Of course, there will still be many occasions when the receiving clerk must consult the purchasing agent, particularly when there are questions as to the specifications or quality of merchandise (usually food) received.

All food and beverage vendors should be instructed that the corresponding invoice must accompany each delivery, or the delivery will be refused. This is particularly important with food, since there is no purchase order, only the quotation sheet, against which to check the delivery.

The person responsible for receiving should be present from the time the delivery truck arrives until all items are safely unloaded and taken into the hotel. All items must be checked against the invoices for quantity and against the quotation sheet for price and, finally, examined to verify quality. All boxed meat must be weighed. It is essential that a scale for this purpose be in the receiving area at all times. Produce and dairy products should be test-checked against specifications for quantity, size, and quality. Delivery of any product that does not meet the quality specified should be refused. All perishable food items should be tagged or marked to indicate date of receipt. Methods of tagging inventories are discussed in the next chapter. If specific types of date coding are used by bakeries, dairies, and so on, these should be checked. A permanent record should be kept in the receiving area of the types of coding used by those vendors.

In addition to verifying the quantities, all deliveries of beverages should be examined for breakage. All broken bottles should be refused and this should be noted on the invoice.

Truck drivers and other delivery personnel should not be permitted in storerooms, refrigerators, or other areas where their products are stored. Empty containers, bottles, and so on, which are to be picked up by the delivery personnel, should be test-checked to ensure that they are actually empty. Deliveries should only be accepted in accordance with previously agreed delivery schedules. In setting these schedules, consideration should, of course, be given to any timing problems that may exist, on a continuing basis, for a specific vendor.

Record of Receipt of Goods			
Quanties checked		Entered on receiving sheet	
Quality checked		Extensions and additions checked	
Prices verified		Approved for payment	

Figure 12–2   Rubber Stamp for Invoice

The imprint of a rubber stamp, designed in the manner shown in Figure 12–2, must be made on the back of each invoice. The areas indicating approval of quantity, quality, and price should be initialed by the receiving clerk after the necessary verification is completed. The remaining areas, covering extensions and final approval for payment, will be subsequently completed.

Each invoice is then entered on a daily receiving sheet, as shown in Figure 12–3. As you can see, the receiving sheet provides a column for the name of the supplier and four columns that separate the incoming shipments into "Beverage Stores," "Food—Direct," "Food—Stores," and "General Stores."

In each column, the monetary amount of the delivery is entered opposite the name of the vendor. "Food—Direct" represents food purchases delivered directly to the kitchen and placed under the control of the chef, as opposed to "Food—Stores," which is food to be placed in the storeroom. Since all beverage purchases should be delivered to the storeroom, only one column is required; "General Stores" represents purchases other than food and beverage. The separation of the direct food charges from the storeroom deliveries is important in establishing proper control over the storerooms. The total of the beverage and food—stores columns shows the dollar value of goods coming into the storerooms; for complete control, all that is needed is to control the issuance of goods from them.

The daily receiving sheet is completed by totaling each column, attaching all invoices, and forwarding it each day to the accounts payable department. The totals of the three food and beverage columns are entered by the food and beverage controller on a worksheet that is used in the final reconciliation of food and beverage activity for the month. The daily receiving sheet also provides a basis for reconciling the total food and beverage purchases for the month, as discussed in Chapter 13.

RECEIVING CLERK'S DAILY REPORT

NO. _____

DATE _____

QUAN.	UNIT	DESCRIPTION	✓	UNIT PRICE	AMOUNT	BEVERAGE STORES	PURCHASE JOURNAL DISTRIBUTION		
							FOOD DIRECT	FOOD STORES	GENERAL STORES

Figure 12–3 Receiving Clerk's Daily Receiving Sheet (Courtesy of William Allen & Company)

EXERCISES

1. What are the differences in procedures for purchasing food versus purchasing beverages and what are the reasons for the differences?

2. Describe the receiving procedures to be followed when receiving a shipment of meat.

3. Circle T or F to indicate whether the following statements are true or false:

   T   F   **a.** Centralized purchasing is most successful when purchasing food.

   T   F   **b.** Prices for fresh produce change continually.

   T   F   **c.** Standards for purchasing meat are issued by the U.S. Department of Agriculture.

   T   F   **d.** The brand a hotel pours when no brand is specified by the customer is termed a *bar brand.*

   T   F   **e.** "Food—direct" is food that goes directly into the storeroom.

4. Circle the correct answer to the following statements:

   a. A purchase order is practical when purchasing:
      (1) Produce
      (2) Dry goods
      (3) Meat

   b. The principal document to be used when ordering meat and fish is:
      (1) A purchase order
      (2) A quotation sheet
      (3) A receiving sheet

   c. The measurement used in specifying the size of shellfish being purchased is:
      (1) The number of units contained in a quart
      (2) The number of units per pound
      (3) The number of ounces per unit

   d. The purchase of liquor is state controlled in:
      (1) All states
      (2) Only Vermont and Massachusetts
      (3) About 50 percent of the states

   e. All food and beverage vendors should be instructed that the invoice should:
      (1) Be sent to the accounting department within 24 hours of delivery
      (2) Should accompany the merchandise
      (3) Should be sent to the hotel at the end of the month

13 Inventory Control and Cost Reconciliation

Proper control does not cease after purchasing and receiving; control over goods in the storeroom is equally important.

FOOD INVENTORIES

The preceding chapter emphasized how many food prices fluctuate on a daily basis. This has been the major deterrent in developing monetary controls over food inventories. Chapter 14 covers the use of point-of-sale systems as a method of inventory control. As you will read, however, the updating of prices due to their volatility is a very time-consuming part of system maintenance. Inventory control over food, therefore, has generally been maintained on a quantity, rather than a monetary, basis.

Meat and Fish

There two important factors in the storage of meat and fish—security and temperature control. All refrigerators and freezers should be securely locked except when inventory is going in or coming out. Hotels with extensive storage facilities will ideally keep the bulk of the inventory in the storeroom area with only limited storage capacity under the control of the kitchen. Thus, only those quantities requisitioned by the chef are issued on a daily basis. The kitchen inventory can then be limited to items, in various stages of preparation, which will be used in the immediate future and leftovers, cooked or uncooked. Action should be taken continuously to plan the best and most rapid utilization of leftovers and, as much as possible, to avoid unnecessary reoccurrence. All other items under kitchen control should be specifically assigned for use in a specific meal period or for a specific banquet function.

A felt-tip pen should be used to mark the day and month on the outside of each container to be stored. Proper rotation on a first-in, first-out basis should be policy for both fresh and frozen products. The best method to control meat and fish in storage is

by using meat tags similar to that shown in Figure 13–1. The meat tag is in two parts which can be separated by tearing along the perforated line. When the meat or fish is weighed and placed in the freezer box, both sections of the tag are completed; one section is attached to the meat or fish, and the other is hung on a board set up in the storage area for that purpose. When the meat or fish is issued to the kitchen, the tag is removed from the board and attached to the requisition. Consequently, at any time, the tags hanging on the board will represent the amount of meat or fish in the freezer. Both refrigerators and freezers, both walk-in and reach-in, should be kept at specified temperatures at all times—34 to 40 degrees for refrigerators and around 0 degrees for freezers is the accepted general range. More specifically, the following are the optimum storage temperatures for specific items:

Meat and poultry	33 to 36 degrees
Fish and shellfish	23 to 30 degrees (for use within 24 to 48 hours)
Frozen foods	0 degrees
Meat being aged	36 degrees
All reach-in coolers	40 degrees

Frozen foods are highly perishable and deteriorate quickly if not handled correctly. They should be stored in the freezer as quickly as possible, preferably in their original shipping cartons. Vapor-proof containers prevent dehydration, oxidation, discoloration, odor absorption, and loss of volatile flavors. Platform racks should be used to keep the food off the floor and permit proper air circulation. Proper grouping by product will reduce handling time, thereby lessening the amount of time the freezer door will be open. A thermometer should be placed where it is easy to see. In walk-in

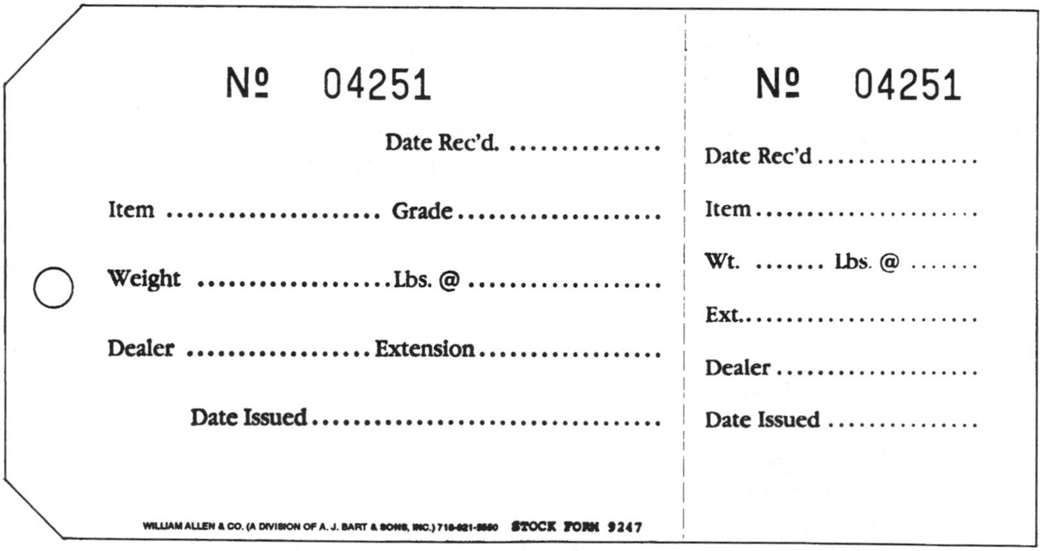
Nº 04251

Date Rec'd. ....

Item .... Grade ....

Weight ....Lbs. @ ....

Dealer .... Extension.................

Date Issued.................................

WILLIAM ALLEN & CO. (A DIVISION OF A. J. BART & SONS, INC.) STOCK FORM 9247

Nº 04251

Date Rec'd ....

Item......................

Wt. .... Lbs. @ ....

Ext.......................

Dealer ....

Date Issued ....

Figure 13–1 Meat Tag (Courtesy of William Allen & Company)

freezers, the thermometer should be attached to the outside, but not next to the condensing unit, as that would affect the temperature reading.

Maximum periods of storage are:

Frozen raw beef, lamb, veal	Up to 1 year
Frozen cooked beef, lamb, veal	Up to 3 months
Frozen pork, fresh	Up to 6 months
Frozen pork, cooked or smoked	Up to 1 month
Frozen fish, raw	Up to 6 months
Frozen fish, cooked	Up to 3 months
Beef, aging	1 month
Beef, other	10 days
Lamb and veal	1 week
Pork	5 days
Fish and seafood	3 days

Dry Goods

Dry goods should also be placed in secure storage under the control of the storekeeper and issued to the kitchen on a requisition basis. All items should be on well-spaced shelving. Physical quantities should be controlled by use of bin cards (Figure 13–2). A bin card should be kept for each individual item, by product and size. The card should show the balance on hand by number or weight, the quantities received (purchases), outgoing quantities (issues to the kitchen), and the resulting balances on hand. The bin cards should be pinned to shelves or hung up in the area where the food is stored. Periodic—weekly or semimonthly—physical counts should be made and the results compared with the bin cards, with variances immediately investigated. Additionally, in order to facilitate proper rotation and pricing of periodic inventories, the date received and the cost of each item should be marked on the top of each can or container. Most canned goods can be kept for six months to a year, but canned fish and seafood, meats, stews, and hash should not be kept longer than three months.

In the food storeroom, pars equal to minimum quantities should be established for items carried in inventory on a continuing basis. When the quantities drop below these par levels, the storekeeper should prepare a requisition to initiate a purchase.

Production Items

The term *production inventory* refers to the inventory of all items under the direct control of the kitchen. Because of the frequency of purchases and the limited life, all bread, produce, fruits, and dairy products usually fall into this category.

The storage time for most dairy products is in the range of three (milk and cream) to ten days (butter and soft cheese). Only hard cheese has a longer life. Fruits and vegetables have a life of three days (mushrooms) up to one month (apples and oranges). Certain items such as onions and bananas should not be stored in any form of refrigeration. While storeroom items are charged to the kitchen as issued on requisitions, production inventory items are treated as "direct" and charged to the kitchen immediately.

BIN CARD

No._____ Product_____ Size_____

Date	Supplier	Quantity Received	Quantity Issued	Balance On Hand

Figure 13–2 Bin Card—Food

BEVERAGE INVENTORIES

Since alcoholic beverages are more susceptible to theft than food, physical security is extremely important. All inventories left in the outlets overnight should be secured in locked cabinets. Locking devices should be placed on wine coolers and draft beer and soda dispensers to prevent unauthorized employee consumption. The outlets themselves should also be completely locked up. Apart from physical security, the liquor laws in most states mandate this when the outlet cannot legally be open for business.

While product loss due to improper temperatures during storage is not a major consideration with beverages, there are certain areas where precautions must be taken. Basic guidelines in those areas are as follows:

White wine and champagne	45 degrees
Red wine	55 degrees

Juices	35 to 40 degrees
Premix and syrups	45 degrees
Draft beer	40 degrees
Carbonated soda	35 degrees

It is particularly important that wines not be subject to extreme temperatures. Freezing will occur below 40 degrees and the bottles will burst; above 70 degrees, the wines will overheat and the corks will pop. In humid weather, it is desirable to remove pourers and seal whiskies and rums as small fruit flies are drawn to these products and enter via the pourers.

Similar to food stores, a bin card (Figure 13–3) should be used to control the receipt and issuance of bottles and the balance on hand, and to identify the minimum balance. The bin cards should be attached to the shelves where the bottles or containers are stored. Only sealed, full bottles should be kept in the storerooms.

WILLIAM ALLEN & CO.
Stock Form 7039

BIN CARD

PRINTED IN U.S.A.

No._____ Size_____ _____

Name

Date	Rec'd	ISSUED TO BAR NO.					Total	Balance
		1	2	3	4	5		

Figure 13–3 Bin Card—Beverages
(Courtesy of William Allen & Company)

In addition to bin cards, the lack of volatility in beverage prices permits a monetary control over the storeroom. This can best be achieved by maintaining a perpetual inventory book or log. This book is also used to detail purchasing, identify par stocks, show shelf location for the product, and provide a record of delivery schedules. The perpetual inventory records (Figure 13–4) are usually maintained by the storekeeper, but in larger hotels they are sometimes kept in the accounting department. They should always be used in counting and checking the physical inventory at period end.

The record should have a page for each brand and size and should be organized in subsections for easy use. A suggested format is as follows:

Whiskies
    Bourbons
    Blends
    Canadian whiskeys
    Irish whiskeys
    Scotch whiskeys
Gin
Vodka
Rum
Brandy and Cognacs
Cordials and Liqueurs
Port Wines and Sherries
Aperitifs and Vermouths
Red Wine
Soft Drinks, Misc.
Premixed Cocktails
Champagne and Sparkling Wines
White Wines
Rosé Wines
Beer

The perpetual record (see Figure 13–4) should indicate the date of receipt, quantity received, amount issued, balance on hand, vendor, and price paid for each purchase. In addition to the storeroom par, the total par for the bars should also be recorded.

Issues to the bars should only be made on the basis of requisitions. All requisitions should be accompanied by empty bottles of a like brand. All bottles issued to the bars must bear color-coded, single-use, peel-proof numbered stickers to identify and control all bottles. Each bar should have a different identifying color and number series. The color identifies the bar and the number can denote the date of issue. Stickers should be numbered by month, that is, 1 to 12.

After being checked against the requisition, the empty bottles returned should be destroyed. All exchanges should be made in the storeroom. If the bottles are redeemable and cannot be destroyed, the sticker should be voided immediately to prevent the empty being reused to obtain another issue. The bars should be restocked to their par levels on a daily basis with two issues if necessary.

Unit Sales Value ____ Sales Price Per Drink ____ No. Drinks Per Bottle ____ Cost Per Drink ____ Par Minimum ____ Par Maximum ____ Sheet No. ____

Vendors 1. ____ 2. ____ 3. ____ 4. ____

PURCHASES				ISSUES		STOREROOM		PURCHASES				ISSUES		STOREROOM	
Date	Vend.	Quan.	Unit Cost	Bar #1	Bar #2	Balance	Value	Date	Vend.	Quan.	Unit Cost	Bar #1	Bar #2	Balance	Value

ITEM ____ BRAND ____ PROOF ____ SIZE ____ BIN NO. ____

Figure 13–4 Perpetual Beverage Inventory Record

All requisitions must be signed by the bartender and the individual making the issue. Bartenders must be responsible for verifying their issues and maintaining their pars.

The hotel controller must keep the official copy of the pars and periodically verify them. The controller and beverage management should review the pars on a periodic basis—at least once every six months.

Bottle sales should only be made by room service and a written order should be turned in showing the room number of the guest. This order can then be used by the bartender instead of an empty bottle to obtain a replacement. It is recommended that a different size of bottle be used for room service than is used in the outlets.

COST RECONCILIATIONS

All requisitions for storeroom issues are priced and extended daily, then totaled separately for food and beverage by the food and beverage controller's office and entered on daily recap sheets. This can be done manually or by feeding the quantities into a computer program in which the prices are preentered. In this case, a computerized printout of issues will be obtained. The total food issue is then added to the total of "direct" purchases delivered to the kitchen. This figure, after a deduction for food consumed by employees, can be compared with the food sales figure and a daily food cost can be obtained. Even though such a comparison on a day-by-day basis will show major fluctuations because of changing inventory levels in the kitchen, nevertheless, after two or three days into the month, a comparison of the cumulative issues to sales will give a fairly accurate indication of the food-cost percentage—issues as a percentage of sales—for the period covered.

Similarly, a comparison can be made of beverage issues to beverage sales. Since all beverages are controlled in the storeroom and issued on requisitions, there are no direct issues with which to contend. Furthermore, the effect of inventory fluctuations is largely avoided by having the bars operate with par stocks. The inventory fluctuations in the bars can be caused only by minor variations in the contents of part bottles, and fairly accurate daily beverage costs can be obtained by comparing issues with sales.

In order to better refine daily food and beverage costs, certain other adjustments should be made to the issues on a daily basis. In particular, adjustments should be made for food issued to the bar—cream, milk, cherries, olives, and the like—and beverages issued to the kitchen, such as wine and brandy used for cooking. Adjustments are also necessary for complimentary drinks, free drinks consumed by management, breakage or spoilage, and the free beer given to the cooks if that is a hotel practice.

Individual reconciliations of beverage cost should be done for each outlet in order to monitor and identify problem areas. A separate reconciliation should be done for wine sales in each outlet so that the cost of sales for wine (normally higher than other alcoholic beverages) can be adjusted out of the total outlet reconciliation in order to better evaluate the costs.

At the end of each period, an overall food and beverage reconciliation (Figure 13–5) should be prepared. In order to better understand these reconciliations, the following is a line-by-line review of the food reconciliation in Figure 13–5 and comments on the beverage reconciliation where it varies.

Hotel Grayscot

Reconciliation of Food and Beverage Costs

Month of _____ 19____

FOOD

	Storeroom	Production	Reconciliation
Opening Inventory - Physical	18722.93	4136.52	22859.45
Purchases	61531.08	43272.22	104803.30
Total Food Available	80254.01	47408.74	127662.75
Less: Store Issues -			
Kitchen	⟨57128.35⟩	57128.35	—
Adver. & Promotion	⟨1436.03⟩		⟨1436.03⟩
Steward Sales	⟨460.00⟩		⟨460.00⟩
Food to Beverage	⟨1956.31⟩		⟨1956.31⟩
Kitchen Credits -			
Entertainment Checks		⟨1528.80⟩	⟨1528.80⟩
Officers Checks		⟨432.60⟩	⟨432.60⟩
Food to Beverage		⟨338.00⟩	⟨338.00⟩
Spoilage		⟨281.75⟩	⟨281.75⟩
Add: Beverage to Food		640.00	640.00
Closing Inventory - Book	19273.32		
Closing Inventory - Physical	⟨19061.20⟩	⟨4721.30⟩	⟨23783.00⟩
Total Food Consumed		97874.14	98086.26
(Overage) Shortage	212.12		
Credit for Employee Meals			⟨3746.00⟩
Total Cost of Sales			94340.26
Sales			314434.20
Food Cost %			30.0%

BEVERAGES

	Storeroom	Bars	Reconciliation
Opening Inventory - Physical	16547.20	4017.32	20564.52
Purchases	18362.10		18362.10
Total Beverages Available	34909.30	4017.32	38926.62
Less: Store Issues -			
Outlet 1	⟨6522.11⟩	6522.11	—
Outlet 2	⟨5731.12⟩	5731.12	—
Banquet Bars	⟨5842.17⟩	5842.17	—
Beverage to Food	⟨640.00⟩		⟨640.00⟩
Steward Sales	⟨116.00⟩		⟨116.00⟩
Credits to Bars -			
Entertainment Checks		⟨841.10⟩	⟨841.10⟩
Officers Checks		⟨106.20⟩	⟨106.20⟩
Beverage to Food		—	—
Breakage & Spoilage		⟨105.00⟩	⟨105.00⟩
Cooks' Beer		⟨581.00⟩	⟨581.00⟩
Add: Food to Beverage		2294.31	2294.31
Closing Inventory - Book	16057.90		
Closing Inventory - Physical	⟨16120.70⟩	⟨3908.00⟩	⟨20028.70⟩
Total Beverage Consumed		18865.73	18802.90
(Overage) Shortage	⟨62.80⟩		
Total Cost of Sales			18802.90
Sales			94014.50
Food Cost %			20.0%

Figure 13–5   Reconciliation of Food and Beverage Costs

Food Reconciliation

The "storeroom" column reflects the activity in the storeroom to arrive at the theoretical inventory which should be on hand at the end of the month. On a line-by-line basis the following takes place:

Opening inventory on hand at beginning of month	$18,722.93
Purchases that went into storerooms	61,531.08
For a total of	$80,254.01
From this amount is deducted issues from the storeroom	
—to the kitchen	$57,128.35
—giveaways for promotional purposes	1,436.03
—sales made at cost to management	460.00
—food sent to bars (cherries, olives, etc.)	1,956.31
These issues are deducted to arrive at the inventory that should be on hand at month end	19,273.32
Actual inventory on hand was	19,061.20
Storeroom reflected a shortage of	212.12

Note: A pattern of continuing shortages must be investigated to determine the cause. The production column reflects actual activity in the kitchen:

Opening inventory on hand at beginning of month	$4,136.52
Direct purchases—went immediately into kitchen	43,272.22
Added: Issues into kitchen from storeroom	57,125.35
Deductions	
Food consumed without revenue	
—entertainment of customers	1,528.80
—by management	432.60
Food issued to bars (e.g., milk, cream)	338.00
Food that has spoiled (usually produce)	281.75
Alcoholic beverages issued to the kitchen for cooking—added in	640.00
The closing kitchen inventory is then deducted	4,721.80

The net result is actual food consumption of $97,874.14 to which is added the storeroom shortage of $212.12 (an overage would be deducted) to arrive at a final cost of food consumed of $98,086.26. The cost of employee meals consumed in other areas than the restaurants can be based on requisitions if there is a cafeteria with its own kitchen. However, for most hotels the deduction is based on an estimated cost per employee meal.

The net result, in this example $94,340.26, can then be matched against the actual sales to arrive at the food cost percentage.

Beverage Reconciliation

The principles followed in arriving at the beverage cost in general follow the same path as the food cost. However, certain comments should be made.

1. As all beverage purchases should go into the storeroom, there is no amount shown under bars.
2. Issues from the storeroom are tabulated by individual outlet and a month-end reconciliation should be done for each outlet, if feasible. This requires careful recording of any transfers that are made between outlets.

3. The credit for cook's beer reflects the long-time practice of giving a cold beer to the cooks at the end of their shift.
4. Employee's meals are not a factor in arriving at the beverage cost.

End-of-Period Entries

While the end-of-period entries required to finalize the financial results are covered in Chapter 8, an exception is the food and beverage reconciliation entries which are described in this chapter in order to be closer to the related rationale.

While an entry is not necessary for the transfers between the storeroom and the outlets, an entry is required for transfers between food and beverage. The appropriate entries for Figure 13–5 are:

a.	Dr	Cost of Food	$640.00	
		Cr Cost of Beverages		$640.00
		To record beverage transfers to food for June		
b.	Dr	Cost of Beverages	$2,294.31	
		Cr Cost of Food		$2,294.31
		To record food transfers to beverages for June		
		Entries must then be made for all other credits:		
a.	Dr	Sales—Entertainment	$2,964.83	
		Accounts receivable	460.00	
		Employee meals (broken down by dept.)	432.60	
		Food—Spoilage	281.75	
		Cr Cost of Food		4,139.18
		To record food credits		
b.	Dr	Employee meals (broken down by dept.)	3,746.00	
		Cr Cost of Food		3,746.00
		To record employee meals credit		
c.	Dr	Sales—Entertainment	841.10	
		Employee meals (broken down by outlet)	106.20	
		Beverage—Breakage and spoilage	105.00	
		Food—Employee meals	581.00	
		Cr Cost of Beverages		$1,633.30
		To record credits to beverages		

Finally, entries must be made to reflect change in inventories.

a.	Dr	Food inventory	$923.55	
		Cr Cost of sales—Food		923.55
		To record increase in food inventory.		
b.	Dr	Cost of sales		
		—Beverages	535.82	
		Cr Beverage inventory		532.82
		To record decrease in beverage inventory.		

In Chapter 14 the use of point-of-sale information to provide additional analyses and controls on food and beverage inventories and costs is reviewed.

1. The Smith Arms had food sales for the month of June in the amount of $137,322.
   Inventories were—at May 31:

storeroom	$19,504
production	4,172

   —at June 30:

storeroom	$21,509
production	3,926

   Purchases for June were:

storeroom	$42,811
kitchen	13,408

   Storeroom issues were:

to kitchen	$41,903
to sales dept.	674
sales to staff	406
to bars	1,711

   Kitchen credits were:

for entertainment checks	$1,113
for officers' checks	218
for spoilage	120

   The kitchen received $442 of cooking wine from the beverage storeroom.
   Employee meals were valued at $3,480.
   Based on this information, prepare a food cost reconciliation for the month and determine the storeroom overage or shortage.

2. What are the maximum periods of storage for:
   a. Pork—frozen after cooking
   b. Beef being aged
   c. Fresh fish
   d. Fresh lamb

3. Circle T or F to indicate whether the following statements are true or false:
   T F a. Meat being aged should be stored at around 36 degrees.
   T F b. Dry goods should be issued to the kitchen on a requisition basis.
   T F c. All production inventories should be under the control of the store-keeper.
   T F d. Bin cards, when used, require the extension of prices times quantities.
   T F e. Bottles issued to the bars should be color coded.
   T F f. Beverage pars should be reviewed at least once every six months.
   T F g. Room service should never be permitted to make bottle sales.
   T F h. Employees' meals are not a factor in arriving at beverage cost.

T F **i.** Food issued to the bars for free snacks for customers must be added into the beverage cost.

T F **j.** Monetary control is easier for beverage inventories than food inventories.

4. Circle the correct answer to the following statements:

   a. Meat tags are used:
   (1) To control meat inventories
   (2) To identify the earliest purchases
   (3) To identify the weight
   (4) All of the above

   b. White wines and champagnes should be stored at:
   (1) Under 35 degrees
   (2) Around 45 degrees
   (3) Around 65 degrees

   c. Which of the following is not categorized as a whiskey:
   (1) Scotch
   (2) Brandy
   (3) Bourbon

   d. Which of the following items usually is included only in the production inventory:
   (1) Canned soup
   (2) Frozen chicken
   (3) Milk

   e. Which of the following fruits should not be stored in any form of refrigeration:
   (1) Oranges
   (2) Bananas
   (3) Grapes

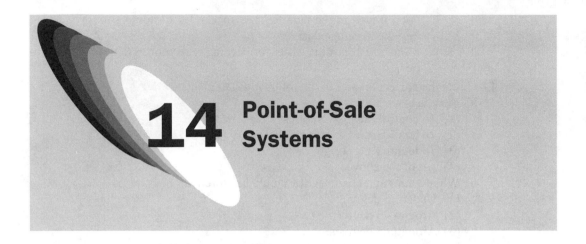

14 Point-of-Sale Systems

Although most restauranteurs view point-of-sale systems as a product of the computer age, it is more accurate to describe them as systems designed to perform historically manual controls more effectively through the use of computer technology.

MANUAL SYSTEMS

The principal element in the manual systems is the use of duplicate orders or duplicate checks, commonly referred to as *dupes*. With the former, the person taking the order uses a duplicate order pad to record it. The order forms in the pad are two identical prenumbered forms; the first copy is carbonized or carbon paper is inserted between the two copies. The server records the details of the customer's order, the table number, the number of guests, the number of the guest check, and the server's initials. One copy is given to the kitchen where it is used to fill the customer's order. If the order must be filled from more than one line or area in the kitchen, it is necessary to use two or more order forms. When the order is complete, the kitchen personnel file their copy of the order. The server uses his or her copy of the order to fill out the guest check in detail for presentation to the customer. At the end of the day, the kitchen copy of the order must be matched up with the guest check. As collusion between a server and a cook can circumvent the system, the process is not complete until, ideally, the orders can also be matched against the actual kitchen consumption. Unless, however, all entrees are precut and counted, it is extremely difficult to verify the consumption.

The task of transferring the order from the order form to a guest check can be eliminated by using a duplicate check whose front copy is a soft tear-off "dupe" that is used to place the kitchen order. Since the complete order is not usually placed at one time, the tear-off copy can be designed (see Figure 14–1) to be used in two or three sections as the different portions of the order are turned in to the kitchen. Since there is no guarantee that what was written on the order copy actually shows up on the check, the match-up process is still necessary.

Hotel Grayscot

RESTAURANT CHECK

Name: ______________________

Room No: ______________________

No. 14379

GUEST RECEIPT — Hotel Grayscot — **No. 14379**

Item 5

Item 4

Item 3

Item 2

Item 1

No. 14379

Figure 14–1 Duplicate Check

Since under either method physical control over guest checks is required, it is necessary to have the servers sign a check-off sheet (Figure 14–2) for each group of checks taken. The servers turn their settled checks in to a cashier who possibly records the check information on a Record of Checks (Figure 14–3) or may only ring the amounts up on some type of cash register.

For many years, restaurants used a *checker* as a means of control. The checker examined the food leaving the kitchen, verified it against what was written on the check, and frequently recorded the amounts on the check. For several reasons, checkers were phased out of practically all operations:

1. On busy days, service was slowed up as servers lined up at the checker.
2. There was almost no way to prevent collusion between the checker and the server.
3. The checker frequently rang up what was written on the check without any physical verification.

ROOM SERVICE
Waiters Daily Check Record

Date_____ / ___ / ___

Outlet_____

Meal_____

Rest. Check #	Room #	Waiter #	Check Retd.	Covers Food	Bev.	Rest. Check #	Room #	Waiter #	Check Retd.	Covers Food	Bev.
01						51					
02						52					
03						53					
04						54					
05						55					
06						56					
07						57					
08						58					
09						59					
10						60					
11						61					
12						62					
13						63					
14						64					
15						65					
16						66					
17						67					
18						68					
19						69					
20						70					
21						71					
22						72					
23						73					
24						74					
25						75					
26						76					
27						77					
28						78					
29						79					
30						80					
31						81					
32						82					
33						83					
34						84					
35						85					
36						86					
37						87					
38						88					
39						89					
40						90					
41						91					
42						92					
43						93					
44						94					
45						95					
46						96					
47						97					
48						98					
49						99					
50						100					
Totals						Totals					

Form No. H-786-5-73

Figure 14–2 Servers' Check-Off Sheet

RESTAURANT CHECK RECORD

OUTLET: RALEIGH ROOM   DATE ___/___/___

BREAKFAST

CHECK NUMBER	ROOM NUMBER	WAITER NUMBER	FOOD COVERS	DISTRIBUTION			SIGNATURE FOR TIPS
				CASH	CHARGE	TIPS	
TOTALS							

H-1037-10-75

Figure 14–3   Record of Checks

These reasons, combined with the increasing labor cost of the checkers, brought about the demise of their position. Efforts were made by some establishments to combine the role of cashier and checker. However, not only did that invite further collusion but it also served to create longer lines of servers at the cashier's station. From these systems, however, the concept of mechanical and, ultimately, electronic prechecking evolved.

INITIAL PRECHECKING SYSTEMS

Prechecking is based on the concept that a check must be rung up in order to initiate the order. This is, in fact, a mechanization of the duplicate check process. With mechanical systems, each item of the order is entered into the register individually and a check is printed. When a check is validated, the machine also prints a tear-off tape. That tape is then taken to the order station in the kitchen where it is used as a requisition to obtain the food. Similarly, a tape can be printed for a beverage order and given to the bartender. While an improvement over the manual systems, the time needed to ring up each item individually and the requirement that each tape be carried to the kitchen by the server slows down the service considerably. Also, corrections are cumbersome on a mechanical register and create problems in balancing the readings.

COMPUTERIZED SYSTEMS

The introduction of computerized point-of-sale systems was a major development for the hotel and restaurant industries. These systems are sold in a large array of sizes and use varying methods of input. Each system uses the same basic methods and concepts and, most important, focuses on the same three goals:

1. To ensure that the product served is exactly what was ordered.
2. To ensure each item served is recorded on a sales check.
3. To ensure that each check is settled in a satisfying manner.

The difference in the systems is in the degree of sophistication. The less sophisticated systems use basic computer hardware with software designed to provide point-of-sale control, while the more sophisticated systems operate with hardware selected and specifically designed to facilitate easy input by the servers and provide the best service possible for the customer. One of the earliest companies (1976) to develop these systems was Remanco and this chapter focuses on its most recent state-of-the-art system, the VISION Series II illustrated in Figures 14–4 and 14–5. This system not only embodies the finer points of earlier systems but utilizes the most recent technological development—the hand-held terminal.

Point-of-sale systems use a combination of terminals and printers that function as input and output devices. The Vision Series II utilizes a processor that can support up to three networks, each of which can have up to 30 connected input and output terminals. Several types of input terminals can be used, the most common of which are touchscreen terminals located at selected locations easily accessible to the servers. The customized screens guide the server through the input process. The essential information input is the identity of the server, the location or table number of the customer, the

REMANCO VISION Series II System Overview

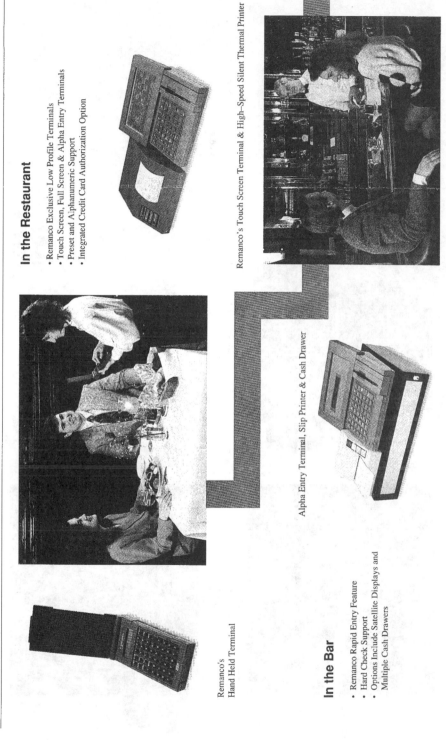

Remanco's
Hand Held Terminal

In the Bar

- Remanco Rapid Entry Feature
- Hard Check Support
- Options Include Satellite Displays and Multiple Cash Drawers

In the Restaurant

- Remanco Exclusive Low Profile Terminals
- Touch Screen, Full Screen & Alpha Entry Terminals
- Preset and Alphanumeric Support
- Integrated Credit Card Authorization Option

Remanco's Touch Screen Terminal & High–Speed Silent Thermal Printer

Alpha Entry Terminal, Slip Printer & Cash Drawer

Figure 14–4 Vision Series II—Bar and Restaurant (Courtesy of Remanco International)

179

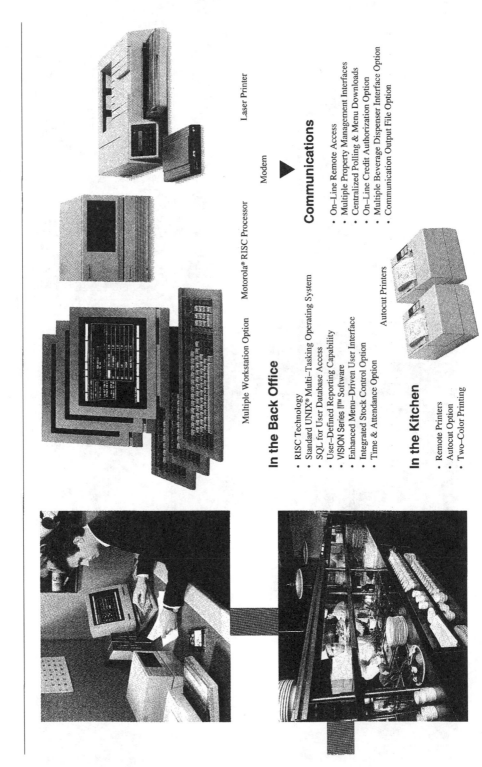

Laser Printer

Modem

Motorola® RISC Processor

Multiple Workstation Option

Autocut Printers

Communications

- On–Line Remote Access
- Multiple Property Management Interfaces
- Centralized Polling & Menu Downloads
- On–Line Credit Authorization Option
- Multiple Beverage Dispenser Interface Option
- Communication Output File Option

In the Back Office

- RISC Technology
- Standard UNIX® Multi–Tasking Operating System
- SQL for User Database Access
- User–Defined Reporting Capability
- VISION Series II™ Software
- Enhanced Menu–Driven User Interface
- Integrated Stock Control Option
- Time & Attendance Option

In the Kitchen

- Remote Printers
- Autocut Option
- Two–Color Printing

Figure 14–5 Vision Series II—Back Office (Courtesy of Remanco International)

number of people being served, and the menu items being ordered. The input program usually provides the ability to put in preparation instructions (i.e., well done for steak, salad dressings, and condiments requested, etc.). Computer cables transmit the orders to the kitchen where they are printed out at the service line. The sophisticated systems permit transmission to several locations, that is, hot items to the hot preparation area, salads to the salad station, and drinks to the bar. Furthermore, several servers can input simultaneously. The computer queues them in order and prints them out. The Vision Series II's hand-held feature permits the server to use an alphanumeric hand-held terminal, really a computerized order pad, with which the orders can be input at the table and transmitted to the kitchen. The hand-held terminals permit the server to spend more time at the tables and less time going to a remote terminal or the kitchen. This speeds up service and permits the server to handle more customers. Another feature of the system permits the server to input the whole order but send parts of it to the kitchen on a delayed basis. Technically, the terminals send a computer signal to antennae located in the ceiling of the restaurant which are connected by cable to the processor.

Prices for all menu items, food and beverage, are stored in memory to be printed on a customer's check. The check is assigned a number at the time of the initial input and can be reprinted on several occasions because of changes or additions to the order. For this reason, many restaurants use a soft-copy check with a computerized print design which is more cost effective than hard checks. However, the hard-check option is available. Multiple checks can be printed and items can be transferred from one check to another.

At the time of settlement, the method of settlement (cash, room charge, designated credit card, etc.) is also entered via the terminal. The larger terminals can be equipped with multiple cash drawers. However, the common practice is to provide the servers with some form of pouch to hold their cash for a drop in a safe at the end of their shift.

At the end of the shift, the server prints a report indicating which checks are still open (unsettled). After all checks are settled, the server can print a settlement report (Figure 14–6) which shows an analysis of his or her total sales and a detailed breakdown of the settlement. This enables the servers to verify their total cash and charges before making their individual drops. The drops should be made in a lock box or drop safe and witnessed by another employee. The employees also use their settlement reports to determine their cash and charge tips. Some hotels provide only the credit sales information to the servers, preferring them to make a "blind," unverified cash drop. While this procedure has merit from a control point of view, it can result in substantially more work for the general cashier in handling and reconciling tips and due-backs. This is particularly true when there is a large number of servers. Charge tips are "due-back" amounts owed by the hotel to the server. Servers normally recover the due-back tips by deducting them from their cash remittance prior to making the drop. However, the cash remittance is sometimes not large enough (this happens frequently at breakfast) to cover the charge tips. When this happens, the server is reimbursed for the shortfall by the general cashier, usually on the following day. The tip amounts are also used to meet the tip declaration and other tip reporting requirements of the IRS. A customized report can be designed (Figure 14–7) to provide the requirement information and facilitate payroll preparation and filing requirements.

Hotel Grayscot

Server: Joan Brown

SETTLEMENT REPORT

Period: 06/03/9x - 06/03/9x

Printed 06/08/9_ 11:41		Current Database		Rpt# 23 Page 1
Sales Summary	Count	GrossAmt	AdjustAmt	NetAmt

—— **SALES SUMMARY** ——

	Count	GrossAmt	AdjustAmt	NetAmt
Category Group Sales				
Food	557	2,798.20	0.00	2,798.20
Beverage	404	1,445.35	0.00	1,445.35
Category Group Totals	961	4,243.55	0.00	4,243.55
			Non-Adjusted Sales	4,243.55
Service Charges				
Service Charge Total	0	0.00		
Discounts				
Store Coupon	6	44.17		
Discount Total	6	44.17		
			Net Adjustments	- 44.17
			Net Sales	4,199.38
Taxes				
Sales Tax	180	187.31		
Tax Total	180	187.31		
			Gross Sales	4,386.69
Tips Collected				
Charge Tips	65	431.12		
Serv Charge Tips	7	31.83		
Tips Collected Total	72	462.95		
			Total Revenue	4,849.64

Figure 14–6   Settlement Report (Courtesy of Remanco International)

At the end of the day, the system must be cleared by running a "z" report. This clears the day's activity from the active file and also clears out the individual server's files. This does not remove the information completely from the system. All information can be reaccessed through the management terminals. The end-of-day function on

SETTLEMENT REPORT

Revenue Summary	Count	GrossAmt	TipAmt	NetAmt

—— REVENUE SUMMARY ——

	Count	GrossAmt	TipAmt	NetAmt
Payment Media				
Cash	158	1,677.02	0.00	1,677.02
Mastercard	21	950.75	156.93	793.82
Visa	10	700.98	62.74	638.24
American Express	18	730.30	93.85	636.45
Room Charge	18	665.26	117.60	547.66
British Pound (15.00)	3	22.73	0.00	22.73
Deutche Mark (30.00)	1	18.60	0.00	18.60
Swiss Franc (200.00)	2	84.00	0.00	84.00
Payment Media Subtotal	231	4,849.64	431.12	4,418.52
Service Charge Tips			31.83	
Payment Media Total	231	4,849.64	462.95	4,386.69
		Total Revenue		4,849.64

	Gross Cash	Tips	Net Cash
Cash less Tips Collected:	1,677.02	462.95	1,214.07
Cash less Tips Paid:	1,677.02	227.82	1,449.20
Tips Collected less Tips Paid:		227.82	

End of Report

Figure 14–6 Settlement Report (*Continued*)

the Vision Series II system is very simple as it utilizes a tape archive system to store the historical information for each recall. The system also has the ability to recreate individual checks through the back-office terminal and either display or print them.

The Vision Series II back-office system uses multiple work-station capabilities and has a laser printer for clear attractive reporting. Updates on menu changes, prices, and so on are also input through a back-office work station. Menu changes, prices, availability, and kitchen preparation can be scheduled based on time of day, day of week, or work station location. The system is designed to interface with most property

Hotel Grayscot

Coffee Shop
Tip Report

Date: April 7, 199x

SERVER No.	SERVER NAME	CASH SALES	CHARGE SALES	CHARGE TIPS
2	John Smith	283.45	79.55	16.00
5	Betty Wills	186.45	110.10	20.50
7	Sally Field	274.60	104.20	18.75
8	Peter Pell	194.80	122.00	24.50
10	Ralph Timms	205.20	90.50	15.00
12	Rolf Thor	188.60	78.60	14.25
15	Jackie Kane	172.20	88.40	16.50
17	Molly Gray	191.10	79.50	13.75
22	Tom Brown	164.80	57.20	12.00
28	Jack Cole	179.50	0	0
33	Jim Wells	130.85	120.70	22.00
	Totals	2171.55	930.75	173.25

Figure 14–7   Tip Report

management systems; in fact, there is a multiple property management system interface capability. The interface provides not only the room charge information to the guest ledger function but also transfers the revenue and city ledger information necessary for the night audit. The system also has a credit card authorization function (optional) which permits the server to swipe the card through the magnetic stripe reader built into the order-entry terminal. The system determines the card type, validity, and expiration date. The credit card vendor is dialed automatically via a modem to obtain an authorization for the amount of the check plus an allowance for a probable gratuity. There is a preauthorization feature where an estimated amount can be authorized prior to the customer's order. However, this step would normally only be used at the customer's request or where there is reason for suspicion on the part of management about the customer's ability to pay, perhaps because of prior problems.

The Vision Series II system, like some of its competitors, provides certain other program options. An electronic time clock capacity allows the server to input the time that he or she starts and finishes work. A detailed report then furnishes the information on each employee required for payroll preparation. This is an attractive feature as it ensures that the employee is actually at his or her station and avoids time lost between punching a time clock and actually starting work. Inventory control is another frequently used option. The mechanics of this function are described in the following section.

All functions are subject to management control with different levels of access necessary to control such things as corrections, voids, entertainment charges, changes to hours worked, and so on.

REPORTS

Operational reports can be printed at any time during the day. This can provide instant sales data, information about workload and performance of individual employees, and product usage. In addition to operational reports produced on an interim basis, four major types of management reports are normally generated: income analysis, employee productivity, inventory control, and cost control.

Income Analysis

Income analysis is the most direct product of the system. It is the breakdown of sales by type (food, liquor, wine, tax, or gratuities) and by outlet, which is then fed into the property management system, either through an interface or by manual input by night audit. It becomes the data source for entry into the general ledger and for the daily revenue report. This information should also be used to provide a daily food and beverage report, which shows daily and cumulative information on food and beverage revenue, numbers of covers, average check, and so on (see Figure 14–8).

Employee Productivity

This report (Figure 14–9) allows management to evaluate the productivity of individual employees with information relative to numbers of covers, average check, total sales, and the ability to promote higher sales with appetizers, desserts, or beverages.

Inventory Control

Since the point-of-sale system specifically identifies each item sold, both food and beverage, this information can provide a full analysis of all inventory consumption.

The ingredients and the quantities used in each recipe are fed into the computer. At the end of a day and on a cumulative basis, a report can be produced in which the ingredients of each food or beverage menu item are multiplied by the number sold to produce the total inventory consumption recorded in the system. This report can be produced in dollars as well as quantities by also feeding the unit costs into the program.

A comparison of the consumption reflected by the report against actual physical consumption (opening inventory plus purchases minus closing inventory) will disclose whether all product usage is being properly recorded and whether or not there are physical inventory shortages.

Obviously, this report has a higher degree of accuracy in the beverage area than in the food area, as actual product mix used in the cooking process is not as exact as in the mixing of drinks. Nevertheless, the same principles apply. Food numbers become particularly useful if the hotel purchases "portion-controlled" entrees.

Portion control is a term used to describe a process where the purveyor prepares the meat or fish in individual portions, in the weight desired, ready for cooking and service to the guest. The number of portions recorded in the point-of-sale system can be matched against the number of portions consumed by the kitchen that day. Portion-controlled products are naturally more expensive than meat or fish pur-

DATE: *March 11, 199___*
DAY: *Tuesday*

Hotel Grayscot

FOOD AND BEVERAGE REPORT

	TODAYS			MONTH TO DATE			YEAR TO DATE		
FOOD REVENUE RESTAURANT	Revenue	Covers	Avg. Check	Revenue	Covers	Avg. Check	Revenue	Covers	Avg. Check
— CAFE —									
Breakfast	522.54	39	13.40	8276.54	828	10.00	29876.65	3208	9.31
Lunch	452.35	28	16.19	1433.86	79	18.15	1492.80	92	16.23
Dinner	855.80	41	20.87	6255.65	322	19.43	9065.45	543	16.70
Room Service	76.85	6	12.81	336.00	38	8.84	762.90	130	5.87
Total Cafe	1908.54	114	16.74	16302.05	1267	12.87	41197.88	3973	10.37
— TAVERN —									
Room Service	86.45	21	4.12	906.54	121	7.49	2406.76	312	7.71
Dinner	522.90	34	15.38	7287.65	386	18.88	28172.45	1976	14.26
Total Tavern	609.35	55	11.08	8194.19	507	16.16	30579.21	2288	13.37
Total Restaurant	2517.89	169	14.90	24496.24	1774	13.81	71777.09	6261	11.46
— BANQUET —									
Banq - Breakfast	62.15	10	6.22	422.89	28	15.10	2076.56	222	9.35
Lunch	0	0		587.55	41	14.33	3208.55	286	11.22
Dinner	220.50	36	8.90	5387.62	182	29.60	13087.66	476	27.50
Other	0	0		1302.76	40	32.57	6134.80	328	18.70
Total Banquet	382.65	46	8.32	7700.82	291	26.46	24507.57	1312	18.68
Total Food	2900.54	215	13.49	32197.06	2065	15.59	96284.66	7573	12.71
BEVERAGE REVENUE									
Cafe	54.20			1244.87			2765.98		
Tavern	240.60			5386.54			21096.54		
Banquet	0.00			3308.72			7634.98		
Total Beverage	294.80			9940.13			31517.50		
TOTAL F&B REVENUE	3195.34			42137.19			127802.16		

Figure 14–8 Daily Food and Beverage Report

Hotel Grayscot

Coffee Shop
Servers' Productivity Report

Date: April 7, 199x

SERVER NO.	SERVER NAME	HRS. WORKED	SALES	NO. OF COVERS	AVG. CHECK	NO. OF APPETIZERS	NO. OF DESSERTS
2	John Smith	5.5	363.00	28	13.96	6	10
5	Betty Wills	4.0	296.55	27	10.98	2	2
7	Sally Field	5.5	378.80	36	10.52	2	1
8	Peter Pell	5.5	316.80	28	11.31	2	5
10	Ralph Timms	5.5	295.70	25	11.82	3	5
12	Rolf Thor	4.0	267.20	27	9.90	0	1
15	Jackie Kane	4.0	260.60	25	10.42	1	1
17	Molly Gray	4.0	270.60	28	9.66	0	2
22	Tom Brown	4.0	222.00	24	9.25	0	0
28	Jack Cole	4.0	179.50	19	9.45	0	1
33	Jim Wells	4.0	251.55	25	10.06	1	1
	Totals	50.0	3102.30	294	10.55	17	29

Highest Average Check—2—John Smith
Most Appetizers   —2—John Smith
Most Desserts   —2—John Smith

Figure 14–9   Servers' Productivity Report

chased in bulk and cut in the kitchen, and a periodic evaluation should be made of the cost of the portion-controlled product versus the prepared product.

Cost Control

The data used to generate the inventory-control information can similarly be used to provide cost-control reports.

The beverage consumption recorded by the point-of-sale system represents theoretical usage (at cost) for inventory purposes. The costs reflected in the reports can be measured against the sales to provide a theoretical or potential cost of sales, which can be compared against the actual cost of sales.

Similarly, a potential cost of sales for food can be generated but again this cost will have a lesser degree of accuracy due to variances in preparation methods, recipe mix, and product yield.

BEVERAGE SYSTEMS

This chapter would not be complete without comments related to systems specifically designed to control beverages.

The shot glass was the first "system" devised to specifically measure the size of a drink and is still frequently used. A more controllable method of measuring is *possipourers,* devices that are locked on the tops of bottles and that control the quantity of the liquor poured.

In the early 1960s, several companies manufactured and marketed systems in which the bottles, usually standing on racks, were equipped with metering devices which not only measured the size of the drink but actually counted the number of drinks poured. The meters are read on a daily basis and a report is prepared showing the opening and closing readings, the number of drinks poured, the selling prices, and a calculation of the potential sales. This system has proved to have several shortcomings. The time required to read the meters and complete the calculations is considerable. In many instances, this resulted in a higher payroll cost. Furthermore, unless every product is metered the sales of the nonmetered items must be rung on a separate key. Obviously, shortages can be hidden if the bartender simply rings a nonmetered sale, even of soft drinks, on the cash register keys assigned to the metered beverages. The earlier versions of these systems also suffered from mechanical problems.

The theory of metering has been improved upon considerably by attaching the meter bottles to point-of-sale systems so that when a drink is poured, not only is it measured, but it triggers the production of a sales check. These systems are quite effective and are widely used in banquets and service bars. Despite efforts to disguise them, their physical appearance usually triggers a negative reaction from the customer. This severely limits their use in bars where they are visible to the customer.

1. List four problems that resulted in the elimination of checkers in restaurants.

2. Briefly describe the various types of reports obtained from a point-of-sale system.

3. Circle T or F to indicate whether the following statements are true or false:

   T   F   **a.** Duplicate orders are commonly referred to as *dupes*.

   T   F   **b.** In a "dupe" system, the kitchen order must be matched up with the check.

   T   F   **c.** In a pre-check system, the drink order is entered by the bartender.

   T   F   **d.** Hand-held terminals send a computer signal directly to the kitchen.

   T   F   **e.** A soft check must be used with prechecking systems.

4. Circle the correct answer to the following statements:

   a. The following is not a goal of precheck systems:
   - (1) To ensure that the product served is exactly what was ordered
   - (2) To ensure that the most profitable menu items are ordered
   - (3) To ensure each item is recorded on a sales check

   b. A server prints a settlement report at the end of the shift in order to:
   - (1) Know which checks are open
   - (2) To verify his or her cash and charges
   - (3) To obtain the credit card authorization codes

   c. When a server prints a "blind" settlement report, he or she cannot:
   - (1) Verify charges
   - (2) Verify tips
   - (3) Verify cash

   d. *Due back* is a term used to describe:
   - (1) Change owed by the server
   - (2) Charges on incorrect credit cards
   - (3) Charge tips owed by the hotel to the server

   e. The point-of-sale system is cleared at the end of the day by running a:
   - (1) "x" report
   - (2) "cd" report
   - (3) "z" report

15 Yields, Potentials, and Other Analyses

In the preceding chapters, the subject of food and beverage costs was addressed. However, many other types of analyses are performed in the food and beverage area for a variety of reasons. Those that find general use throughout the hotel and restaurant industry are reviewed in this chapter.

YIELDS

Yield calculations are made for two primary reasons:

1. To determine the exact cost of a menu item which, in the course of preparation, has required cutting and trimming and has also possibly suffered weight loss in the cooking.
2. To compare the total cost of an item processed in the kitchen against the cost of purchasing the same product already portion cut.

While the first calculation deals only with the food cost element, the second must also take into account the labor and overhead involved in processing.

Yield Percentage

The yield percentage is the basic formula used in the calculation of yields. Simply stated, the formula is as follows:

$$\text{Total Yield Percentage} = \frac{\text{Remaining Weight} \times 100}{\text{Original Weight}}$$

The full test is only completed when the remaining weight is computed after cooking, while the original weight is the weight in the original state in which it was purchased.

Yield tests can be performed at any point during the processing. However, if the tests are going to be used for comparison of two products, it is mandatory that the tests be performed at exactly the same stage of processing. As an example, yields can be calculated to measure the trim, that is, the excess fat which must be removed. In this calculation, the formula is:

$$\text{Trimming Yield} = \frac{\text{Weight after Trimming Fat}}{\text{Weight before Trimming Fat}}$$

Similarly, a boning yield would be calculated as follows:

$$\text{Boning Yield} = \frac{\text{Weight after Bones Are Removed}}{\text{Weight before Bones Are Removed}}$$

The federal government uses yields to grade live cattle. The yield is based on the weight of the major cuts, trimmed and deboned, against the weight of the live animal. Since hotels normally buy primal (primary) cuts rather than live animals, the most common yield calculation performed in a hotel is calculated on a comparison of the usable meat and the primal cut. In addition to beef, the federal government also uses yields to determine grades for lamb and pork. In the case of the latter, the grade is based on a combination of yield from the cuts and the quality. Lamb, like beef, is graded based on usable cuts measured against the live animal.

Calculation of Butcher's Yield Cost

In determining the final cost of beef products, most hotels use a *butcher's yield cost* calculation sheet (Figure 15–1) to record the step-by-step basis:

1. The general information indicates that the product being tested is two legs of veal, choice grade, with a total weight of 35 pounds, purchased from Smith Meats at $3.15 per pound for a total cost of $110.25.
2. The breakdown indicates the byproducts obtained—bones, stew fat, and stew meat—and the final product—veal cutlets.
3. The weight column indicates the breakdown of the total weight by product.
4. The ratio column indicates the relative weight of each product, the yield on the end product, veal cutlets, being 45.7 percent.
5. The value per pound column shows the relative values assigned to each byproduct.
6. The total value column shows the total value of the byproducts; the remaining cost of $102.80 is the true cost of the cutlets.
7. This cost then breaks down to $6.42 per pound or 40 cents per ounce.
8. In order to obtain the total cost, four hours of labor at $6 per hour for a total of $24 must be added to the product cost of $102.80.
9. The total cost of $126.80 for 16 pounds of cutlets is $7.92 per pound.

A final step in this evaluation would be to cook the cutlets and cut them to portion size. (In the case of veal cutlets, they would probably be precut to portion size, but in the case of roasts, the portioning would be done after cooking.) The final portion

cost is arrived at by dividing the total cost of the end product by the number of portions obtained. A ratio known as the *portion cost factor* is arrived at as follows:

$$\text{Portion Cost Factor} = \frac{\text{Portion Cost}}{\text{Supplier's Price per Pound}}$$

Using this factor, the new portion cost can quickly be calculated any time the supplier's price changes.

The final portion cost can also be compared to the cost of purchasing precut portions. In making this comparison, it is important to remember that the butchering process results in certain indirect overhead costs (e.g., cutting utensils, clean up, cost of space required, etc.) which do not occur when precut portions are used. However, the end quality must also be evaluated.

Poultry and Fish

Yield calculations are also used to evaluate poultry with emphasis on turkey rather than chicken. Since the aging process is not used in preparing poultry, yields are obtained in relation to various stages of processing: cutting, deboning, and cooking. In general, the better yields are obtained on the medium-sized birds. While the unused parts (e.g., the head) constitute too large a percentage of the small birds, the very large birds tend to have excessive bone and fat. Turkey produces a lean meat yield of over 60 percent, while the same evaluation on chicken results in a yield of under 50 percent.

Similarly, yield calculations can be made on fish. Since, however, fish is not subject to federal grading standards, there is very little effective use of yield calculations in this area.

Produce

Yield calculations are also used to evaluate fresh and canned vegetables. Aging and packing procedures are the primary factors impacting yields of fresh produce, while the degree to which the product has been drained impacts canned products. The Department of Agriculture publishes a book of standards for both these areas.

Frozen Food

While the yield on frozen products is very high, the amount of glazing can impact the results. Glazing involves covering the vegetables with a butter and sugar coating which melts in the cooking process.

POTENTIALS

The development of point-of-sale systems has greatly simplified the calculation of potentials, but the concept is one of the oldest food and beverage control procedures. It is important to understand that there is a basic difference in the approach to beverage potentials and food potentials. Beverage potentials attempt to arrive at the expected sales for a day, while food potentials take the actual sales and attempt to arrive at the poten-

BUTCHER'S YIELD COST

Product __Leg of Veal__ Grade __Choice__ Date __3/18/9X__

Number __2__ Weight __35__ Lbs. ____ Ozs. Specification ____

Item Cost __$110.25__ At __$3.15__ Per __lb.__ Supplier __Smith Meats, Albany__

BREAKDOWN	Weight		Ratio To Total Weight	Value Per Lb.	Total Value	Cost Of	
	Lb.	Oz..				Lb.	Oz..
Bones	8	0	22.8	.10	$0.80		
Stew Fat	6	4	17.9	–	–		
Stew Meat	4	12	13.6	1.40	6.65		
Veal Cutlets	16	0	45.7		102.80	6.42	.40
TOTAL			100%	110.25			

LABOR COST: No. Hours Spent __4__ X $ __6__

FINISHED PRODUCT COST: Cost of Food $ __102.80__ + (Labor) $ __24.00__ = $ __126.80__

COST PER LB. (Including Labor) = $ __7.92__

I.M. Butcher
Signed

Figure 15–1 Calculation of Butcher's Yield Cost

tial cost. Simply stated, beverage potentials are calculated on a sales basis, while food potentials are calculated on a cost basis.

Beverage Potentials

Beverage potentials (Figure 15–2) are calculated by taking the beverage consumption for a day and multiplying it by the selling price to arrive at a figure for potential sales which then can be compared to the actual sales. The calculation is simplified greatly if par stocks are maintained for each bar. When the same level of inventory is kept in the

Hotel: _Grayscot_	Outlet: _Lounge_			Date: _3/21/9-_		Completed By: _J. Smith_		
Item	Brand	Quantity	Cost Price	Total Cost	Selling Price	Potential Sales	Potential Cost %
Vodka	Bar	11	8.65	95.15	35.00	385.00	24.7
Gin	Bar	5	6.20	31.00	35.00	175.00	17.7
Rum	Bar	3	5.10	15.10	35.00	105.00	14.9
Scotch	Bar	6	9.40	58.40	40.00	240.00	24.3
Scotch	B&W	1	12.10	12.10	55.00	55.00	22.0
Scotch	Dewars	2	11.30	22.60	55.00	110.00	20.5

Figure 15–2 Daily Potential Beverage Sales Calculation

bar on a daily basis, the requisition written, after the end of business, to replenish the stock equals the beverage consumption for that day. While this is not a hundred percent correct because of part bottles, this does not create a significant degree of error. Over 90 percent of a bar's sales are composed of beverages of which several bottles are consumed each day. Additionally, the part bottle factor tends to level itself out: a bottle of one liquor is finished one day and another brand on the following day. If the bar stock changes on a daily basis, it is necessary to take an inventory each day so that the increases and decreases can be factored in to arrive at the consumption. Since this is time consuming, the potentials usually become a weekly or monthly comparison to actuals. However, for several reasons discussed in preceding chapters, maintaining a par stock for each bar is a strongly recommended practice.

The conversion of the requisition to the sales equivalent is usually done by the food and beverage controller at the same time that a calculation of consumption is made on a cost basis. The consumption is stated in terms of full bottles and where part bottles are involved in the calculation, tenths of a bottle. (Tenths is the normal manner in which consumption or inventory of part bottles is stated.) The selling price of a bottle can be calculated by multiplying the individual drink price by the number of drinks that can be obtained from a bottle. As an example, Figure 15–2 reveals that 11 bottles of bar vodka were consumed at a cost of $8.65 each. One shot of vodka in a drink measures 1 1/4 ounces and sells for $1.75. Since the bottle contains 25.6 ounces, about 20

drinks are obtained from a bottle. Multiplying 20 times $1.75, we get the selling price of $35 for a bottle for a potential sales for the 11 bottles of $385 (11 × $35).

Mixed cocktails will cause variances if the selling price is not purely a reflection of the combined selling prices of the alcoholic ingredients. The impact of these variances can be avoided by using specific brands only for the cocktails and not for regular drinks or by premixing the more popular cocktails and issuing them to the bars on a premixed basis. Overages will be created if additional charges are made for certain nonalcohol mixes, such as orange juice, on which no potential sales value has been calculated. Additionally, the sale of a material amount of straight soft drinks also results in overages unless the bottled product is used for such sales while soda guns are used for mixes with alcoholic beverages. In order to avoid distortions, it is essential to record sales for all entertainment or promotion giveaways. (The sales can then be reversed as part of the night audit house account procedure).

Food Potentials

As previously mentioned, food potentials are calculated at cost. It is necessary, therefore, to analyze the sales for the day or period by menu item. Prior to the advent of sophisticated point-of-sale systems, this was done by abstracting the checks, that is, the cashier or host/hostess would go through the checks manually and tabulate the quantity sold of each menu item. In most hotels and restaurants, these numbers can now be obtained from an end-of-day printout of the point-of-sale system readings. While previously it was then necessary to multiply the cost of each item by the quantity sold, this information is now obtained from the point-of-sale system as a byproduct of the inventory control function described in the preceding chapter. While calculated costs are used for the appetizers, soups, entrees, and desserts, fixed estimates (standard costs) are used for such items as vegetables, bread, butter, coffee, or tea.

A total potential cost can then be determined by adding the individual costs of each item. The potential is then compared against the total actual cost of food consumed by the kitchen that day, that is, the total cost of storeroom issues and direct purchases.

It is necessary to make adjustments for any food consumed for which there is no potential revenue—in particular any food used for employee meals or issued to the bars.

OTHER ANALYSES

Several other food and beverage analyses are used as part of the control process. While many such analyses are customized to suit a specific property, the following are some of the more common in use.

Menu Profitability Analysis

The procedure of analyzing sales by menu item can also be used to measure the profitability of the sales mix. The potential cost of the restaurant's sales can be matched against the actual sales to obtain a cost percentage. On selected dates over a period of

time, the selling price of menu items can be changed, which produces a new cost percentage and new sales volume numbers.

While an increase or decrease in the selling price of an item will obviously change the cost percentage, the more sophisticated information to be obtained is the impact of the changed prices on customers' menu selections. Careful study of these changes can permit the restaurant to set prices for each item to deliver the optimum profitability from the mixture of item cost and customer selection.

Cost Index Utilization

In the discussion on yields, reference was made to the use of the portion cost factor to recalculate item costs in the event of a price change. This theory can be extended to deveop an easily adjustable cost index for the main items on the menu.

The initial step is to develop a cost index (Figure 15–3) based on the cost and selling price of one serving of each menu item. In the same manner as described in the preceding section on menu profitability, the quantity column in the index can be adjusted daily based on actual menu selections to provide a daily overall potential cost.

The final step is to use the portion cost factor to interrelate the unit cost column to actual purchase price paid to the vendor so that the effect of a change in the vendor's price is immediately reflected in the potential cost percentage on a daily basis.

Popularity Index

Another use of an analysis of daily sales by menu item is the preparation of a popularity index. Using the numbers in Figure 15–3 for main-course items only, the total num-

| Item | Quantity Sold | New Daily Cost | | Prior Daily Cost | | Actual Sales | Cost % | |
		Per Unit	Total	Per Unit	Total		New	Prior
Steak	36	4.80	172.80	4.52	162.72	396.00	43.6	41.1
Fish	11	2.10	23.10	2.10	23.00	77.00	30.0	29.9
Lobster	12	4.00	48.00	4.00	48.00	144.00	33.3	33.3
Chicken	8	1.75	14.00	1.70	13.60	48.00	29.2	28.3
Pasta	15	1.30	19.50	1.30	19.50	75.00	26.0	26.0
Omelette	4	1.50	6.00	1.50	6.00	20.00	30.0	30.0
Soup	9	0.50	4.50	0.50	4.50	13.50	33.3	33.3
Pie	12	0.60	7.20	0.55	6.60	24.00	30.0	27.5
Ice Cream	20	0.40	8.00	0.40	8.00	40.00	20.0	20.0
Coffee	72	0.15	10.80	0.15	10.80	72.00	15.0	15.0
TOTAL	199	—	313.90	—	302.72	909.50	34.5	33.3

Hotel: Hotel Grayscot MENU COST INDEX Date: 3/22/9_

Figure 15–3   Menu Cost Index

ber of entrées sold was 86 of which 36 were steaks. Using those numbers as a basis for a popularity index, the index number for steaks is 0.418, or 36 divided by 86.

However, a proper index should be calculated based on the numbers for a test period of one to two weeks rather than one day. Also, it is valuable to develop indexes for each day of the week and seasonal indexes throughout the year. The primary purposes of a popularity index are forecasting and budgeting. Variances from the index should be documented to identify changing patterns in customer preference as well as the impact of selling price changes.

Average Check Analysis

An analysis of the average check on a daily basis and its relationship to cost may also be of value in identifying trends and in making decisions relative to selling price or menu changes.

Daily Portion Control Report

Earlier in the chapter, reference was made to the option of purchasing precut portions. The merits of using portion-controlled cuts are wasted if a proper audit procedure is not conducted using a daily portion control report. This report (Figure 15–4) is a simple reconciliation of the purchases and sales of the portion-cut items. All differences that show a recurring pattern should be investigated in depth.

Inventory Turnover

Establishing standards for inventory turnover will result in optimum use of storage space, increased security, and control over the amount of funds tied up in inventories.

Inventory turnover is the average time period during which inventories on hand are consumed. Because of the limits on the varying useful life of food items, the overall food inventory should turn over at least twice per month. This is a combination of a short life on produce and bakery and dairy products and a longer life on other items.

The speed with which the beverage inventory turns over is more a function of storage space. Provided space is available, most items should turn over on a once-per-month basis. Beer is ordered more frequently and, therefore, will have a higher turnover rate, but a large wine inventory, particularly of vintage wines, can materially reduce the overall turnover rate.

A lower than average turnover in food could be indicative of dead stock, possibly no longer usable because of age or menu changes. On the other hand, it may simply indicate that too much money is tied up in inventory.

Special buys in liquor because of volume discounts or impending price increases may justify carrying a larger than normal beverage inventory with a resultant low turnover. However, a low beverage turnover is frequently due to stocking wines that are no longer on the wine list; these should be used up in banquet.

Inventory turnover can be calculated on a monthly basis using the following calculation: Divide cost of sales by average inventory (opening inventory plus closing inventory divided by 2).

Hotel Grayscot	DAILY PORTION CONTROL REPORT						DATE 3/18/9—
ITEM	Opening Inventory	Purchased	Closing Inventory	Quantity Used	Quantity Sold	Difference	Comment
Filet mignon 6 oz.	16	24	10	30	29	-1	Returned by guest
Filet mignon 8 oz.	18	12	5	25	24	-1	Overcooked
New York Strip 12 oz.	16	36	8	44	44		
Chicken cordon bleu	12	12	10	14	14		

Figure 15–4 Daily Portion Control Report

Assume cost of food sold for July to be $92,500 with an opening inventory of $28,300 and a closing inventory of $31,700. Then, the turnover is:

$$\frac{92,500}{28,300 + 31,700/2} \quad = \quad \frac{92,500}{30,000} \quad = \quad 3.083$$

Converted to an average number of days that inventory is held, the calculation is:

$$\frac{31 \text{ days}}{3.083} \quad = \quad 10.05 \text{ days}$$

However, it is desirable to set turnover standards for various types of inventories. Acceptable standards are shown in Figure 15–5.

Labor Cost Analysis

The use of daily labor reports to evaluate restaurant and kitchen productivity is discussed in detail in Chapter 6.

Rental and Purchase Comparisons

Although the decision as to whether to buy or lease linen and/or uniforms is usually made before the hotel opens, many hotels make a periodic operating analysis.

To function with the highest level of efficiency, a hotel laundry should be integrated into the original design and not added on at a later date. Since the leasing concept embodies laundering and leasing as a combined service, the construction of a laundry normally ends any consideration thereof. However, the reverse is not necessarily true; many hotels that originally use a linen service ultimately make the decision

Inventory Turnover Standards as at March 21, 199x		
FOOD	DAYS AVAILABLE	MONTHLY TURNOVER
Dry goods	24	1.2
Bakery	4	7.0
Dairy & eggs	4	7.0
Fresh produce	4	7.0
Frozen fruits & vegetables	12	2.3
Meats	21	1.3
Prepared, processed items	12	2.3
Seafood	21	1.3
BEVERAGE		
Cordials, liqueurs	28	1.0
Brandy, cognacs	28	1.0
Port Wine, sherries	28	1.0
Appetizer Wine, vermouth	28	1.0
Red, White, & Rosé Wines	21	1.3
Sparkling Wines & Champagnes	21	1.3
Whiskey, Gin, Vodka, & Rum	28	1.0
Soft Drinks	10	2.8
Beer	7	4.0

Figure 15–5   Inventory Turnover Standards

to add a laundry. However, a laundry built during the overall construction is not only cheaper but usually more functional.

The analysis itself should be done for a period of one year in the following manner:

1. Capital cost of laundry—construction and equipment divided by 10 (based on average 10-year life of equipment),

   plus

   Total cost of linen divided by average number of months of use life (for most items 1 to 3 years) multiplied by 12 equals annual linen cost,

   plus

   Annual operating cost of laundry after crediting income from guest laundry, equals

   Total Annual Cost if linen is owned compared to:

2. Total cost of using an outside linen service for one year.

It is important to note that when a hotel owns the linen the quality and, therefore, the customer perception is higher.

Breakage Analysis

Every hotel should inventory the china, glassware, and silver twice per year and prepare a loss/breakage analysis on each item.

The calculation is very simple; for example,

Beginning inventory	420 cups
Purchases	200 cups
	620 cups
Less: Closing inventory	370 cups
Loss/Breakage	250 cups

Breakage rate = 250 divided by 6 months =
    41.6 per month (actually very low)

Negative results in this analysis should prompt hotels to consider using china or glass less susceptible to breakage.

Equipment Analysis

When considering purchase alternatives for new equipment, it is important to prepare a cost analysis for comparison purposes. The following is a recommended format for such an analysis using a 10-year useful life for a piece of kitchen equipment.

Original cost of broiler	$12,700
Life	10 years
Costs to train staff on usage	$ 1,350
Annual operating costs	
Payroll to operate	$ 6,000
Parts and maintenance	720
Total annual costs	$ 6,720

Year 1 Cost—1/10 of original cost	$ 1,270
Training	1,350
Annual operating	6,720
Total	$ 9,340
Years 2–10 Annual Cost	
1/10 of original cost	1,270
Annual operating	6,720
Total	$ 7,990
Total 10-year cost	
Year 1	$ 9,340
Year 2–10 9 × 7,990	71,910
Total	$81,250
Annualized cost	$ 8,125

This final number should be compared to the annual cost of the other option.

1. Complete a butcher's yield cost calculation and arrive at a cost per pound based on the following information:
   a. Three striploins weighing a total of 77 pounds are purchased at a price of $3.20 per pound.
   b. The striploins are deboned and trimmed resulting in the following byproducts:
      9 pounds of bone valued at 10 cents per pound
      3 pounds of sirloin tips for stroganoff valued at $1.80 per pound
      5½ pounds of stew beef valued at $1.35 per pound
   c. Labor cost is 2½ hours at $7.50 per hour.

2. A bar orders six bottles of gin at $5.35 per bottle. Each bottle yields 20 drinks selling at $2.25 per drink. What is the potential cost percentage on the gin?

3. Circle T or F to indicate whether the following statements are true or false:
   T F a. A yield percentage is calculated by dividing the remaining weight by the original weight and multiplying by 100.
   T F b. Chicken produces a higher lean meat yield than turkey.
   T F c. The use of par stocks simplifies calculations of daily potentials.
   T F d. Mixed cocktails can cause variances in potential calculations.
   T F e. Using a food cost index can speed up the analysis of the impact of an increase in a vendor's price.
   T F f. Whether to buy or lease linen is primarily a preopening decision.
   T F g. Beverage inventories turn over more frequently than food inventories.
   T F h. China, glassware, and silver should be inventoried on a monthly basis.

4. Circle the correct answer to the following statements:
   a. The federal government uses quality as well as yield in grading:
      (1) Lamb
      (2) Beef
      (3) Pork
   b. Federal grading standards are not used for:
      (1) Poultry
      (2) Fish
      (3) Canned vegetables
   c. Beverage potentials are calculated on a:
      (1) Sales price basis
      (2) Cost basis
      (3) Quality basis
   d. The term *abstracting checks* means:
      (1) Tabulating by hand the quantity of each item sold
      (2) Listing the amount of each check
      (3) Pulling out the house entertainment checks

e. If cost of food sold is $65,000 and the average of the opening and closing inventories is $32,500, the inventory turnover for the month is:

(1) 0.5

(2) 21,125

(3) 2.0

16 Telephone and Other Sources of Income

TELEPHONE

Historically, telephone service, although an operated department, could not be deemed a "profit center." Instead, it was regarded as a department which must, of necessity, be operated at a loss in order to service the guests. However, in the 1970s and early 1980s, the federal and state governments made sweeping changes in the laws pertaining to telephone service. These changes resulted in the telephone department becoming a true profit center.

Call Accounting Systems

As a direct result of the various rulings, several companies started marketing call accounting systems. While the majority of the companies had previous involvement in the telephone field, several new companies were also active in the call accounting market. The new companies were not, however, necessarily at a disadvantage because a call accounting system is not telephone equipment.

Properly defined, a call accounting system is a time-measuring machine which has the ability not only to measure the length of a telephone call but also to recognize the number that is called. Each area code has a specific preprogrammed rate per minute. The computer function in the system then multiplies the rate per minute by the measured length of the call to arrive at a specific charge for the call. The systems are usually programmed to charge fixed amounts for local calls and 800 number calls rather than compute a charge based on the length of the call. The system is linked to a printer that will print out the room numbers, number called, and the charge immediately, at specific intervals (usually every 30 minutes), or only as requested. Interfaces to property management systems facilitate direct posting of the charge to the guest folio while at the same time storing the information for use by the night auditors. Practically all systems have a limited storage capacity requiring purging of all information

on guest-room calls on a daily basis. A summary printout (see Figure 16–1) at the end of the day provides a detailed listing of calls, total revenue (for audit purposes), and the actual cost of the calls. The charges are based on the programmed rates that produce the desired markup for the hotel. It is customary to make fixed charges for local calls ($.50 to $1) and 800-number calls ($.75 to $1.50). The justification for these charges is that even though hotels are not charged for these calls, they are providing the use of their equipment for which they are entitled to some reimbursement. It is important that the rates be revised whenever telephone rates change.

The more sophisticated systems also provide a control over administrative calls. Calling codes are assigned either to individuals or to extensions and the administrative calls are recorded in the same manner as guest-room calls. Such systems usually have the ability to print out a listing of calls by guest-room number and administrative code. Administrative calls print out the cost of the call rather than a marked up amount. Furthermore, while most systems, due to limited capacity, store guest-room calls for only 24 hours, many store administrative calls for a week. This permits the printing of the cost of administrative calls by assigned code on a weekly basis. This printout can then be used as a basis for an accounting entry charging telephone expense in each department and crediting the cost of long-distance and local calls.

In recent years, telecommunications fraud has become a major problem. Because the hotel systems provide automatic access to long-distance service from the guest

Hotel Grayscot

September 19, 199X

Time	City Called	State	Number Called	Length	Charge
8:02	Albuquerque	NM	505-428-7113	3:10	$4.07
8:17	New York City	NY	212-759-1103	2:10	2.00
8:28	Baltimore	MD	800-629-1714	3:20	1.00
9:17	Bennington		442-8075	1:10	0.50
9:19	Bennington		442-8163	2:10	0.50
9:39	Miami	FL	305-628-7133	2:20	3.13
10:06	New York	NY	212-754-2116	4:60	4.05
10:22	San Francisco	CA	707-629-2108	3:80	5.22
11:11	Chicago	IL	312-725-6408	6:40	8.08
11:13	Bennington		447-9023	4:10	0.50
11:22	Toronto	ON	519-813-7482	3:30	5.15
11:29	N. Bennington		442-6218	3:20	0.50
11:51	Boston	MA	617-924-8226	4:20	3.80
12:03	St. Louis	MO	314-908-7262	5:30	7.60
12:17	New York City	NY	212-754-2116	4:20	3.75
12:23	Hartford	CT	203-625-8142	6:30	4.80
12:29	Bennington		442-7182	1:20	0.50

Figure 16–1   Call Accounting Printout

rooms, they have been a major target of telephone service thieves. This has necessitated the restricting of access from the guest rooms to certain areas. The ability of telephone system maintenance service companies to dial into a hotel's system from a remote location has also resulted in losses. By duplicating the maintenance company's method of access, a thief can obtain full access to the hotel's system and use it as a relay for long-distance calls. Problems have also occurred because controls built into the normal service are not effective when heavy traffic results in calls being transferred to an overflow provider.

The outshoot of these problems is that hotels audit their telephone bills in depth to the point of matching all calls over a specified amount (e.g., $15) against guest records.

STORES AND CONCESSIONS

Store rentals and income from concessions are the most common form of other income in the hotel industry. In certain parts of the world (e.g., Hong Kong), the rental income from the stores can sometimes surpass, on a net basis, the income from any other department in the hotel. Leases are executed for varying periods of time, usually at least two years, and the rents are determined in three basic formats.

Fixed rental.   This consists of fixed monthly payments for the full term of the lease. It is best suited for a tenant whose gross receipts are difficult to verify or whose potential volume is limited because of the nature of the business or the size of the space to be occupied. Often included in this category are checkroom concessionaires and individual proprietors operating small newsstands with a very limited selling area in or off the main lobby. This type of lease is also used for any office spaces available in the hotel and for lobby display cases.

Minimum rental plus a percentage of the gross receipts over a specified amount.   Most store tenants are offered this type of rental agreement. If proper records are kept, enabling the hotel controller to verify the gross receipts with reasonable accuracy, then it is the best type of arrangement for both parties. The tenants, because the minimum rental is usually low, can function properly and stay solvent even during a protracted period of poor sales. When business is good and the gross revenue high, they can easily afford the additional rent. The hotel operators benefit because they are ensured of a steady, dependable income, since the minimum rentals are not subject to fluctuations and the possibility of tenant failures is lessened.

Straight percentage of the gross sales.   This type of rental agreement is usually offered only to concessionaires, such as the valet, whose gross receipts are entirely derived from the guests and charged on their bills. This ensures complete control of the gross receipts by the hotel's accounting staff. Where the hotel does not provide in-house facilities, a similar percentage agreement should be negotiated with outside valets, car-rental agencies, florists, and the like.

CONTROL OF REVENUE

The tenants and concessionaires routinely permit guests to charge their purchases or fees for services to their hotel bills. This is expected, and the leases should provide for it. The hotel operators must agree to accept the charges and, subject to some restrictions, reimburse the tenants in full for them. The most common restriction is the amount they will accept without prior credit approval.

These charges, like all other charges incurred by the guests, are then processed through the hotel's normal accounting and collection system, at no cost to the tenants or concessionaires. But problems can and do arise. Guests will occasionally dispute the charges, often as they are checking out and there is no time to investigate the complaints. The hotel will incur collection expenses over and above their employees' salaries and other normal operating expenses. They may have to pay commissions to credit card companies, collection agencies, or attorneys and pay legal fees and court costs for any lawsuits. Some guest accounts will not be paid at all and will have to be written off as bad debts. Serious disputes between tenants and the hotel executives cannot be avoided unless agreement is reached in the initial negotiations as to the procedures to be followed, financial responsibility for any additional expenses or losses is clearly established, and the agreement is incorporated in the leases. Such disputes will unquestionably adversely affect guest relations and future earnings of both parties.

The problems and some available options follow. Solutions can be reached only in direct negotiations between the two parties.

Disputes over Charges

Guest disputes of any charge should, if time permits, be referred to the credit or assistant managers for whatever action is deemed necessary. An immediate settlement of these questions is the only way to satisfy the guests and keep their good-will. However, few guests have the time at checkout to wait for their complaints to be investigated. Often, the front-office cashiers have no alternative but to deduct the amount of the disputed charge from the total due and have the guest settle the remaining net balance. The disputed amount is left as an open balance on the bill, transferred to city ledger, and investigated on the following day by the clerk in the accounting department.

Any disputes involving tenant or concessionaire charges must obviously be reviewed with them. At this point, guidelines for adjustments and collections are needed. Disputes involving the amount charged are relatively simple to settle and can be handled by the investigation clerks as part of their daily routine. But if a guest refuses to pay the original or adjusted amount, certified as being correct by the tenant or concessionaire, special collection efforts are called for. Who determines if they are worth making, who absorbs any unusual expenses, and who takes the loss if they are deemed to be uncollectible? These questions must be settled as part of the original agreement.

Credit Cards

A substantial number of guests settle their bills at departure by charging the total amount due on an acceptable credit card. Obviously, many of these accounts include charges from a tenant or concessionaire. The credit card company's discount is based

on the total charges submitted. Does the hotel absorb the total expense, or does it charge the tenants and concessionaires their prorated share?

Sound credit procedures mandate that all guest accounts that are unpaid after a specified period be turned over to a collection agency or attorney for collection, usually for a fee consisting of a percentage of the amount collected. Again, these amounts will undoubtedly include some charges by the tenants and concessionaires. Who is responsible for the collection fees on these charges? The same question arises in cases where legal action is required, but it is further complicated by the fact that court costs and legal fees are sometimes incurred for lawsuits that do not recover the amount due. Finally, the same problem exists on accounts that, after all collection efforts have failed, are deemed to be uncollectible and are written off as bad debts.

Solutions are difficult after the fact. Hotel operators would be well advised to discuss these problems with all prospective tenants, resolve them, and include the agreements in the leases.

Audit of Gross Income

Of the three types of rental agreements described earlier, only the second, calling for a minimum rental plus a percentage, requires an audit of gross income. This function is the responsibility of the hotel controller. However, the leases should clearly outline the obligations of the tenants regarding reporting requirements, records to be kept, hours they must be available to the hotel's accounting staff, and so on. Finally, the leases should be very specific as to the exact method of calculating the additional rent. Unfortunately, too many are not, creating another area of potential disagreement between the two parties.

These poorly worded leases call for a minimum rental, payable monthly, and a percentage of the gross sales over a specified annual amount. Tenants often interpret such a clause to mean that the additional rent is due only at the end of each year. Management, on the other hand, usually insists on a monthly calculation, based on one-twelfth of the gross sales figures called for in the leases. Some regard each month's calculations as final. Others accumulate the monthly sales figures, calculate the exact additional rent due at the end of the year, and make an adjustment at that time for any difference between the actual amount and the total paid to date. Serious disputes have arisen because of these different interpretations.

Reporting Requirements Vary

Most leases obligate the tenants to report their gross sales monthly. In addition, they are usually required to submit a statement from a certified public accountant, at least once a year, of the audited gross receipts.

Hotel controllers can verify the reported gross income only through an audit of the tenant's books and records. Cash-register readings and available tapes should be checked against the daily sales as entered in the sales journal. If sales are subject to a sales tax, the records, forms, and returns required by the state, city, or local authorities should be examined during the audit. The gross sales on the returns should be compared with the reported amount, and payment of the tax called for on the return should

be confirmed by the canceled checks. However, the products they offer—prescriptions, drugs, and flowers—are often ordered by the guests by telephone or through a member of the hotel's staff. These and other charge sales for items personally picked by the guests can at least give the hotel controller an indication of what the total commissionable sales should be.

GUEST LAUNDRY AND VALET

Most hotels regard guest laundry as a necessary service to be provided rather than a profit center. In fact, many hotels that have in-house laundries will nevertheless send the guest laundry and dry cleaning to an outside supplier. During peak occupancies, there is usually heavy pressure on in-house laundries to service both housekeeping and the food and beverage department. This is particularly true in convention hotels where the heavy banquet volume places a strong but uneven demand on the laundry. On such occasions, the last thing the laundry manager wants to deal with is guest laundry.

Furthermore, both guest laundry and dry cleaning require specialized equipment. Hotels only use this equipment to clean uniforms, which does justify the investment required. A more logical approach is to concession out both the guest laundry and the dry cleaning to a local laundry service.

When guest laundry and dry cleaning are handled by an outside service, the hotel usually receives a commission (10–15%) of the charges to the guest. The concessionaire is responsible for printing the laundry and valet slips which are placed in the guest rooms and completed by the guest. When the laundry and dry cleaning is returned to the hotel, one of two procedures is normally followed. (1) The outside laundry returns one copy of the slip attached to the laundry and the second copies are grouped and totaled so that they can be used as a basis to post the charges to the guest's account. (2) Instead of the second copy, a control list showing room number and charge is provided to the hotel to be used for posting. When the hotel pays the billing from the laundry, it automatically deducts the commission and credits it to a concession revenue account. When the hotel actually does the laundry in house, the most correct accounting procedure would be to establish a guest laundry department, crediting the revenue thereto and charging it with the applicable labor and supplies. Since, however, determining those costs is difficult, a common approach is to credit all income against laundry costs. The net laundry cost is then allocated as laundry expense to rooms, food and beverage, and any other departments using linen.

GARAGE

When faced with competition from motor hotels, many of the older city hotels elected to include a garage in their buildings. They offered the convenience of in-house parking either free to their guests or at a nightly charge. While the number of hotels offering free parking has increased (in fact some downtown hotels with no garage provide their guests with free parking in a nearby garage), most also, except during peak occupancy, offer parking to the general public at the prevailing rates.

Controlling garage revenue is difficult at all times. In a motor hotel, it is further complicated by the need to differentiate between the guests' cars, parked free, and those of the paying public. (Where a hotel garage is operated by an outside firm, the firm will thoroughly check the daily revenue as part of its normal operating procedure, but this does not relieve the hotel controller from the responsibility of checking all revenue generated in any department of the hotel.)

Controlling the income properly requires two separate and entirely different procedures: (1) the verification of revenue and (2) an actual inspection of the parked cars. Revenue (cash sales and charges) is shown on the garage cashier's daily report. This report is merely a listing, in numerical sequence, of all issued and outstanding tickets with the amount charged or collected that day next to each ticket. A garage ticket should be printed in at least three parts: one for the guest, another for the car, and the third filed in numerical order in a rack at the cashier's station. All three parts should be time-stamped to indicate when the car was brought in. The guest's and rack's segments should be stamped when the car is taken out. In addition, the garage attendant should record, on the back of the rack portion of the ticket, the license number, color and make, and location of the parked car. For a hotel guest, the name and room number should also be recorded.

The garage tickets are issued in numerical sequence, but they can only be canceled by a second time stamp when the guests check out. To assist the accounting clerks in controlling the tickets, garage cashiers are usually required to list first on a tally sheet the unused tickets from prior days, and then the tickets issued on that day. Any checkouts from prior days are indicated by entering the amount charged or designated code next to the ticket number.

Except where free parking is offered, the clerks can only check the amount charged by calculating, on as many tickets as possible each day, the total number of hours the cars were parked. Where free parking is offered, additional steps must be taken. Hotel guests should be required to present their garage tickets to the front-office cashiers for validation when they check out. The cashiers should time-stamp the tickets, enter the room number, and initial each one. Time-stamping and initialing the ticket serves a dual purpose: first, to authorize the garage attendants to release the car without a charge; and second, to prevent overtime parking by the guest.

The regulations in most motor hotels call for a charge to be assessed if guests do not remove their cars within a specified time after checking out, or after a certain hour of the day. All cars parked in the garage, or, on a more frequent test-check basis, the cars parked on a particular floor or section of the garage, should be checked. All cars inspected should be ticketed, and the ticket time-stamped. Particular notice should be taken of the date stamped on the ticket, and any car parked for a period of more than, say, three days, or a week, should be noted. The checker should record the ticket number, license number, make, and color of the car and turn this information over to the garage manager or the chief of security for investigation. As a final test, this information on at least 25 percent of the cars inspected, should be recorded and compared with the entries on the tickets filed in the cashier's racks.

Garage operations, unfortunately, lend themselves to employee theft. Frequent surprise inspections are the only tool available to minimize these losses.

Commission on Parking

In order to compete for the business generated by the traveling public, hotels without an in-house garage must make some arrangements for parking cars. This usually takes the form of an agreement with the operators of a nearby garage or parking lot for the needed parking spaces. Most of these agreements require the guests to pay for parking their cars, with the hotel receiving a percentage of the total charges as a commission. The normal procedure is for the guest to leave the car with the doorman who then calls the garage to send one of its employees to pick up the car and, when desired by the guest, to deliver it to the hotel.

Parking fees are usually charged to the guests' accounts. Depending on the agreement, they can be posted on the bill daily or at departure. For daily posting, a garage attendant must deliver a list of the guest cars in the garage to the front-office cashiers or night auditors each night. The list should show the room numbers, guest names, and amount due, which, in effect, would be the daily rate. Otherwise, the parking charge for the full stay can be brought over at checkout by the garage attendants delivering the cars.

Likewise, reimbursements for the parking fees can be made in one of two ways:

1. Payment in full may be given to the garage attendants delivering the charges, in which case the front-office cashiers treat each transaction as a paid-out and post them as such on the guest bill. Periodically, the hotel receives payment for the commission due.

2. The garage charges are accumulated for a specified period, and payment for the net amount due, total charges less commission, is sent to the garage operator.

Control and verification of the commissions due obviously present no problems. The hotel controllers need only keep a worksheet listing the total daily charges or paid-outs. Occasionally a guest will insist on getting his or her own car from the garage and paying the parking charge directly to the garage cashier. However, these cash payments are so few that most hotels will accept the figures for cash receipts submitted to them by the garage operators.

Parking charges for guest cars can be an expense rather than a substantial commission income. As noted, some hotels offer free parking to their guests even though they have no in-house garage. Again, an agreement for the needed spaces must be negotiated with the operator of a garage or parking lot. The procedures for parking cars are the same, except that the hotel assumes the responsibility for paying the charges, usually at a special rate.

SALE OF USED FURNITURE AND EQUIPMENT

Periodically, hotels decide to sell certain used furniture or equipment. Usually, this results from a room or restaurant renovation program, but in the case of glassware or china it may result in the sale of odd pieces due to a change in design.

Such sales are most successful when the unneeded items are accumulated until there is enough volume to justify advertising the event. Good employee relationships usually dictate that the sale be restricted to employees on the first day and then opened to the public. In either case, the control procedure is the same. Potential customers identify the items they wish to buy and then go to a cashier who collects the money and writes a receipt in duplicate. One copy is given to the purchaser who shows the receipt to the guard at the door when taking the item out, while the other copy is retained by the cashier and used to balance the day's receipts.

All sales should be on a cash-and-carry basis. At the end of the sale, any items left should be sold to used furniture and equipment dealers for whatever price they offer. Items that simply can't be sold should be given away for charitable purposes. The proceeds of the sale of fully depreciated furniture and equipment should be credited to "Salvage Sales" in the Store Rentals and Other Income Department.

1. Describe in detail the concept and operation of a call accounting system.
2. Explain the relative advantages and disadvantages of the following types of store leases:
   a. Fixed rental
   b. Minimum rental plus a percentage of the gross receipts over a specified amount
   c. Straight percentage of the gross sales
3. Circle T or F to indicate whether the following statements are true or false:
   T F a. Prior to 1970, hotels could not make a profit on telephone operations.
   T F b. Commissions received from a guest laundry concessionaire should be credited to laundry expense.
   T F c. Sales tax returns can be used to verify a tenant's gross revenue.
   T F d. Inspection of the parked cars is an important control procedure over garage revenue.
   T F e. Hotels cannot charge the guest for calls to an 800 number.
4. Circle the correct answer to the following statements:
   a. A store lease provides for a minimum rental of $1,200 per month plus 10 percent of revenue over $14,000 per month. The rent must be computed monthly. If revenues are $11,000 in January, $16,000 in February and $13,000 in March, the total rent for the three months is:
      (1) $4,000
      (2) $3,800
      (3) $4,100
   b. The usual method of controlling free parking for guests is to:
      (1) Give the guests a different color ticket
      (2) Have the ticket validated by the front-office cashier
      (3) Ask guests to park in a separate section of the garage
   c. It is impractical to charge for guest parking:
      (1) Only when the guest checks in
      (2) On a nightly basis
      (3) Only when the guest checks out
   d. The proceeds of the sale of fully depreciated furniture and equipment should be credited to:
      (1) Fixed Assets—Furniture and Equipment
      (2) Fixed Assets—Accumulated Depreciation
      (3) Other Income—Salvage Sales
   e. When guest laundry and dry cleaning are handled by a concessionaire, the laundry and valet slips are printed:
      (1) By the hotel
      (2) By the concessionaire

17 Recreational: Golf, Tennis, and Spas

It would be difficult to address the accounting needs for all possible forms of recreational activities found at a resort hotel. This chapter, therefore, discusses three of the more common—golf, tennis, and spas—while Chapter 19 addresses the accounting and control requirements for a casino operation.

GOLF

Other than swimming, usually a non-revenue-producing activity, golf is the most popular activity for the vacation traveler. According to the National Golf Foundation (NGF) in Jupiter, Florida, there are now more than 27 million golfers in the United States. A golf course is a basic requirement if a resort is to be successful.

Most golf operations have two department heads working somewhat independently under the supervision of the general manager or possibly a director of recreational activities.

The first department head, the golf superintendent, is a full-time employee responsible for the maintenance and upkeep of the golf course, facilities, and equipment. The superintendent's staff will usually consist of a core of permanent employees supplemented by some seasonal employees. However, in areas where golf is a year-round activity, the staff will be relatively fixed. In seasonal operations, the staffing reaches a peak prior to the reopening of the course. At that time, there is extensive grass cutting, trimming, sand trap refilling, and other maintenance necessary to restore the course to its proper playing condition. Prior to closing at the end of the season, reseeding and fertilizing may again increase the level of staffing. During the closed period, the work of the full-time employees is limited to overhauling equipment, inside painting of the facilities, and any other work that can be done inside. In northern locations, it is not uncommon for the golf course maintenance staff to be responsible for snow removal for the entire resort. Some of the vehicles and equipment used in golf course maintenance can be readily adapted for snow removal.

The second department head, the golf professional, is responsible for the pro shop operation and all areas related to actual play. In seasonal operations, the professional frequently is not employed during the closed period and may indulge in other types of work. Furthermore, the method by which the professional is compensated varies from resort to resort.

Almost all professionals receive an annual retainer from the resort, the amount of which depends on the opportunities for the professional to receive income in other areas. The most lucrative of these areas is the operation of the golf shop or pro shop, as it is more commonly called. In a resort operation, the pro shop sells not only golf equipment (e.g., clubs, bags, and golf balls) but also a large array of clothing and shoes. Much of the clothing is either designer styles or identity items, that is, bearing the name or logo of the resort. A large percentage of the clothing sales is for items to be used as gifts, souvenirs, or prizes. As a result, the pro shop becomes a major retail outlet.

In some resorts, the pro shop is operated by the resort and its management is one of the functions for which the professional receives his or her retainer. However, in many operations the pro shop is operated as a business by the professional. No rent is charged, but the professional buys and owns the merchandise and is reponsible for staffing and other operating costs which, depending on the agreement negotiated with the resort, may or may not include utilities.

Financial arrangements for golf carts vary from resort to resort. Following are the three alternatives most commonly in use:

1. The resort owns the golf carts and retains all the revenue.
2. The resort owns the golf carts but pays the professional a commission for handling the carts.
3. The golf professional owns and operates the carts and receives all the revenue.

Greens fees, the charges made for the right to play the course, are usually 100 percent revenue to the resort as is revenue derived from any form of membership. On the other hand, the professional almost always retains any revenue received for giving golf lessons.

From the preceding paragraph, it is clear that the accounting and the format of the departmental statement will vary depending on the arrangements. In Figure 17–1, a departmental statement for a golf operation, it is assumed that the resort owns and operates the pro shop and the golf cart rental operation but pays the professional a 10 percent commission on each.

Control of Revenue

As in all areas of a hotel operation, proper controls must be in place to ensure that revenue is correctly recorded.

In the pro shop, controls are similar to those used in upscale retail operations where the pricing structure justifies an inventory control system. All merchandise should be tagged with a two-part price tag (see Figure 17–2) which is attached to the merchandise. When an item is sold, one part of the tag is separated and fed through a scanning device connected to an electronic cash register. Each tag should be encoded

Hotel Grayscot

Departmental Statement—July 19, 19xx
Golf Course

Revenue			
Pro shop merchandise sales	$ 19,752		
Greens fees	122,608		
Golf carts	61,722		
Memberships	16,104		
		$220,186	
Cost of Sales			
Cost of pro shop merchandise sold		9,821	
Gross Profit		210,365	
Salaries and Wages			
Pro shop	8,943		
Course maintenance	19,460	28,403	
Payroll Taxes and Benefits		7,122	
Total Payroll		35,525	
Other Expenses			
Cart fuel	478		
Commissions	8,147		
Electricity	485		
Equipment maintenance	2,173		
Fertilizer	6,112		
Golf cart maintenance	762		
Grounds and landscaping	1,371		
Irrigation	1,063		
Operating supplies	674		
Sand	708		
Seeding	533		
Telephone	276		
Water	492	23,274	58,799
Departmental Profit			$151,566

Exhibit 17–1   Departmental Statement—Golf Course

with the category of the merchandise (e.g., golf clothing), the description of the item, the cost, and the selling price. Thus, when the scanner reads the tag it sends the information to the register to print a sales check and also puts into the computer memory the identity and cost of the item.

Sales information can be printed out on a daily basis by a partial clearing of the register. At the same time, the computer automatically deducts the sale from the shop's inventory which is stored in memory. Prior to the end of the period, all items added to inventory (i.e., purchases) must, again through a scanner, be fed into the computer. At

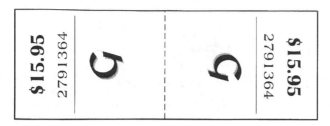

Figure 17–2   Price Tag

the end of the period, a theoretical inventory can then be printed out. The computer's storage capacity will determine how frequently the daily activity must be purged. The period-end theoretical inventory should then be matched against the actual physical inventory to identify overages and shortages. While overages are usually caused by improper tagging or scanning, shortages are primarily due to pilferage. Excessive and unexceptable losses require a tightening of the physical controls over the merchandise and may justify the installation of an exit alarm system activated by the tags. However, for image reasons, this latter step should be initiated only as a last resort.

Control can be exercised over greens fees and carts by issuing the player two-part tags (Figure 17–4) which can be attached to the golf bag, for greens fees, and the carts, for rentals. These tags should be numerically controlled and issued through the pro

Figure 17–3   Starter Collecting Bag Tag (Photograph by Chris Alexopoulos)

Figure 17–4 Golf Bag Tag

shop. This should be done at the same time that the revenue is input into the register under the proper identity key. One part of each tag should then be removed by the starter when the players tee off at the first hole. The tags should be forwarded to the night-audit staff who utilize them to reconcile the revenue and record the number of rounds in the daily statistics. It is important that tags be issued for members and complimentary rounds also. This is done not only for control purposes but also to compute the proper number of rounds for the statistics. However, they should be rung up as a "zero" amount on the cash register. Marshals, used to patrol the course, should be required to periodically check for bag tags and cart tags.

The control process is much easier in a resort that restricts play to members and hotel guests. In such circumstances, the volume of cash transactions is low as items are usually charged to a guest room or a member's account. Charges are then processed through night audit, reconciled and balanced in the same manner as other hotel charges. If the pro shop registers are not interfaced to the front-office system, it is essential that the charges be delivered to the hotel front office for posting on a timely basis.

Membership revenue is recorded at the beginning of the season when the members are billed. The accounts receivable should be carried in a separate section in the hotel city ledger. A monthly reconciliation should be prepared to balance the membership types and fees to the total membership revenue.

Expenditure

The departmental statement (Figure 17–1) shows typical revenues and matching expenditures. Expenditures can be recorded through the hotel accounts payable

and payroll systems in the same manner as the expenses of any other operating department.

The departmental numbers can vary heavily from month to month, depending on the time of the year and the weather conditions. Prior to the course opening, the income will be restricted to memberships while expenses are high. Not only is payroll high, but the allotments for fertilizer, seeding, sand, and so on needed to put the course into playable condition are primarily expended prior to opening or just before closing. The cost of these items can, if desired, be spread over the entire season. Payroll is, however, the primary cost throughout the year.

There is some inconsistency in the treatment of the golf course as an operated department compared to the other operated departments. While repairs and energy costs related to the other departments are charged to the property operation and maintenance and energy costs departments, respectively, such costs related to the golf course are charged directly to the golf department.

Food and beverage operations in the golf course clubhouse should be handled in the same manner as the other food and beverage operations and not incorporated into the golf course statements.

TENNIS

The accounting and controls required for a tennis operation are very similar to those for a golf operation but usually on a much smaller scale. This is particularly true for a tennis shop operation. Similar to the golf shop, the tennis shop can be operated by either the tennis professional or by the hotel. If the hotel is the operator, the rules set out earlier in this chapter relative to sales and inventory control in a golf pro shop are equally applicable to a tennis shop operation.

While some hotels sell memberships to local residents, the primary source of revenue is court rentals which are normally on a "per hour" or "per half-hour" basis. Since the volume of business frequently does not justify extensive controls, it is important that a log of court activity be maintained and that charges be promptly processed through the tennis shop. A representative of the accounting department can visually verify court usage on a random basis and later check that the usage was logged and revenue recorded. Complimentary usage must be logged.

Payroll, cost of sales, and other expenses charged to the tennis department are usually limited to those related to the tennis shop operation. Court upkeep is normally absorbed into the property operation and maintenance department as payroll or tennis court expense as applicable. All expenses, payroll and other, are processed through the regular hotel systems in the same manner as golf expenditures.

SPAS

Spa operations must be viewed with two completely different concepts in mind: spa hotels and spas operated as a guest amenity at both resort and commercial hotels.

Spa hotels cater exclusively to spa clientele. An example of such operations is the Golden Door in Escondido, California. Similar operations, perhaps not of the same

scale, can be found in California, Arizona, and other states where year-round outdoor activity is normal. While the ability to conduct outside activities on a year-round basis is not mandatory—some spas are operated in colder surroundings—temperate climates permit a much larger scope of activities.

In spa hotels, the guest is charged an overall rate including room, meals, and spa participation. The guest's ability to have unlimited use and access to all spa services eliminates the need for heavy financial controls in the area. From an accounting point of view, a spa department could be set up as a profit center, but its revenue would be simply an allocation of a portion of the room rate. There is, therefore, considerable logic to only allocating a portion of the revenues to the food department and leaving the balance of the package revenue in the rooms department. The spa would then be treated as a non-revenue-producing overhead department.

In a hotel or resort where the spa is simply another service offered the guest, accounting for the operation as an operating department (see Figure 17–5) is necessary.

Revenue, as illustrated, is usually derived from four basic sources. The first of these—sale of merchandise—is somewhat similar to the operation of a golf pro or ten-

Hotel Grayscot

Departmental Statement—July 19, 19xx
Spa

Revenue			
Sale of merchandise		$ 2,797	
Facility usage charges		2,572	
À la carte services		9,246	
Packages		2,309	$16,924
Cost of Sales			
Cost of merchandise sold			1,172
Gross Profit			15,752
Payroll			
Salaries and wages	6,652		
Payroll taxes and benefits	1,711	8,363	
Other Expenses			
Fitness supplies	699		
Laundry	482		
Pool supplies	429		
Linen	208		
Electricity	1,756		
Water	462		
Equipment repair	719	4,755	13,118
			$ 2,634

Figure 17–5   Departmental Statement—Spa

nis shop. While the product focus is on oils and other spa treatments, it is not unusual for the spa to sell items of clothing such as bathing suits or athletic footwear. Once again, the controls described for the other two retail shops are equally applicable.

Many visitors to the spa are only interested in using the pool or the nautilus machines or participating in aerobics—particularly "step aerobics," a new form of workout to improve cardiovascular fitness. For such use, the spa charges a daily usage or admittance charge called a *facility usage charge*. Each entrant should be issued one half of a two-part ticket, the remaining half being retained for audit purposes. The revenue, cash or charge, should be recorded immediately upon admission to the spa. Any complimentaries must be recorded as such.

Spa attendants, massage personnel, dieticians, and so on also provide certain à la carte services for specific set prices. These services include dietary consultation, massages, herbal rubs, and various types of skin treatments. The charge for each service provided should be recorded immediately upon completion.

Finally, the hotel may sell packages that include free spa usage and some or all of the à la carte services. The guest should receive, at check-in, a card indicating exactly what is included in the package. This card should be produced and validated immediately upon visiting the spa. The property management system, in recording the daily room revenue, should be programmed to allocate an appropriate amount of revenue to the spa for the services included in the package.

As can be seen from Figure 17–5, most of the expenses, other than reception payroll, relate principally to the à la carte services (some payroll relates to management and aerobics). Since utility costs are materially impacted by a spa operation, they are usually monitored separately and charged to the department. From an accounting point of view, this is similar to the treatment of the golf course, a deviation from the normal accounting for an operated department.

1. Draw a small organization chart illustrating a resort golf operation.

2. Explain the difference between the concepts of a spa hotel and a spa operated as an amenity for guests.

3. Circle T or F to indicate whether the following statements are true or false:

   T   F **a.** A golf superintendent's staff is at a peak prior to reopening the course.

   T   F **b.** Golf professionals are always employed on a year-round basis.

   T   F **c.** Almost all golf professionals receive a retainer from the golf club.

   T   F **d.** Normally, the golf professional retains revenue received from giving lessons.

   T   F **e.** The primary cause of inventory shortages in a golf pro shop is pilferage.

4. Circle the correct answer to the following statements:

   a. The number of golfers in the United States is:
      (1) Between 5 and 10 million
      (2) Between 25 and 30 million
      (3) Over 50 million

   b. Golf professionals in many resorts earn the major portion of their income from:
      (1) Operation of the pro shop
      (2) Lessons
      (3) Greens fees

   c. The largest expense in a golf operation is:
      (1) Fertilizer
      (2) Course maintenance payroll
      (3) Sand

   d. The principal source of tennis revenue for hotels is usually:
      (1) Local memberships
      (2) Sale of clothing
      (3) Court rentals

   e. Tennis court rental charges are used based on:
      (1) The number of players
      (2) The length of the playing time
      (3) The final score of the match

18 Self-Standing Restaurants and Private Clubs

Since there is a close similarity between self-standing restaurants and private clubs, it seemed appropriate to address both types of operations in the same chapter.

There are thousands of country clubs in North America, the principal element of which is golf. The control and accounting aspects of a golf operation were addressed in the preceding chapter. The rest of the private clubs are mostly downtown membership clubs in which the focal point is the restaurant. Some of the older and more traditional clubs have accommodations, rooms or suites, available for rental by members either by the night or for extended periods stretching from a week to a year. They are, in fact, small private hotels and must be considered as such from an accounting point of view. While many clubs also have recreational facilities, such as handball or racquetball, their use is normally included in the annual membership dues and they cannot be considered as independent profit centers.

CORPORATE STRUCTURE

Many restaurants are sole proprietorships. This is particularly true where the premises are leased, thus limiting the financial exposure due to operating losses. The sole proprietor format is used in the example of financial statements for a restaurant (Figure 18–1). Other restaurants may be partnerships or corporations. Normally, the larger restaurants and, of course, the restaurant chains, are corporations. In fact, most of the major chains such as McDonalds or Kentucky Fried Chicken have gone public and are traded actively on the stock exchange. Many of the small, privately owned restaurants that have been incorporated are Chapter "S" corporations, entities in which liability exposure is limited by the corporate structure but the tax treatment is very similar to that of a sole proprietorship.

The corporate structures of private clubs are more complex. Most are member-owned clubs where the shares are held by members under various covenants that restrict the transfer or sale of the shares. In many cases, the shares are subject to

Cafe West

Balance Sheet
as at January 31, 199X

Assets		
Cash—Petty Cash	$ 50.00	
House Bank	100.00	
Operating Account	3,081.73	$3,231.73
Accounts Receivable		71.41
Inventories—Food	1,494.71	
Beverage	570.98	
Supplies	410.00	2,475.69
Prepaids—Rent	1,400.00	
Insurance	2,172.09	3,572.09
Security Deposits		1,390.00
Fixed Assets—Furniture & Equipment	2,568.55	
Automobile	8,590.00	
	11,158.55	
Accumulated Depreciation	2,085.94	9,072.61
		$19,813.53
Liabilities & Equity		
Accounts Payable—Trade	$509.00	
Sales Tax Payable	683.57	
Payroll Taxes Payable	231.90	1,424.47
Accrued—Salaries & Wages	595.00	
Utilities	300.00	
Other	806.00	1,701.00
Bank Loan		15,000.00
Proprietors Equity—Opening Balance	7.71	
Profit, YTD	2,680.35	
	2,688.06	
Withdrawals	1,000.00	1,688.06
		$19,813.53

Figure 18–1   Balance Sheet—Restaurant

repurchase by the club. Any operating profits are usually reinvested in the club operation, although there is nothing to prevent a distribution to the shareholders, unless such is limited by the bylaws. Usually, however, major distributions occur only in the event of the sale of club property. There are also many not-for-profit clubs where there is no ownership interest.

INTERNAL CONTROLS

Internal controls necessary for most restaurants are described in Section IV. Additional comments are, however, required relative to fast food operations which are rarely found in hotels. Those that do exist within the confines of a hotel are usually leased out to fast-food operators.

Fast-food kitchens should only issue food after a check has been rung up, similar in principle to prechecking procedures described in Chapter 14. The singular difference is that actual payment is also required prior to receiving the food. In some of the operations, a single person is responsible for taking the order, collecting the cash, and issuing the food—the normal procedure at take-out windows unless the order is placed in advance at a remote terminal. In other operations, the order and cash is taken by one person and the food delivered by a second. Very few fast-food operations accept credit cards as the time involved negates the principle of fast food. This situation is, however, changing as fast operations are installing terminals where the customer can automatically key in the order and automatically pay using a credit card in a manner similar to bank ATM machines.

Private clubs do not require the same level of control needed in hotels or restaurants. Very few clubs accept payment in cash; the charge is signed and charged to the member's account. Even tips added to members' checks are subsequently paid through the payroll. Since most clubs add an automatic service charge to the check, the amount of discretionary tipping is minimal. The absence of cash greatly reduces the exposure to server fraud. Caution is, however, advised. It should not be assumed that the absence of cash eliminates all potential for fraud. A server may still omit charging for an item or charge for a lesser item than served. Inflating the check in order to increase the applicable service charge is also a possibility.

Very little control procedure is necessary in the area of memberships. Each member should be assigned a permanent membership number and billing, whether monthly or annually, should be automatic. A master control list should be maintained and balanced to the revenue each time a billing is made.

Collection procedures are similar to those described for golf operations. The names of members with overdue accounts are posted on a notice board and if not settled within the requisite time, membership privileges can simply be terminated. Legal action can, of course, be instituted to effect collection but many clubs, as a manner of policy, refrain from such action. In member-owned clubs, the bylaws usually provide for the automatic repurchase of the member's share in the event of failure to sustain membership obligations.

As mentioned in Section IV, procedures for purchasing, receiving, and inventory control are similar to those needed in a hotel. However, due to a lesser volume, some of these functions are performed by the same person which, unfortunately, reduces control. Review by the controller and management should be performed on a continuing basis to minimize exposure. Traditionally, the atmosphere present in private clubs has resulted in a less than desirable focus on internal control with resulting losses. A contributing factor is also the emphasis on food quality and service with very little membership focus on profitability.

ACCOUNTING PROCEDURES AND FINANCIAL STATEMENT PRESENTATION

Accounting procedures for recording revenue and expenditure in restaurants and restaurant operations in clubs are similar to those for food and beverage operations in hotels. The processing of accounts payable and payroll, in addition to revenue record-

ing, is described in the sections applicable to those procedures. The primary difference, therefore, is not in the actual procedures, but in the format of the charts of accounts and financial presentation.

Most restaurants, rather than using a departmental format, have opted for a single income statement that shows the results at different operating levels. This format is used in Figure 18-2. In a manner similar to a hotel departmental statement, levels in-

Cafe West
Statement of Income
for the Period Ending January 31, 199–

Revenue		
Sales—Restaurant Food	$6,858.60	
Take Out Food	1,634.82	
Beverage	890.60	$9,384.02
Cost of Sales		
Food	2,501.58	
Beverage	104.15	2,605.73
Gross Profit		6,778.29
Operating Expenses		
Salaries and wages	1,587.88	
Cleaning supplies	14.41	
Utensils	40.00	
Linen service	104.60	
Office supplies	117.74	
Paper supplies	65.36	
Credit card commissions	15.20	
Guest entertainment	37.35	
Advertising	121.25	
Legal and accounting	77.26	
Telephone	96.35	
Kitchen fuel	172.62	
Short (over)	< 2.49 >	
Menus	6.30	
Kitchen supplies	24.49	2,478.32
Operating Profit		4,299.97
Occupancy Expenses		
Heat	96.45	
Repairs	84.45	
Electricity	70.00	250.90
		4,049.07
Fixed Charges		
Rent	1,000.00	
Insurance	206.72	
Interest	140.00	
Depreciation	22.00	1,368.72
Net Profit		$2,680.35

Figure 18–2   Income Statement—Restaurant

clude revenue, cost of sales, gross profit, and direct operating expenses to arrive at an operating profit level. Marketing expenses, such as advertising and guest entertainment, are deducted at this level. This is not a complete departure from hotel procedures as many hotels also treat advertising solely for the restaurants as direct expenses of the food and beverage department.

Two more groups of expenditures are then deducted to arrive at net profit. Utilities and repairs and maintenance costs are grouped under the heading of "Occupancy Costs." The final grouping of fixed charges includes the traditional rent, insurance, depreciation, and real estate taxes. If the entity is a corporation, income taxes will be a later deduction. The balance sheet (Figure 18–1) is a smaller version of a hotel balance sheet.

Most member-owned clubs prefer to have a separate schedule for the food and beverage operations, similar to a hotel food and beverage departmental statement. This is appropriate as the responsibility for those operations is usually in the hands of a restaurant manager. Grouping of the results in a separate schedule is, therefore, consistent with levels of management responsibility. The net results of the food and beverage operation are then transferred to the final income statement (Figure 18–3) which includes membership income and all other expenses.

The Members' Club West
Statement of Income
for the Month of January 31, 199x

Revenue		
Membership dues	$7,128.00	
Profit (loss) from restaurant	2,680.35	
Interest income	322.00	$10,130.35
Operating Expenses		
Administrative salaries and wages	3,756.08	
Printing and stationery	272.15	
Advertising	128.00	
Legal fees	200.00	
Telephone	116.22	
Travel and entertainment	61.10	4,533.55
Operating Profit		5,596.80
Building Operations		
Heating	1,326.11	
Electricity	872.03	
Repairs and maintenance	613.21	
Garbage removal	125.00	2,936.35
		2,660.45
Fixed Charges		
Insurance	312.00	
Taxes	873.06	
Depreciation	1,322.00	2,507.06
Net Income		$ 153.39

Figure 18–3   Income Statement—Members' Club

The format for financial statements for not-for-profit clubs follows the rules established in FASB Statement No. 117. These requirements include a statement of financial position, a statement of activities, and a statement of cash flows. The statement of financial position must reflect total assets, new assets, and liabilities. Net assets must be categorized as permanently restricted as to their use, temporarily restricted, or unrestricted. The statement of activities must show changes in net assets, which can be done in a revenue, expenses, and change in net equity format. The cash flow statement must follow the FASB Statement No. 95 Statement of Cash Flows format. The intent of these requirements is clearly to place the not-for-profit clubs in the same category for financial presentation as charities, churches, and similar organizations.

SUMMARY

While restaurants do not have the advantage of a high profit margin on lodging operations, they are normally able to maintain a higher margin of profit on restaurant operations than hotels. The primary reason for this is flexibility in hours and staffing. Restaurants, unlike hotels, are not obliged to stay open for new periods that are unprofitable (e.g., room service in a hotel). Also, restaurants have a greater flexibility in closing certain days of the week that are normally unprofitable. Additionally, restaurants are less likely to be locked into labor contracts or employee agreements and, therefore, have a greater flexibility in reducing staffing.

Private clubs normally look to the membership dues to provide their main source of revenue and have traditionally been very happy if the restaurant operations achieve a break-even level.

19 Casinos

Casinos are the fastest growing area of the resort industry. In December 1993, casinos (including those on Indian reservations) were legal in 35 states while another 6 states permitted them only on river boats. *The Harrah's Survey of U.S. Casino Entertainment* (1944, Second Edition) indicated that not only did 90 percent of American adults approve of legalized casino gaming, but that a large number of them had paid at least one visit to a casino in the preceding year. In other words, casinos have become a major element of the entertainment business.

While casino operations do not necessarily require a hotel location, both hotel and casino operators, dating back to the early days in Las Vegas, have recognized that casinos and hotel operations are closely interrelated, one element serving and at the same time feeding off the other.

CASINO ORGANIZATION

From a structural point of view, casino management usually has a higher degree of independence than the management of a normal hotel-operated department.

The magnitude of operations of a casino hotel dictates that there be a level of authority above the hotel general manager, usually a managing director or a vice president of operations. The casino manager also reports to this individual, and is essentially at the same authority level as the hotel general manager. The relationship between the two managers can be somewhat delicate, requiring both to display a strong sense of cooperation and understanding. The hotel provides many areas of service to the casino, including rooms and food and beverages to the casino clientele and the services of the overhead departments, that is, engineering and marketing. Other recreational departments, such as the golf course and the spa, also provide recreational activities to casino customers.

Most of the services provided by the hotel take place outside the physical confines of the casino. The reservations, front-desk, and housekeeping staff and most of

the food and beverage staff operate within their respective areas. However, beverage service is usually provided inside the casino. The employees providing that service primarily report to food and beverage management but also have a dotted line of authority to casino management.

All staff directly involved in the operation of the games are completely under the authority of the casino manager. This includes assistant managers, supervisors or "pit bosses" as they are commonly referred to, and the dealers who operate the games. It also includes hosts, public relations personnel, and casino security. Two further categories of staff deal with the financial and control functions of the casino: the cage staff and the casino credit personnel.

THE CAGE

In every casino, there is a location where chips and cash are stored and transactions are settled. This area usually consists of a room adjacent to the casino, with a window or windows that open into the casino, and it is usually called the *casino cage*.

The cage is the control center for the flow of chips to and from the tables. Such transfers are made whenever a table has a shortage or an excess of chips, and they are controlled in a systematic fashion that is described later in this chapter. The cage is also the focal point for the handling of credit granted to individual players for the purpose of gambling.

The cage is under the authority of a cage manager, who has the overall responsibility for the cage personnel and for the total casino bank. The casino bank consists principally of three forms of money: chips, cash, and markers (outstanding debts owed by gamblers). An initial chip bank in a predetermined amount is issued to the cage and, together with an adequate supply of cash, forms the initial casino bank.

From the chip bank, chips are issued to the tables to be exchanged with the players for cash or markers. At the end of each shift, the number of house chips kept at each table is restored to the original amount either by issuing additional chips from the cage or by returning excess chips to the cage. Thus, the amount of the chip float at each table remains fixed and forms a part of the total cage bank.

Cash floats are issued to cashiers who staff change booths in the slot-machine areas. Change booths provide change to slot-machine customers to speed up play and avoid congestion at the cage windows. The change-booth floats also form a part of the total cage bank.

CASINO CONTROL

In many ways, a casino operation is similar to that of a bank. The high volume of cash and credit transactions and the volatile activity of play necessitates a high level of control. The heart of casino control is based on two fundamental rules. First, the cage operates as a giant bank which, while its three elements may vary, remains unchanged in total amount and must be balanced on a daily basis. (Occasionally, because of increased volume or an increase in the number of games, it may be necessary to increase the total bank but this is unusual. Second, each game or table is, in itself, a profit cen-

ter that must be accounted for individually as well as in total with individual subtabulation being done for each type of game played.

While chips can, of course, be exchanged for cash or approved credit at the cage window, every effort should be made to sell chips at the individual table. Each table is equipped with a steel lockbox beneath the table. While the box is in place, it has an open slot through which all cash received from players is dropped. When the box is removed from the table, the slot is automatically locked and can be reopened only by keys that are under the control of the count team. The boxes are locked up in the countroom and, at a specific time, all boxes are opened and the contents counted carefully under strict supervision.

When chips are issued to a player for credit, the player is required to sign a marker acknowledging the debt (see Figure 19–1). A duplicate copy of this marker is dropped through the table slot, so the combined total of the cash and the markers in the box equals the income of the table for chips issued.

However, this figure does not reflect the final result for the table. If the table returns excess chips to the cage during or at the end of a shift, the table must receive a credit for these chips. A credit slip denoting the chips returned is completed and sent in duplicate to the cage along with the chips. When the count is verified by the cage, the duplicate is signed and sent back to the table, where it is dropped through the slot. An example of a credit slip is shown in Figure 19–2.

Finally, winnings by players may deplete the supply of chips at a table, necessitating the issuance of more chips by the cage. When an additional supply of chips is required, a *fill slip* (Figure 19–3) is completed in duplicate and sent to the cage. The cage keeps the original and returns the initialed duplicate with the chips to the table. The duplicate is then dropped through the slot. Thus, the net result of any table is the cash plus markers and credit slips, known as the *drop,* less the total of the fill slips. The net is known as the *win*.

The individual results, by shift, for each table game are recorded on a form known as the *stiff sheet*. This form is used to tabulate the opening and closing inventories of chips, the drop, credit and fill slip totals, and markers for each table. The re-

To ______________________ Bank
Name of Bank

Check No. A 42173

Acct. Number ______________________

Date ______________, 19____

______________________ Branch

City and State ______________________

PAY TO THE ORDER OF: Hotel Grayscot

$ ____________

______________________ Dollars

The undersigned agrees that he or she is personally responsible for this indebtedness and agrees to pay in full without objection and relinquishes all legal rights to contest this obligation in all Federal, State and foreign courts or jurisdictions.

Address ______________________

Telephone ______________________

Signed

Figure 19–1 Casino Marker

Hotel Grayscot
CREDIT SLIP

DATE			TIME	

SHIFT	GYD	DAY	SWING

Game	Number	Denomination	Amount
CRAPS			
21			
ROULETTE			
BIG WHEEL			
TOTAL			

MEMO   RETURN CHIPS ☐

RUNNER	FLOOR MAN
CASHIER	DEALER - BOXMAN

B 7061

Figure 19–2 Credit Slip for Chips Returned

sulting win is calculated for each table game and the totals for the shift, by game, are determined. The individual stiff sheets for each shift are then combined in the preparation of the casino balance sheet.

The calculation of the drop and the win for the slot operation is tabulated in a different manner. The drop is determined, not by the amount of coins inserted into the machine, but by the amount contained in the *drop buckets* that are removed at the end of each shift. When coins are inserted into a machine, they fall into a holding area known as a *hopper*. Only when the hopper is full do the coins get diverted to the drop bucket. When the hopper is emptied due to a jackpot, it is replenished with a "fill" of coins or tokens, similar to the chip fills replenishing table inventories. Very large jackpots are usually paid by hand. The "win" for the slot operation is the drop minus the machine fills and hand-paid jackpots.

Hotel Grayscot

FILL SLIP

DATE		TIME	

SHIFT	GYD	DAY	SWING

Game	Number	Denomination	Amount
CRAPS			
21			
ROULETTE			
BIG WHEEL			
TOTAL			

MEMO

RETURN CHIPS ☐

RUNNER	FLOOR MAN
CASHIER	DEALER - BOXMAN

C 1611

Figure 19–3   Fill Slip for Chips Issued

The completion of the daily cage balance sheet (Figure 19–4) is the responsibility of the cage manager, or appointee. This sheet is a mathematical summary of the results by table and by game in the manner explained in the preceding paragraph. The time-consuming but most important part of the daily process is the physical count. The number of shifts operated for each table (normally a maximum of three) will determine the number of actual boxes to be counted. The boxes should, for proper control, be replaced with an empty box at the end of each shift. The locking mechanisms on the tables require that a new box be inserted in order to remove the old box.

A separate subcount sheet (Figure 19–5) should be prepared for each box. The physical count of all currency dropped should be rechecked by a second individual. The counting should also be observed by supervisors who do not participate in the actual count. The individual table counts are then combined for each table and carried forward to the master sheet.

Hotel Grayscot

CASINO BALANCE SHEET FOR September 19 ___ , 19 ___

Game	Cash Drop	I.O.U.s	Gross Play	Credit Slips	Less Fills	Net Wins	%
CRAPS							
Table 1	2,486,000	758,000	1,728,000	53,000	1,559,000	222,000	12.3
Table 2	637,000	62,000	575,000	11,000	503,000	83,000	10.9
Table 3	103,571	---	103,571	2,000	90,000	15,571	15.0
Total Craps	3,226,571	820,000	2,406,571	66,000	2,152,000	320,571	13.3
BLACKJACK							
Table 1	493,400	72,000	421,100	7,000	366,000	62,100	14.7
Table 2	83,500	11,500	72,000	3,000	66,000	9,000	12.5
Table 3	114,100	13,000	101,100	6,000	91,000	16,100	15.9
Table 4	7,223	---	7,223	800	4,800	3,223	44.6
Table 5							
Total Blackjack	698,223	96,800	601,423	16,800	527,800	90,423	14.8
ROULETTE							
Table 1	683,300	51,000	632,300	11,500	552,500	91,300	14.7
Table 2			---			---	
Table 3	184,123	---	184,123	2,000	169,000	17,123	9.3
Total Roulette	867,423	51,000	816,423	13,500	721,500	108,423	13.3
SLOTS	322,911	✕	322,911	✕	Jackpots 42,300	280,611	86.9
Total Casino	4,247,705	967,800	5,215,505	96,300	3,441,600	800,028	15.3

Figure 19–4 Daily Casino Balance Sheet

The results of each shift by table number should be tabulated on a day-by-day basis for review of variances and unusual results. This tabulation is facilitated by use of a computer. It is important that the names of the actual personnel working that shift also be included in the tabulation. Thus, by regrouping, a record of results by individual dealer and/or supervisor can also be obtained.

The last tabulation that must be completed on a daily basis is the nightly balancing of the cage bank. This balancing can also be facilitated by the use of a specially designed form (Figure 19–6). Certain items on the bank count sheet require explanation.

Hotel Grayscot

Count Sheet

Date: _____ **Table:** _____ **Shift:** _____

CURRENCY	No. of Bills	TOTAL
$1		
$5		
$10		
$20		
$50		
$100		
$500		
$1,000		

Fill Slips
No.   Amount

Credit Slips
No.   Amount

Signatures of Counters   Signature of Supervisor

Figure 19–5   Casino Shift Count Sheet

Hotel Grayscot

Casino Bank Count for September 19XX

Opening bank		$12,930,300
Add: IOUs received		967,800
LESS: IOUs collected		930,300
Net change in IOUs		$12,967,800
Closing bank		
Bank count		

CURRENCY	No. OF BILLS	TOTAL	
$1	25,000	25,000	
$5	5,000	25,000	
$10	10,000	100,000	
$20	5,000	100,000	
$50	5,000	250,000	
$100	5,000	500,000	
$500	4,000	2,000,000	
$1,000	5,000	5,000,000	8,000,000

TOTAL CURRENCY CHIPS IN CAGE	No. OF CHIPS	TOTAL	
$1	3,500	3,500	
$5	19,200	96,000	
$10	30,000	300,000	
$20	20,000	400,000	
$50	20,000	1,000,000	
$100			
$500			
Table banks	80,000		
Slot banks	40,000		
Slot change banks	60,000		
Foreign chips	21,500		
Total chips	2,000,000		
Checks held	−		
IOUs	2,967,800	4,967,800	
Total checks & IOUs			
Closing bank		$12,967,800	

DAILY DEPOSIT RECONCILIATION

Net win	800,028	
Net change in IOUs	37,500	
Actual deposit	$ 762,528	

Figure 19–6 Casino Daily Bank Count

Foreign Chips

In locations where more than one casino is in operation, it is common practice to accept chips from the other casino(s). Those chips must be exchanged at the cage window for the casino's own chips. Those chips are then returned to the originating casino in exchange for cash. Until that exchange is completed, they are carried in the casino bank as *foreign chips*.

Checks Held

Frequently, a player, normally known to the casino personnel, will cash a check but ask that it be held and not deposited until a specific date. This must be a relatively short period of time, possibly one to two weeks or until the end of the month. Beyond that length of time, the normal practice is to have the player sign a marker since legally a postdated check is simply a promise to pay.

Good casino practice mandates that all travelers' checks and foreign currency be deposited as part of the deposit on a daily basis.

It is important to understand that the exact net win cannot be deposited since the markers (IOUs) included in it must be added to the casino bank. However, the markers collected are deposited. Thus, the casino bank will fluctuate to the degree that the markers increase or decrease. The total chips counted will differ from the total chips in circulation by the amount of uncashed chips still in the hands of customers. The casino bank is simply holding additional cash in substitution for uncashed chips. Over a period of time, the amount of uncashed chips will increase as they are lost, misplaced, or kept for souvenirs. When a casino completely changes its chips (by changing design, color, etc.), the amount of the uncashed chips can, in accordance with sound accounting practice, be written into income. The income should not, however, be realized for at least three months, permitting the chips that are "floating," but with the intention of ultimate cashing, to be actually redeemed.

ISSUANCE AND COLLECTION OF MARKERS

In the preceding section, the term *IOU* is sometimes used instead of markers. While *markers* is the more correct term, *IOU* is a part of the normal casino language used internally between gaming employees. The terms are synonymous.

The mechanics of issuing markers was addressed, but it is now necessary to review their control within the overall casino credit and collection procedure.

All players desiring credit are required to provide the information necessary to complete a credit application, specifying the credit limit desired and providing bank references and a history of credit limits previously obtained in other casinos. After checking these references, the casino credit office can make a judgment as to whether to grant the full amount of credit requested, a lower amount, or no credit.

A player should never be permitted to exceed his or her credit limit. Should a casino negligently or knowingly permit a player to exceed the requested limit, the player may, with some justification, refuse to pay the excess. Most players are not local residents but visit the hotel periodically, either on their own or on junkets (casino-

sponsored trips). On a return visit, it is desirable to ask a player to settle any markers outstanding from a prior visit before granting additional credit.

Since markers form a portion of the casino bank, they are physically kept and controlled in the casino cage. Each player has a marker envelope on the front of which a record of all markers issued, payments, and the current balance is displayed. Careful recording of issuance and payment must be made. If the markers are removed from the envelope for delivery, upon payment, to the player, this must be carefully noted. Some casinos prefer to have only the records in the cage while the actual markers are under the control of the casino credit manager who has the responsibility for collection. This can create problems, however, since players go to the cage to redeem their markers at any time, day or night.

Because casino debts are usually of a rather confidential nature, much of the collection effort must be made by telephone, with a careful record kept of all calls. Letters requesting settlement can also be used, particularly if the debtor has resisted efforts to collect by telephone.

Before a debt is written off as uncollectible, consideration should be given to using an outside collection agency. However, the degree of success is limited since, in many locations, payment of casino debts is not enforceable under the law.

ACCOUNTING PROCEDURE

Casino operating results (see Figure 19–7) are presented in a similar manner to other recreational departments. Payroll and other expenditures are recorded through the hotel systems in the same manner as other operated department expenses. A revenue entry can readily be prepared on a daily or monthly basis from the daily casino balance sheet (Figure 19–4) and the daily bank count (Figure 19–6). The latter report is only required for the numbers of the daily deposit and the net change in markers outstanding. In journal entry format, using the numbers reflected in the two reports, the entry for September 19, 19xx would be as follows:

Dr.	Casino Bank Account	$762,528	
	Accounts receivable—Markers	37,500	
Cr.	Casino revenue		$800,028

To record casino results for September 19.

It is important to note that the net win is considered revenue rather than the total gross play or drop. *Drop* is an industry term frequently used instead of *gross play*.

The accounting treatment for uncollectible markers sometimes differs from that reflected in Figure 19–7. However, treating the write-offs as a reduction of total revenue is the conservative approach which avoids inflation of revenue due to the granting of excess credit. An explanation is required of some of the expenses shown.

Paid outs. In table games this is the actual winnings paid to players. In slot machines it represents only the jackpots paid and machine fills as the incidental winnings of smaller amounts automatically paid out by the machines are considered adjustments to gross play and not paid outs or winnings.

Payroll. Casino staff as described earlier in the chapter but not including food and beverage personnel.

Hotel Grayscot

Casino Department Statement
for the Month Ending September 30, 199–

Gross Play	$103,548,632	
LESS: Paid out	81,406,139	
Net Win		$22,142,493
LESS: Markers written off		96,500
Total Revenue		22,045,993
Payroll		
Cash payroll	3,685,420	
Payroll taxes and benefits	822,643	
Total Payroll		4,508,063
Other costs and expenses		
Advertising	721,538	
Commissions	136,850	
Credit and collection	82,171	
Data processing	68,407	
Entertainment	645,382	
Equipment rental	11,156	
Insurance	69,125	
Legal fees	104,000	
Music and entertainment	2,580,400	
Operating supplies	7,461	
Printing and stationery	3,122	
Telephone	31,802	
Travel	68,211	
Uniforms	5,680	
Total Other Costs and Expenses		4,535,305
Total Expense Before Casino Taxes		9,043,368
Profit Before Casino Taxes		13,062,625
Casino Taxes		4,409,200
Net Profit (Loss)		$8,653,425

Figure 19–7 Casino Department Statement

Advertising. Advertising that is primarily for the casino.

Commissions. Commissions paid to junket operators. Junket operators bring groups or individual gamblers to the casino for which they are paid a commission.

Entertainment. The cost of complimentary rooms, food and beverage, and transportation provided to qualified players including those brought by junket operators. The rooms and food and beverage revenues are recorded in the specific operated departments and charged to the casino at agreed rates—usually somewhat discounted.

Music and entertainment. The costs of an act or acts featured at the hotel in order to attract players to the casino are usually charged to the casino.

Operating supplies. The cost of cards, chips, dice, and other supplies consumed during casino play.

Casino taxes. Casinos are usually subject to additional taxes imposed by the various taxing bodies.

The net results of a casino operation can, depending on the mix of the games, vary substantially when measured as a percentage of revenue. Table games produce a net win of 12 to 18 percent, while slot machines produce a net win of over 85 percent. Yet, the operating costs are much more a function of the volume of the table games than the slots. Therefore, a high volume of slot machine play will result in a much higher margin of net profit.

USE OF COMPUTERS

In addition to the various recording procedures related to producing financial results, computers are used in two major areas in casino operations: compiling the forecast and controlling credit.

The term *forecast* relates to tabulations of the drop made by the staff in the pit during the course of play. While the only legitimate number for the drop is the final result of the count, the pit staff is expected to produce an accurate estimate. Traditionally, the forecast was a manual procedure carried out by the supervisors following play at each table. Computers have greatly simplified the process by requiring only that the type and amount be input each time cash, markers, fill slips, or credit slips are dropped through the slot. An updated forecast of play can, therefore, be printed out, by table, at any time.

The use of computers has greatly simplified the control of credit during the course of play. The play of any player utilizing credit must be tracked to ensure that any winnings at the end of the evening be applied first to redeem the outstanding markers. Otherwise, the casino would face the possibility that a player could cash in his or her chips and exit the premises leaving behind a substantial debt. Since most major players move from table to table, particularly when fortune is not smiling on them, the manual tracking of an individual was difficult and time-consuming. By continually inputting an individual player's activity at each table, an updated status report on one or all credit players can be printed out at any time.

For slot machines, the use of electronics has resulted in each machine being a minicomputer that provides a multitude of options as to the type of game and the manner in which it is played.

1. The following information relates to the play at a blackjack table. Calculate the net win:
   a. Cash in the drop box $38,710
   b. Markers in the drop box $8,000
   c. Fill slips in the drop box $2,600
   d. Credit slips in the drop box $3,350

2. Describe three uses of computers in casino operations.

3. Circle T or F to indicate whether the following statements are true or false:
   T   F   a. A credit slip is completed when additional chips are issued to a table.
   T   F   b. *Markers* are another name for *IOUs*.
   T   F   c. Slot machines produce the highest margin of profit.
   T   F   d. Individual table results are tabulated on a stiff sheet.
   T   F   e. When people visit a casino on a junket, they pay their travel agent.

4. Circle the correct answer to the following statements:
   a. The location where chips are stored and transactions settled is termed:
      (1) The pit
      (2) The cage
      (3) The count room
   b. When a table returns excess chips to the cage, the slip completed is called:
      (1) A marker
      (2) A fill slip
      (3) A credit slip
   c. Foreign chips are:
      (1) Chips from another country
      (2) Chips from a different table
      (3) Chips from another casino
   d. Floating chips are:
      (1) Chips that float in water
      (2) Chips that have not been redeemed by customers before the casino closed
      (3) Chips carried to a different table
   e. When coins are dropped into a slot machine, they fall into:
      (1) The drop bucket
      (2) The hopper
      (3) The coin counter

20 Departmental Statements

The computerization of the hotel general ledger has greatly facilitated the preparation of the financial statements. Not only was it necessary to add and balance a manual or mechanical general ledger, often a time-consuming process, but the individual balances then had to be transferred to a financial statement. A look back at the chart of accounts displayed in Chapter 3 reveals 10 or more departments, either operated or overhead. Some of the larger departments contain 30 to 50 individual accounts, making the transfer of all balances extremely time-consuming. Additionally, the statements had to be balanced, department by department, an equally time-consuming process. Utilizing a computer program, the financial statements can be updated and printed in 30 to 40 minutes, the sole determining factor being the speed of the printer.

Another important feature of computerized software is the ability to format and reformat the structure of the financial statements. Most systems have a feature or option by which the prior year's numbers can be transferred over to the current year and used to provide comparisons. Similarly, budget numbers for the current year can be input (usually done for the entire year at the beginning of the year) to provide either the actual budget numbers for comparison purposes or to show the variances from budget. The decision as to whether to show actual budget numbers or variances therefrom depends on management preference. The width limitations prescribed by the software usually prevent printing both budget and variance. Furthermore, it would make the individual departmental schedule cumbersome and, in fact, there is no real value to having both.

This chapter deals exclusively with the various departmental schedules and their percentages which can be presented in various formats to provide information for an analysis of the results. Figure 20–1 shows a complete set of departmental schedules for a full-service hotel with a golf course and a hotel-operated gift shop.

In Chapter 22, each department is analyzed from an operational results point of view. In this chapter, the format and organization and the various options related thereto are examined.

Hotel Grayscot

DEPARTMENTAL STATEMENT - SEPTEMBER 199X

ROOMS

	Month Actual	%	Month Budget	%	Prior Yr Actual	%	YTD Actual	%	YTD Budget	%	Prior Yr Actual	%
Revenue												
Transient - Individual	305624	52.3	116054	22.4	139065	33.0	1498765	54.0	1124543	46.5	1312675	54.1
Golf - Individual	3602	6.1	58092	11.2	5687	1.3	88765	3.2	254376	10.5	32541	1.3
Corporate - Individual	9703	1.6	4721	0.9	18056	4.2	87654	3.1	33275	1.3	88706	3.6
Group - Corporate	102881	17.6	192087	37.2	132986	31.6	537645	19.4	504768	20.9	402546	16.6
Group - Tour & Travel	28072	4.8	77098	14.9	93766	22.2	212768	7.6	231548	9.5	287659	11.8
Group - Association	101322	17.3	68054	13.1	31067	7.3	345212	12.4	265098	10.9	298703	12.3
Total Revenue	583676	100.0	516106	100.0	420627	100.0	2770809	100.0	2413608	100.0	2422830	100.0
Salaries & Wages												
Salaries & Wages - Front Office	19877	3.4	22108	4.2	15431	3.6	142342	5.1	156432	6.4	137658	5.6
Salaries & Wages - Housekeeping	31062	5.3	27665	5.3	26098	6.2	187659	6.7	181243	7.5	156438	6.4
Salaries & Wages - Bell Staff	4103	0.7	6361	1.2	4432	1.0	23108	0.8	27085	1.1	28796	1.1
Total Salaries & Wages	55042	9.4	56134	10.8	45961	10.9	353109	12.7	364760	15.1	322892	13.3
Payroll Taxes & Empl. Relations												
Holiday & Vacation Pay	1722	0.3	1655	0.3	765	0.1	11212	0.4	11207	0.4	4987	0.2
Employee Meals	1944	0.3	2245	0.4	1685	0.4	13675	0.4	14325	0.5	13265	0.5
Payroll Taxes & Related Expenses	12994	2.2	11306	2.1	5446	1.2	89616	3.2	73993	3.0	39399	1.6
Total Benefits & Payroll Taxes	16660	2.8	15206	2.9	7896	1.8	114503	4.1	99525	4.1	57651	2.3
Other Expenses												
Cable TV	695	0.1	658	0.1	687	0.2	4432	0.2	5987	0.2	6123	0.3
China & Glassware	0	0.0	112	0.0	0	0.0	0	0.0	543	0.0	0	0.0
Cleaning Expense	1371	0.2	2354	0.5	1987	0.5	7123	0.3	12543	0.5	13241	0.5
Commissions	8654	1.4	9987	1.9	6754	1.6	22108	0.8	47654	2.0	42387	1.7
Contract Cleaning	0	0.0	0	0.0	0	0.0	564	0.0	2543	0.1	5648	0.2
Contract Services	22	0.0	345	0.1	132	0.0	123	0.0	0	0.0	546	0.0
Decorations	856	0.1	1235	0.2	777	0.2	7432	0.3	7659	0.3	8879	0.4
Drycleaning	362	0.0	342	0.1	465	0.1	1978	0.1	2207	0.1	1976	0.1
Equipment Rental	675	0.1	126	0.0	67	0.0	4187	0.2	1215	0.1	1870	0.1
Guest Supplies	6687	1.2	6152	1.2	6548	1.6	38665	1.4	44582	1.8	27697	1.1
Walked Guests	0	0.0	0	0.0	175	0.0	0	0.0	0	0.0	187	0.0
Laundry	6705	1.2	4365	0.8	4268	1.0	31683	1.1	35909	1.5	28828	1.2
Licenses & Permits	0	0.0	0	0.0	0	0.0	154	0.0	0	0.0	0	0.0
Linen	2110	0.4	8867	1.7	8769	2.1	3654	0.1	21365	0.9	15643	0.6
Office Supplies	1275	0.2	254	0.0	377	0.1	3765	0.1	1985	0.1	3327	0.1
Printing & Stationery	433	0.0	1265	0.2	4537	1.1	5132	0.2	9870	0.4	13265	0.5
Reservation Expense	4876	0.8	1377	0.3	0	0.0	11254	0.4	13212	0.5	0	0.0
Telephone Expense	0	0.0	432	0.1	2079	0.5	5123	0.2	3786	0.2	14648	0.6
Travel Expense	976	0.1	231	0.0	0	0.0	5546	0.2	1769	0.1	2546	0.1
Uniforms	0	0.0	1450	0.3	1436	0.3	17684	0.6	13800	0.6	4987	0.2
Utensils	1967	0.4	169	0.0	342	0.1	0	0.0	0	0.0	388	0.0
Miscellaneous Expense	0	0.0	788	0.2	687	0.2	354	0.0	1437	0.1	1435	0.1
Data Processing expense	76	0.0	0	0.0	131	0.0	6243	0.2	6574	0.3	4565	0.2
Dues & Subscriptions	1208	0.2	0	0.0	0	0.0	508	0.0	0	0.0	453	0.0
Vehicles	567	0.1	487	0.1	433	0.1	7154	0.2	4534	0.2	3546	0.1
Total Other Expenses	39515	6.5	40996	7.9	40651	9.6	179866	6.4	239174	9.9	202184	8.3
Total Expenses	111217	18.7	112336	21.7	94508	22.4	647478	23.3	703459	29.1	582727	24.0
Profit (Loss)	472459	81.3	403770	78.2	326119	77.5	2123331	76.6	1710149	70.8	1840103	75.9

Figure 20–1 Departmental Statements

Hotel Grayscot

DEPARTMENTAL STATEMENT - SEPTEMBER 199X

	Month Actual	%	Month Budget	%	Month Prior Yr	%	YTD Actual	%	YTD Budget	%	YTD Prior Yr	%
FOOD AND BEVERAGE												
Revenue												
Food - Outlet 1	66908	20.7	57064	28.6	49903	20.8	256661	18.6	382824	35.8	334973	24.8
Food - Outlet 2	81873	25.4	34888	17.5	35340	14.7	379081	27.5	177731	16.6	203359	15.0
Food - Banquet	93312	28.9	55259	27.7	93654	39.0	402170	29.2	257941	24.1	501205	37.0
Total Food	241593	75.0	147211	73.8	178897	74.5	1037912	75.3	818499	76.5	1039537	76.8
Beverage - Outlet 1	7456	2.3	15908	3.0	6714	2.8	31337	2.3	36761	3.4	31863	2.4
Beverage - Outlet 2	42491	13.2	26122	13.1	21740	9.1	177912	12.9	122362	11.5	137185	10.1
Beverage - Banquet	29853	9.3	17288	8.7	29321	12.2	115622	8.4	80938	7.6	123239	9.1
Total Beverage	79800	24.8	49318	24.8	57775	24.1	324871	23.6	240061	22.5	292287	21.6
F&B Misc. Income - Public Room Rental	1110	0.3	3036	1.5	1350	0.6	4339	0.3	8028	0.8	7475	0.6
- Audio/Visual	68	0.0			1493	0.6	7971	0.6			8200	0.6
- Other					734	0.3	1806	0.1	2233	0.2	5706	0.4
Total Revenue	322571	100.0	199565	100.0	240249	100.0	1376899	100.0	1068821	100.0	1353205	100.0
Cost of Sales												
Food - Cost of Food	93587	38.7	57094	38.8	71705	40.1	413053	39.8	314929	38.5	413635	39.8
Employee Meals	(8246)	73.4	(8400)	5.7	(5814)	3.2	(47365)	4.6	(53647)	6.6	(41753)	4.0
Net Cost of Food	85291	35.3	48694	33.1	65891	35.8	365688	35.2	261282	31.9	371882	35.8
Cost of Beverages	20015	25.1	11552	23.4	15760	27.3	90188	27.8	56618	23.6	79847	27.3
Total Cost of Sales	105306	32.6	60246	30.2	81651	34.0	455876	33.1	317900	29.7	451729	33.4
Salaries and Wages												
Salaries & Wages - Kitchen	56150	17.4	42437	21.3	38346	15.0	303590	22.1	266352	24.9	246424	18.2
Salaries & Wages - Service	33392	10.4	17311	8.7	28701	12.0	168605	12.2	109283	10.2	174782	12.9
Salaries & Wages - Bartenders	4073	1.3	3864	1.9	3558	1.5	21551	1.6	24900	2.3	31588	2.3
Salaries & Wages - F&B Admin.	5527	1.7	9479	4.7	8119	3.4	55323	4.0	80287	7.5	98935	7.3
Total Salaries & Wages	99142	30.8	73091	36.6	78724	32.9	549069	39.9	480822	36.6	551729	40.7
Payroll Taxes & Empl. Relations												
Holiday & Vacation Pay	2974	0.9	2193	1.1	733	0.3	16934	1.2	14425	1.4	8910	0.7
Employee Meals	3747	1.2	2919	1.5	2918	1.2	20611	1.5	18379	1.7	18269	1.4
Payroll Taxes & Related Expenses	16028	5.0	16164	8.1	12320	5.1	111987	8.1	129192	12.1	88900	6.6
Total Benefits & Payroll Taxes	22749	7.1	21276	10.7	15971	5.6	149532	10.8	161996	15.2	116079	8.7
Other Expenses												
Banquet Expenses	863	0.3	0	0.0	0	0.0	1106	0.1	0	0.0	570	0.0
Bar Expense	213	0.1	658	0.3	280	0.1	4495	0.3	3015	1.3	3135	0.2
China & Glassware	1421	0.4	1230	0.6	1459	0.6	6652	0.5	11234	1.0	9778	0.7
Cleaning Expense	2728	0.9	1181	0.6	1014	0.4	6051	0.4	7715	0.7	8112	0.6
Contract Cleaning	0	0.0	200	0.1	111	0.1	0	0.0	1350	0.1	2736	0.2
Decorations	979	0.3	2444	1.2	1932	0.8	5581	0.4	14712	1.4	14802	1.1
Dry Cleaning	641	0.2	300	0.2	746	0.3	2394	0.2	2100	0.2	2207	0.2
Equipment Rental	822	0.3	166	0.1	634	0.3	4925	0.4	1494	0.1	3760	0.3
Guest Supplies	627	0.2	239	0.1	842	0.4	2814	0.2	2187	0.2	1457	0.1
Ice	0	0.0	82	0.0	0	0.0	962	0.1	750	0.1	424	0.0
Kitchen Fuel	517	0.2	1500	0.8	342	0.1	8807	0.6	13700	1.3	3492	0.3
Laundry	3436	1.1	3312	1.7	722	0.3	20590	1.5	19310	1.8	15699	1.2
Licenses & Permits	0	0.0	30	0.0	0	0.0	1414	0.1	1274	0.1	1652	0.3
Linen	445	0.1	1200	0.6	350	0.2	3960	0.3	10960	1.0	6775	0.5
Menus & Wine Lists	925	0.3	910	0.5	3723	1.5	6774	0.5	9190	0.9	9886	0.7
Music & Entertainment	6359	2.0	5646	2.8	4661	1.9	28686	2.1	26129	2.4	29946	2.2

Figure 20–1 Departmental Statements *(continued)*

Hotel Grayscot

DEPARTMENTAL STATEMENT - SEPTEMBER 199X

FOOD AND BEVERAGE

	Month Actual	%	Month Budget	%	Month Prior Yr	%	YTD Actual	%	YTD Budget	%	YTD Prior Yr	%
Other Expenses - Continued												
Office Supplies	622	0.2	110	0.1	206	0.1	3330	0.2	990	0.1	1658	0.1
Paper Supplies	1754	0.5	1225	0.6	1747	0.7	10371	0.8	7964	0.8	13838	1.0
Printing & Stationery	902	0.3	532	0.3	0	0.0	3103	0.2	3663	0.3	2315	0.2
Spoilage	0	0.0	200	0.1	0	0.0	6200	0.5	1800	0.2	0	0.0
Silver	1100	0.3	820	0.4	61	0.0	8017	0.6	7487	0.7	435	0.0
Telephone Expense	1140	0.4	200	0.1	671	0.3	5044	0.4	1500	0.1	3993	0.3
Travel Expense	762	0.2	250	0.1	12	0.0	1652	0.1	2250	0.2	1089	0.1
Uniforms	1399	0.4	2229	1.1	2378	1.0	22504	1.6	20356	1.9	6840	0.5
Utensils	1683	0.5	700	0.4	2102	0.9	7205	0.5	5000	0.5	12984	1.0
Miscellaneous Expense	0	0.0	150	0.1	1517	0.6	718	0.1	1369	0.1	6379	0.5
Data Processing Expense	1198	0.4	500	0.3	449	0.2	3292	0.2	4500	0.4	5597	0.4
Dues & Subscriptions	0		0		0		500	0.0	100	0.0	630	0.0
Total Other Expenses	30536	9.5	26014	13.0	25959	10.8	177150	12.9	182099	17.0	170109	12.6
Total Expenses	152427	47.4	120381	60.3	120654	50.3	875751	63.6	824917	67.1	837917	62.0
Total Cost of Sales & Expense	257733	80.0	180627	90.5	202305	84.3	1331627	96.7	142817	102.0	1289646	95.4
Profit (Loss)	64838	20.0	18938	9.5	37944	15.7	45272	3.3	(73996)	(2.0)	63559	4.6

Figure 20–1 Departmental Statements *(continued)*

Hotel Grayscot

DEPARTMENTAL STATEMENT · SEPTEMBER 199X

TELEPHONE DEPARTMENT

	Month Actual	%	Month Budget	%	Prior Yr Actual	%	YTD Actual	%	YTD Budget	%	Prior Yr Actual	%
Revenue												
Revenue - Local	368	4.7	280	2.6	160	2.6	1973	4.5	1393	2.5	1346	2.7
Revenue - Long Distance	5614	71.3	9885	90.2	5023	80.3	32867	74.8	50066	89.0	41836	84.4
Revenue - Commissions	1896	24.1	800	7.3	1072	17.1	9127	20.8	4800	8.5	6366	12.8
Total Revenue	7878	100.0	10965	100.0	6255	100.0	43967	100.0	56259	100.0	49548	100.0
Cost of Sales												
Cost of Local Calls	0	0.0	140	1.3	0	0.0	130	0.3	697	1.2	0	0.0
Cost of Long Distance	3187	40.5	5931	54.1	1675	26.8	21582	49.1	30039	53.4	28911	58.3
Rental of Equipment	0	0.0	50	0.5	0	0.0	0	0.0	450	0.8	0	0.0
Total Cost of Sales	3187	40.5	6121	55.8	1675	25.8	21712	49.4	31186	55.4	28911	58.3
Salaries and Wages												
Salaries & Wages - Tel Operators	1942	24.7	2625	23.9	0	0.0	4489	10.2	10875	19.3	0	0.0
Total Salaries & Wages	1942	24.7	2625	23.9	0	0.0	4489	10.2	10875	19.3	0	0.0
Payroll Taxes & Empl. Relations												
Holiday & Vacation Pay	58	0.7	79	0.7	0	0.0	104	0.2	327	0.6	0	0.0
Employee Meals	90	1.1	107	1.0	0	0.0	151	0.3	436	0.8	0	0.0
Payroll Taxes & Related Expenses	604	7.7	559	5.1	0	0.0	1047	2.4	2325	4.1	0	0.0
Total Benefits & Payroll Taxes	752	9.5	745	6.8	0	0.0	1302	3.0	3088	5.5	0	0.0
Other Expenses												
Contract Services & Labor	561	7.1	575	5.2	561	9.0	5049	11.5	5175	9.2	4530	9.1
Equipment Charges	270	3.4	200	1.8	426	6.8	2935	6.7	1800	3.2	3907	7.9
Office Supplies	0	0.0	30	0.3	0	0.0	0	0.0	274	0.5	100	0.2
Printing & Stationery	0	0.0	86	0.8	0	0.0	0	0.0	652	1.2	0	0.0
Miscellaneous Expense	0	0.0	30	0.3	0	0.0	0	0.0	274	0.5	0	0.0
Total Other Expenses	831	10.5	921	8.4	987	15.8	7984	18.2	8175	14.5	8537	17.2
Total Exoenses	3525	44.7	4261	39.1	987	15.8	13775	31.3	22138	39.4	8537	17.2
Total Cost of Sales & Expense	6712	85.2	10412	95.0	2662	42.6	35487	80.7	53324	94.8	37448	75.6
Profit (Loss)	1166	14.8	553	5.0	3593	57.4	8480	19.3	2935	5.2	12100	24.4

Figure 20–1 Departmental Statements *(continued)*

Hotel Grayscot

DEPARTMENTAL STATEMENT - SEPTEMBER 199X

GIFT SHOP

	Month Actual	%	Month Budget	%	Month Prior Yr	%	YTD Actual	%	YTD Budget	%	Prior Yr Actual	%
Revenue												
Sales - Clothing & Gifts	11677	70.6	16904	90.7	6219	74.4	53414	73.3	71640	89.3	29031	69.6
Sales - Other	4861	29.4	1732	9.3	2136	25.6	19459	26.7	8615	10.7	12651	30.4
Total Revenue	16538	100.0	18636	100.0	8355	100.0	72873	100.0	80255	100.0	41642	100.0
Cost of Sales												
Cost of Clothing & Gifts	3930	33.7	7607	45.0	3627	58.3	25261	47.3	32102	44.8	15562	53.6
Cost of Sales Other	6557	134.9	1421	82.0	2237	104.7	18121	93.1	7066	82.0	8362	66.1
Total Cost of Sales	10487	40.5	9028	55.8	5864	70.2	43382	59.5	39168	48.8	23924	57.4
Salaries and Wages												
Salaries & Wages Gift Shop	3449	20.9	4514	24.2	2069	24.8	17640	24.2	23946	29.8	17162	41.2
Total Salaries & Wages	3449	2.09	4514	24.2	2069	24.8	17640	24.2	23946	29.8	17162	41.2
Payroll Taxes & Empl. Relations												
Holiday & Vacation Pay	103	0.6	135	0.7	0	0.0	528	0.7	719	0.9	375	0.9
Employee Meals	126	0.8	171	0.9	84	1.0	610	0.8	911	1.1	558	1.3
Payroll Taxes & Related Expenses	859	5.2	953	5.1	226	2.7	4165	5.7	5054	6.3	1967	4.7
Total Benefits & Payroll Taxes	1088	6.6	1259	6.8	310	3.7	5303	7.3	6684	8.3	2900	6.9
Other Expenses												
Cleaning Expense	0	0.0	30	0.2	0	0.0	0	0.0	274	0.3	91	0.2
Decorations	0	0.0	0	0.0	0	0.0	559	0.8	0	0.0	0	0.0
Contract Services & Labor	0	0.0	0	0.0	0	0.0	0	0.0	0	0.0	18	0.0
Office Supplies	60	0.4	0	0.0	15	0.2	586	0.8	0	0.0	31	0.1
Paper Supplies	116	0.7	225	1.2	108	1.3	843	1.2	2057	2.6	900	2.2
Postage & Telegrams	34	0.2	150	0.8	0	0.0	117	0.2	1370	1.7	0	0.0
Printing & Stationery	0	0.0	281	1.5	0	0.0	368	0.5	1278	1.6	0	0.0
Telephone Expense	26	0.2	30	0.2	18	0.2	373	0.5	270	0.3	36	0.1
Travel Expense	34	0.2	130	0.7	0	0.0	422	0.6	1170	1.5	0	0.0
Uniforms	0	0.0	369	2.0	0	0.0	0	0.0	1891	2.4	4	0.0
Miscellaneous Expense	37	0.2	0	0.0	0	0.0	858	1.2	0	0.0	126	0.3
Data Processing	18	0.1	0	0.0	0	0.0	18	0.0	0	0.0	0	0.0
Total Other Expenses	325	2.0	1215	6.5	141	1.7	4144	5.7	8310	10.4	1206	2.9
Total Expenses	4862	29.4	6988	37.5	2520	30.2	27087	37.2	38940	48.5	21268	51.0
Total Cost of Sales & Expense	15349	92.8	16016	85.9	8384	100.4	70469	96.7	78108	97.3	45192	108.4
Profit (Loss)	1189	7.2	2620	14.1	(29)	(0.4)	2404	3.2	2147	2.7	(3510)	(8.4)

Figure 20–1 Departmental Statements *(continued)*

Hotel Grayscot

DEPARTMENTAL STATEMENT - SEPTEMBER 199X

GOLF

	Month Actual	%	Month Budget	%	Month Prior Yr	%		YTD Actual	%	YTD Budget	%	YTD Prior Yr	%
Revenue													
Pro Shop Sales	20648	12.2	14042	5.9	11078	8.2		76441	13.0	49245	5.9	44710	8.6
Greens Fees	112985	66.8	183914	77.7	94112	69.3		399377	68.0	642748	77.2	385612	74.6
Cart Rentals	35394	20.9	38724	16.4	30710	22.6		104126	17.8	140854	16.9	86710	16.8
Golf Memberships	0	0.0	0	0.0	0	0.0		1100	0.2	0	0.0	0	0.0
Total Revenue	169027	100.0	236680	100.0	135900	100.0		580044	100.0	832848	100.0	517032	100.0
Cost of Sales													
Pro Shop Cost of Sales	12041	58.3	8425	60.0	6414	57.9		47525	62.2	29547	60.0	27108	60.6
Total Cost of Sales	12041	58.3	8425	60.0	6414	57.9		47525	62.2	29547	60.0	27108	60.6
Salaries and Wages													
Salaries & Wages - Maintenance	19481	11.5	20245	8.6	18720	13.8		164113	28.3	170567	20.5	152820	29.6
Salaries & Wages - Pro Shop	8943	5.3	11338	4.8	8108	6.0		47468	8.2	44392	5.3	41082	7.9
Total Salaries & Wages	28424	18.8	31583	13.4	26828	19.8		211581	36.5	214959	25.8	193902	37.5
Payroll Taxes & Empl. Relations													
Holiday & Vacation Pay	853	0.5	948	0.4	744	0.5		6291	1.1	6449	0.8	5820	1.1
Employee Meals	748	0.4	943	0.4	682	0.5		3534	0.6	6579	0.8	5617	1.1
Payroll Taxes & Related Expenses	3758	2.2	4426	1.9	2810	2.1		35039	6.0	29965	3.6	21052	4.1
Total Benefits & Payroll Taxes	5359	3.1	6317	2.7	4236	3.		44864	7.7	42993	5.2	32489	6.3
Other Expenses													
Cleaning Expense	0	0.0	100	0.0	0	0.0		47	0.0	610	0.1	0	0.0
Commissions	0	0.0	1404	0.6	0	0.0		275	0.0	4924	0.6	0	0.0
Contract Services & Labor	275	0.2	83	0.0	105	0.1		599	0.1	747	0.1	310	0.1
Decorations	144	0.1	0	0.0	0	0.0		25	0.0	0	0.0	0	0.0
Dry Cleaning	0	0.0	0	0.0	0	0.0		669	0.1	0	0.0	0	0.0
Equipment Rental	26	0.0	250	0.1	0	0.0		607	0.1	750	0.1	0	0.0
Office Supplies	32	0.0	0	0.0	0	0.0		110	0.0	0	0.0	0	0.0
Paper Supplies	0	0.0	0	0.0	0	0.0		2870	0.5	1865	0.2	848	0.2
Printing & Stationery	892	0.5	460	0.2	622	0.5		2164	0.4	2250	0.3	648	0.1
Telephone Expense	176	0.1	250	0.1	170	0.1		1490	0.3	1125	0.1	521	0.1
Travel Expense	0	0.0	125	0.1	0	0.0		4090	0.7	2000	0.2	1672	0.3
Uniforms	694	0.4	250	0.1	480	0.4		1879	0.3	378	0.0	142	0.0
Miscellaneous Expense	0	0.0	42	0.0	0	0.0		655	0.1	900	0.1		0.0
Dues & Subscriptions	0	0.0	100	0.0	0	0.0		4760	0.8	5000	0.6	100	0.0
Consultants	945	0.6	0	0.0	0	0.0		45	0.0	900	0.1	7210	1.4
Licenses & Permits	0	0.0	100	0.0	0	0.0		5964	1.0	9378	1.1	8615	1.7
Operating Supplies	1391	0.8	1042	0.4	982	0.7		6763	1.2	10690	1.3	3820	0.7
Electricity	114	0.1	1850	0.8	280	0.2		1202	0.2	4563	0.6	810	0.2
Fuel	297	0.2	507	0.2	160	0.1		2816	0.5	3078	0.4	60	0.0
Sewage/Drainage	0	0.0	342	0.1	0	0.0		627	0.1	0	0.0	728	0.1
Water	(66)	0.0	0	0.0	180	0.1		1362	0.2	747	0.1	9186	1.8
Building Repairs	412	0.2	83	0.0	1180	0.9		12729	2.2	12375	1.5	308	0.1
Electrical & Mechanical Equip	1837	1.1	1375	0.6	90	0.1		2221	0.4	900	0.0	128	0.0
Engineering Supplies	754	0.5	100	0.0	85	0.1		414	0.1	0	0.0	2176	0.4
Furniture	0	0.0	0	0.0	0	0.0		5666	1.0	2628	0.3	6220	1.2
Golf Cart Maintenance	6	0.0	292	0.1	172	0.1		5760	1.0	7920	1.0	1654	0.3
Grounds & Landscaping	1371	0.8	880	0.4	860	0.6		2518	0.4	1872	0.2	1580	0.3
Irrigation Systems	35	0.0	208	0.1	110	0.1		1892	0.3	1100	0.1	180	0.0
Removal of Waste	642	0.4	220	0.1	508	0.4		79	0.0	900	0.1	700	0.1
Snow Removal	0	0.0	0	0.0	70	0.1		1352	0.2	0	0.0	180	0.0
Vehicles	646	0.4	100	0.0	620	0.5		24443	4.2	32960	4.0	19012	3.7
Compounds	88	0.1	0	0.0	100	0.1		28780	4.9	28105	3.4	22111	4.3
Fertilizer	6118	3.6	6592	2.8	5200	3.8		582	0.1	2145	0.3	1652	0.3
Gasoline - Carts	0	0.0	5621	2.4	380	0.3		432	0.1	602	0.1	182	0.0
Roads & Paths	0	0.0	429	0.2	0	0.0							
Sand	227	0.1	240	0.1	176	0.1		1259	0.2	2160	0.3	976	0.2
Total Other Expenses	17056	10.2	23112	9.4	12650	9.3		127146	21.7	143572	17.4	91549	17.7
Total Expenses	50839	32.1	61022	24.5	43714	32.2		383591	65.9	401524	48.4	317940	61.5
Total Cost of Sales & Expense	62880	37.2	69447	29.4	50128	36.9		431116	74.3	431071	51.8	345048	66.7
Profit (Loss)	106147	62.8	167233	70.6	85772	63.1		148928	25.7	401777	48.2	171984	33.3

Figure 20–1   Departmental Statements *(continued)*

Hotel Grayscot

DEPARTMENTAL STATEMENT - SEPTEMBER 199X

ADMINISTRATIVE AND GENERAL

	Month Actual	%	Month Budget	%	Month Prior Yr	%	YTD Actual	%	YTD Budget	%	YTD Prior Yr	%
Salaries & Wages												
Salaries & Wages - Accounting	13715	21.8	10965	16.6	10138	12.6	111137	24.4	93817	19.0	85760	17.2
Salaries & Wages - Administrative	4494	7.1	6137	9.3	308	0.4	40088	8.8	49626	10.0	67129	13.5
Total Salaries & Wages	18209	28.9	17102	25.9	10446	13.0	151225	33.2	143443	29.0	152889	30.7
Payroll Taxes & Empl. Relations												
Holiday & Vacation Pay	546	0.9	513	0.8	300	0.4	4345	1.0	4303	0.9	3480	0.7
Employee Meals	404	0.6	420	0.6	358	0.4	3347	0.7	3337	0.7	2803	0.6
Payroll Taxes & Related Expenses	2718	4.3	3084	4.7	1044	1.3	26859	5.9	26055	5.3	23215	4.7
Total Benefits & Payroll Taxes	3668	5.8	4017	6.1	1702	2.1	34551	7.6	33695	6.8	29498	6.0
Other Expenses												
Cleaning Expenses	0	0.0	0	0.0	0	0.0	0	0.0	0	0.0	0	0.0
Contract Services & Labor	970	1.5	0	0.0	7850	9.8	9092	2.0	0	0.0	16656	3.3
Dry Cleaning	315	0.5	250	0.4	421	0.5	1290	0.3	2250	0.5	1170	0.2
Equipment Rental	0	0.0	150	0.2	0	0.0	551	0.1	1350	0.3	150	0.0
Licenses & Permits	0	0.0	0	0.0	0	0.0	65	0.0	0	0.0	5	0.0
Office Supplies	954	1.5	510	0.8	533	0.7	10317	2.3	4658	0.9	5685	1.1
Postage & Telegrams	632	1.0	150	0.2	238	0.3	3058	0.7	1370	0.3	2879	0.6
Printing & Stationery	1062	1.7	600	0.9	184	0.2	4589	1.0	5480	1.1	3373	0.7
Telephone Expense	958	1.5	315	0.5	906	1.1	5185	1.1	2805	0.6	2526	0.5
Travel Expense	38	0.1	800	1.2	20	0.0	2617	0.6	7200	1.5	2267	0.5
Uniforms	0	0.0	150	0.2	7	0.0	541	0.1	1370	0.3	398	0.1
Miscellaneous Expense	194	0.3	83	0.1	0	0.0	1045	0.2	754	0.2	2614	0.5
Audit Fees	1000	1.6	1500	2.3	0	0.0	9485	2.1	13500	2.7	0	0.0
Bank Charges	17	0.0	0	0.0	0	0.0	137	0.0	0	0.0	89	0.0
Cashiers Short & Over	(600)	-1.0	60	0.1	(10)	-0.7	(1552)	-0.3	548	0.1	806	0.2
Credit Card Commissions	21605	34.3	19018	28.8	9568	11.9	79770	17.5	87946	17.8	65367	13.1
Credit & Collection Expense	0	0.0	0	0.0	0	0.0	(27)	0.0	0	0.0	14560	2.9
Data Processing Expense	781	1.2	300	0.5	124	0.2	6093	1.3	2700	0.5	4008	0.8
Donations & Contributions	235	0.4	416	0.6	0	0.0	2641	0.6	3744	0.8	466	0.1
Dues & Subscriptions	650	1.0	80	0.1	106	0.1	720	0.2	720	0.1	266	0.1
Guest Loss & Damage	152	0.2	83	0.1	0	0.0	416	0.1	754	0.2	641	0.1
Legal Fees	714	1.1	1214	1.8	4016	5.0	11768	2.6	10926	2.2	8123	1.6
Professional Fees	0	0.0	0	0.0	0	0.0	375	0.1	754	0.2	0	0.0
Managers' Expenses	12098	19.2	16500	25.0	41326	51.4	118502	26.0	148500	30.1	134730	27.1
Bad Debt Expense	100	0.2	1001	1.5	2000	2.5	3868	0.8	4629	0.9	6963	1.4
Total Other Expenses	42095	65.3	45930	68.0	66712	84.9	279237	59.2	325954	64.2	273742	63.3
Total Expenses	63972	100.0	67049	100.0	78860	100.0	465013	100.0	503092	100.0	456139	100.0
Profit (Loss)	(63972)	-100.0	(67049)	-100.0	(78860)	-100.0	(465013)	-100.0	(503092)	-100.0	(456139)	-100.0

Figure 20–1 Departmental Statements *(continued)*

Hotel Grayscot

DEPARTMENTAL STATEMENT - SEPTEMBER 199X

SALES AND MARKETING	Month Actual	%	Month Budget	%	Month Prior Yr	%	YTD Actual	%	YTD Budget	%	Month Prior Yr	%
Salaries and Wages												
Salaries & Wages - Sales	10037	11.9	8852	16.3	5528	10.4	74784	17.3	81261	16.7	72218	12.5
Total Salaries & Wages	10037	11.9	8852	16.3	5528	10.4	74784	17.3	81261	16.7	72218	12.5
Payroll Taxes & Empl. Relations												
Holiday & Vacation Pay	301	0.4	266	0.5	0	0.0	2222	0.5	2438	0.5	3165	0.5
Employee Meals	177	0.2	171	0.3	76	0.1	1419	0.3	1564	0.3	1091	0.2
Payroll Taxes & Related Expenses	1314	1.6	1404	2.6	440	0.8	12449	2.9	12898	2.6	8091	1.4
Total Benefits & Payroll Taxes	1792	2.1	1841	3.4	516	0.9	16090	3.7	16900	3.5	12347	2.1
Other Expenses												
Decorations	0	0.0	0	0.0	0	0.0	0	0.0	0	0.0	3	0.0
Contract Services & Labor	0	0.0	0	0.0	809	1.5	435	0.1	0	0.0	3635	0.6
Dry Cleaning	90	0.1	75	0.1	215	0.4	374	0.1	675	0.1	606	0.1
Equipment Rental	209	0.2	375	0.7	184	0.3	2175	0.5	3375	0.7	2477	0.4
Office Supplies	572	0.7	250	0.5	408	0.8	7586	1.8	2250	0.5	3820	0.7
Paper Supplies	0	0.0	0	0.0	0	0.0	0	0.0	0	0.0	72	0.0
Postage & Telegrams	0	0.0	0	0.0	0	0.0	0	0.0	0	0.0	0	0.0
Printing & Stationery	0	0.0	250	0.5	202	0.4	486	0.1	2250	0.5	2220	0.4
Telephone Expense	3262	3.9	1000	1.8	1503	2.8	11788	2.7	9000	1.8	11234	1.9
Travel Expense	817	1.0	900	1.7	475	0.9	8367	1.9	17600	3.6	5857	1.0
Uniforms	0	0.0	0	0.0	0	0.0	14	0.0	0	0.0	122	0.0
Miscellaneous Expense	0	0.0	250	0.5	45	0.1	536	0.1	2250	0.5	1045	0.2
Data Processing Expense	0	0.0	0	0.0	0	0.0	559	0.1	0	0.0	0	0.0
Donations & Contributions	0	0.0	0	0.0	0	0.0	0	0.0	0	0.0	140	0.0
Dues & Subscriptions	1530	1.8	600	1.1	25	0.0	6537	1.5	5400	1.1	3370	0.6
Postage & Telegrams - Sales	2094	2.5	1500	2.8	1510	2.8	13965	3.2	13500	2.8	12414	2.1
Guest Entertainment	4486	5.3	2500	4.6	6269	11.7	29451	6.8	15000	3.1	22117	3.8
Guest History	0	0.0	0	0.0	0	0.0	0	0.0	0	0.0	110	0.0
Photography	143	0.2	291	0.5	67	0.1	1129	0.3	2619	0.5	1822	0.3
Trade Shows	1450	1.7	1000	1.8	1850	3.5	10675	2.5	6000	1.2	3153	0.5
Agency Fees	3150	3.7	4000	7.4	2389	4.5	24014	5.6	36000	7.4	10057	1.7
Brochures	2390	2.8	2083	3.8	3406	6.4	10077	2.3	18747	3.8	42170	7.3
Direct Mail	900	1.1	417	0.8	0	0.0	3671	0.8	3753	0.8	6807	1.2
Hotel Representatives	319	0.4	250	0.5	286	0.5	4689	1.1	2250	0.5	5377	0.9
Local Media	942	1.1	3300	6.1	351	0.7	18775	4.3	28050	5.7	10340	1.8
Newsletter	0	0.0	0	0.0	0	0.0	20	0.0	0	0.0	367	0.1
Public Relations	2500	3.0	2917	5.4	2543	4.8	22004	5.1	26253	5.4	8891	1.5
Print - Directories	5597	6.6	1100	2.0	166	0.3	16794	3.9	9900	2.0	14447	2.5
Print - Magazines	22081	26.1	8333	15.3	0	0.0	60551	14.0	74997	15.4	948	0.2
Print - Newspapers	21241	25.1	12544	23.1	15409	28.9	80187	18.6	112896	23.1	234007	40.4
Production	325	0.4	1666	3.1	3280	6.2	19864	4.6	14994	3.1	59439	10.3
Radio & TV	746	0.9	0	0.0	600	1.1	1528	0.4	0	0.0	15084	2.6
Trade Agreements	0	0.0	0	0.0	5250	9.8	2797	0.6	0	0.0	10769	1.9
Total Other Expenses	74844	86.0	45601	80.3	47252	88.7	359046	79.0	407759	79.8	492920	85.4
Total Expenses	86673	100.0	56294	100.0	53296	100.0	449920	100.0	505920	100.0	576855	100.0
Profit (Loss)	(86673)	-100.0	(56294)	-100.0	(53296)	-100.0	(449920)	-100.0	(505920)	-100.0	(576855)	-100.0

Figure 20–1 Departmental Statements (*continued*)

Hotel Grayscot

DEPARTMENTAL STATEMENT - SEPTEMBER 199X

ENERGY COSTS

Other Expenses	Month Actual	%	Month Budget	%	Month Prior Yr	%	YTD Actual	%	YTD Budget	%	Month Prior Yr	%
Electric Light Bulbs	565	2.0	417	1.6	274	1.2	3086	1.3	2652	1.1	3461	1.6
Electricity	18231	64.6	16800	64.6	15893	69.6	159880	67.7	147300	61.1	133202	61.0
Fuel	0	0.0	5000	19.2	2559	11.3	22253	9.4	39500	16.4	63060	28.9
Propane Gas	3399	12.0	1000	3.8	0	0.0	26323	11.1	26500	11.0	0	0.0
Sewage	2540	9.0	800	3.1	3000	13.2	9023	3.8	7200	3.0	8007	3.7
Water	3505	12.4	2000	7.7	1000	4.4	15546	6.6	18000	7.5	10781	4.9
Total Other Expenses	28240	100.0	26017	100.0	22726	100.0	23611	100.0	241152	100.0	218511	100.0
Total Expenses	28240	100.0	26017	100.0	22726	100.0	23611	100.0	241152	100.0	218511	100.0
Profit (Loss)	(28240)	-100.0	(26017)	-100.0	(22726)	-100.0	(23611)	-100.0	(241152)	-100.0	(218511)	-100.0

Figure 20–1 Departmental Statements *(continued)*

Hotel Grayscot

DEPARTMENTAL STATEMENT - SEPTEMBER 199X

PROPERTY OPERATION AND MAINTENANCE	Month Actual	%	Month Budget	%	Month Prior Yr	%	YTD Actual	%	YTD Budget	%	YTD Prior Yr	%
Salaries & Wages												
Salaries & Wages - Engineering	15050	26.7	12885	33.7	11329	35.8	105940	31.5	109336	33.7	91349	33.0
Salaries & Wages - Security	3316	5.9	2738	7.2	2269	7.2	32975	9.8	25427	7.8	22768	8.2
Total Salaries & Wages	18366	32.6	15623	40.8	13598	42.9	138915	41.3	134763	41.6	114117	41.2
Payroll Taxes & Empl. Relations												
Holiday & Vacation Pay	551	1.0	469	1.2	0	0.0	4016	1.2	4044	1.2	4125	1.5
Employee Meals	461	0.8	386	1.0	344	1.1	3647	1.1	3261	1.0	2776	1.0
Payroll Taxes & Related Expenses	3079	5.5	2519	6.6	1173	3.7	28960	8.6	21792	6.7	14147	5.1
Total Benefits & Payroll Taxes	4091	7.3	3374	8.8	1517	4.8	36623	10.9	29097	8.9	21048	7.6
Other Expenses												
Contract Services & Labor	722	1.3	833	2.2	622	2.0	5653	1.7	7467	2.3	8109	2.9
Dry Cleaning	0	0.0	0	0.0	0	0.0	149	0.0	0	0.0	58	0.0
Equipment Rental	0	0.0	83	0.2	0	0.0	286	0.0	747	0.2	144	0.1
Guest Supplies	0	0.0	0	0.0	0	0.0	0	0.0	0	0.0	66	0.0
Office Supplies	6	0.0	42	0.1	0	0.0	119	0.0	378	0.1	65	0.0
Paper Supplies	0	0.0	0	0.0	0	0.0	0	0.0	0	0.0	0	0.0
Printing & Stationery	0	0.0	42	0.1	0	0.0	2	0.0	378	0.1	0	0.0
Telephone Expense	40	0.1	30	0.0	47	0.1	645	0.2	270	0.1	196	0.1
Travel Expense	0	0.0	0	0.0	0	0.0	54	0.0	0	0.0	0	0.0
Uniforms	546	1.0	247	0.6	522	1.6	2113	0.6	2254	0.7	1608	0.6
Miscellaneous Expense	0	0.0	60	0.2	44	0.1	792	0.2	548	0.2	491	0.2
Dues & Subscriptions	0	0.0	0	0.0	0	0.0	0	0.0	0	0.0	75	0.0
Heating, Ventilation & Air Cond.	5087	9.0	2083	5.4	403	1.3	17543	5.2	18747	5.8	16932	6.1
Building Repairs	7907	14.0	2083	5.4	2062	6.5	19687	5.9	18747	5.8	12721	4.6
Curtains & Drapes	0	0.0	125	0.3	0	0.0	32	0.0	1125	0.3	249	0.1
Electrical & Mechanical Equipment	2292	4.1	833	2.2	420	1.3	6157	1.8	7497	2.3	4113	1.5
Elevators	374	0.7	660	1.7	281	0.9	3308	1.0	6028	1.9	5266	1.9
Engineering Supplies	1426	2.5	250	0.7	142	0.4	4924	1.5	2250	0.7	1452	0.5
Exterminating	350	0.6	180	0.5	0	0.0	1575	0.5	1620	0.5	175	0.1
Floor Covering	217	0.4	166	0.4	261	0.8	947	0.3	1494	0.5	640	0.2
Furniture	3177	5.6	246	0.6	333	1.1	4484	1.3	2246	0.7	1899	0.7
Grounds & Landscaping	4341	7.7	3524	9.2	5885	18.6	19496	5.8	19789	6.1	22210	8.0
Kitchen Equipment	1405	2.5	1250	3.3	250	0.8	10024	3.0	8100	2.5	10142	3.7
Laundry Equipment	1020	1.8	813	2.1	641	2.0	3961	1.2	5478	1.7	7377	2.7
Painting & Decorating	858	1.5	2000	5.2	8	0.0	1613	0.5	19930	6.2	775	0.3
Plumbing	598	1.1	833	2.2	535	1.7	4114	1.2	5598	1.7	7634	2.8
Removal of Waste	2065	3.7	1250	3.3	1139	3.6	12102	3.6	8100	2.5	12549	4.5
Refrigeration	16	0.0	0	0.0	0	0.0	465	0.1	0	0.0	0	0.0
Service Contracts	0	0.0	480	1.3	394	1.2	290	0.0	4384	1.4	3181	1.1
Snow Removal	0	0.0	0	0.0	0	0.0	0	0.0	6400	2.0	4250	1.5
Swimming Pool	0	0.0	0	0.0	717	2.3	0	0.0	0	0.0		
Television	656	1.2	600	1.6	48	0.2	945	0.3	5480	1.7	4908	1.8
Vehicles	819	1.5	560	1.5	553	1.7	5009	1.5	5040	1.6		
Total Other Expenses	33922	60.2	19273	50.4	15307	48.3	126489	47.8	160125	49.4	127285	47.1
Total Expenses	56379	100.0	38270	100.0	30422	100.0	302027	100.0	323985	100.0	262450	100.0
Profit (Loss)	(56379)	-100.0	(38270)	-100.0	(30422)	-100.0	(302027)	-100.0	(323985)	-100.0	(262450)	-100.0

Figure 20-1 Departmental Statements *(continued)*

Hotel Grayscot

DEPARTMENTAL STATEMENT - SEPTEMBER 199X

FIXED CHARGES	Month Actual	%	Month Budget	%	Month Prior Yr	%	YTD Actual	%	YTD Budget	%	Month Prior Yr	%
Capital Expenses												
Insurance - Bldg & Contents	20036	10.6	28409	14.3	29386	16.1	189074	11.0	255681	14.3	227514	13.3
Taxes - Real Estate	12652	6.7	12436	6.3	10194	5.6	112634	6.6	111924	6.3	97508	5.7
Interest - Mortgage	77500	40.9	77500	39.1	79588	43.6	697500	40.8	697500	39.1	716250	41.9
Depreciation	79127	41.8	80000	40.3	63288	34.7	712149	41.6	720000	40.3	669599	39.1
Total Capital Expenses	189315	100.0	198345	100.0	182456	100.0	1711357	100.0	1785105	100.0	1710871	100.0
Profit (Loss)	189315	-100.0	198345	-100.0	182456	-100.0	1711357	-100.0	1785105	-100.0	1710871	-100.0

Figure 20–1 Departmental Statements *(continued)*

252

Hotel Grayscot

DEPARTMENTAL STATEMENT - SEPTEMBER 199X

LAUNDRY

	Month Actual	%	Month Budget	%	Month Prior Yr	%	YTD Actual	%	YTD Budget	%	Month Prior Yr	%
Revenue												
Sales - Laundry	(181)	100.0	0	0.0	(741)	100.0	501	100.0	0	0.0	212	100.0
Total Revenue	(181)	100.0	0	0.0	(741)	100.0	501	100.0	0	0.0	212	100.0
Salaries and Wages												
Salaries & Wages - Guest Laundry	7347	71.2	5880	62.1	3651	61.3	31405	60.7	35224	63.8	32328	60.2
Total Salaries & Wages	7347	71.2	5880	62.1	3651	61.3	31405	60.7	35224	63.8	32328	60.2
Payroll Taxes & Empl. Relations												
Holiday & Vacation Pay	220	2.1	176	1.9	256	4.3	941	1.8	1056	1.9	893	1.7
Employee Meals	281	2.7	214	2.3	163	2.7	1332	2.6	1258	2.3	1035	1.9
Payroll Taxes & Related Expenses	1859	18.0	1257	13.3	427	7.2	8555	16.5	7557	13.7	4269	7.9
Total Benefits & Payroll Taxes	2360	22.9	1647	17.4	846	14.2	10828	20.9	9870	17.9	6197	11.5
Other Expenses												
Cleaning Expense	0	0.0	0	0.0	0	0.0	280	0.5	0	0.0	12	0.0
Paper Supplies	0	0.0	0	0.0	0	0.0	0	0.0	0	0.0	942	1.8
Laundry Supplies	567	5.5	1817	19.2	1141	19.2	8402	16.2	9053	16.4	9160	17.1
Uniforms	0	0.0	60	0.6	0	0.0	9	0.0	548	1.0	689	1.3
Miscellaneous Expense	48	0.5	60	0.6	43	0.7	848	1.6	548	1.0	273	0.5
Laundry Transfer to Rooms	(6705)	-65.0	(6152)	-65.0	(4268)	-71.7	(31683)	-61.2	(35934)	-65.0	(34114)	-63.5
Laundry Transfers to F&B	(3436)	-36.8	(3312)	-35.1	(722)	-23.7	(20590)	-37.7	(19310)	-35.1	(15699)	-28.9
Total Other Expenses	(9526)	-95.8	(7527)	-79.5	(3806)	-75.5	(42734)	-80.6	(45133)	-81.7	(38737)	-71.7
Total Expenses	(181)	-1.8	0	0.0	0	0.0	501	1.0	0	0.0	212	0.0
Profit (Loss)	(0)	0.0	0	0.0	0	0.0	0	0.0	0	0.0	0	0.0

Figure 20–1 Departmental Statements *(continued)*

Hotel Grayscot

DEPARTMENTAL STATEMENT - SEPTEMBER 199X

HUMAN RESOURCES DEPARTMENT

	Month Actual	%	Month Budget	%		YTD Actual	%	YTD Budget	%
Salaries and Wages									
Salaries & Wages	4436	16.1	3890	14.8		30726	15.3	35010	14.9
Total Salaries & Wages	4436	16.1	3890	14.8		30726	15.3	35010	14.9
Payroll Taxes & Empl. Relations									
Holiday & Vacation Pay	133	0.5	0	0.0		913	0.5	467	0.2
Employee Meals	83	0.3	0	0.0		575	0.3	177	0.1
Payroll Taxes & Related Expenses	355	1.3	310	1.2		2729	1.4	2146	0.9
Health Insurance	12765	46.2	13630	52.0		104129	51.8	122670	52.2
401K and Flexible Benefits	502	1.8	600	2.3		8013	4.0	4509	1.9
Workmen's Compensation	2830	10.2	3853	14.7		21708	10.8	34677	14.8
Total Benefits & Payroll Taxes	16668	60.3	18393	70.2		138067	68.6	164646	70.1
Other Expenses									
Dry Cleaning	32	0.1	0	0.0		211	0.1	0	0.0
Office Supplies	101	0.4	0	0.0		993	0.5	0	0.0
Paper Supplies	0	0.0	0	0.0		0	0.0	0	0.0
Printing & Stationery	425	1.5	667	2.5		3384	1.7	6003	2.6
Telephone Expense	357	1.3	100	0.4		1087	0.5	900	0.4
Travel Expense	300	1.1	133	0.5		1100	0.5	1197	0.5
Miscellaneous Expense	0	0.0	0	0.0		227	0.1	0	0.0
Data Processing Expense	0	0.0	0	0.0		75	0.0	0	0.0
Dues & Subscriptions	0	0.0	0	0.0		135	0.1	0	0.0
Legal Fees	0	0.0	0	0.0		0	0.0	0	0.0
Professional & Consultants Fee	0	0.0	800	3.1		125	0.1	7200	3.1
Employee Relations	194	0.7	0	0.0		6017	3.0	0	0.0
Employee Relocation	1788	6.5	1250	4.8		10923	5.4	11250	4.8
Medical Expenses	0	0.0	800	3.1		1301	0.6	7200	3.1
Personnel Recruitment	1725	6.2	166	0.6		5192	2.6	1494	0.6
Total Other Expenses	4922	17.8	3916	14.9		30770	15.3	35244	15.0
Department Allocation									
Alloc to Rooms	(6508)	-23.6	(6524)	-24.9		(47709)	-23.7	(58494)	-24.9
Alloc to F&B	(16028)	-63.8	(16164)	-61.7		(111987)	-58.2	(129192)	-55.0
Alloc to Telephone	(327)	-1.2	(341)	-1.3		(598)	-0.3	(3057)	-1.3
Alloc to Gift Shop	(436)	-1.6	(524)	-2.0		(2189)	-1.1	(4698)	-2.0
Alloc to A&G						(12349)	-6.1	(15735)	-6.7
Alloc to Sales	(436)	-1.6	(655)	-2.5		(5381)	-2.7	(5874)	-2.5
Alloc to Engineering	(1309)	-4.7	(1310)	-5.0		(14600)	-7.3	(11745)	-5.0
Alloc to Laundry	(982)	-3.6	(681)	-2.6		(4750)	-2.4	(6105)	-2.6
Total Departmental Allocations	(25576)	-100.0	(26199)	-100.0		(199563)	-100.0	(234900)	-100.0
Total Expenses	0	0	0	0.0		0	0	0	0.0
Profit (Loss)	0	0	0	0.0		0	0	(0)	0.0

Figure 20–1 Departmental Statements (continued)

THE STRUCTURE OF THE STATEMENTS

First, and most important, the format follows the Uniform System of Accounts (see Figure 3–1) both as to departments and as to accounts contained within each department. The departments are either operated or overhead departments. The operated (i.e., income producing) departments are:

Rooms
Food and Beverages
Telephone
Gift Shop
Golf
Rents and Other Income

The overhead (i.e., support) departments are:

Administrative and General
Sales and Marketing
Property Operation and Maintenance
Energy Costs

There are also two allocated departments, Laundry and Human Resources. These two departments can also be considered to fill a support function for the operated departments. The difference is that a logical allocation of the costs of these departments to certain operated departments can be made. The costs of the Laundry department, net of any income derived from guest laundry, can be allocated based on the volume of work done for the respective departments. The total cost of the Human Resources department is allocated based on the number of employees administered in each department. Another allocated department found in many hotels is Employee's Cafeteria. This department is used if the cafeteria has its own food preparation area and requires specific employees. Finally, the Fixed Charges or Capital Expenses (the terms are synonymous) are reflected on the last schedule.

The structure of the operated departments groups the accounts within various subheadings:

Revenue
Cost of Sales
Salaries and Wages
Payroll Taxes and Employee Relations
Other Expenses

As previously mentioned, it is not necessary to show every individual revenue or expense on the departmental schedules. However, groupings, particularly of expenses, should not be done unless no analytical value can be derived by showing the accounts separately, the individual amounts are insignificant, or they are being compared to a budget number in which they were combined. In the first two examples, the question must be raised as to the value of having two separate general ledger accounts. The third situation is valid but care should be taken in subsequent years to budget these expenses separately, particularly if the amounts in question are significant.

Overhead departments normally have no revenue or cost of sales; they are broken down, therefore, between Salaries and Wages, Payroll Taxes and Related Expenses, and Other Expenses.

In all departments, totals are provided for each subheading. Additionally, a total expense combined, excluding cost of sales, is provided in addition to a total of expenses and cost of sales.

While Figure 20–1 does not reflect a gross profit, that is, revenue minus cost of sales, clearly this option should be considered. As stressed earlier, the final design of the departmental statements depends entirely on management preference, subject, of course, to limitations of the software. However, in general, software packages for hotel back-office systems provide great flexibility in the area of statement design. In fact, several options are usually provided with the package. Of these, a most useful feature is the system's ability to automatically distribute the allocated departments based on preset formats.

Figure 20–1 provides comparisons, on a monthly and year-to-date basis, against budget and against prior year. An alternative format would be to show the variance from budget or from both budget and prior year. However, most hotels prefer to show the actuals rather than the variances. Management usually finds this format easier to understand and work with.

Most software packages provide the opportunity to show percentages opposite each number. Management must decide, department by department, which numbers will be used as a base on which the percentages are calculated. The operated departments in Figure 20–1 follow the format most commonly used by hotels:

1. Percentages opposite individual revenue classifications reflect that revenue segment measured against total revenue (sometimes termed *vertical analysis.*)
2. Individual cost of sales is measured against the applicable revenue. Total cost of sales is measured against total revenue.
3. Salaries and wages, payroll taxes and benefits, and other expenses are shown as a percentage of total departmental revenue.
4. Departmental profit is shown as a percentage of total departmental revenue.

Two approaches are commonly used in the overhead departments for percentages:

1. Each individual expense within the department is shown as a percentage of the total departmental expense. This is the approach used in Figure 20–1.
2. All expenses in all overhead departments are shown as a percentage of total revenue.

The problem with the latter approach is that the percentages on many of the smaller items lose their significance. It should be noted, however, that in the area of advertising expenditures a comparison against total hotel revenue, whether reflected on the departmental schedules or on a separate analysis, does have a high level of validity as a measurement of comparison.

While percentages are valuable tools in measuring such expenditures as cost of sales or payroll, the primary focus should always be on comparisons to budget and prior years. The impact of such comparisons is explored more fully in Chapter 22 in relation to a complete analysis of operating results.

In the next chapter, the remaining elements of the financial statement package—the balance sheet, the statement of income, and recommended statistics—are reviewed.

1. Describe the differences between operated departments, overhead departments, and allocated departments.

2. Name two allocated departments commonly used in hotels and describe the basis for the allocations.

3. Circle T or F to indicate whether the following statements are true or false:

   T   F   **a.** Telephone is an operated department.

   T   F   **b.** Golf is an overhead department.

   T   F   **c.** The Human Resources department is normally allocated.

   T   F   **d.** Vertical analysis is the comparison of departmental expenses against total department revenue.

   T   F   **e.** Software packages provide very little flexibility in the manner in which percentages are shown.

4. Circle the correct answer to the following statements:

   a. The following expenditure is not found in an overhead department:

   (1) Salaries and wages

   (2) Cost of sales

   (3) Other expenses

   b. Expenses should not be grouped in a departmental statement if:

   (1) They are insignificant

   (2) They were combined in the budget

   (3) The amounts are material

   c. The most valuable comparison to be made of advertising expenses is:

   (1) As a percentage of room revenue

   (2) As a percentage of total revenue

   (3) As a percentage of total payroll

21

The Income Statement, Balance Sheet, and Statistics

In the preceding chapter, we saw how the individual operating accounts in the general ledger are translated into departmental statements, operated and overhead, in accordance with the Uniform System of Accounts. The next step in the process of preparing meaningful and informative financial statements is to combine the departmental statements into a statement of income.

Traditional accounting practice involved the use of a worksheet to record adjustments and divide the trial balance accounts into the statement of income and the balance sheet. The requirement that the income and expenses be separated into departmental statements rendered the worksheet format impractical for hotel accounting. The ability of computerized software to assemble general ledger accounts in the proper grouping and sequence has rendered the worksheet obsolete.

Several formats for the income statement are in use in the hotel industry. As a result of hotel companies being acquired by conglomerates with interests other than hotels, hotel companies in such situations have resorted to preparing a condensed income statement which can readily be consolidated with those of manufacturing operations or financial institutions. However, the income statement format that most closely follows the principles of the Uniform System is displayed in Figure 21–1.

In this format, the results of each department are carried over in some detail to the income statement. In fact, the totals for each subsection—revenue, cost of sales, payroll and related expenses (on a combined basis), other expenses, and net profit (loss) or total expenditure—are all reflected on the statement. Percentages are shown, in the operated departments, as a percentage of the departmental revenue, sometimes referred to as *vertical analysis,* and in the overhead departments, as a percentage of total revenue. Similarly, fixed charges (i.e., property taxes, insurance, interest, and depreciation) are shown also as percentages of total revenue.

Subtotals are provided for the operated departments and the overhead departments; they also combine the totals of both types of departments. The net result at that

Hotel Grayscot

STATEMENT OF INCOME
FOR THE MONTH OF SEPTEMBER 199__

Department	Revenue	%	Cost of Sales	%	Payroll & Related Expenses	%	Other Expenses	%	Net Profit (Loss)	%
Rooms	583,676	52.6	-----		71,702	12.3	39,515	6.8	472,459	80.9
Food & Beverages	322,571	29.1	105,306	32.6	121,891	37.8	30,536	9.5	64,838	20.1
Telephone	7,878	0.7	3,187	40.5	2,694	34.2	831	10.5	1,166	14.8
Gift Shop	16,538	1.5	10,487	63.4	4,537	27.4	325	2.0	1,189	7.2
Golf	169,027	15.2	12,041	7.1	33,783	20.0	17,056	10.1	106,147	62.8
Rents & O/I	9,134	0.8	-----		-----		-----		9,134	100.0
Total Operator Departments	1,108,824	100.0	131,021	11.8	234,607	21.2	88,263	8.0	654,933	59.1
Administrative & General	-----		-----		21,877	2.0	42,095	3.8	63,972	5.8
Sales & Marketing	-----		-----		11,829	1.1	74,844	6.7	86,673	7.8
Property Operation & Maintenance	-----		-----		22,457	2.0	33,922	3.1	56,379	5.1
Energy Costs	-----		-----		-----		28,240	2.5	28,240	2.5
Total Overhead Departments					56,163	5.1	179,101	16.2	235,264	21.2
House Profit	1,108,824	100.0	131,021	11.8	290,770	26.2	267,364	24.1	419,669	37.8
Property Taxes									<12,652>	1.1
Insurance									<20,036>	1.8
Gross Operating Profit (Loss)									386,981	34.9
Interest									<15,833>	1.4
Depreciation									<79,127>	7.1
Net Profit (Loss)									292,021	26.4

Figure 21–1   Statement of Income

level (i.e., after operated departments and overhead departments) is referred to as the *house profit*. The house profit is further reduced by property taxes and insurance to arrive at the *gross operating profit* or *gross operating loss*. This level of income is widely used as a measurement of the profitability of the operation. It is also used in making economic appraisals or valuations of the property. Use of these ratios is discussed in more detail in the next chapter. The gross operating profit or loss is then reduced by interest and depreciation, sometimes referred to as *financial charges,* in order to arrive at the net income or loss.

One of the negative factors in using an income statement with this amount of detail is that there is no easy manner in which to show comparisons against budget or

prior year. In order to do so, it is necessary to prepare two more statements in the same format. Similarly year-to-date figures, actual, budget, and prior year require three more statements. In order to solve this problem, some hotels list each department under headings of revenue, cost of sales, payroll, and related and other expenses. The totals for each department are listed in a six-column format, month on the left and year to date on the right. Subtotals are provided in each category. This is not a recommended format as the actual results for each department are not reflected and the statement loses much of its meaning.

The condensed form of income statement is displayed in Figure 21–2. This format is usually referred to as a "Condensed Statement of Operations." While the net results of the operated departments are not shown, the combined costs (i.e., cost of sales, payroll and related expense, and other expense) are shown as percentages of departmental income, which permits easy determination of departmental results. The individual revenue categories are shown as a percentage of total revenue (this information is also provided in Figure 21–1, Statement of Income).

The totals for each overhead department are shown as a percentage of total revenue as are the fixed charges. This format permits the easy presentation of budget and prior year with comparable year-to-date numbers shown on the second page.

THE BALANCE SHEET

The balance sheet combines asset, liability, and capital accounts to provide a statement of financial position for the operation at a specific period of time, normally the end of a financial period and certainly at the end of the financial year. An example of a balance sheet is provided in Figure 21–3. While some hotel companies actually prepare a budget for their balance sheet, this is not common industry practice. Although it is useful to try to set guidelines for certain balance-sheet items such as accounts receivable, the value of a complete budget for the balance sheet is questionable because balance-sheet numbers are not subject to separate control but remain purely a function of the results of the operation. A historical comparison to prior year's numbers is usually provided.

As previously mentioned, general ledger accounts are frequently grouped into a single balance-sheet heading. This contrasts with the departmental statements where all revenue and expense accounts are shown individually. Common groupings are as follows:

1. All bank accounts are grouped under "Cash in Bank."
2. City ledger and guest ledger are grouped under "Accounts receivable—trade." Other accounts receivable ledger accounts will either be included in the same category or grouped under "Sundry Receivables" dependent on their nature.
3. Individual prepaid accounts, other than insurance, will be grouped under "Prepaid—Other."
4. Separate ledger accounts will be maintained for each payroll tax liability but grouped on the balance sheet under "Payroll Taxes Payable."
5. Ledger accounts for accruals that are not of a significant amount will be grouped under "Other accruals."

Hotel Grayscot

Condensed Statement of Operations
as at September 30, 199X

	YTD CURRENT	%	YTD BUDGET	%	YTD PRIOR YEAR	%
Revenues						
Rooms	2,770,809	56.2	2,413,608	53.4	2,422,830	60.5
Food (including Other Income)	1,072,028	21.7	828,760	18.3	1,060,918	26.5
Beverage	324,871	6.6	240,061	5.3	292,287	7.3
Telephone	43,967	0.9	56,259	1.2	49,548	1.2
Other Operated Departments	652,917	13.2	913,103	20.2	113,532	2.8
Rentals and Other Income	68,422	1.4	67,334	1.5	66,518	1.7
Total Revenues	4,933,014	100.0	4,519,125	100.0	4,005,633	100.0
Departmental Costs and Expenses:						
Rooms	647,478	23.4	703,459	29.1	582,727	14.5
Food and Beverage	1,331,627	95.3	1,142,817	106.9	1,289,646	32.2
Telephone	35,487	80.7	53,324	94.8	37,448	0.9
Other Operated Departments	501,585	76.8	509,179	55.8	144,669	3.6
Total Costs and Expenses	2,516,177	51.0	2,408,779	53.3	2,054,490	51.3
Total Operated Departmental Income	2,416,837	49.0	2,110,346	46.7	1,951,143	48.7
Undistributed Operating Expenses:						
Administrative and General	465,013	9.4	503,092	11.1	456,139	11.4
Sales and Marketing	449,920	9.1	505,920	11.2	576,855	14.4
Property Operation and Maintenance	302,027	6.1	323,985	7.2	262,420	6.6
Energy Costs	236,111	4.8	241,152	5.3	218,511	5.5
Total Overhead Expenses	1,453,071	29.5	1,574,149	34.8	1,513,925	37.8
Income before Fixed Charges	963,766	19.5	536,197	11.9	437,218	10.9
Fixed Charges:						
Property Taxes	112,634	2.3	111,924	2.5	97,508	2.4
Insurance	189,074	3.8	255,681	5.7	227,514	5.7
Interest	147,416	3.0	147,416	3.3	149,170	3.7
Depreciation	712,149	14.4	720,000	15.9	669,599	16.7
Total Fixed Charges	1,161,273	23.5	1,235,021	27.4	1,143,791	18.5
Net Income (Loss)	(197,507)	(4.0)	(698,824)	(15.5)	(706,573)	(17.6)

Figure 21–2   Condensed Statement of Operations

Hotel Grayscot

Condensed Statement of Operations
as at September 30, 199X

	MONTH CURRENT	%	MONTH BUDGET	%	MONTH PRIOR YEAR	%
Revenues						
Rooms	583,676	52.6	516,106	52.1	420,627	61.6
Food (including Other Income)	242,771	21.9	150,247	15.2	182,474	26.7
Beverage	79,800	7.2	49,318	5.0	57,775	8.5
Telephone	7,878	0.7	10,965	1.1	6,255	0.9
Other Operated Departments	185,565	16.7	255,316	25.8	8,355	1.2
Rentals and Other Income	9,134	0.8	8,122	0.8	8,324	1.2
Total Revenues	1,108,824	100.0	990,074	100.0	683,810	100.0
Departmental Costs and Expenses:						
Rooms	111,217	19.1	112,336	21.8	94,508	22.5
Food and Beverage	257,733	79.9	180,627	90.5	202,305	84.2
Telephone	6,712	85.2	10,412	95.0	2,662	42.6
Other Operated Departments	78,229	42.2	85,463	33.5	9,475	113.4
Total Costs and Expenses	453,891	40.9	388,838	39.3	308,950	45.2
Total Operated Departmental Income	654,933	59.1	601,236	60.7	374,860	54.9
Overhead Expense:						
Administrative and General	63,972	5.8	67,049	6.7	78,860	11.5
Sales and Marketing	86,673	7.8	56,294	5.6	53,296	7.8
Property Operation and Maintenance	56,379	5.1	38,270	3.9	30,422	4.5
Energy Costs	28,240	2.5	26,017	2.6	22,726	4.8
Total Overhead Expenses	235,264	21.2	187,630	18.8	185,304	28.6
Income before Fixed Charges	419,669	37.8	413,606	41.9	189,556	26.3
Fixed Charges:						
Property Taxes	12,653	1.1	12,436	1.3	10,194	1.5
Insurance	20,036	1.8	28,409	2.9	29,386	4.3
Interest	15,833	1.4	15,833	1.6	16,250	2.4
Depreciation	79,127	7.1	80,000	8.1	63,288	9.3
Total Fixed Charges	127,648	11.4	136,678	13.9	119,118	17.5
Net Income (Loss)	292,021	26.4	276,928	28.0	70,438	8.8

Figure 21–2 Condensed Statement of Operations *(continued)*

Hotel Grayscot

BALANCE SHEET AS AT SEPTEMBER 30, 199 __

Assets / Current Assets	This Year	Last Year
Cash		
House Banks	12,000	12,000
Cash in Bank	26,924	6,149
Total Cash	38,924	18,149
Accounts Receivable		
Accounts Receivable - Trade	551,559	473,745
Sundry Receivables	66,895	0
Travel Advances	200	200
Reserve for Bad Debts	(27,239)	(17,757)
Total Accounts Receivable	591,415	456,188
Inventories		
Food	22,481	23,786
Beverages	14,122	9,416
Gift Shop	20,313	8,252
Golf Pro Shop Inventory	26,151	10,018
Total Inventories	83,067	51,472
Prepaid Expenses		
Prepaid Insurance	83,213	96,478
Prepaid Advertising	7,985	17,317
Prepaid Other	56,913	30,128
Total Prepaids	148,111	143,923
Total Current Assets	861,517	669,732
Fixed Assets		
Land	4,000,000	4,000,000
Buildings	8,232,000	8,232,000
Furniture and Equipment	3,171,624	3,011,719
Operating Equipment	368,722	368,722
	15,722,346	15,612,441
Accumulated Depreciation	3,507,767	2,608,711
Total Fixed Assets	12,264,579	13,003,730
Total Assets	$13,126,096	$13,673,462

Liabilities & Equity / Current Liabilities	YTD This Month	YTD Last Year
Accounts Payable Trade	277,260	274,304
Advance Deposits	238,006	125,232
Gift Certificates	38,760	29,347
Sales Taxes Payable	79,092	50,553
Accrued Salaries & Wages	37,839	6,376
Payroll Taxes Payable	24,227	38,318
Accrued Utilities	33,298	24,462
Accrued Interest	31,666	32,500
Accrued Credit Card Commissions	30,053	22,118
Total Current Liabilities	790,201	603,210
Long-term Liabilities		
Mortage Payable	1,900,000	1,950,000
Total Long-term Liabilities	1,900,000	1,950,000
Total Liabilities	2,690,201	2,553,210
Equity		
Capital Stock	8,000,000	8,000,000
Retained Earnings (Deficit)		
Balance - Jan. 1, 199-	2,633,402	3,826,825
Profit (loss) for the year	(197,507)	(706,573)
	10,435,895	11,120,252
Total Liabilities & Equities	$13,126,096	$13,673,462

Figure 21-3 Balance Sheet

The balance sheet is segmented into five major sections:

1. Current assets—assets with an expected life of less than one year.
2. Fixed assets—assets with an extended life.
3. Current liabilities—liabilities expected to be settled within one year.
4. Long-term liabilities—liabilities of an extended life such as loans and mortgages.

It should be noted that at year end, proper presentation dictates that the current portion of long-term debt be shown under current liabilities. This is not done in Figure 21–3 as it is an interim statement, that is, a period ending during the course of the fiscal year.

5. Equity—includes capital stock and retained earnings or deficit. The equity represents the excess of assets over liabilities.

The current assets section of the balance sheet is subdivided into four sections: cash, accounts receivable, inventories, and prepaid expenses. Another possibility would be to divide current liabilities into subsections for accounts payable and accrued expenses. The content and calculation of the balance sheet was previously discussed in Chapter 8, relative to year-end work papers. Balance sheet ratios and other formulas used to analyze balance-sheet accounts are discussed in Chapter 22.

The financial statements, balance sheet, statement of income, and supporting departmental statements constitute the end product of the accounting process. However, no set of hotel financial statements is complete without certain statistics, usually shown on a separate page (Figure 21–4).

STATISTICS

While many operating ratios are used in the analytical process (Chapter 22) the format of the statistics page in the financial statements normally follows those in common usage throughout the industry and is understandable to the various levels of management.

The most significant statistics in the hotel industry is the percentage of occupancy—the ratio of rooms occupied to rooms available. To illustrate, Hotel Grayscot (Figure 21–4) has 200 rooms. Thus, the total rooms available for September is 200 multiplied by 30 days or 6,000 rooms available. Actual room nights occupied was 4,108. Therefore, occupancy is as follows:

$$\frac{\text{Occupied Rooms} \times 100\%}{6,000 \text{ Available Rooms}} = 68.5\% \text{ Occupancy}$$

Similarly, calculations can be made of the two main segments of business, transient and group.

Average rate is determined by dividing the actual revenue by the number of rooms. If we take the room revenue figure for September, $583,676 (Figure 20–1), the calculation is as follows:

$$\frac{\$583{,}676 \text{ Room Revenue}}{4{,}108 \text{ Rooms Occupied}} = \$142.08 \text{ Average Rate}$$

The average rate, like occupancy, can be calculated on a market segment basis. The costs of sales for the various departments are available in the departmental schedules but they are also included on the statistics page as most hoteliers consider such percentages to be of particular significance. The number of golf rounds is also a statistic considered highly significant in resort operations.

Hotel Grayscot

**Statistics
as at September 30, 199–**

MONTH ACTUAL	MONTH BUDGET	MONTH PRIOR YR		YTD ACTUAL	YTD BUDGET	YTD PRIOR YR
6,000	6,000	6,000	Rooms available	54,600	54,600	54,600
			Rooms occupied			
2,301	1,295	1,437	Transient	9,926	8,714	9,581
1,807	2,467	1,872	Group	9,292	9,108	8,331
4,108	3,762	3,309	Total	19,218	17,822	17,912
			Percentage of occupancy			
38.4%	21.6%	24.0%	Transient	18.2%	16.0%	17.5%
30.1%	41.1%	31.2%	Group	17.0%	16.7%	15.3%
68.5%	62.7%	55.2%	Total	35.2%	32.7%	32.8%
			Average rate			
$152.72	$138.12	$113.30	Transient	$168.77	$162.06	$149.66
$128.54	$136.70	$137.72	Group	$117.91	$109.95	$118.70
$142.08	$137.19	$127.12	Total	$144.18	$135.43	$135.26
			Number of			
7,206	6,951	6,038	guests	34,111	30,218	30,178
35.3%	33.1%	36.8%	Food cost	35.2%	31.9%	35.8%
25.1%	23.4%	27.3%	Beverage cost	27.8%	23.6%	27.3%
			Cost of sales			
40.5%	55.8%	26.8%	Telephone	49.4%	55.4%	58.3%
63.4%	48.4%	70.2%	Gift shop	59.5%	48.8%	57.4%
58.3%	60.0%	57.9%	Golf	62.6%	60.0%	60.6%
			Total golf			
2,982	4,196	3,025	rounds	10,128	14,732	10,171

Figure 21–4 Statistics

1. Explain the difference between an income statement following the format of the Uniform System and a Condensed Statement of Operations.

2. List four types of account groupings commonly used on a balance sheet and explain which general ledger accounts are usually grouped under which headings.

3. Circle T or F to indicate whether the following statements are true or false:

    T F **a.** House profit is the total profit of the operated departments before deduction of the overhead departments..

    T F **b.** Gross operating profit is house profit less interest and depreciation.

    T F **c.** Net income is gross operating profit less interest and depreciation.

    T F **d.** Fixed assets are assets with a life of less than one year.

    T F **e.** Current liabilities are liabilities expected to be settled within one year.

4. Circle the correct answer to the following statements:

    a. The equity section of the balance sheet does not include:
      (1) Long-term liabilities
      (2) Capital stock
      (3) Retained earnings

    b. Which of the following is not a current asset:
      (1) Cash
      (2) Accounts receivable
      (3) Accrued expenses

    c. In the month of June, a 300-room hotel has 5,210 rooms occupied. The occupancy percentage is:
      (1) 177%
      (2) 86.8%
      (3) 57.8%

    d. The hotel in item c had room revenue of $746,000. The average rate was:
      (1) $248.66
      (2) $143.19
      (3) $82.88

22 Financial Statement Analysis and Review

The most important responsibility of a hotel controller is to provide management with operational advice based on financial analysis. This requires the dissection of the operating results on a department-by-department basis.

Analysis of results calls for comparisons against budget, prior year's results, and industry standards. Comparisons against budget can be misleading, the results depending on whether the budget is realistic, overcautious, or much too optimistic. Several studies of industry averages and standards are published annually. These studies provide industry information within many different categories: by type of hotel, number of rooms, age, and geographical location. While the studies are invaluable in preparing projections for new hotel projects, they only provide industry averages or means. In other words, they are a combination of the good and the bad, the successful and the unsuccessful. To be willing to accept achievement of only these averages is, in many cases, to be willing to accept a certain level of mediocrity. The emphasis, therefore, in any analysis should be on improvement against prior results. The more in-depth analysis, not only of the current year against a prior year, but of the continuing trend of operating results is ultimately the key to whether the operation is on a proper course to success.

While cost controls are essential, there is no quicker road to success than a continuing improvement in volume. In the hotel industry, improved volume in most operating departments depends on increasing the occupancy. Increased room revenue is a function of some combination of improved occupancy, average rate, or both. In Chapter 26, a section is devoted to yield management. While it has always been recognized that optimum room revenue requires the best combination of occupancy and average rate, computer technology has provided hotels with a method, termed *yield management,* by which the proper combination can be identified and achieved.

The initial step in analyzing results should, therefore, be directed to comparisons of occupancy and average rate. In Figure 21–4, an example of a statistics schedule, the occupancy and average rate are broken down into the two main segments, individual

and group. While this meets the requirements of good financial reporting, in-depth analysis requires that a further segmentation take place. Both categories should be further subdivided: individual into transient, golf, and corporate; group into corporate, tour, and travel; and association. This requires research beyond the level of the statistical information provided with the financial statements. However, the daily revenue reports in a hotel operation should readily provide the necessary information on rooms occupied. By analyzing the market segments both in terms of occupancy and average rate, a better insight can be obtained into the sources of the substantial increase in room revenue over the prior year.

In analyzing expenses in all departments, the first consideration is to properly define the expenditure within three classifications: variable, semivariable and nonvariable. Variable expenses should be expected to increase or decrease in relation to increases or decreases in volume; semivariable expenses vary to some degree relative to change in volume, while fixed expenses have no direct relationship to volume changes.

ROOMS

Within the rooms department it is, once more, important to note that increased volume is a combination of higher occupancy and higher average rate. However, some expenses are variable only in terms of occupancy while others may be directly related to increased dollar volume. For example, guest supplies should not, except for price increases, be expected to increase because of increased revenue if solely attributed to higher room rates. However, higher occupancy will result in an increase in quantities consumed. On the other hand, travel agents' commissions, calculated as a percentage of the actual rates charged, should vary directly in relation to dollar volume.

Within the rooms department, salaries and wages and related payroll taxes and benefits comprise over 60 percent of the expenses. Since the payroll taxes and benefits normally increase or decrease in relation to cash payroll (although certain departments may carry a higher benefit cost), the focus of the analysis should be placed on salaries and wages. It should, however, be noted that throughout all departments in Figure 20–1 there was a disproportionate increase in payroll taxes and benefits. This should be investigated but was probably caused by an addition being made to benefits provided (e.g., a pension plan, etc.). The first step should be to place the current year's cash payroll on a real salaries and wages comparison against the prior year, that is, by eliminating the impact of rate increases. If we assume that there was an actual average rate increase in salaries and wages of 5 percent, the current year's payroll shown in Figure 20–1 can be restated for comparison purposes as follows:

Category	Current	Prior Yr.
Front Office	$18,930	$15,431
Housekeeping	29,583	26,098
Bell Staff	3,908	4,432

Once again, the question of variable versus nonvariable must be addressed. While the housekeeping staff and bell staff required should be almost directly proportionate to rooms occupied and check-ins, the front-office staff includes reservations

which normally has only a limited relationship to current volume. Furthermore, there is a basic staffing requirement in the front office at all times. Therefore, the front-office payroll should not vary with volume to the same degree as bell staff. A comparison of the restated payroll against occupancy reveals the following:

Occupancy	increased by 13.3%
Payroll	
Front Office	increased by 3.3%
Housekeeping	increased by 19.9%
Bell Staff	decreased by 20.0%

It is difficult to reconcile a 19.9 percent increase in housekeeping payroll to a 13.3 percent increase in occupancy. This must be investigated to determine whether there was a loss in productivity or an increase in services provided. The material drop in bell staff payroll, while favorable, is difficult to understand in view of a higher occupancy. The combined effect suggests that the housekeeping department may have assumed certain duties previously assigned to the bell staff. Further investigation is definitely called for.

Many of the other expenses in the rooms department are of a consumable nature and should be expected to vary with volume. The most material of these is usually guest supplies which has become a major cost item for hotels because of the increased emphasis on bathroom amenities (e.g., shampoo, body lotion). Since the departmental statement shows other expenses as a percentage of room revenue, abnormal variances are easy to stop.

Looking again at Figure 20–1, reservation expense did not appear in the prior year. This may be a new cost, possibly due to a new arrangement with a reservation service or possibly a reclassification of certain expenses. The drops in both telephone and printing and stationery suggest the latter. However, this should be fully investigated. Laundry expense has increased from 1.0 to 1.2 percent. However, laundry is an allocation of part of the cost of the laundry department rather than being a directly controllable expense. The cause of the increase can, therefore, be more easily discerned by an analysis of the laundry department. Certain expenditures such as licenses and permits, dues and subscriptions, and cable TV are more of a fixed expense and cannot be expected to increase as occupancy increases. On an overall basis, the "Other Expenses" level of 6.5 percent of room revenue compared to 9.6 percent the preceding year is very favorable and is the principal reason for the higher percentage of departmental profit.

FOOD AND BEVERAGE

The substantial increase in revenue, both food and beverage, in Outlet 2 (Figure 20–1) suggests a major change either in physical design or in method of operation. When either of these circumstances occurs, a separate analysis is warranted, comparing actual results to the original projections made to justify the changes and perhaps recover capital costs related to them. An overall comparison against occupancy indicates that food and beverage revenue increased approximately 34 percent over the preceding year, while rooms occupied increased by 13.3 percent. Such a result cannot be achieved only

by price increases and suggests that either guests are eating (and drinking) in the hotel more frequently or there has been a substantial increase in nonguest business or perhaps a combination of both. A further study should be made to identify the sources of the increase.

Both food and beverage costs dropped slightly from the preceding year. However, both appear to exceed industry averages for this type of operation. A poor mixture of restaurant and banquet business can cause a higher than normal food cost; banquets, because of their preset nature, have a lower food cost. However, in our example, banquet business is approximately 40 percent of total food revenue which is fully acceptable. Further studies should be made to determine the causes for the high costs.

Since there has been a major change in the operation, it is difficult to make a comparison of payroll costs against the prior year. Again, comparisons against original projections for the changed operation would be more useful. Total cash payroll dropped from 32.9 percent of revenue to 30.8 percent. It is interesting to note that despite an expanded operation administrative payroll dropped substantially—not necessarily desirable in such circumstances. This should be reviewed as it may only be the result of payroll reclassification.

Other expenses dropped from 10.8 to 9.5 percent. Almost all expenses in this department are of a variable nature. Because of the apparent operational changes, definitive analysis is difficult. Cleaning expense shows a major jump and should be investigated. The increase in Music and Entertainment is probably due to the operational change as this expense is relatively fixed. Laundry shows an increase similar to that found in the rooms department.

While prior months would have been analyzed on a month-by-month basis, the year-to-date numbers shown are not impressive at the profit level. However, the current month suggests that the operational changes and their impact are starting to be realized.

TELEPHONE

Telephone revenue is directly related to occupancy levels, subject, of course, to any price increases. In Figure 20–1, revenue increased by approximately 36 percent compared to an occupancy increase of 13.3 percent, indicating either a higher markup on calls, a more efficient capture of revenue, or increased volume due to a particular group or type of guest.

Cost of sales for both the current month and the prior year are very low. However, it would appear that both numbers contain errors or possibly corrections as on a year-to-date, 49.4 percent figure is much closer to budget and prior year. The cost of sales should be easily controlled as it is a function of the markup programmed in the call accounting system.

There was no payroll in the prior year, indicating that it is probable that the switchboard was previously handled by front-office employees rather than an operator. Other expenses are immaterial; they consist of the telephone maintenance contract, a normally fixed expense, and charges for additional equipment charges outside the contract.

GIFT SHOP

Increases in gift shop revenue are normally a function of higher occupancy and price increases. However, the increase of almost 100 percent over the prior year suggests that the gift shop in Figure 20–1 underwent some organizational changes including, possibly, an expansion. The cost of sales for the month, at 63.4 percent, is somewhat high and the individual elements of the cost do not relate properly to the revenues. This requires an investigation as apparently there are errors. However, it should be understood that the cost of sales in a gift shop relates to the actual mix of sales. If the volume of low-profit items such as newspapers, magazines, and candy is high in proportion to the sale of gifts, the cost of sales will be higher. The year-to-date cost in our example is reasonable for a high-volume gift shop.

The substantially higher level of payroll, and, therefore, taxes and benefits is fully justified by the increase in volume.

Other expenses are mostly supplies which will also vary in relation to volume.

GOLF

Since golf operations are discussed in detail in an earlier chapter, the following comments are limited to a review of Figure 20–1.

Despite a higher volume, the payroll, as could be expected, remained virtually constant, the slight increase in the dollar amount not being enough to suggest any increase in the number of employees. Other expenses show an increase for the month of about 35 percent, and only slightly less on a year-to-date basis. However, it is difficult to point to any specific area as a major problem. Furthermore, the higher budget suggests some planned maintenance programs expected to be covered by a major increase in revenue—budgeted but unfortunately not achieved.

RENTS AND OTHER INCOME

Rental income is an odd amount, slightly higher than prior year. This suggests that the rent is subject to some form of percentage calculation and should, of course, be audited in accordance with procedures described in Chapter 16. Forfeit deposits can vary from month to month and may even be a negative figure, as seen, when deposits are refunded that were previously absorbed in income. Miscellaneous revenue comes from varied sources (see Chapter 16) and no consistent level of income can be anticipated.

ADMINISTRATIVE AND GENERAL

The overhead departments are much more fixed in nature than other expenses in operated departments. While certain expenses vary in relation to volume, the major portion thereof does not.

This applies equally to the payroll and taxes and benefits and to other expenses. In administrative and general, it is reasonable to find a small increase in payroll, due probably to additional staffing in accounts receivable to handle a higher volume and

possibly an increase in night-audit requirements. The substantial increase in payroll in the example (Figure 20–1) does, in view of the preceding statement, require serious investigation. A clue can perhaps be found in other expenses where the preceding year had a very high figure for manager's expenses. This account covers all costs other than payroll related to the general manager (e.g., car expenses, living allowance, entertainment, etc.). However, the higher amount in the prior year, combined with the lack of administrative payroll, suggests that all management costs were included in that account. Further investigation is, of course, required. Similarly, the contract services amount in the prior year was $7,850, while it is less than $1,000 in the current year.

In reviewing the remainder of other expenses, increases are found where expected. Higher credit commissions are a direct reflection of higher volume while increases in printing and stationery and office supplies can also be rationalized.

SALES AND MARKETING

Activity in the sales and marketing department bears little relationship to volume. In fact, many hoteliers follow the theory that less expenditure is required in this area when volume is high, that is, at a satisfactory level. However, others will point to Coca Cola's famous experiment in reducing advertising. The lesson learned there was that marketing is required to sustain volume as well as to increase it.

The key to analyzing the sales and marketing numbers lies in a comparison to budget rather than prior year. The budget should be based on the annual marketing plan, the preparation of which is vital for all hotels. Not only does the marketing plan set the philosophy and goals for the year but it time phases expenditures to meet these goals. The sales and marketing department budget is a key element of the marketing plan. All variations, therefore, and there are several in our example, require thorough investigation. Increased expenditures in the advertising area are usually necessitated by failures in attaining the original goals.

ENERGY COSTS

Energy levels should be expected to increase with higher occupancy. However, the weather and the time of year play a larger role in energy costs than volume. A very cold winter will increase fuel consumption or electricity, depending on the type of heating used. A very hot summer requiring an increased load on air conditioning can have a dramatic impact on electricity costs.

PROPERTY OPERATION AND MAINTENANCE

Maintenance costs, like energy, are usually a function of seasonal changes rather than volume. It is difficult to carry out major maintenance programs when the hotel is running a high occupancy because such programs normally require that selected rooms or public areas be taken out of service. As a result, expenses, including payroll, are frequently higher in slower periods.

Unfortunately, a hotel cannot forecast major repairs necessitated by equipment failure or an unusual occurrence. Expenditures such as grounds and landscaping or snow removal are seasonal in nature. Similarly, excessive heat will increase the number of air conditioning problems.

The most realistic approach from a financial point of view is to expect that on an annual basis the engineering department will carry out a continuing program of preventive maintenance which will keep costs, measured as a percentage of total revenue, at a constant level.

LAUNDRY

Prior comments were made under the rooms and food and beverage areas relative to the substantial increase in laundry expense. At this point in reviewing Figure 20–1, it is now appropriate to examine the cause or causes for this increase. An examination of the laundry department shows a substantial increase in payroll costs in the monthly but not in year-to-date numbers. This requires investigation to determine the cause. There may be a change in the operation, possibly an addition to management which would account for the increase. On the other hand, there is perhaps an accounting error. A retroactive increase in wage rates is another possibility. The basis for allocation between the rooms department and the food and beverage department appears consistent with budget.

HUMAN RESOURCES

An initial look at the figures for the human resources department indicates that this is a newly created department which in prior years was either absorbed in administrative and general or the operated departments. The creation of the department suggests increased staffing and creation of a separate department entity.

The allocation of this department also explains the substantial increase seen throughout all departments in payroll taxes and benefits.

BALANCE SHEET

While the operating results must be the focus of a hotel controller's financial analysis, it is also necessary to look at the balance sheet.

The determination of turnover ratios requires the extraction of numbers both from the operating results and the balance sheet. In particular, inventory turnover is a key element of the monthly analysis process. Inventory turnover is calculated by dividing the average inventory for a period (determined by averaging the total of the opening and closing inventories) into the cost of sales. In Figure 21–3 we find the inventory totals as at September 30. In order to illustrate the determination of the various turnovers, opening inventories (i.e., as at August 31) have been provided.

Inventory	August 31	September 30	Average
Food	23,101	22,481	22,791
Beverages	13,628	14,122	13,875

Gift Shop	19,797	20,313	20,055
Golf Pro Shop	28,053	26,151	27,102

The turnover ratios for each inventory can now be calculated as follows:

Inventory	Cost of Sales	Average Inventory	Turnover Ratio
Food	93,537	22,791	4.14
Beverages	20,015	13,875	1.44
Gift Shop	10,487	20,055	0.52
Golf Pro Shop	12,041	27,102	0.45

The food turnover of approximately 4.1 means that the average food inventory is being consumed 4.1 times in a month or every 7.3 days (30 days in a month divided by 4.1). This is extremely satisfactory; a ratio over 3.5 is acceptable in the industry. A low ratio is indicative of carrying too high an inventory which is not only reflective of poor cash management but also creates a risk of spoilage of products not being used within their usable lifetime period. It may also indicate nonmoving or obsolete stock. The impact of inventory theft can also be hidden by continuous inflating of the inventories.

The beverage turnover of 1.4 is also an acceptable level within the industry. Beverage inventories, since spoilage is not a factor, tend to be higher, relative to consumption, due to purchasing in larger quantities to obtain volume discounts. Hotels that have a high volume of wine sales will also have lower turnover ratios due to the need to carry a satisfactory range of wines, some of which have a high-dollar cost.

Retail inventories, as might be found in gift shops or sports outlet pro shops, frequently represent two to three months sales due to the large range of products that must be carried. Caution should be exercised, however, relative to high levels of clothing in the inventories. Changing styles can render the product obsolete or at least take it out of favor. This is particularly a concern in pro shops if the season is drawing to a close.

The accounts receivable turnover ratio is a measurement of the effectiveness of collection efforts. It measures credit sales against average trade accounts receivable. Similar to average inventories, average receivables is the total of the opening and closing accounts receivable balances. Figure 21–1 reveals only the total sales, not the amount of credit sales. However, if we assume the level of trade accounts receivable—$551,559—to be relatively unchanged and estimate credit sales at 50 percent of total revenue, a norm in the industry, the turnover ratio is $504,414 (50 percent of $1,108,824) divided by $551,559 or 0.92. Converted to days, this means that the average age of the accounts receivable is 30 days multiplied by 0.92 or 27.6 days, a highly acceptable number.

Certain other ratios are measurements of the liquidity of the operation. The more common of these are the following:

1. Current ratio (current assets divided by current liabilities) for Hotel Grayscot is 1.1. Less than 1.0 is regarded as a poor ratio.
2. Debt to equity is 0.26. This indicates a strong overall position.
3. Interest coverage (gross operating profit to interest—YTD) is 2.4. This is also a strong liquid situation indicating no problems in payment of interest on long-term obligations.

The acid test ratio (cash plus accounts receivable and inventories measured against current liabilities) is less than 1.0. This, in some circumstances, would indicate a weak situation. However, the low debt to equity ratio indicates clearly that additional borrowings to improve the cash position could be easily accomplished.

While the lack of a positive net income results in no return on the equity or, in the case of a public company, no earnings per share, this is a function of the high level of depreciation. The actual cash flow is strong; this will be discussed in greater detail in Chapter 23.

Two other commonly used ratios are the profit margin, the relationship of net profit to revenue (26.4 percent in Figure 21–1) and the operating efficiency ratio, the relationship of income before fixed charges to revenue (37.8 percent in Figure 21–1).

SUMMARY

In this chapter, analysis and review have been approached by examining the financial statements and departmental schedules seen in Figures 21–1, 21–2, and 21–3 and Figure 20–1. Those statements are a composite of rational numbers that can be found in an average hotel operation but do not reflect any specific operation on a composite basis. Consequently, there are some instances of unusual numbers, the reason for which would normally be ascertained through actual investigation. It must be stressed that while possible causes have been hypothesized in this chapter, in a real hotel situation it is the duty and responsibility of the hotel controller to make in-depth investigations to pinpoint the causes.

1. List all expenses in the rooms department in Figure 20–1 which you consider to be normally variable.

2. List all expenses in the food and beverage department in Figure 20–1 which you consider to be normally fixed.

3. Circle T or F to indicate whether the following statements are true or false:

   T   F   **a.** Housekeeping payroll should vary proportionately to occupancy.

   T   F   **b.** If food sales increase due to a higher average check, payroll can be expected to increase, even if wage rates do not.

   T   F   **c.** Banquets have a higher food cost than restaurant operations.

   T   F   **d.** The call accounting system can be used to control the markup on telephone sales.

   T   F   **e.** A proportionately large volume of sales of newspaper and candy will reduce the cost of sales in a gift shop.

   T   F   **f.** Accounts receivable turnover is measured by dividing the average accounts receivable outstanding into total sales.

4. Circle the correct answer to the following statements:

   a. A hotel has a cost of sales—food in the month of August of $103,000. The food inventory at July 31 was $31,722 and at August 31 was $19,733. The inventory turnover was:

   (1) 2.0

   (2) 5.2

   (3) 4.0

   b. The best analysis of the sales and marketing expenditures comes from a:

   (1) Comparison to the previous year

   (2) Comparison to budget

   (3) Comparison to the prior month

   c. The following department is sometimes allocated to the operated and overhead departments:

   (1) Energy costs

   (2) Administrative and general

   (3) Employee cafeteria

23 The Statement of Cash Flow

While the financial statements of a hotel (and other businesses) have traditionally consisted of a balance sheet and a statement of income, or profit and loss, the accounting profession has struggled to find another method of presentation which would be more easily understood by management in general.

One of the earlier attempts was the introduction of a "Statement of Sources and Application of Funds" which focused on analyzing the causes and results of an increase or decrease in the net working capital. Working capital is the excess of current assets over current liabilities. If we examine the comparative balance sheets in Figure 23–1, we find that the working capital as at December 31, 199X, was $45,300 ($431,500 minus $385,200) and as at December 31, 199Y, $34,200, a decrease of $11,100. While the statement of sources and application of funds was definitely a step in the right direction, it was never accorded the level of management enthusiasm hoped for by accountants. This is probably because the concept of working capital was in itself part of the accountant's vocabulary, not readily understood or accepted by the layman.

The statement of source and application of funds was replaced by the "Statement of Changes in Financial Position (SCFP)." The SCFP provided further flexibility in that it could be prepared on the basis of working capital or cash. While the two alternatives permitted the accountant to exercise his or her own preference in the format presented, the variances in presentation from operation to operation contributed to increased confusion on the part of operational management.

Happily, the Financial Accounting Standards Board (FASB) has now mandated that hotels, and companies in general, present a "Statement of Cash Flow (SCF)" in addition to the balance sheet and income statement. The SCF focuses purely on the underlying causes for the change in the cash position from the preceding year and explains the various sources and uses of cash that have occurred during the year. Additionally, it divides the cash activity into three main segments: operating activities, investing activities, and financing activities. The intent of this segmentation is clear: to permit management to focus on cash flow derived directly from operations and to un-

COMPARATIVE BALANCE SHEETS
AS AT DECEMBER 31, 199X AND 199Y

Assets	199X	199Y	Net Increase (Decrease)
Current Assets:			
Cash	26,300	39,400	13,100
Accounts Receivable (net)	192,500	292,300	99,800
Inventories	71,100	83,700	12,600
Prepaid Expenses	141,600	148,200	6,600
Total Current Assets	431,500	563,600	132,100
Property and Equipment:			
Land	4,000,000	4,000,000	---
Buildings	8,015,000	8,232,000	217,000
Furniture and Equipment	3,171,600	3,212,400	40,800
Operating Equipment	368,700	368,700	---
SUBTOTAL	15,555,300	15,813,100	
Less: Accumulated Depreciation	2,903,000	3,507,000	<604,000>
Total Property and Equipment	12,652,300	12,306,100	
Investments	317,000	106,000	<211,000>
TOTAL ASSETS	13,400,800	12,975,700	<425,100>
Liabilities and Owners' Equity			
Current Liabilities:			
Accounts Payable	148,700	244,100	95,400
Taxes Payable	51,200	79,100	27,900
Accrued Expenses	135,300	156,200	20,900
Current Portion of Long-Term Debt	50,000	50,000	---
Total Current Liabilities	385,200	529,400	144,200
Long-Term Debt:			
Mortgage Payable	1,900,000	1,850,000	<50,000>
TOTAL LIABILITIES	2,285,200	2,379,400	
Owners' Equity:			
Common Stock	8,000,000	8,000,000	---
Retained Earnings	3,115,600	2,596,300	<519,300>
Total Owners' Equity	11,115,600	10,596,300	
TOTAL LIABILITIES AND OWNERS' EQUITY	13,400,800	12,975,700	<425,100>

Figure 23–1 Comparative Balance Sheets

derstand the cause and effect relationship that other activities have had relative to the overall cash position.

In order to illustrate the use of an SCF, Figure 23–1 shows comparative balance sheets of Hotel Grayscot as at the end of two successive years and the increases or decreases in assets, liabilities, and capital from one year to the next. Figure 23–2 is a

Hotel Grayscot

STATEMENT OF INCOME
FOR THE YEAR ENDED DECEMBER 31, 199Y

Total Revenue	$7,982,600
Rooms:	
Revenue	4,446,700
Payroll and Related Expenses	413,100
Other Expenses	301,500
Departmental Income	3,732,100
Food and Beverage:	
Revenue	2,272,100
Cost of Sales	561,100
Payroll and Related Expenses	1,022,600
Other Expenses	284,600
Departmental Income	413,800
Telephone:	
Revenue	107,100
Cost of Sales	58,200
Payroll and Related Expenses	10,400
Other Expenses	11,100
Departmental Income	27,400
Minor Operated Departments	366,400
Rentals and Other Income	101,400
Total Income: Operated Departments	4,641,100
Overhead Expenses:	
Administrative and General	642,300
Sales and Marketing	601,400
Property Operation and Maintenance	403,500
Energy Costs	302,100
Total Overhead Expense	1,949,300
Income Before Fixed Charges	2,671,800
Property Taxes	152,200
Insurance	239,600
Interest	194,900
Depreciation	604,000
Total Fixed Charges	1,190,700
Income Before Income Taxes	1,481,100
Income Taxes	592,400
Net Income	888,700

Figure 23–2 Statement of Income

statement of income created for the year in question. In Figure 23–3, the impact on cash of both the balance sheet changes and the statement of income are analyzed following the format dictated for preparation of a statement of cash flow. It should be noted that the hypothetical numbers for the Hotel Grayscot are not identical to the set of numbers used to illustrate the balance sheet and income analysis covered in Chapter 21. Rather, a new set of numbers has been created which will better serve to illustrate the specific objectives of this chapter. Included in these changes is the addition of investments in the balance sheet and the introduction of income taxes in the statement of income.

There are certain basic rules or accounting principles which, if followed, will facilitate the preparation of the statement of cash flow and the reconciliation of the net change in cash to the increase or decrease in the balance-sheet figure for cash from one year end to the next. In listing the more common of these rules, the starting point must always be the net income (or a negative amount if a loss) reflected on the statement of income.

1. All noncash expenditures must be added back; the most commonly found example is depreciation expense.
2. Increases in current assets, other than cash, reduce the availability of cash and must be deducted; decreases are added.
3. Increases in current liabilities result in increases in available cash and must be added; conversely, decreases must be deducted.
4. Any sale of a long-term asset will produce an increase in cash and must be added; conversely any purchase of a long-term asset reduces cash.
5. Settlement of a long-term liability reduces cash.
6. Payment of a dividend reduces cash.
7. Long-term borrowing (not part of the example in Figure 23–3) will result in an increase in cash.

The simplification of the effect of all activities to the level of their impact on cash is a relatively simple concept which management can readily comprehend and, therefore, the concept finds general acceptance.

ANALYSIS OF THE STATEMENT OF CASH FLOW

Since adequate cash flow to meet obligations is critical to a hotel operation, certain ratios have been developed. Although there may be a detrimental effect on the ability of the hotel to increase or even maintain earnings levels, nevertheless the use of cash for capital expenditures, that is, purchase of fixed assets, is, at least on a short-term basis, discretionary. The real focus of analysis must, therefore, be on cash flow from operations (CFO) and the margin of safety with which the CFO covers certain obligations. The ratios are as follows:

1. The ratio of cash flow from operations to current liabilities. While this ratio is, in Figures 23–3 and 23–1, less than 1 (0.77 to be precise), a ratio exceeding 0.50 is considered acceptable. The current ratio (current assets over current liabilities) of 1.06 assures liquidity. An improved rate of collection of

Hotel Grayscot

STATEMENT OF CASH FLOW FOR YEAR ENDED DECEMBER 31, 199Y

Cash Flow from Operating Activities:

Net Income (loss)	<$219,300>

Adjustments to Reconcile Net Income to
Cash Provided by Operations

Depreciation expense	604,000
Increase in accounts receivable	< 99,800>
Increase in inventories	< 12,600>
Increase in prepaid expenses	< 6,600>
Increase in accounts payable	95,400
Increase in taxes payable	27,900
Increase in accrued expenses	20,900
Net Cash from Operating Activities	$409,900

Cash Flow from Investing Activities:

Disposal of investments (at cost)	211,000
Acquisition of buildings	<217,000>
Acquisition of furniture and equipment	< 40,800>
Net Cash from Investing Activities	< 46,800>

Cash Flow from Financing Activities:

Payment of dividends	<300,000>
Payment of mortgage	< 50,000>
Net Cash from Financing Activities	<350,000>

Net Increase in Cash	13,100
Cash - Beginning of Year	26,300
Cash - End of Year	39,400

Figure 23–3　Statement of Cash Flow

accounts receivable with a corresponding reduction in accounts payable could, however, improve the ratio.

2. The ratio of cash flow from operations to total liabilities—0.17—is low. However, in itself this is not problematic if the interest coverage (following ratio) is satisfactory.

3. The ratio of cash flow from operations before interest expense to interest expense, termed *interest coverage*—3.10—is financially comfortable.

4. Cash flow from operations to dividends—1.36—indicates that a major portion of the discretionary cash flow was used to pay dividends. This is not a desirable policy on a continuing basis as it deprives the hotel of the cash required to make capital expenditures. Such expenditures were, in fact, only feasible in the year under review because the required cash was generated by the sale of $211,000 of investments.

With their complete focus on cash and the availability of cash to meet necessary obligations or make discretionary expenditures, these ratios are relatively easy for management to understand and provide the general manager with green lights or warning signals as they improve or deteriorate from one year to the next.

1. What is the main difference between a statement of cash flow, a statement of changes in financial position, and a statement of source and application of funds?

2. List six basic rules that can be followed in preparing a statement of cash flow.

3. Circle T or F to indicate whether the following statements are true or false:

   T   F   **a.** A statement of cash flow is required by the Financial Accounting Standards Board.

   T   F   **b.** In preparing an SCF, depreciation expense must be deducted from net income.

   T   F   **c.** In preparing an SCF, increases in current assets must be deducted from net income.

   T   F   **d.** In preparing an SCF, proceeds of the sale of a long-term asset must be deducted from net income.

   T   F   **e.** The starting point in preparing an SCF is always net income (loss).

4. Circle the correct answer to the following statements:

   a. Interest coverage is:

   (1) The ratio of net income to interest expense

   (2) The ratio of cash flow from operations to interest expense

   (3) The ratio of cash flow from operations before interest expense to interest expense

   b. An acceptable ratio of cash flow from operations to current liabilities is:

   (1) In excess of 1.00

   (2) In excess of 0.50

   (3) In excess of 1.50

   c. The current ratio is:

   (1) Current assets divided by current liabilities

   (2) Current assets divided by net income

   (3) Current assets divided by capital

24 Preparing a Budget

Once a year, the hotel controller is called upon to orchestrate one of the most important elements of a hotel operation: the preparation of the annual budget. The budget is not, however, solely the responsibility of the controller. The successful budget requires the participation of all members of the management staff. Without their participation, it is impossible to obtain a commitment to the budget. Without such a commitment, the budget is merely numbers on some pieces of paper.

THE INITIAL STEPS

Successful completion of a budget can be compared to the successful completion of a building project; it requires a critical path. A calendar must be established, pinpointing the date by which each phase of the budget must be completed. The calendar must contain some leeway for error—an allowance for time lost due to unforeseen circumstances. At the same time, this allowance should not be built into any particular section or time period that is so visible that the purpose is lost. This can best be achieved by establishing a final completion date that is earlier than required. This necessitates pushing forward the deadline for submission of each section and advancing the initial starting date.

In Chapter 22 there was reference to the hotel's annual marketing plan. It is essential that the marketing plan be completed prior to starting the budget. This is necessary because the marketing plan not only defines the hotel's mission statement, it describes the strategies and goals, that is, the means by which the mission will be achieved.

The goals in the marketing plan set certain measurable objectives that are the foundation upon which the budget is built. Such objectives should include the following:

Occupancy—by market segment
Average rate—by market segment

Pricing structure—rooms, food and beverage, and other income-producing areas (e.g., golf course prices for rounds and carts)

Numbers of covers for each outlet

Other sales goals

In addition to the measurable goals, the marketing plan must set out the strategies required to reach these goals. The most basic of these strategies is the planned marketing and advertising, the timing thereof, and the markets at which the thrust will be directed. An important part of this, which carries directly over into the total budget preparation, is the completion, on a period-by-period basis, of the sales and marketing budget for the coming year.

Other strategies may be of a nonrecurring nature but nevertheless critical to the results of the final budget. Such strategies can include projects to upgrade or refurbish rooms or public areas, changes in staffing to upgrade or improve service, planned new outlets, or planned development of new revenue sources or markets.

Committees must be appointed, first to complete the marketing plan and second to assist the controller in policing and directing the budget preparation process. One of the first responsibilities of the budget committee is to establish the schedule. Since the commencement of the budget preparation depends on the completion of the marketing plan, the first concern of the budget committee must be whether, in fact, the date set for completion of the marketing plan permits adequate time for the proper scheduling of the preparation of the budget. For most hotels, this means a date no later than the middle of August (assuming that the hotel operates on a calendar-year basis). If such a deadline is not projected for completion of the marketing plan, pressure must immediately be brought to bear on management to change the planned completion date of the marketing plan. In view of this, it is apparent that the budget committee must be appointed and hold its first meeting no later than mid-July.

THE BUDGET SCHEDULE

The following is a suggested schedule for preparation of a hotel budget based on a calendar year operation:

July	10	First meeting of budget committee
	20	Issuance of the budget package including requests for capital budget approvals
	31	Review of marketing plan goals
Aug	20	Submission and approval of occupancy and average rate on a period-by-period and market-segment-by-market-segment basis
	31	Submission of capital budget requests
Sept	10	Preliminary approval of capital budget requests
	15	Submission of revenues for rooms and food and beverage departments
	25	Approval of rooms and food and beverage revenues
Oct	5	Submission of revenues for all other operated departments

	10	Approval of all revenues
	25	Submission of departmental budgets for all operated departments
Oct	5	Review and approval of operated departments (detailed schedule to be issued on a department-by-department basis)
Oct	15	Submission of overhead department budgets
	31	Review and approval of all overhead departments (detailed schedule to be issued on a department-by-department basis)
Nov	10	First review of total budget
	15	Final review and approval of budget and final approval of capital budget
	25	Completion of cash flows and budget submission exhibits
	30	Submission of budget to owners

This budget schedule is very tight and delays can result from difficulties in reaching concurrence at any of the approval levels. Therefore, the schedule is prepared on the assumption that the deadline for submission to the owners is December 10 or later. If this final deadline is earlier than that date, then the total budget schedule must be moved forward.

BUDGET PHILOSOPHIES

A survey of management throughout the industry would uncover varied opinions relative to the overall approach to a budget. These include the concept that the budget should be extremely optimistic, setting almost unattainable goals. Proponents of this philosophy argue that only by setting very high goals will management strive to attain optimum success. The opposite end of the scale is that the budget should be very conservative, setting goals that can readily be attained even if the year is not as successful as expected. Advocates of this approach argue that not only will it provide management with a sense of achievement, but the success will draw praise and possibly financial rewards from the owners.

Neither approach is admirable or recommended. While senior management may have become acclimatized to excessive optimism, junior managers, realizing early in the year that the goals are unattainable, become disillusioned and even resentful. Extreme conservatism, on the other hand, results in complacency and eliminates incentive to strive for higher targets. The ideal budget philosophy is to produce a budget that is challenging but, with effort and lack of serious mishap, can be attained.

On a more technical level, there are also two approaches to the actual budget preparation. Some hotels adopt a policy of predetermining their profit goals prior to completing the budget detail. Preparation of the budget then becomes a process of massaging the expenditures in order to arrive at the prescribed results.

A much more desirable approach is a "ground-up" budget with the various levels developed in an orderly fashion based on the revenue data. This type of approach permits easy identification of the problems when, in the course of the year, budgeted results are not achieved.

The Budget Package

The budget package usually consists of three main elements:

1. The revenue section where, utilizing the predetermined goals, the total revenue numbers are developed.
2. A payroll budget package where departmental payroll figures are calculated based on the revenue information.
3. Detailed departmental schedules.

Revenue. The room revenue worksheets (Figure 24–1) provide historic information and, in certain areas, related formulae in order to aid the budgeting of future revenue.

At the rate and occupancy level, the historical information is provided for three preceding years to better view historical trends. As stressed in Chapter 22, the successful hotel shows continually improving trends. This philosophy must carry over to the budget process. In terms of room sales, both budget and actual information are provided for the preceding year. For many hotels, the prior year's budget information may not be considered useful. However, in some instances it can provide warnings or indicators of prior undue optimism or pessimism which should not be repeated.

Since overall goals have been agreed to in the marketing plan, the principal objective now faced is to properly time phase the level of business within the preset perimeters. However, if in so doing it becomes apparent that the marketing plan goals are unrealistic, immediate action is necessary to review and amend those targets.

The objective in Figure 24–1 is simply to show a pattern of a combination of occupancy, rate, and market mix for a period of years and produce a budget which could reasonably be compiled based on the trends reflected in those numbers. The most critical factor in arriving at a breakdown is the division of rooms occupied between transient and group. The marketing plan must set a specific allocation of rooms to group sales on a month-by-month basis. Since individual business usually results in a higher room rate, group allocations must not be allowed to supplant individual bookings. Therefore, it can be anticipated that group allocations will be smaller in periods of higher occupancy. Some hotels set a policy that group bookings can exceed the allocated number of rooms provided that the group pays the full transient rate. There is some logic to this approach as group business normally results in higher food and beverage income. The negative effect is that it is difficult to fill the nights immediately preceding and following group dates.

Because of the various factors related to group bookings, the proper approach to budgeting occupied rooms is to require the group sales department to budget the group occupancy before rooms division management budgets the transient rooms. Since many groups will have already booked their dates, group sales has a strong foundation on which to build its budget. In budgeting transient rooms, historical trends are the principal guide to be used.

The worksheets provided for food and beverage revenue (Figure 24–2) follow a presentation format using historical data in a manner similar to the format used for room revenue. Budgeting by market segment is replaced by budgeting by outlet and in-

Hotel Grayscot 199___
ROOM REVENUE BUDGET - Page 1

	JAN	FEB	MAR	APR	MAY	JUNE	JULY	AUG	SEPT	OCT	NOV	DEC	TOTAL
Rooms Available													
Year 1	6200	5800	6200	6000	6200	6000	6200	6200	6000	6200	6000	6200	73200
Year 2	6200	5600	6200	6000	6200	6000	6200	6200	6000	6200	6000	6200	73000
Prior Year	6200	5600	6200	6000	6200	6000	6200	6200	6000	6200	6000	6200	73000
Budget	6200	5600	6200	6000	6200	6000	6200	6200	6000	6200	6000	6200	73000
Rooms Occupied													
Transient ―――													
Individual ―――													
Year 1	1050	1008	882	966	1088	1121	1562	1481	1508	1472	1211	1028	14377
Year 2	1070	1120	980	1074	1106	1232	1611	1592	1660	1469	1206	1192	15312
Prior Year	1105	1316	990	1081	1214	1250	1708	1604	1671	1508	1222	1183	15852
Budget	1220	1345	1124	1200	1322	1400	1800	1700	1800	1600	1350	1400	17261
Golf ―――													
Year 1	—	—	—	—	76	180	206	271	262	202	—	—	1197
Year 2	—	—	—	—	84	176	228	282	249	242	—	—	1261
Prior Year	—	—	—	—	88	194	215	265	261	213	—	—	1236
Budget	—	—	—	—	120	200	300	300	275	250	—	—	1445
Corporate ―――													
Year 1	102	110	115	117	116	109	106	92	123	121	131	104	1346
Year 2	110	110	115	120	120	112	117	98	119	108	111	97	1337
Prior Year	118	122	115	125	108	98	121	79	137	139	141	111	1414
Budget	125	125	115	150	150	110	110	90	150	150	150	110	1535
Total Transient													
Budgeted	1345	1470	1239	1350	1592	1710	2210	2090	2225	2000	1500	1510	20241
Transient Occupancy													
Budgeted	21.7%	26.3%	20.0%	22.5%	25.7%	28.5%	35.6%	33.7%	37.1%	32.3%	25.0%	24.4%	27.7%

Figure 24-1   Room Revenue Budget

Hotel Grayscot 199__
ROOM REVENUE BUDGET - Page 2

	JAN	FEB	MAR	APR	MAY	JUNE	JULY	AUG	SEPT	OCT	NOV	DEC	TOTAL
Rooms Occupied													
Group ----													
Corporate ----													
Year 1	502	517	508	565	517	482	474	468	517	416	368	307	5641
Year 2	522	511	516	711	662	522	492	475	480	602	512	392	6403
Prior Year	531	498	521	582	728	716	678	522	641	638	508	308	6871
Budget	550	525	525	600	850	950	800	600	625	650	525	325	7525
Tour & Travel													
Year 1	412	462	481	462	172	192	182	206	242	317	202	231	3561
Year 2	462	472	262	248	108	178	191	171	261	362	190	247	3152
Prior Year	471	481	240	312	216	215	380	202	281	381	207	218	3604
Budget	600	600	400	400	300	350	550	325	400	500	325	350	5100
Association													
Year 1	—	—	322	394	592	580	640	380	628	513	301	282	4632
Year 2	132	162	480	572	660	528	718	508	790	711	122	260	5643
Prior Year	121	140	508	726	672	812	872	761	882	961	208	272	6935
Budget	150	150	700	800	700	900	1000	800	1100	1050	225	300	7875
Total Group													
Budgeted	1300	1275	1625	1800	1850	2200	2350	1725	2125	2200	1075	975	20500
Occupancy													
Budget	21.0%	22.8%	26.2%	30.0%	29.8%	36.7%	37.9%	27.8%	35.4%	35.5%	17.9%	15.7%	28.1%
Overall ----													
Rooms Occupied	2645	2745	2864	3150	3442	3910	4560	3815	4350	4200	2575	2485	40741
Occupancy	42.7%	49.0%	46.2%	52.5%	55.5%	65.2%	73.5%	61.5%	72.5%	67.7%	42.9%	40.1%	55.8%

Figure 24–1 Room Revenue Budget *(continued)*

Hotel Grayscot 199__
ROOM REVENUE BUDGET - Page 3

	JAN	FEB	MAR	APR	MAY	JUNE	JULY	AUG	SEPT	OCT	NOV	DEC	TOTAL
Rooms Occupied													
Transient ---													
Individual ---													
Year 1	81.51	84.08	78.22	87.16	98.16	101.71	124.62	131.06	129.72	133.11	106.11	103.12	
Year 2	84.62	86.15	88.31	89.03	101.22	103.82	127.85	137.18	134.08	137.15	109.12	114.17	
Prior Year	87.80	91.08	86.14	91.82	104.83	102.90	131.42	139.50	140.22	146.12	108.32	117.08	
Budget	90.00	93.00	90.00	94.00	110.00	110.00	140.00	150.00	150.00	150.00	110.00	120.00	
Golf ---													
Year 1	—	—	—	—	94.82	95.08	117.29	119.16	111.22	112.88	—	—	
Year 2	—	—	—	—	96.17	94.82	121.11	124.08	119.38	110.71	—	—	
Prior Year	—	—	—	—	99.03	97.22	122.04	131.11	121.08	111.82	—	—	
Budget	—	—	—	—	105.00	105.00	130.00	135.00	125.00	115.00	—	—	
Corporate ---													
Year 1	78.02	76.16	79.20	82.08	91.02	92.02	111.12	113.04	115.11	112.02	71.11	81.16	
Year 2	76.12	74.12	79.19	81.12	93.12	93.11	108.19	117.62	116.08	109.17	82.08	84.92	
Prior Year	77.15	77.72	81.03	83.02	92.02	91.08	117.32	119.08	118.12	111.38	83.15	91.03	
Budget	80.00	80.00	85.00	85.00	95.00	95.00	120.00	120.00	120.00	120.00	95.00	95.00	
Overall ---													
Transient Rate													
Budgeted	89.07	91.89	89.54	93.00	108.21	108.45	137.65	146.56	144.89	143.38	108.50	118.18	119.06
Average Rate													
Group ---													
Corporate ---													
Year 1	64.11	76.11	77.14	82.02	97.11	88.13	113.08	123.62	131.08	133.17	97.11	98.02	
Year 2	71.10	78.03	79.08	84.61	99.08	93.79	121.72	129.77	136.71	139.02	99.12	101.11	
Prior Year	77.18	82.12	83.13	88.73	103.62	99.81	134.19	141.82	144.12	138.22	101.13	97.63	
Budget	85.00	85.00	85.00	90.00	105.00	105.00	140.00	150.00	150.00	150.00	105.00	105.00	

Figure 24–1 Room Revenue Budget *(continued)*

Hotel Grayscot 199___

ROOM REVENUE BUDGET - Page 4

	JAN	FEB	MAR	APR	MAY	JUNE	JULY	AUG	SEPT	OCT	NOV	DEC	TOTAL
Tour & Travel													
Year 1	66.12	67.18	73.02	78.81	83.13	88.21	129.05	126.14	138.15	141.12	89.11	91.08	
Year 2	71.08	69.31	71.16	80.04	96.01	89.15	133.11	136.12	141.71	139.18	88.03	94.12	
Prior Year	74.72	77.53	78.05	81.12	92.11	94.67	137.08	144.03	148.03	146.54	96.52	97.17	
Budget	80.00	80.00	80.00	85.00	100.00	100.00	140.00	150.00	150.00	150.00	100.00	100.00	
Association													
Year 1	91.52	93.17	91.51	92.02	94.08	107.22	111.28	129.11	138.12	136.51	91.03	96.02	
Year 2	94.08	97.02	94.06	97.63	99.22	105.16	121.62	131.16	144.62	146.08	98.11	94.81	
Prior Year	100.00	100.00	99.12	101.11	98.71	118.03	138.52	148.17	151.18	148.12	101.15	99.22	
Budget	100.00	100.00	105.00	105.00	105.00	115.00	145.00	155.00	155.00	150.00	105.00	105.00	
Overall —													
Group Rate Budgeted	84.42	84.41	92.38	95.56	104.19	108.30	142.13	152.32	152.59	150.00	103.49	103.21	118.70
Room Revenue													
Transient —													
Individual —													
Prior Year —													
Budget	95000	120000	90000	100000	125000	130000	250000	250000	225000	225000	150000	150000	1910000
Actual	97019	119861	85279	99257	127264	128625	224465	223758	234308	220349	132367	138506	1831058
This Year —													
Budget	109800	125085	101160	112800	145420	154000	252000	255000	270000	240000	148500	168000	2081765
Golf —													
Prior Year —													
Budget	—	—	—	—	8000	20000	30000	30000	30000	25000	—	—	143000
Actual	—	—	—	—	8715	18861	26239	34744	31602	23818	—	—	143978
This Year —													
Budget	—	—	—	—	12600	21000	39000	40500	34375	28750	—	—	176225

Figure 24–1　Room Revenue Budget *(continued)*

Hotel Grayscot 199__
ROOM REVENUE BUDGET – Page 5

	JAN	FEB	MAR	APR	MAY	JUNE	JULY	AUG	SEPT	OCT	NOV	DEC	TOTAL
Corporate —													
Prior Year —													
Budget —	10000	10000	10000	10000	10000	10000	10000	10000	10000	10000	10000	10000	120000
Actual	9104	9482	9318	10378	9938	8926	14196	9407	16182	15482	11724	10104	134241
This Year —													
Budget	10000	10000	9775	12750	14250	10450	13200	10800	18000	18000	14250	10450	151925
Total Transit													
Prior Year —													
Budget —	105000	130000	100000	110000	143000	160000	290000	290000	265000	260000	160000	160000	2173000
Actual	106123	129343	94597	109635	145916	156412	264900	267909	282092	259648	144091	148610	2109276
This Year —													
Budget	119800	135085	110935	125550	172270	185450	304200	306300	322375	286750	162750	178450	2409915
Room Revenue													
Transient —													
Individual —													
Prior Year —													
Budget —	40000	40000	45000	50000	75000	80000	90000	90000	90000	90000	60000	30000	760000
Actual	40983	40896	43311	51641	75435	71464	90981	74030	92381	88184	51374	30070	750749
This Year —													
Budget	46750	44625	44625	54000	89250	99750	112000	90000	93750	97500	55125	34125	861500
Tour & Travel													
Prior Year —													
Budget —	35000	35000	15000	25000	20000	20000	50000	50000	50000	50000	20000	20000	390000
Actual	35193	37292	18732	25309	19896	20354	52090	29094	41596	55832	19980	21183	376552
This Year —													
Budget	48000	48000	32000	34000	30000	35000	77000	48750	60000	75000	32500	35000	555250

Figure 24–1 Room Revenue Budget *(continued)*

Hotel *G*rayscot 199___
ROOM REVENUE BUDGET - Page 6

	JAN	FEB	MAR	APR	MAY	JUNE	JULY	AUG	SEPT	OCT	NOV	DEC	TOTAL
Association													
Prior Year ---													
Budget	10000	10000	50000	65000	65000	100000	100000	100000	100000	100000	30000	30000	760000
Actual	11384	13583	50353	73406	66333	95840	120789	112757	133341	142343	21039	26988	868157
This Year ---													
Budget	15000	15000	73500	84000	73500	103500	145000	124000	170500	157500	23625	31500	1016625
Total Group													
Prior Year ---													
Budget	85000	85000	110000	140000	160000	200000	240000	240000	240000	240000	110000	80000	1910000
Actual	87559	91770	112396	150356	161664	187658	263861	215881	267318	286359	92393	78241	1995458
This Year ---													
Budget	109750	107625	150125	172000	192750	238250	334000	262750	324350	330000	111250	100625	2433375
SUMMARY													
Total Revenue													
Prior Year ---													
Budget	190000	215000	210000	250000	303000	360000	530000	530000	505000	500000	270000	240000	4098000
Actual	184578	211632	197674	249614	288928	316283	488326	439639	501626	506780	224760	216747	3826515
This Year ---													
Budget	229550	242710	261060	297550	365020	423700	638200	569050	646625	616750	274000	279075	4843290
Occupancy													
Prior Year ---													
Actual	37.8%	45.7%	38.2%	47.2%	48.8%	54.7%	64.1%	55.5%	64.6%	61.0%	38.1%	33.7%	51.9%
This Year ---													
Budgeted	42.7%	49.0%	46.2%	52.5%	55.5%	65.2%	73.5%	61.5%	72.5%	67.7%	42.9%	40.1%	55.8%
Average Rate													
Prior Year ---													
Actual	78.50	82.77	83.39	88.08	95.48	96.28	123.09	127.69	129.18	131.43	98.32	103.61	100.93
This Year ---													
Budgeted	86.79	88.42	91.15	94.46	106.05	108.36	139.96	149.16	148.65	146.85	106.41	112.30	118.88

Figure 24-1 Room Revenue Budget (*continued*)

Hotel Grayscot 199___
FOOD AND BEVERAGE BUDGET – Page 1

OUTLET 1

	JAN	FEB	MAR	APR	MAY	JUNE	JULY	AUG	SEPT	OCT	NOV	DEC	TOTAL
Breakfast Covers													
Year 1	3003	2994	2721	3420	3792	4861	5791	4910	5418	5701	2711	3170	48492
Year 2	3110	3079	2880	3740	4017	4922	5922	5140	5721	5923	2802	3391	50647
Prior Year	3320	3299	3320	4102	4290	5120	6310	5320	5982	6107	2917	3582	53669
Budget	3400	3580	3600	4500	5000	5860	6900	5500	6300	6300	3400	3700	57980
Lunch Covers													
Year 1	472	511	401	412	463	488	671	642	608	596	418	440	6122
Year 2	480	562	372	408	511	513	691	631	643	649	412	491	6363
Prior Year	511	601	451	458	592	611	703	620	713	711	521	472	6964
Budget	600	650	500	550	650	700	750	750	750	750	450	500	7600
Dinner Covers													
Year 1	—	—	—	—	508	521	608	706	646	511	—	—	3500
Year 2	—	—	—	—	514	511	711	812	782	649	—	—	3979
Prior Year	—	—	—	—	622	535	822	917	821	802	—	—	4515
Budget	—	—	—	—	900	1000	1100	1200	1100	900	—	—	6200
Other Covers													
Year 1	—	—	—	—	—	—	—	—	—	—	—	—	
Year 2	—	—	—	—	—	—	—	—	—	—	—	—	
Prior Year	—	—	—	—	—	—	—	—	—	—	—	—	
Budget	—	—	—	—	—	—	—	—	—	—	—	—	
Total Covers													
Year 1	3475	3505	3122	3832	4763	5870	7070	6253	6672	6808	3129	3610	58114
Year 2	3590	3641	3252	4148	5042	5946	7324	5583	7146	7221	3214	3882	60989
Prior Year	3831	3900	3771	4560	5504	6266	7825	5851	7516	7620	3438	4054	65146
Budget	4000	4230	4100	5050	6550	7500	8750	7450	8150	7950	3850	4200	71780

Figure 24–2   Food and Beverage Budget

Hotel *G*rayscot 199___
FOOD AND BEVERAGE BUDGET - Page 2

OUTLET 1 Average Check	JAN	FEB	MAR	APR	MAY	JUNE	JULY	AUG	SEPT	OCT	NOV	DEC	TOTAL
Breakfast ——													
Year 1	8.22	8.11	9.08	8.12	8.41	8.64	8.78	8.79	8.62	8.59	8.01	8.11	—
Year 2	8.61	8.48	8.81	8.72	8.61	8.72	8.88	8.68	8.71	8.38	8.11	8.72	—
Prior Year	8.66	8.71	7.97	8.68	8.73	8.73	8.68	8.53	8.88	8.62	8.13	8.08	—
Budget	9.01	9.01	9.01	9.01	9.01	9.01	9.25	9.25	9.25	9.25	9.25	9.25	—
Lunch ——													
Year 1	9.02	9.13	90.6	9.08	9.16	9.13	9.14	9.06	9.17	9.05	9.21	9.36	—
Year 2	9.61	9.42	9.41	9.38	9.48	9.33	9.27	9.38	9.82	9.79	9.38	9.42	—
Prior Year	10.08	10.11	9.79	10.41	10.53	10.22	10.38	10.21	10.44	10.39	10.22	10.41	—
Budget	11.01	11.01	11.01	11.01	11.01	11.01	11.01	11.01	11.01	11.01	11.01	11.01	—
Dinner ——													
Year 1	—	—	—	—	14.88	14.79	14.33	14.37	14.39	14.22	—	—	—
Year 2	—	—	—	—	16.12	15.91	15.72	15.61	15.49	15.16	—	—	—
Prior Year	—	—	—	—	16.62	16.48	16.12	16.08	16.07	16.31	—	—	—
Budget	—	—	—	—	17.51	17.51	17.51	17.51	17.51	17.51	—	—	—
Other ——													
Year 1	—	—	—	—	—	—	—	—	—	—	—	—	—
Year 2	—	—	—	—	—	—	—	—	—	—	—	—	—
Prior Year	—	—	—	—	—	—	—	—	—	—	—	—	—
Budget	—	—	—	—	—	—	—	—	—	—	—	—	—
OUTLET 1 Revenue													
Breakfast ——													
Year 1	24685	24281	21986	27770	31891	41999	50845	43159	46703	48972	21715	25709	409714
Year 2	26777	26110	25373	32613	34586	42920	52587	44615	49830	49635	22724	29570	437340
Prior Year	28751	28734	26460	35605	37452	44698	54771	45380	53120	52642	23715	28493	460271
Budget	30634	32256	32436	40545	45050	52258	63825	50875	58275	58275	31450	34225	530104

Figure 24-2   Food and Beverage Budget *(continued)*

Hotel Grayscot 199___

FOOD AND BEVERAGE BUDGET – Page 3

	JAN	FEB	MAR	APR	MAY	JUNE	JULY	AUG	SEPT	OCT	NOV	DEC	TOTAL
Lunch —													
Year 1	4257	4665	3633	3741	4241	4455	6133	5817	5574	5394	3850	4118	55880
Year 2	4613	5294	3501	3827	4844	4786	6406	5919	6314	6354	3865	4625	60347
Prior Year	5151	6076	4415	4768	6234	6244	7297	5330	7444	7387	5325	4914	71585
Budget	6606	7157	5505	6055	7157	7707	8258	8258	8258	8258	4955	5505	83676
Dinner —													
Year 1	—	—	—	—	7559	7706	8713	10145	9296	7266	—	—	50685
Year 2	—	—	—	—	8286	8130	11177	12675	12113	9839	—	—	62220
Prior Year	—	—	—	—	10338	8817	13251	14649	13193	13081	—	—	73328
Budget	—	—	—	—	15759	17510	19261	21012	19261	15769	—	—	108562
Other —													
Year 1	—	—	—	—	—	—	—	—	—	—	—	—	—
Year 2	—	—	—	—	—	—	—	—	—	—	—	—	—
Prior Year	—	—	—	—	—	—	—	—	—	—	—	—	—
Budget	—	—	—	—	—	—	—	—	—	—	—	—	—
Total Revenue													
Year 1	28942	28946	25619	31511	43691	54160	65691	59121	61574	61532	25565	29827	516279
Year 2	31390	31404	28874	36440	47716	55836	70170	63209	68257	65828	26589	34195	559907
Prior Year	33902	34810	30875	40373	54024	59759	75319	66359	73757	73110	29040	33407	605184
Budget	37240	39413	37941	46601	67966	77475	91344	80145	85794	82302	36405	39730	722342
OUTLET 1 **Beverage Revenue**													
Lunch —													
Year 1	213	233	182	187	212	223	307	291	279	270	192	206	2794
Year 2	231	265	175	191	242	239	320	296	316	318	193	231	3017
Prior Year	258	304	221	238	312	312	365	317	372	369	266	246	3579
Budget	330	358	275	303	358	585	413	413	413	413	248	275	4184

Figure 24–2 Food and Beverage Budget (*continued*)

Hotel Grayscot 199___
FOOD AND BEVERAGE BUDGET – Page 4

	JAN	FEB	MAR	APR	MAY	JUNE	JULY	AUG	SEPT	OCT	NOV	DEC	TOTAL
Dinner ——													
Year 1	—	—	—	—	1512	1541	1743	2029	1859	1453	—	—	10137
Year 2	—	—	—	—	1657	1626	2235	2532	2423	1968	—	—	12444
Prior Year	—	—	—	—	2068	1763	2650	2930	2639	2616	—	—	14666
Budget	—	—	—	—	3152	3502	3852	4202	3852	3152	—	—	21712
Other ——													
Year 1	—	—	—	—	—	—	—	—	—	—	—	—	—
Year 2	—	—	—	—	—	—	—	—	—	—	—	—	—
Prior Year	—	—	—	—	—	—	—	—	—	—	—	—	—
Budget	—	—	—	—	—	—	—	—	—	—	—	—	—
Total Revenue													
Year 1	213	233	182	187	1724	1764	2049	2320	2138	1723	192	206	12931
Year 2	231	265	175	191	1899	1865	2556	2831	2738	2285	193	231	15461
Prior Year	268	304	221	238	2379	2076	3015	3246	3011	2985	266	246	18245
Budget	330	358	275	303	3510	3887	4265	4615	4265	3565	248	275	25896
OUTLET 2													
Breakfast Covers													
Year 1	—	—	—	—	—	—	—	—	—	—	—	—	—
Year 2	—	—	—	—	—	—	—	—	—	—	—	—	—
Prior Year	—	—	—	—	—	—	—	—	—	—	—	—	—
Budget	—	—	—	—	—	—	—	—	—	—	—	—	—
Lunch Covers													
Year 1	—	—	—	—	—	—	—	—	—	—	—	—	—
Year 2	—	—	—	—	—	—	—	—	—	—	—	—	—
Prior Year	—	—	—	—	—	—	—	—	—	—	—	—	—
Budget	—	—	—	—	—	—	—	—	—	—	—	—	—

Figure 24–2   Food and Beverage Budget *(continued)*

Hotel Grayscot 199__

FOOD AND BEVERAGE BUDGET - Page 5

	JAN	FEB	MAR	APR	MAY	JUNE	JULY	AUG	SEPT	OCT	NOV	DEC	TOTAL
Dinner Covers													
Year 1	1811	1963	2302	2854	2733	2411	2412	2321	2654	2711	1861	1854	27887
Year 2	2003	2082	2651	2976	2862	2917	2801	2514	2822	2615	1942	1917	30102
Prior Year	2171	2270	2711	3011	3025	3017	2762	2643	2921	2817	2062	2011	31421
Budget	2280	2491	2819	3312	3171	3286	3151	3062	3171	3022	2191	2081	34035
Other Covers													
Year 1	—	—	—	—	—	—	—	—	—	—	—	—	—
Year 2	—	—	—	—	—	—	—	—	—	—	—	—	—
Prior Year	—	—	—	—	—	—	—	—	—	—	—	—	—
Budget	—	—	—	—	—	—	—	—	—	—	—	—	—
Total Covers													
Year 1	1811	1963	2302	2854	2733	2411	2412	2321	2654	2711	1861	1854	27887
Year 2	2003	2082	2651	2976	2862	2917	2801	2514	2822	2615	1942	1917	30102
Prior Year	2171	2270	2711	3025	3025	3017	2762	2643	2921	2817	2062	2011	31421
Budget	2280	2491	2819	3312	3171	3286	3151	3062	3171	3022	2191	2081	34035
OUTLET 2													
Average Check													
Breakfast —													
Year 1	—	—	—	—	—	—	—	—	—	—	—	—	—
Year 2	—	—	—	—	—	—	—	—	—	—	—	—	—
Prior Year	—	—	—	—	—	—	—	—	—	—	—	—	—
Budget	—	—	—	—	—	—	—	—	—	—	—	—	—
Lunch —													
Year 1	—	—	—	—	—	—	—	—	—	—	—	—	—
Year 2	—	—	—	—	—	—	—	—	—	—	—	—	—
Prior Year	—	—	—	—	—	—	—	—	—	—	—	—	—
Budget	—	—	—	—	—	—	—	—	—	—	—	—	—

Figure 24-2   Food and Beverage Budget *(continued)*

Hotel Grayscot 199__
FOOD AND BEVERAGE BUDGET - Page 6

	JAN	FEB	MAR	APR	MAY	JUNE	JULY	AUG	SEPT	OCT	NOV	DEC	TOTAL
Dinner ---													
Year 1	15.08	14.92	15.11	15.08	21.03	21.61	22.08	23.12	22.17	21.91	15.82	15.91	
Year 2	15.22	15.22	15.78	15.71	22.18	21.82	22.71	23.18	22.31	22.72	15.79	16.37	
Prior Year	15.17	15.81	16.81	16.92	23.11	23.91	23.81	23.62	23.91	23.62	16.33	17.03	
Budget	17.51	17.51	17.51	17.51	24.51	24.51	24.51	24.51	24.51	24.51	18.01	18.01	
Other ---													
Year 1	—	—	—	—	—	—	—	—	—	—	—	—	
Year 2	—	—	—	—	—	—	—	—	—	—	—	—	
Prior Year	—	—	—	—	—	—	—	—	—	—	—	—	
Budget	—	—	—	—	—	—	—	—	—	—	—	—	
OUTLET 2													
Revenue													
Breakfast ---													
Year 1	—	—	—	—	—	—	—	—	—	—	—	—	
Year 2	—	—	—	—	—	—	—	—	—	—	—	—	
Prior Year	—	—	—	—	—	—	—	—	—	—	—	—	
Budget	—	—	—	—	—	—	—	—	—	—	—	—	
Lunch ---													
Year 1	—	—	—	—	—	—	—	—	—	—	—	—	
Year 2	—	—	—	—	—	—	—	—	—	—	—	—	
Prior Year	—	—	—	—	—	—	—	—	—	—	—	—	
Budget	—	—	—	—	—	—	—	—	—	—	—	—	
Dinner ---													
Year 1	27310	29288	34783	43038	57475	52102	53257	53662	58839	59398	29441	29497	528090
Year 2	30486	31688	41833	46753	63479	63649	63611	58275	62959	59413	30664	31381	584190
Prior Year	32934	35889	45572	50946	69908	72136	65763	62428	69841	66538	33672	34247	639874
Budget	39923	43617	49326	57993	77721	80540	77231	75050	77721	74069	39460	37479	730130

Figure 24–2 Food and Beverage Budget (*continued*)

Hotel Grayscot 199___
FOOD AND BEVERAGE BUDGET – Page 7

	JAN	FEB	MAR	APR	MAY	JUNE	JULY	AUG	SEPT	OCT	NOV	DEC	TOTAL
Other —													
Year 1	—	—	—	—	—	—	—	—	—	—	—	—	
Year 2	—	—	—	—	—	—	—	—	—	—	—	—	
Prior Year	—	—	—	—	—	—	—	—	—	—	—	—	
Budget	—	—	—	—	—	—	—	—	—	—	—	—	
Total													
Year 1	27310	29288	34783	43038	57475	52102	53257	53662	58839	59398	29441	29497	528090
Year 2	30486	31688	41833	46753	63479	63649	63611	58275	62959	59413	30664	31381	584190
Prior Year	32934	35889	45572	50946	69908	72136	65763	62428	69841	66538	33672	34247	639874
Budget	39923	43617	49326	57993	77721	80540	77231	75050	77721	74069	39460	37479	730130
OUTLET 2 **Beverage Revenue**													
Lunch —													
Year 1	—	—	—	—	—	—	—	—	—	—	—	—	
Year 2	—	—	—	—	—	—	—	—	—	—	—	—	
Prior Year	—	—	—	—	—	—	—	—	—	—	—	—	
Budget	—	—	—	—	—	—	—	—	—	—	—	—	
Dinner —													
Year 1	6827	7322	8696	10760	14369	13025	13314	13415	14710	14850	7360	7374	132022
Year 2	7621	7922	10458	11638	15870	15912	15903	14569	15740	14853	7666	7845	146047
Prior Year	8234	8972	11393	12737	17477	18034	16441	15607	17460	16634	8418	8562	159969
Budget	9981	10904	12331	14498	19430	20135	19308	18762	19430	18517	9865	9370	182532
Other —													
Year 1	—	—	—	—	—	—	—	—	—	—	—	—	
Year 2	—	—	—	—	—	—	—	—	—	—	—	—	
Prior Year	—	—	—	—	—	—	—	—	—	—	—	—	
Budget	—	—	—	—	—	—	—	—	—	—	—	—	

Figure 24-2 Food and Beverage Budget (*continued*)

Hotel Grayscot 199___
FOOD AND BEVERAGE BUDGET – Page 8

	JAN	FEB	MAR	APR	MAY	JUNE	JULY	AUG	SEPT	OCT	NOV	DEC	TOTAL
Total													
Year 1	6827	7322	8696	10760	14369	13025	13314	13415	14710	14850	7360	7374	132022
Year 2	7621	7922	10458	11688	15870	15912	15903	14569	15740	14853	7666	7845	146047
Prior Year	8234	8972	11393	12737	17477	18034	16441	15607	17460	16634	8418	8562	159969
Budget	9981	10904	12331	14498	19430	20135	19308	18762	19430	18517	9865	9370	182532
BANQUET													
Breakfast Covers													
Lunch —													
Year 1	906	921	918	1008	1075	1108	1068	1071	1106	1181	1103	1006	12471
Year 2	922	917	933	1072	1069	1117	1128	1131	1143	1508	1131	662	12733
Prior Year	933	961	963	1383	1421	1309	1320	1291	1472	1562	1202	799	14615
Budget	1000	1000	1000	1400	1500	1700	1600	1500	1700	1700	1200	1000	16300
Lunch Covers													
Year 1	413	463	451	507	581	553	541	531	553	582	549	508	6232
Year 2	451	451	461	531	539	548	581	561	528	711	579	348	6289
Prior Year	471	482	481	702	722	657	674	648	736	768	603	422	7366
Budget	500	500	500	700	750	850	800	750	850	850	600	600	8250
Dinner Covers													
Year 1	812	862	812	908	991	1071	1072	982	1062	1088	1002	1068	11730
Year 2	918	951	942	972	1077	1083	1005	1091	1008	1442	1070	1073	12632
Prior Year	922	981	961	968	1022	1288	1331	1198	1421	1599	1168	1081	13940
Budget	1000	1050	1050	1200	1450	1600	1750	1550	1700	1700	1200	1200	16450
Other Covers													
Year 1	503	406	589	672	608	728	798	709	791	808	772	783	8167
Year 2	517	429	588	692	662	888	872	871	838	817	822	711	8647
Prior Year	550	490	562	711	628	881	949	908	979	902	873	733	9166
Budget	600	600	600	700	700	900	1000	1000	1000	1000	900	900	9900

Figure 24-2 Food and Beverage Budget (*continued*)

Hotel Grayscot 199__

FOOD AND BEVERAGE BUDGET - Page 9

	JAN	FEB	MAR	APR	MAY	JUNE	JULY	AUG	SEPT	OCT	NOV	DEC	TOTAL
Total Covers													
Year 1	2634	2652	2770	3095	3255	3460	3479	3293	3512	3659	3426	3365	38600
Year 2	2808	2748	2924	3267	3287	3636	3586	3654	3517	4478	3602	2794	40301
Prior Year	2876	2914	2967	3764	3792	4135	4274	4045	4608	4831	3846	3035	45087
Budget	3100	3150	3150	4000	4400	5050	5150	4800	5250	5250	3900	3700	50900
BANQUET													
Average Check													
Breakfast ——													
Year 1	8.88	8.79	8.91	8.88	8.68	9.03	8.93	8.89	8.97	9.04	8.98	9.03	
Year 2	9.63	9.52	9.71	9.58	9.39	9.28	9.68	9.38	9.72	9.79	9.69	9.58	
Prior Year	9.82	9.79	9.69	9.66	9.76	9.92	9.96	10.03	10.11	10.13	9.88	10.01	
Budget	10.01	10.01	10.01	10.01	10.01	10.51	10.51	10.51	10.51	10.51	10.01	10.01	
Lunch ——													
Year 1	12.88	12.63	12.72	12.88	12.59	13.15	13.46	13.12	13.35	13.61	13.03	12.96	
Year 2	13.02	13.11	13.13	13.26	13.91	13.88	14.04	14.16	14.05	13.92	13.71	13.88	
Prior Year	13.61	13.43	13.36	13.72	14.08	14.46	14.72	14.74	14.65	14.46	14.31	14.28	
Budget	14.01	14.01	14.01	14.01	15.01	15.01	15.01	15.01	15.01	15.01	14.51	14.51	
Dinner ——													
Year 1	26.28	26.71	27.33	27.41	28.62	28.71	29.02	29.82	29.99	29.62	29.71	29.82	
Year 2	27.38	27.77	28.11	28.12	29.91	30.03	30.11	30.66	31.07	30.97	30.61	30.57	
Prior Year	29.08	28.82	29.08	29.18	31.03	31.51	30.92	33.08	33.41	33.05	31.12	31.31	
Budget	30.01	30.01	30.01	30.01	32.01	32.01	34.01	34.01	34.01	34.01	32.01	32.01	
Other ——													
Year 1	4.87	4.91	5.03	4.72	5.19	5.08	5.11	5.08	5.01	4.78	4.69	4.78	
Year 2	5.22	5.11	5.12	5.03	5.31	5.28	5.23	5.17	5.09	5.03	4.99	5.01	
Prior Year	5.63	5.31	5.52	5.42	5.63	5.72	5.65	5.49	5.59	5.23	5.17	5.39	
Budget	6.01	6.01	6.01	6.01	6.01	6.01	6.01	6.01	6.01	6.01	6.01	6.01	

Figure 24–2   Food and Beverage Budget *(continued)*

Hotel Grayscot 199__
FOOD AND BEVERAGE BUDGET - Page 10

	JAN	FEB	MAR	APR	MAY	JUNE	JULY	AUG	SEPT	OCT	NOV	DEC	TOTAL
BANQUET													
Revenue													
Breakfast ——													
Year 1	8045	8096	8179	8951	9331	10005	9537	9521	9921	10676	9905	9084	111252
Year 2	8879	8730	9059	10377	10038	10366	10919	10609	11110	14763	10959	6342	122151
Prior Year	9162	9408	9331	13360	13859	12985	13147	12949	14882	15823	11876	7998	144781
Budget	10010	10010	10010	14014	15015	17867	16816	15765	17867	17867	12012	10010	167263
Lunch ——													
Year 1	5319	5848	5737	6530	7315	7272	7282	6967	7383	7921	7153	6584	81310
Year 2	5872	5913	6053	7041	7497	7606	8157	7944	7418	9897	7938	4830	86167
Prior Year	6410	6473	6426	9631	10166	9500	9921	9552	10782	11105	8629	6026	104683
Budget	7005	7005	7005	9807	11258	12759	12008	11258	12759	12759	8706	8706	121033
Dinner ——													
Year 1	21339	23024	22192	24888	28362	30748	31109	29283	31849	32227	29769	31848	336640
Year 2	25135	26409	26480	27333	32213	32552	30261	33450	31319	44659	32753	32802	375334
Prior Year	26812	28272	27946	28246	31713	40585	41155	39630	47476	52847	36348	33846	434875
Budget	30010	31511	31511	36012	46415	51216	59518	52716	57817	57817	38412	38412	531365
Other ——													
Year 1	2450	1993	2963	3172	3156	3698	4078	3602	3963	3862	3621	3743	40299
Year 2	2699	2192	3011	3481	3197	4689	4561	4503	4265	4110	4102	3562	44370
Prior Year	3097	2602	3102	3854	3536	5039	5362	4985	5473	4717	4513	3951	50230
Budget	3606	3606	3606	4207	4207	5409	6010	6010	6010	6010	5409	5409	59499
Total													
Year 1	37154	38961	39071	43541	48164	51724	52006	49373	53116	54686	50449	51258	569502
Year 2	42584	43244	44603	48231	52945	55183	53897	56506	54112	73469	55752	47536	628023
Prior Year	45481	46756	46806	55091	59273	68110	69585	67115	78613	84493	61366	51821	734509
Budget	50631	52132	52132	64040	76894	87251	94352	85748	94453	94453	64539	62537	879159

Figure 24–2 Food and Beverage Budget (*continued*)

BANQUET	JAN	FEB	MAR	APR	MAY	JUNE	JULY	AUG	SEPT	OCT	NOV	DEC	TOTAL
Beverage Revenue													
Lunch ——													
Year 1	532	585	574	653	731	727	728	697	738	792	715	658	8131
Year 2	587	591	605	704	750	761	816	794	742	990	794	483	8617
Prior Year	641	647	643	963	1017	950	992	955	1078	1111	863	603	10462
Budget	701	701	701	981	1126	1276	1201	1126	1276	1276	871	871	12103
Dinner ——													
Year 1	6402	6907	6658	7466	8509	9225	9333	8785	9555	9668	8931	9554	100992
Year 2	7540	7923	7944	8200	9664	9757	9078	10035	9396	13398	9826	9840	112600
Prior Year	8044	8482	8384	8474	9514	12175	12346	11889	14243	15854	10904	10154	130463
Budget	9003	9453	9453	10804	13924	15365	17855	15815	17345	17345	11524	11524	159409
Other ——													
Year 1	980	797	1185	1269	1262	1479	1631	1441	1585	1545	1448	1497	16120
Year 2	1079	877	1204	1392	1279	1875	1824	1801	1706	1644	1641	1425	17748
Prior Year	1239	1041	1241	1541	1414	2016	2145	1994	2189	1887	1805	1580	20692
Budget	1442	1442	1442	1683	1683	2164	2404	2404	2404	2404	2164	2164	23800
Total													
Year 1	7914	8289	8416	9388	10502	11431	11692	10322	11878	12005	11094	11710	125243
Year 2	9207	9391	9753	10296	11692	12393	11718	12631	11844	16031	12260	11748	138966
Prior Year	9923	10170	10267	10978	11945	15141	15483	14838	17510	18852	13573	12337	161017
Budget	11146	11596	11596	13467	16733	18804	21460	19344	21025	21025	14558	14558	195312
LOUNGE													
Beverage Revenue													
Year 1	24810	25112	26113	25008	31530	32710	56112	52018	54180	51210	26122	29513	434428
Year 2	26032	27033	28012	29109	34728	35168	61980	59133	61116	58720	30076	33714	484821
Prior Year	28111	29041	32110	33116	38114	40802	64729	64711	68072	66512	35122	37122	537544
Budget	33500	33500	37000	37000	44250	44250	73750	73750	73750	73750	39000	39000	602500

Figure 24–2 Food and Beverage Budget *(continued)*

Hotel *G*rayscot 199___
FOOD AND BEVERAGE BUDGET – Page 12

	JAN	FEB	MAR	APR	MAY	JUNE	JULY	AUG	SEPT	OCT	NOV	DEC	TOTAL
Total Food Revenue													
Year 1	93406	97295	99473	118091	149330	157986	170954	162155	173529	175716	105454	110583	1613871
Year 2	104460	106336	115309	131424	164141	174668	187678	177989	185329	198669	113005	113112	1772119
Prior Year	112317	117455	123353	146410	183204	200005	210667	195901	222211	224141	124079	119925	1979567
Budget	127794	135161	139398	168634	225581	245265	262926	240942	257967	250813	140403	139746	2334630
Total Beverage Revenue													
Year 1	39764	40957	43407	45343	58125	58936	83168	78676	82906	79787	44759	48803	704624
Year 2	43091	44611	48399	51285	64189	65338	92156	89163	91438	91890	50196	53539	785295
Prior Year	46525	48487	53991	57069	69915	76053	99650	98402	106053	104983	57379	58266	876774
Budget	54957	56358	61203	65268	83923	87077	118783	116472	118470	116857	63671	63203	1006241
Food & Beverage Misc. Income													
Prior Year ——													
Budget													
Public Rooms	400	400	400	400	500	500	500	500	500	400	400	400	5300
Audio/Visual	500	500	500	500	600	600	600	600	600	500	500	500	6500
Other	100	100	100	100	200	200	200	200	200	100	100	100	1700
Total	1000	1000	1000	1000	1300	1300	1300	1300	1300	1000	1000	1000	13500
Prior Year ——													
Actual													
Public Rooms	400	550	450	600	525	600	750	775	700	675	400	300	6725
Audio/Visual	530	480	620	580	640	570	890	975	850	660	480	380	7655
Other	–	–	300	–	375	60	–	2010	805	180	–	920	4650
Total	930	1030	1370	1180	1540	1230	1640	3760	2355	1515	880	1600	19030
This Year ——													
Budget													
Public Rooms	600	600	600	600	600	600	600	600	600	600	600	600	7200
Audio/Visual	600	600	600	600	600	600	600	600	600	600	600	600	7200
Other	400	400	400	400	400	400	400	400	400	400	400	400	4800
Total	1600	1600	1600	1600	1600	1600	1600	1600	1600	1600	1600	1600	19200

Figure 24-2 Food and Beverage Budget *(continued)*

dividual meal period. Numbers of covers and average check replace numbers of occupied rooms and average rate.

Certain correlations should be made between numbers of food covers and occupancy. Restaurant covers can be expected to increase or decrease in relation to transient occupancy while banquet volume has a similar relationship to group occupancy. Close attention must be paid to policies or initiatives detailed in the marketing plan. Particular consideration should be given to any programs aimed at increasing non-hotel-guest business and the impact of such programs must be reflected in the forecasted volume and/or average check. Miscellaneous food and beverage income, public room rentals, and income from audio/visual equipment usage can be expected to increase proportionately to increases in banquet volume, that is, numbers of covers as differed from sales increases caused only by increases in the average check.

Telephone revenue (Figure 24–3) and gift shop revenue (Figure 24–4) are budgeted based on sales per occupied rooms. An exception is pay phone commissions, which are difficult to budget as revenue depends on an assortment of factors, most of which cannot be measured. The conservative approach to budgeting pay phone commissions is to budget the same revenue as the preceding year.

Golf revenues, pro shop sales, greens fees, and cart rentals are all a function of the activity on the golf course (i.e., number of rounds played) and can be budgeted in relation thereto. Membership income depends on policy decisions relative to increases in the number of members. Such policy matters should be reflected in the marketing plan and budgeting should be completed with due reference thereto.

A worksheet is not normally necessary for rentals and other income as the amounts can be entered directly on the departmental worksheet. Rental income should be budgeted with proper reference to existing and/or planned leases or changes in existing leases. The remaining categories of other income should, unless there is information to the contrary, be budgeted in line with the preceding year.

Throughout the preceding comments on budgeted revenue and in the various figures, there is repeated reference to the prior year's actual results. Since the budget is completed before the end of the prior year, it is always necessary to use "best estimates" for the portion of the year that has not been completed at the time the budget is prepared.

Finally, the initial revenue budgeting for each operating department should be the responsibility of the head of that department. Without this complete and direct involvement, the proper commitment to the achievement of the budgeted goals cannot be obtained.

Payroll.   Payroll is the largest single cost in a hotel operation and should, accordingly, be budgeted as diligently as possible. Fortunately, for most operations this can be done with a very high level of accuracy, subject, of course, to the achievement of budgeted revenues.

In Chapter 7 the importance of the staff planning function and the use of staffing guides is given great emphasis. One of the most important uses of the staffing guide is to prepare the budget. The importance, therefore, of maintaining staffing guidelines on a current and accurate basis cannot be overstated.

Hotel Grayscot 199___
TELEPHONE REVENUE BUDGET

	JAN	FEB	MAR	APR	MAY	JUNE	JULY	AUG	SEPT	OCT	NOV	DEC	TOTAL
LOCAL													
Prior Yr. – Actual													
Revenue Per Occ. Room	.90	.85	.88	1.02	1.28	1.18	1.40	1.62	1.58	1.78	1.16	1.08	
Total Revenue	2111	2166	2089	2883	3873	3876	5582	5561	6075	6835	2652	2259	45963
This Yr. – Budget													
Revenue Per Occ. Room	1.25	1.25	1.25	1.25	1.25	1.25	1.25	1.50	1.50	1.50	1.25	1.25	
Total Revenue	3306	3431	3580	3938	4303	4888	5700	5723	6525	6300	3219	3106	54018
LONG DISTANCE													
Prior Yr. – Actual													
Revenue Per Occ. Room	1.72	1.81	1.78	1.65	2.46	2.62	2.58	1.40	1.45	2.05	1.71	2.08	
Total Revenue	4035	4612	4226	4663	7444	8607	10286	4806	5575	7872	3909	4351	70387
This Yr. – Budget													
Revenue Per Occ. Room	2.00	2.00	2.00	2.00	2.00	2.00	2.00	2.00	2.00	2.00	2.00	2.00	
Total Revenue	5290	5490	5728	6300	6884	7820	9120	7630	8700	8400	5150	4970	81482
COMMISSIONS													
Prior Yr. – Actual	530	610	580	640	780	860	1250	1190	1385	1210	760	640	11135
This Yr. – Budget	600	600	600	600	800	900	1300	1200	1400	1200	800	600	10600
TOTAL REVENUE													
Prior Yr. – Actual	6677	7388	6895	8185	12917	13343	17118	11558	12035	15917	7321	7251	127485
This Yr. – Budget	9196	9521	9908	10838	11987	13608	16120	14553	16625	15900	9169	8676	146100

Figure 24–3 Telephone Revenue Budget

Hotel Grayscot 199__
GIFT SHOP REVENUE BUDGET

	JAN	FEB	MAR	APR	MAY	JUNE	JULY	AUG	SEPT	OCT	NOV	DEC	TOTAL
SALES - GIFTS													
Prior Yr. - Actual													
Revenue Per Occ. Room	3.81	3.78	3.96	4.22	6.08	5.17	4.29	4.62	5.31	4.87	4.02	7.85	
Total Revenue	8938	9631	9401	11926	18398	16983	17104	15860	20417	18701	9190	16422	172972
This Yr. - Budget													
Revenue Per Occ. Room	4.00	4.00	4.00	4.00	6.00	6.00	5.00	5.00	5.00	5.00	4.00	8.00	
Total Revenue	10580	10980	11456	12600	20652	23460	22800	19075	21750	21000	10300	19880	204533
SALES - OTHER													
Prior Yr. - Actual													
Revenue Per Occ. Room	1.06	1.14	1.08	1.35	1.72	1.61	1.70	1.85	1.71	1.82	1.60	1.85	
Total Revenue	2487	2905	2564	3759	5205	5289	6778	6351	6575	6989	3658	3870	56428
This Yr. - Budget													
Revenue Per Occ. Room	1.25	1.25	1.25	1.25	2.00	2.00	2.00	2.00	2.00	2.00	2.00	2.00	
Total Revenue	3306	3431	3580	3938	6884	7820	9120	7630	8700	8400	5150	4970	72929
TOTAL REVENUE													
Prior Yr. - Actual	11425	12536	11965	15684	23603	22272	23882	22212	26992	25690	12847	20292	229400
This Yr. - Budget	13886	14411	15036	16538	27536	31280	31920	26705	30450	29400	15450	24850	277462

Figure 24–4 Gift Shop Revenue Budget

Hotel Grayscot 199___
GOLF REVENUE BUDGET - Page 1

	JAN	FEB	MAR	APR	MAY	JUNE	JULY	AUG	SEPT	OCT	NOV	DEC	TOTAL
No. of Rounds													
Prior Yr.- Actual	—	—	—	—	1280	3658	2980	3271	3708	2480	—	—	
This Yr. - Budget	—	—	—	—	1500	4000	3500	3500	4000	2500	—	—	
Pro Shop Sales - Per Round													
Prior Yr.- Actual	—	—	—	—	3.61	4.08	3.92	4.16	3.82	4.06	—	—	
This Yr. - Budget	—	—	—	—	4.00	4.00	4.00	4.00	4.00	4.00	—	—	
Total Sales													
Prior Yr.- Actual	—	—	—	—	4621	14925	11682	13607	14165	9776	—	—	68775
This Yr. - Budget	—	—	—	—	6000	16000	14000	14000	16000	10000	—	—	76000
Green Fees - Per Round													
Prior Yr.- Actual	—	—	—	—	32.90	37.80	36.95	38.05	38.60	33.20	—	—	
This Yr. - Budget	—	—	—	—	35.00	40.00	40.00	40.00	40.00	40.00	—	—	
Total Green Fees													
Prior Yr.- Actual	—	—	—	—	42112	138272	110111	124462	143129	79946	—	—	638031
This Yr. - Budget	—	—	—	—	52500	160000	160000	160000	160000	160000	—	—	752500
Cart Rental Rev - Per Round													
Prior Yr.- Actual	—	—	—	—	14.72	15.10	16.20	16.30	16.25	16.40	—	—	
This Yr. - Budget	—	—	—	—	15.00	16.00	17.00	17.00	17.00	17.00	—	—	
Total Cart Rental													
Prior Yr.- Actual	—	—	—	—	18842	55236	48276	60255	39491		—	—	275417
This Yr. - Budget	—	—	—	—	22500	64000	59500	68000	42500		—	—	316000

Figure 24–5   Golf Revenue Budget

Hotel *G*rayscot 199___

GOLF REVENUE BUDGET - Page 2

	JAN	FEB	MAR	APR	MAY	JUNE	JULY	AUG	SEPT	OCT	NOV	DEC	TOTAL
MEMBERSHIPS													
No. of Members													
Prior Yr.- Actual	—	—	80	180	140	—	—	—	—	—	—	—	
This Yr. - Budget	—	—	100	150	100	—	—	—	—	—	—	—	
Annual Dues													
Prior Yr.- Actual	—	—	870	890	860	—	—	—	—	—	—	—	
This Yr. - Budget	—	—	1000	1000	1000	—	—	—	—	—	—	—	
Membership Income													
Prior Yr.- Actual	—	—	69600	160200	120400	—	—	—	—	—	—	—	
This Yr. - Budget	—	—	100000	200000	150000	—	—	—	—	—	—	—	
Total Golf Revenue													
Prior Yr.- Actual	—	—	69600	160200	185974	208433	170069	191386	217598	129213	—	—	1332424
This Yr. - Budget	—	—	100000	200000	231000	240000	213500	213500	244000	152500	—	—	1594500

Figure 24–5 Golf Revenue Budget *(continued)*

Briefly restating material covered in Chapter 5, hotel staffing, like most expenses, can be deemed to be variable or nonvariable. The variable positions can be found in the operating departments while variations in staffing in the overhead departments are usually of a preplanned seasonal nature. The staffing in the operating departments varies heavily in direct relation to various measurements of volume or levels of productivity. The standards established for staffing levels subject to such variations are set out in the staffing guide.

The budget worksheets for payroll preparation should, therefore, be laid out in a manner that permits calculation of budgeted payroll based on numbers of hours anticipated (based on the guidelines established) and the budgeted volume level. For example, a payroll budget worksheet for the rooms department (Figure 24–6) will, in addition to being divided into the sub departments (i.e., front office, housekeeping, and bell staff), also provide for budgeting by position based on a combination of hours worked and established rates of pay. In this schedule, each hotel should maintain a pay scale (with two to three rate levels) for each job category. This pay scale should, prior to budget preparation, be reviewed and amended as necessary on an annual basis.

Each month, or period, can then be budgeted through a combination of calculated hours required and average hourly rate. Budgeted payroll positions such as maids or bell staff, where the required staffing varies directly with volume, should be widely differing amounts from period to period. The payroll for receptionists will also vary, but not to the same degree, as staffing is less flexible while hours for reservationists will vary only on a seasonal basis rather than in relation to occupancy. Management payroll is relatively fixed, subject only to a possible seasonal modification.

Pay rates may be changed during the year if that has historically been the pattern. Payroll budget worksheets similar to Figure 24–6 must be completed for all departments. Again, it should be emphasized that completion of these worksheets is the responsibility of the department head who must be committed to the staffing reflected therein.

DEPARTMENTAL SCHEDULES

The last responsibility for a department head is to complete the departmental budget schedule. This requires the inserting of period-by-period numbers for each account following the financial statement format. (See Figure 24–7 for an example of a rooms department budget.) Revenue and payroll numbers must be copied from the respective worksheets to the final schedule.

Since payroll taxes and benefits are subject to change due to changes in tax rates and benefit costs, the controller should issue a department-by-department guideline for calculating this section of the departmental budget.

The remaining task is to budget the other expenses. The department head should budget other expenses making constant reference to the current year's financial statement and being cognizant of any cost impacts or savings due to policy changes. Expenses of a variable nature, such as guest supplies, should reflect the impact of higher occupancies in addition to price increases which may, to some degree, impact practically all expense areas.

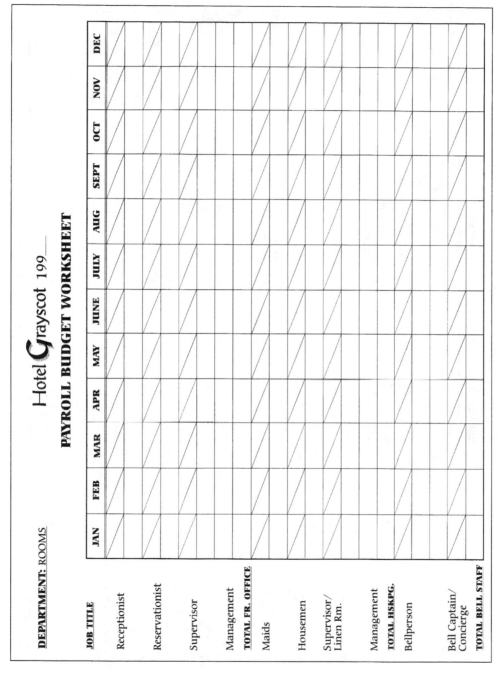

Figure 24–6 Payroll Budget Worksheet

Hotel Grayscot
DEPARTMENTAL BUDGET 199X - ROOMS

CRITERIA		JAN	FEB	MAR	APR	MAY	JUNE	JULY	AUG	SEPT	OCT	NOV	DEC	TOTAL	PRIOR YR.
	Revenue														
	Individual - Transit	109800	125085	101160	112800	145420	154000	252000	255000	270000	240000	148500	168000	2081765	1831058
	- Golf					12600	21000	39000	40500	34375	28750			176225	143978
	- Corporate	10000	10000	9775	12750	14250	10450	13200	10800	18000	18000	14250	10450	151925	134241
	- Total	119800	135085	110935	125550	172270	185450	304200	306300	322375	286750	162750	178450	2409915	2109276
	Group - Corporate	46750	44625	44625	54000	89250	99750	112000	90000	93750	97500	55125	34125	861500	750749
	- Tour & Travel	48000	48000	32000	34000	30000	35000	77000	48750	60000	75000	32500	35000	555250	376552
	- Association	15000	15000	73500	84000	73500	103500	145000	124000	170500	157500	23625	31500	1016625	868157
	- Total	109750	107625	150125	172000	192750	238250	334000	262750	324250	330000	111250	100625	2433375	1995458
	Total Room Revenue	229550	242710	261060	297550	365020	423700	638200	569050	646625	616750	274000	279075	4843290	3826515
	Salaries & Wages														
Per	Front Office	13012	12760	12950	14182	18500	18820	20118	19722	19967	20118	12545	12482	195176	162591
Schedule	Housekeeping	11112	10080	11002	14008	19000	19110	21012	20008	20520	21012	10012	10310	187196	158012
	Bell Staff	3608	3612	3666	3610	3600	3620	3820	3710	3760	3820	2107	2112	41045	37564
	Total	27732	26452	27618	31810	41100	41550	44950	43440	44247	44950	24664	24904	423417	358167
	Payroll Taxes and Benefits														
3% of Payroll	Vacation Pay	832	794	829	954	1233	1247	1349	1303	1327	1349	740	747	12703	10745
3.5% of Payroll	Employee Meals	971	926	967	1113	1439	1454	1573	1520	1549	1573	863	872	14820	12536
Allocation	Payroll Taxes	3328	3174	3314	3817	4932	4986	5394	5213	5310	5394	2960	2988	50810	42980
	Total	5130	4894	5109	5885	7604	7687	8316	8036	8186	8316	4563	4607	78332	66261
	Total Payroll	32862	31346	32727	37695	48704	49237	53266	51476	52433	53266	29227	29511	501749	424428
	Other Expenses														
Fixed	Cable TV	800	800	800	800	800	800	800	800	800	800	800	800	9600	9143
Fixed	China & Glass	350	350	350	350	350	350	350	350	350	350	350	350	4200	3654
0.25% of Rev.	Cleaning Supplies	574	607	653	744	913	1059	1596	1423	1617	1542	685	698	12108	10232
1.0% of Rev.	Commissions	2296	2427	2611	2976	3650	4237	6382	5691	6466	6168	2740	2791	48433	44545
Fixed	Contract Cleaning	200	200	200	500	200	200	200	200	500	500	200	200	3000	2657
Fixed	Decorations	850	850	850	850	850	850	850	850	850	850	850	850	10200	9876
Fixed	Equipment Rental	150	150	150	150	150	150	150	150	150	150	150	150	1800	1547
2.5% of Rev	Guest Supplies	5739	6068	6527	7439	9126	10593	15955	14226	16166	15419	6850	6977	121082	95663
Allocation	Laundry	5810	6371	6853	7811	9582	11122	16753	14938	16974	16190	7193	7326	126921	118769
0.2% of Rev.	Linen	459	485	522	595	730	847	1276	1138	1293	1234	558	558	9687	8876
0.1% of Rev.	Office Supplies	230	243	261	298	365	424	638	569	647	617	274	279	4843	4538
0.1% of Rev.	Paper Supplies	230	243	261	298	365	424	638	569	647	617	274	279	4843	4472
0.2% of Rev.	Printing & Stationery	459	485	522	595	730	847	1276	1138	1293	1234	548	558	9687	9857
0.5% of Rev.	Reservation Expense	1148	1214	1305	1488	1825	2119	3191	2845	3233	3084	1370	1395	24216	21768
0.2% of Rev.	Telephone	459	485	522	595	730	847	1276	1138	1293	1234	548	558	9687	8897
Fixed	Travel	200	200	200	200	200	200	200	200	200	200	200	200	2800	2765
Fixed	Uniforms	600	600	600	600	600	600	600	600	600	600	600	600	7200	7033
Fixed	Walked Guests	100	100	100	100	100	100	100	100	100	100	100	100	1200	978
	Total Other	20652	21878	23686	26387	31265	35769	52232	46925	52879	50886	24280	24669	411507	365270
	Total Expense	53515	53224	56414	64082	79969	85006	105498	98401	105311	104151	53506	54180	913256	789698
	Profit (Loss)	176035	189486	204646	233468	285051	338694	532702	470649	541314	512599	220494	224895	3930034	3036817

Figure 24-7 Rooms Department Budget

In budgeting the impact of inflation, that is, price increases, it is important that there be consistency throughout all departments in regard to the inflation factor. Therefore, based on economic conditions, the controller should issue an inflation factor to be used as a guideline. It must be recognized, however, that department heads may be cognizant of price increases expected to exceed the guideline and should budget accordingly.

While volume changes are the basis for budgeting, many of the operating department expenses and overhead department expenses do not, for the most part, vary with volume. As can be seen in Figure 24–7, there should be a column on the departmental budget schedule that indicates the criteria for each expense. In the income-producing departments, this criteria will usually be a relationship to sales or "fixed." "Fixed" does not mean that each month or period will be the same amount but rather that the amounts are predetermined independent of volume. Numbers of occupied rooms or numbers of covers served are other criteria that are used. The department heads responsible for budgeting overhead departments should, therefore, budget each expense on a "ground-up" basis, identifying each element of all expenses.

When completed, the departmental schedules along with the supporting worksheets are submitted by the department head to the controller who is responsible for combining the departments and completing the budgeted income statement. The controller also assumes the responsibility for compiling the budget for the administrative and general department and budgeting the fixed charges.

Before submitting the completed budget for review to the budget committee, the controller reviews each department for mathematic accuracy and to catch any obvious errors in the handling or treatment of an item of income or expenditure. The budget is then subject to a lengthy review by the budget committee and it can be anticipated that budgets for certain departments may be returned to the responsible department heads for revision. Since overhead departments can to some degree be affected by the budgets of operated departments, the initial submission of departmental budgets for overhead departments is frequently scheduled after an initial review of the operated department budgets.

When the overall budget is finally approved, the controller must compile a cash flow (reviewed in Chapter 25) and other schedules normally including some long-range projections. A satisfactory cash flow is necessary in order to permit final approval of the capital budget for the coming year.

The final step is to deliver the completed budget and accompanying documents to the owners or, in the case of a hotel chain, to regional management for their approval. As part of the budget package, there must be a narrative explaining the rationale used in each department to arrive at both revenue and expense. This rationale must be in adequate detail to avoid excessive questioning of individual items with the final goal of speeding up the approval process.

1. Using the budgeted revenue numbers in Figure 24–2, prepare a departmental budget schedule for food and beverage. The department statements in Figure 20–1 can be used as a guideline in setting the budget format.

2. Circle T or F to indicate whether the following statements are true or false:

    T F **a.** Historical trends are very important in preparing a budget.

    T F **b.** Banquet volume should be budgeted lower during periods of group occupancy.

    T F **c.** A "ground-up" approach develops a budget in an orderly fashion based on revenue data.

    T F **d.** Payroll should be budgeted based on estimated hours and hourly rates.

    T F **e.** The most variable payroll in the rooms department is reservationists.

3. Circle the correct answer to the following statements:

    a. The goals for budgeted occupancy and average rate should first be determined:

    (1) At the first meeting of the budget committee

    (2) In the capital budget request

    (3) In the marketing plan

    b. A schedule for budget preparation should ideally cover a period of:

    (1) One to two months

    (2) Two to three months

    (3) More than four months

    c. The best approach to a budget is to set:

    (1) Extremely optimistic goals

    (2) Goals that are challenging but attainable

    (3) Very conservative goals

    d. Group allocations should:

    (1) Be given preference over individual bookings

    (2) Not be allowed to supplant individual bookings

    (3) Should be on the same basis as individual bookings

25 Long-Term Projections and Cash Flow Forecasts

While all businesses have become increasingly concerned with long-range planning, the heavy investment by major corporations has accelerated the process in the hotel industry. While the individual hotel sets goals for future years relative to capital improvements and possible expansion of capacity, the hotel chains must think in terms not only of increased profits from existing operations, but also of new acquisitions or construction of new properties. Simply stated, long-range planning is a combination of existing operations and development. While both areas must ultimately be combined in the final plan, the projections for new development are much more complex than projecting future results for existing operations. Existing operations are principally concerned with new approaches to marketing, possible changes in existing market segmentation, the impact of new competition, and the overall business climate with focus on inflation, interest rates, and the business cycle. New development involves construction costs, sources of funding, site location, feasibility studies, and tax planning.

EXISTING OPERATIONS

Most hotel companies combine their marketing plan, the results of the budget process, and long-range planning into a total package referred to as their *business plan*. The most commonly used time period for the operational projections of a business plan is five years. The detailed budget for the coming year provides a base upon which to build years 2 through 5. Any planned major changes in the method of operation in those years must, of course, be built into the operating projections. However, if such changes involve construction necessitating the borrowing of funds, it is advisable to budget the capital project separately in the development/expansion part of the business plan.

The format for the five-year projections (Figure 25–1) involves showing the expected results for the current year, the budget for the coming year, and the projections for years 2 through 5. This format is frequently referred to as a "Five-Year Summary of Projected Income." The assumptions or rationale used to develop the budget for the

Hotel Grayscot

FIVE YEAR FORECAST

1999___ to 1999___

	Actual This Year	Budget	Year 2	Year 3	Year 4	Year 5
Occupancy	49.2%	55.8%	59.7%	63.9%	67.7%	71.8%
Average Rate	$106.57	$118.88	$123.64	$128.58	$133.72	$139.07
Rooms - Revenue	3826515	4843290	5389613	5997562	6611712	7288751
Payroll & Benefits	424424	501479	531568	563462	597270	633106
Other Expenses	365270	411507	432082	453686	476371	500189
Dept. Profit	3036821	3930304	4425963	4980413	5538072	6155456
Food & Beverage - Revenue	2856341	3337872	3714384	4133367	4556623	5023221
Cost of Sales	875412	9701065	1080601	1202493	1325628	1461373
Payroll & Benefits	1211903	1462712	1550475	1643503	1742113	1846640
Other Expenses	260712	301062	316115	331921	348517	365943
Dept. Profit	504314	603033	767193	955450	1140365	1349266
Telephone - Revenue	116350	135500	150784	167793	184975	203916
Cost of Sales	66012	71400	79454	88416	97470	107451
Payroll & Benefits	39011	41620	44117	46764	49570	52544
Other Expenses	8125	8277	8691	9125	9582	10061
Dept. Profit	3202	14203	18522	23487	28353	33860
Gift Shop - Revenue	229400	277462	308760	343588	378771	417557
Cost of Sales	118310	141012	156918	174619	192499	212211
Payroll & Benefits	53018	59112	62659	66418	70403	74628
Other Expenses	4119	43325	4541	4768	5007	5257
Dept. Profit	53953	73013	84642	97783	110862	125461
Golf - Revenue	1332424	1594500	1774360	1974507	2176697	2399591
Cost of Sales	35722	38513	42857	47692	52575	57959
Payroll & Benefits	611105	692322	733861	777893	824567	874041
Other Expenses	408712	531629	558210	586121	615427	646198
Dept. Profit	276885	332036	439431	562802	684128	821393
Other Income	96012	101500	112949	125690	138561	152749
Total Dept. Profits	3971187	5054089	5848700	6745624	7640340	8638186
Overhead Depts.						
Administrative & General						
Payroll & Benefits	232111	244300	258958	274495	290965	308423
Other Expense	262513	271312	282164	293451	305189	317397
Total	494624	515612	541122	567947	596154	625820
Sales & Marketing						
Payroll & Benefits	121602	125350	132871	140843	149294	158251
Other Expense	421018	425600	446880	469224	492685	517319
Total	542620	550950	579751	610067	641979	675571
Property Operation						
Payroll & Benefits	191018	201713	213816	226645	240243	254658
Other Expense	205112	210118	218523	327264	340355	353969
Total	396130	411831	432339	553909	580598	608627
Energy Costs	272112	281018	292259	303949	316107	328751
Total Overhead	1705486	1759411	1845471	2035872	2134838	2238769
House Profit	2265701	3294678	4003229	4709753	5505501	6399417
Taxes	112000	112000	115360	118821	122385	126057
Insurance	76318	80000	82400	84872	87418	90041
Total	188318	192000	197760	203693	209804	216098
Gross Operating Profit	2077383	3102678	3805469	4506060	5295698	6183319
Interest	184500	172500	160500	148500	136500	124500
Depreciation	842112	862018	882018	902018	912018	922018
Net Profit	1235271	2240660	2923451	3604042	4383680	5261301

Figure 25–1   Five-Year Projections

coming year, together with the detailed budget and supporting worksheets, must be explained in detail in a section of the business plan devoted to the budget for the following year. The additional assumptions used to extend the budget for the coming year into projections for years 2 through 5 must accompany the 5-year summary of projected income. In Figure 25–1, the assumptions made were as follows:

REVENUE:

1. Room occupancy will increase at the rate of 7 percent in years 2 and 3 and 6 percent in years 4 and 5.
2. Room rates will increase at 4 percent per year (the expected maximum rate of inflation).
3. All other revenues will continue to maintain the same relationship to room revenue they have in the budget for the coming year.

EXPENSES:

1. Payroll and related expenses will increase at a rate of 6 percent. While it is expected that cash payroll can be limited to increases under 5 percent because of turnover, benefits will increase at a much higher rate because of taxation or government-mandated benefit programs related to Social Security and health insurance.
2. Other expenses in the operated departments will increase at a rate of 5 percent, being a combined effect of higher volume on the variable expenses and inflation impact on the nonvariable expenses.
3. Other expenses in administrative and general will increase at a rate of 4 percent.
4. Sales and marketing costs, other than payroll and related expenses, will increase at the rate of 5 percent per year.
5. Property operation and maintenance, other than payroll and operated expense, will increase by 4 percent per year plus an additional expenditure of $100,000 in year 3 for the repainting of the entire interior of the hotel.
6. Energy costs will increase at 4 percent per year.

FIXED CHARGES:

1. Property taxes and insurance will increase at 3 percent per year.
2. As no debt financing is planned, interest expense will continue to reduce in line with the current debt repayment schedule.
3. Expenditures on furniture and equipment will remain at a relatively conservative level resulting in increases in depreciation expense of $20,000 per year.

After completion and approval of the five-year summary of projected income, the hotel chains usually prepare a combined summary on a regional or divisional basis and ultimately an overall summary for the chain.

Since no new debt financing is planned and the level of capital expenditures is limited, the preparation of a five-year cash flow forecast for operations (Figure 25–2)

Hotel *G*rayscot

5 YEAR PROJECTION - CASH FLOW FROM OPERATIONS

	Budget	Year 2	Year 3	Year 4	Year 5
Net Profit	$2240660	2923451	3604042	4383680	5261301
Add: Depreciation	862018	882018	902018	912018	922018
	3102678	33805469	4506060	5295698	6183319
Less: Debt Repayment	<120000>	<120000>	<120000>	<120000>	<120000>
Purchases of Furniture & Equipment	<200000>	<200000>	<200000>	<200000>	<200000>
Available for Dividends and Investment	2782678	3485469	4186060	4975698	5863319

Figure 25–2 Five-Year Cash Flow from Operations

is relatively simple. It involves adding back noncash expense, that is, depreciation, and deducting cash outlays for furniture and equipment purchases and debt repayment. Changes in the amounts of current assets other than cash and in the amounts of current liabilities must also be taken into account. While there is nothing to prevent showing projected dividend payments, it is preferable to show the total cash flow as "Available for Dividends and Investment."

DEVELOPMENT AND EXPANSION

New hotel construction or major additions to existing properties normally require substantial debt financing, that is, the borrowing of funds to be repaid over a number of years, usually extending well beyond the five-year period used for projecting existing operations. The goal of long-term forecasts for such projects must be to evaluate the ability of the project not only to meet debt repayment but also to provide an adequate return on any initial capital investment required—in short, to determine the economic feasibility of the project. Such a requirement necessitates that projections of income and cash flow extend at least until the final repayment of all long-term financing.

The initial step in analyzing and projecting a new hotel project is to prepare the feasibility study. Most hotel companies retain experts in project analysis on their corporate staffs. However, banks, insurance companies, and other sources of long-term financing usually require that a feasibility study also be prepared by an independent firm. Several companies specialize in the field. The feasibility study contains various elements, all of which are critical to the credibility of the study and the development of meaningful projections based on the research conducted in preparing the study.

1. *Site evaluation*—an analysis of the feasibility of the site for the proposed hotel. Factors considered are size and location, access, availability of utilities, natural attractions, and proximity to shopping, historic sites, and other places of interest.
2. *Market*—a study of the existing market for the site and a determination of probable market sources.
3. *Competition*—a review of existing hotels that would possibly provide competition for the proposed facility. This must be a comprehensive review as it will also help to determine existing and potential markets.
4. *Labor situation*—an analysis of the existing labor supply focusing on the availability of both skilled and unskilled labor. Costs are also evaluated. Housing and transportation factors also influence the labor supply.
5. *Room demand*—a projection of market demand for rooms is made based upon the preceding analysis of the market and the competition, with consideration to the relative merit of the site.
6. *Facilities*—the proposed facilities must correspond to the anticipated room demand and the requirements of the anticipated market segments.

After the research is completed, a detailed projection of operating results is prepared. This projection must cover at least the first three years of operation and ideally the first five. New hotels are not expected to reach normal operating levels until at least the third year. The projections take basically the same format as the five-year summary of projected income, except that the bottom line will be the gross operating profit as neither interest expense nor depreciation are known at this time. Income taxes have been ignored for purposes of this exercise. Instead of using historical data, the projections must be entirely based on information and rationale developed in the feasibility study. However, during the study of the competition, a certain amount of valuable historical information can be obtained.

CAPITAL COST AND FINANCING

Before financing can be obtained for a project, it is also necessary to compile acceptable estimates of total project costs. This is sometimes a time-consuming process, particularly if initial estimates are unacceptable and revisions must be made both to the envisioned facilities and the projections of operating results based thereon. It is, however, common practice to utilize the services of a general contractor experienced in hotel construction or a project management company with experience in the field. Since these companies are hoping to be hired for the project in their specific field or area of expertise, they are usually willing to participate without charge in the preparation of estimates.

Estimates must be subdivided into the various elements of cost that are commonly used in the hotel industry:

1. *Land*—presumably this cost is readily available but should include the cost of any actions necessary to prepare the site for construction.

2. *Building*—as discussed in the preceding paragraph. The construction costs must include the cost of all building equipment which will be permanently affixed to or built into the construction (e.g., elevators and boilers).
3. *Interest during construction*—as construction progresses, it becomes necessary to start borrowing. Since no income is received in the construction period which can be used to cover the interest on the borrowing, the costs are capitalized as part of the total project cost.
4. *Furniture, fixtures, and equipment*—this includes furniture and furnishings for the rooms and public areas and all moveable equipment used in the back of the house.
5. *Operating equipment*—as stated in a prior chapter, this is the term used to cover linen, china, glass, and silver. The initial cost of uniforms is sometimes also included in this category.
6. *Inventories*—this includes the opening inventories of food and beverages and operating supplies (e.g., paper goods, stationery, fuel, etc.).
7. *Preopening expenses*—this includes all expenses incurred prior to opening. Principal items are salaries and office expenses of hotel personnel, advertising, sales, and public relations. Administrative costs of project management should, however, be included in the construction cost.
8. *Working capital*—no hotel can open without sufficient funds to cover the costs of day-to-day operations and any initial cash losses.

Thus, the summary of costs for a new 200-room hotel could appear as follows:

Land	$ 1,200,000
Building	9,600,000
Interest during construction	1,000,000
Furniture, fixtures and equipment	6,600,000
Operating equipment	800,000
Inventories	250,000
Preopening expenses	500,000
Working capital	500,000
	$20,450,000

These numbers are approximate costs for an average first-class hotel in United States.

While the normal approach to financing is to attempt to borrow as high a percentage of the project as possible, the 20-year projections for this project (Figure 25–3) are based on an equity investment of $3,450,000 and a 20-year mortgage of $17,000,000 at 7 percent. The interest rate used in any projections should, of course, approximate current rates being charged on new hotel construction loans.

For illustrative purposes, the five-year projections in Figure 25–1 are extended an additional 15 years. Debt service is restated to reflect repayment, in equal installments, of a $17,000,000 mortgage over the 20-year period.

In order to evaluate the quality or feasibility of the project, certain key data can be derived from the cash flow. Of major interest to any lender is the *payback period,* the number of years required to recover the total cost of the project. From an investment point of view, the most common analysis used by hotel companies to evaluate the

Hotel Grayscot

20 - YEAR CASH FLOW PROJECTIONS

Project Cost: $20,450,000
Equity: 3,450,000
Proposed Financing: . . . . 17,000,000 at 7%

Year	Gross Operating Profit	Debt Service	Capital Expenditure	Cash Flow
1	3,102,678	1,604,679	20,450,000	<18,952,001>
2	3,805,469	1,604,679	200,000	2,400,790
3	4,506,060	1,604,679	200,000	3,101,381
4	5,295,698	1,604,679	200,000	3,891,019
5	6,183,319	1,604,679	200,000	4,778,640
6	6,430,651	1,604,679	200,000	5,025,972
7	6,687,877	1,604,679	200,000	5,283,198
8	6,955,392	1,604,679	200,000	5,550,713
9	7,233,608	1,604,679	200,000	5,828,929
10	7,522,953	1,604,679	200,000	6,118,274
11	7,823,871	1,604,679	200,000	6,419,192
12	8,136,825	1,604,679	200,000	6,732,146
13	8,462,299	1,604,679	200,000	7,057,620
14	8,800,790	1,604,679	200,000	7,396,111
15	9,152,822	1,604,679	200,000	7,748,143
16	9,518,935	1,604,679	200,000	8,114,256
17	9,899,692	1,604,679	200,000	8,495,013
18	10,295,679	1,604,679	200,000	8,891,000
19	10,701,506	1,604,679	200,000	9,302,827
20	11,135,807	1,604,679	<5,800,000>(Note 1)	15,731,128

Payback Period: 5.95 years
Return of Discounted Cash Flow Basis: 19.9%

Note 1: *Represents $200,000 annual expenditure on furniture and equipment less residual value of $6,000,000.*

Figure 25–3   20-Year Projection and Cash Flow

project is the rate of return on a discounted cash flow basis. In order to complete this analysis, the total cost of the project is applied as a capital expenditure in year 1 and a residual value is added back as incoming cash in year 20.

In Figure 25–3, a residual value of $6,000,000 is used to complete a cash flow which provides a return on a discounted basis of 19.9 percent.

Projects are evaluated by hotel companies based on comparative rates of return and length of payback. A short payback period eliminates the risk that changes in demographics or market patterns will have a negative impact on the proposed hotel. Overseas projects usually require a higher projected rate of return because of risks related to political upheaval or currency fluctuations. However, the desire of a hotel chain to have a "presence" in a certain market may result in a marginal project gaining approval.

Common sources of financing for North American projects are banks, insurance companies, and pension funds. Tax advantages through use of depreciation to provide savings also makes some projects attractive to individual investors or partnerships. Government-aided or -subsidized financing is frequently available for overseas projects, particularly in underdeveloped countries looking for aid in developing tourism as an industry and reducing unemployment.

1. A hotel project is budgeted at $18,000,000. Proposed equity is $4,000,000 and proposed borrowing is $14,000,000 for 20 years at 7.5 percent, payable in equal installments. Gross operating profit for the first year is projected at $400,000 and is expected to grow at 5 percent per year. Prepare a 20-year cash flow (ignore income taxes).

2. Calculate the payback period and the discounted rate of return on the project above. Use a residual value of $3,000,000 in year 20.

3. Circle T or F to indicate whether the following statements are true or false:
   T   F   **a.** Elevators should be considered part of the construction cost.
   T   F   **b.** In preparing a cash flow, interest and depreciation must be added back.
   T   F   **c.** Preopening expenses must be included in the total budget for a project.
   T   F   **d.** The *payback period* is the number of years required to recover the equity.
   T   F   **e.** New hotels are not expected to reach normal operating levels until at least the third year.

4. Circle the correct answer to the following statements:
   a. The most commonly used time period for the operational projection in a business plan is:
   (1) 5 years
   (2) 10 years
   (3) 20 years
   b. Cash flow projections for a new hotel project should cover at least:
   (1) 5 years
   (2) 20 years
   (3) The length of the long-term financing
   c. Interest during the construction period must be:
   (1) Treated as an operating expense
   (2) Added to the capital cost
   (3) Ignored
   d. The budget for operating equipment in a new project should not include:
   (1) China
   (2) Furniture
   (3) Silver

26 Systems Management

With the advent of the computer age, hotels now find themselves using a wide range of computer systems. While property management and point-of-sales systems constitute, for most hotels, a major part of the total systems in use, there are many other systems that are either only indirectly or not at all related to the accounting or financial reporting systems. Although some large properties have an MIS (Management Information Systems) department completely independent of the accounting function, the final responsibility for systems management rests, in most hotels, with the controller. This can easily be rationalized because the organization and administration of the front office and accounting systems calls for considerable expertise in the computer field. This expertise can usually be utilized in the other areas.

Thus, in larger hotels a systems manager reports to the controller. In other properties, there may be an assistant controller—systems. In smaller properties, systems management may be only one of the responsibilities of the assistant controller and, in some instances, it is a direct responsibility of the hotel controller. The intent of this final chapter is to identify the more common systems and the responsibilities of the controller's office in performing its role as manager.

COMMUNICATIONS

For many years, the term *communication systems* in a hotel environment meant telephones and perhaps the telex. Telex machines have disappeared from most hotels, being replaced by fax machines. The fax is a quieter, cheaper, and much more versatile method of transmitting messages. While the telex could only send messages in the system's own type format, the fax transmits messages exactly as created. This includes graphs, charts, and even photographs. A copy of a document sent by fax constitutes a legal copy of the document. Furthermore, a fax operates over a regular telephone line and can easily be moved around an office, requiring no special wiring or installation.

Telephones remain a major element of hotel systems. However, the combination of deregulation and improved technology has resulted in many more options and versatility in their use. The controller's department is now called upon to evaluate the costs and merits, not only of the various long-distance providers, but also the relative merits of the various service options offered. In Chapter 16, the use of call accounting technology to process guest charges and control profitability was described. Call accounting systems are also programmed to control administrative use and provide accurate allocations of the total cost of administrative calls.

Major developments have taken place in the realm of telephone answering systems. The earlier concept of a tape recorder activated by the telephone to record incoming calls and provide recorded responses has evolved into the science of *voice mail*. Computer storage replaces the tape recorder in capturing and responding to calls and transmits the information within its own communications network.

Electronic mail provides a somewhat related communication network. Many hotels now have their own computer network that provides a method of communication between all the computer terminals throughout the property. Messages can be sent directly from location to location or simply stored in the computer either for delivery at a future time or merely as information that can be accessed if and when needed.

For some time, hotels have been providing guests with the ability to use modems to communicate by computer with their home office or customers. However, communication technology has now actively invaded the guest room via the television set. In recent years, hotels have used designated channels on the guest room sets to furnish prerecorded advertising and guest information. Now guests can use the television set to obtain their messages and view their account. This allows them to call the desk to query charges, obtain corrections, and institute an automatic checkout.

YIELD MANAGEMENT

Yield management is a program to restrict or eliminate low-rated business when demand is high and to seek lower rated market segments when demand is low. The reader may wonder about the involvement of a member of the accounting staff, even when functioning as systems manager, since the description clearly suggests that yield management is simply an advanced reservation technique.

Unfortunately, yield management fails in many operations for two reasons. First, the front-office personnel have preset ideas about how and from where business is derived, and second, they lack the technical skills to properly understand or use the related software. These two reasons alone issue a call for help, but a third reason is that yield management is a profit-improvement plan that must have the benefit of the best technical mind on a hotel staff.

Before yield management was fully refined and specific software was designed, the concept was already in use in many metropolitan hotels. Contrary to what much of the public believes, many hotels do not set a specific rate on each room from which they discount but rather regard the total hotel as having a range of rates from A (the minimum) to D or E (the maximum). As demand on a specific day increased, the hotels first ceased offering rate A, and gradually the other rates, until as occupancy reached the 90 percent level only the top rate was being sold.

This procedure did, in a rather unrefined manner, and on a short lead-time basis, achieve part of the first goal of yield management: to maximize rates when demand is high. However, the hotels did not react to demand patterns, only immediate short-term demand, and the goal of yield management, to develop lower rated market segments in periods of low demand, was not a related element of the procedure. Which is not to say that the hotels did not seek low rated business in periods of low occupancy, but rather that there was no coordination in the two programs.

The proper use of yield management first requires an evaluation of overall demand. Too low a level of overall demand negates much of the value of yield management. Second, it calls for a careful definition of the individual market segments applicable to the property and the accurate tracking of the demand patterns of each segment. The proper definition of each segment and accurate tracking of the demand related to it is essential to the success of the program. Demand statistics should include not only rooms occupied but business refused. For example, they may reveal that a large amount of corporate transient business, a high rated segment, is being turned away because of early booked low-rate tour business.

Once the demand is properly defined by market segment, room availability can be programmed on a long-term basis to refuse or severely restrict low-rate market segments in high-demand periods and to open up to otherwise refused low-rate segments (e.g., package tours) in periods of low demand.

As can readily be seen, errors in defining the segments can result in room availability while low-rate business has been turned away, which can be very costly. The role of the systems manager, after the program is functioning, is to continually audit and monitor the market segments.

BANQUET SPACE MANAGEMENT

Several software companies have designed software packages to control and manage the available banquet space. These programs replace the old "book" found in every banquet office. The programs can usually be run as another menu off the property management system, which limits the hardware investment to terminals for each of the banquet staff. The benefit of the program is the ability to store and provide, on demand, all the physical attributes and restrictions of each area and to permit flexibility in switching groups around. The most important control feature in such programs is the respective authorization levels for moving a function from one area to another. These programs are very simple to operate and the systems manager is usually involved only in the set-up stage or if major changes in facilities take place.

SECURITY

The security of the hotel guest is a widely discussed topic receiving media coverage even on "60 Minutes." As a result, a multitude of electronic locking devices have become available to the hotel industry. Hotels that have not resorted to electronic locking devices can be placed in two categories: the low-rate properties that cannot afford or justify the cost of the system, and those fortunate hotels who are in rural or isolated areas with no history and very limited risk of criminal activity.

The earlier systems used some form of plastic card or key which activated the lock. Anyone who stood in a lonely hallway trying to get a poorly cut card to activate an unwilling lock will remember the cards. A new card had to be cut each time a guest checked in. The level of system failure and guest complaint on such systems is high.

Newer and more effective systems require the guest to activate the lock mechanism by punching in a series of precoded numbers similar to those on an ATM. These systems are frequently tied in to the property management system and are automatically activated when the guest checks in and receives a printed copy of the access code.

The role of the systems manager in this area is usually determined by the degree to which the system is interfaced with other systems.

ENERGY MANAGEMENT

Over the last decade, the cost of utilities in a hotel operation has increased dramatically. As a result, there has been a heavy emphasis on systems designed to control and reduce energy costs, with an emphasis on electricity or natural gas.

Most vendors of property management systems provide certain optional programs for energy control. One of the more common of these programs is a direct interface with the registration process where the checking in of a guest activates the utilities in the room. This includes turning on the heat or air conditioning, both of which already have preset minimum and maximum levels. Guests are permitted individual control within those ranges.

Similar systems use the activation by the guest of the electronic lock to turn on the utilities. Other energy management systems focus on overall management of the total energy consumption in the hotel. A major factor in determining the total electricity cost for a hotel is the demand charge. The demand charge is calculated based on the highest demand for power (usually the average of the two highest readings) in a particular period.

The function of the energy management system is to monitor the demand and when the demand increases toward a predetermined acceptable limit, the system initiates a *shedding* process. Shedding involves the turning off of certain nonvital equipment (e.g., air conditioning in certain areas for a period of time) in order to keep the demand from exceeding the desired limit.

The systems manager works closely with the engineer in monitoring the system. Since many such systems are operated as an interface off the property management system hardware, night audit is sometimes called upon to print readings, monitor the system, and even initiate or turn off certain functions.

IN-ROOM MOVIES

Another interface to the property management systems found in many hotels is in-room movies. Since the movies and the operating software are usually provided by a vendor who pays the hotel a commission based on the guest charges, very little involvement is required from systems management. However, in the future the concept of providing entertainment directly to the guest room may be widely expanded. The obvious area where this will eventually happen is gaming operations where the guest will

be able to gamble via the television screen directly from the comfort of his or her room. This will possibly include off-track betting on horse racing and other forms of sports betting.

CONCLUSIONS AND A LOOK TO THE FUTURE

The heaviest involvement of the controller's office in systems will continue to be in the area of food and beverage. In Chapter 13, a variety of management information reports related thereto are illustrated. The ability of the new point-of-sales systems to capture a wealth of information can lead to a highly expanded use of this information in menu planning and marketing. Some experts in the restaurant field have already developed formulas relative to the level of customer preference of various menu items and how this information can be used to adjust the menu to best satisfy and, therefore, maximize the largest segment of the market while at the same time still retaining the smaller but higher spending customers. To date, these theories have relied principally on menu item counts. By using technology not only to count specific items but to analyze the customer's preference in seasonings, ingredients, sizes of portions, vegetable selection, and so on, menu content can be developed to a very fine science.

The area of purchasing can also benefit from increased technology. Direct on-line communication with a selection of vendors will not only speed up the ordering process, but also will feed directly into the accounts payable process, eliminating the need for manual processing of invoices.

However, a major use of technology in the hotel field still remains in the future. Labor costs continue to escalate, the minimum wage will continue to climb, and in order to obtain quality staffing, the hotel and restaurant field must remain competitive in the labor market. The lesson to be learned from other industries is not to continue to suppress labor rates, but to increase productivity through the use of technology. Hotels have made some steps in this direction with automatic checkout procedures and simplified registration. However, the back of the house continues to be labor intensive. The use of robots to wash dishes and clean floors is not science fiction but a realistic approach that must be pursued. While the role of a server will remain in quality restaurants, increased self-ordering and self-service can be expected in coffee shops and family restaurants. The kitchen is a high payroll cost area. Increased use of technology and the availability of higher quality prepared foods can allow staff reductions. The laundry is certainly an area where technology can be used.

The fruits of higher productivity levels can be used to provide increased wages and satisfactory benefits to the necessary workers in the hotel and restaurant field. The positive response received from employees will, in turn, result in further increases in productivity and a higher level of profitability. The goal of a controller in a hotel operation must be exactly that—a higher level of profitability combined with a high level of customer service. The days of wearing an eyeshade and adding columns of figures are gone forever.

1. Suggest two possible operations in a hotel, other than those described in Chapter 26, where the quality and efficiency could possibly be improved through new technology and describe the technology to be used.

2. Circle T or F to indicate whether the following statements are true or false:

   T   F   **a.** Fax messages are transmitted over telephone lines.

   T   F   **b.** *Shedding* is the process of reducing electrical demand by turning off some nonvital equipment.

   T   F   **c.** Hotels always charge a specific rate for a specific room.

   T   F   **d.** Statistics on room demand should include refused business.

   T   F   **e.** Guest room utilities are sometimes activated at check-in.

3. Circle the correct answer to the following statements:

   a. The concept of communicating from department to department by computer is known as:
   (1) Voice mail
   (2) Telecommunications
   (3) Electronic mail

   b. Yield management is a technique used in hotels to:
   (1) Obtain the highest number of portions from a cut of beef.
   (2) To maximize the combination of rate and occupancy.
   (3) Obtain the best use of available banquet space.

   c. The demand charge for electricity in a hotel is calculated based on:
   (1) Total kilowatt hours consumed
   (2) The average highest readings of demand for power
   (3) The total number of air conditioning units in use

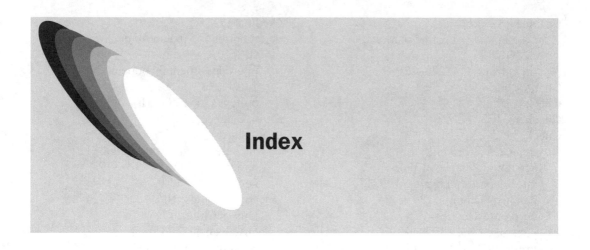

Index

Management reports, 94–96
Markers, 236–237
Market list, 154
Menu abstracting, 12
Menu profitability analysis,
    195–196
Metering, 188
Modems, 327
Modified Accelerated Cost Recovery
    System (MACRS), 107
Money orders, 142
Monthly journal, 33–34

National Restaurant Association, 16
NCR Class, 42, 45–47
Night auditors, 43, 52
Night audits, 11, 32, 43
    accounting office review, 53
    advance deposits, 52–53
    banquet controls, 57–58
    charge codes, 50–52
    computerized, 47–50
    daily revenue report, 58–61
    deposit procedures, 54–55, 57
    and entry into general ledger, 58
    food and beverages, 54
    hand transcript, 45
    posting, 50–52
    property management systems,
        47–50

One-write payroll systems, 79
On-line transmission, 119
Open balance, 75
Operating accounts, 29
Operating efficiency ratio, 276
Operations analyst, 13
Organization chart, 9
Outstanding checks, 100
Outstanding deposits, 100
Overtime, 84–85, 94

Parking. See Garage
Par stocks, 156
Payback period, 322

Payroll, 14, 78
    budget worksheet, 313
    cash payments, 86–87
    control, 81
    deductions, 88, 90–92
    management reports, 94–96
    overtime, 84–85
    recording of, 92–94
    staffing, 81–82
    systems, 79–81
    test-checks, 85–86
    time cards, 84
    tips and, 82, 84
    vacations, 85
Pegboard payroll systems, 79
Perpetual record, 166
Point-of-sale systems:
    computerized, 178–184
    manual, 174–178
    prechecking, 178
    VISION Series II, 178–181
Popularity index, 196–197
Portion control, 185
Possipourers, 188
Posting, 31, 50–52
Potentials, 192–195
Preauthorization, 118
Prechecking, 178
Prepaids, 100, 101
Production inventory, 163
Productivity report, 94
Profit margin, 276, 276
Property management systems, 47–50,
    273–274
Purchase journals, 72
Purchasing, 65–70
    beverage, 156–157
    food, 153–156

Receiving, 70–72, 157–159
Reconciliations, 168–171
Rental and purchase comparisons,
    198–199
Rental income, 272
Reporting states, 90